JEWS, ANTISEMITISM AND CULTURE IN VIENNA

Jews, Antisemitism and Culture in Vienna

Edited by

Ivar Oxaal, Michael Pollak and Gerhard Botz

ROUTLEDGE & KEGAN PAUL
LONDON AND NEW YORK

First published in 1987 by
Routledge & Kegan Paul Ltd
11 New Fetter Lane, London EC4P 4EE

Published in the USA by
Routledge & Kegan Paul Inc.
in association with Methuen Inc.
29 West 35th Street, New York, NY 10001

Set in Sabon
by Columns Ltd, Reading
and printed in Great Britain
by Richard Clay Ltd.,
Bungay, Suffolk

Library of Congress Cataloging in Publication Data
Jews, Antisemitism, and culture in Vienna.
   Bibliography: p.
   Includes index.
1. Jews – Austria – Vienna – History – 20th century.
2. Antisemitism – Austria – Vienna.
3. Jews – Austria – Vienna – Intellectual life.
4. Vienna (Austria) – Ethnic relations.
I. Oxaal, Ivar. II. Pollak, Michael, 1948– . III. Botz, Gerhard.
DS135.A92V543   1987   943.6′004924   87–4756

British Library CIP Data also available

ISBN 0-7102-0899-5

CONTENTS

ACKNOWLEDGMENTS

Twelve of the thirteen contributions to this volume were presented at a public colloquium entitled *Les Juifs Viennois – De La Fin de Siècle à la Deuxième Guerre Mondiale* held at the Institut Autrichien in Paris, 26-28 March 1985. Bruce Pauley later kindly offered to fill a historical gap in the conference papers with his chapter on political antisemitism in the interwar period. Bernd Marin's contribution is presented here in the form of a revised and updated version of his important theoretical paper first published in *Political Psychology*, Summer, 1980, pp. 57-74, reprinted here with permission of the editor, Alfred M. Freedman, and the Plenum Publishing Corporation, New York. The colloquium was funded through subventions from the Institut Autrichien; the Austrian Federal Ministry of Science and Research under the Minister, Dr Heinz Fischer; and the Ludwig Boltzmann Institut für Historische Sozialwissenschaft, University of Salzburg, Professor Gerhard Botz, Director.

The editors would like to express their thanks to all the participants at the conference, and would like to express their special gratitude to Dr Rudolf Altmüller, Director of the Institut Autrichien, and his staff, for their unfailing encouragement and professional assistance in the difficult tasks of staging a multilingual and well-attended public symposium of this type. Thanks are also due to Professor Eugène Fleischmann, Centre National de la Recherche Scientifique (CNRS) – Programme Comparaisons Internationales, Paris – and Dr Victor Karady, *directeur de recherche* (CNRS), Maison des Sciences de l'Homme, Paris, for their advice and assistance. Allan Janik played a major role, as he frequently does, as intellectual catalyst and intermediary in bringing together this very diverse collection of scholars who he thought shared important basic concerns.

We are grateful for the assistance of Dr Martin Goldenberg, and Eva Goldenberg, London, for providing the first draft translation from the German of chapter 10; and to Frances Williams Lacroix, University of Rennes, for her translation from the French of chapter 3.

CONTRIBUTORS

STEVEN BELLER is a Fellow of Peterhouse, and former Fellow of Trinity, at Cambridge University. His recent PhD thesis on Jewish influences in Viennese culture is to be published.

GERHARD BOTZ is Professor of Austrian history, with particular reference to contemporary history, at the University of Salzburg. Born in Schärding am Inn in 1941 he completed his PhD at the University of Vienna in 1967. Author of a number of major studies of interwar Austria, he has a strong interest in quantitative and oral history methods of research. He was Visiting Professor at the University of Minnesota in 1985 and Stanford University in 1986–7.

GEORGE CLARE is best known as the author of the prize-winning *Last Waltz in Vienna*, first published in 1981 and subsequently issued in French, German, Italian, Brazilian and Israeli editions. Born in Vienna in 1920, he emigrated to the Irish Republic in 1938; subsequently served in the British army and information services in Berlin and was employed by the Axel Springer Verlag 1954-83. He now lives near Cambridge, England.

ALLAN JANIK is Visiting Professor at the Brenner Archiv, University of Innsbruck. Born in the United States in 1941 he was educated at St Anselm's College, New Hampshire, and attended Villanova, Pennsylvania and Brandeis universities. In 1973 he was co-author, with Stephen Toulmin, of the highly influential *Wittgenstein's Vienna*, recently reissued in a revised German translation. Recent appointments have been to the Department of Philosophy, University of Bergen, and the Arbetslivscentrum, Stockholm. *How Not To Interpret a Culture*, Bergen, 1986, contains major new essays.

FRANÇOISE KREISSLER is a Lecturer in the German Department, University of Paris III. Born in Vienna in 1949, she has studied Chinese in Peking and the University of Shanghai, and Yiddish language and literature at Columbia University and the University of Paris. She obtained a PhD through research at the École des Hautes Études en Sciences Sociales on 'German Cultural Activities in China from the End of the Nineteenth Century to World War II'.

BERND MARIN is Professor in the Department of Political and Social Sciences, European University Institute, Florence; and a research associate of the Institut für Politik und Sozialforschung, Vienna. His researches into post-Fascist antisemitism in Austria have reached a wide public. He is co-author, with John Bunzl, of *Antisemitismus in Österreich: Historische und Soziologische Studien*, Innsbruck, 1983.

IVAR OXAAL is an honorary research associate of the Institute of European Studies, University of Hull, England, where he was formerly Senior Lecturer in Sociology. Born in the United States in 1931, he spent his childhood in Norway; was educated at Ohio State University, Oberlin College, and UCLA, where he obtained a PhD in 1965. He is the author of studies on inter-ethnic relations and development in the British Caribbean, but for the past decade has been chiefly engaged with research into primary sources dealing with Viennese social history.

BRUCE F. PAULEY is Professor of History at the University of Central Florida, Orlando. He is the author of a number of major publications on Austrian fascism including *Hahnenschwanz und Hakenkreuz: Steirischer Heimatschutz und österreichischer National-sozialismus, 1918-1934*, Europa Verlag, 1972; and *Hitler and the Forgotten Nazis: a History of Austrian National Socialism*, University of North Carolina Press, 1981; the latter including material on Austrian antisemitism and the treatment of Jews.

MICHAEL POLLAK was born in Vienna in 1948 and is chargé de recherche at the Centre National de la Recherche Scientifique (CNRS) in Paris, and a staff member of the Institut d'histoire du temps présent. He is the author of *Vienne 1900: Une identité blessée*, Éditions Gallimard/Julliard, 1984, and other studies into the history and sociology of culture. Recent publications include investigations of Auschwitz survivors.

SIGURD PAUL SCHEICHL is widely recognized as a leading authority on the work of the Viennese satirist Karl Kraus. Born in 1942, he studied in Innsbruck, Vienna and the University of Kansas. He taught at the University of Bordeaux from 1967 to 1971 and now teaches at the Institut für Germanistic at the University of Innsbruck. Dr Scheichl's publications closely relevant to the concerns of this volume include 'Aspekte des Judentums im "Brenner" (1910-1937)', *Untersuchungen zum 'Brenner'*, Salzburg, 1981. He is editor, with Edward Timms, of *Karl Kraus in neuer Sicht: Londoner Kraus Symposium*, Munich, 1986.

RICHARD THIEBERGER was Professor and Head of the Department of German and Austrian Studies, University of Nice, France, until his retirement in 1982. Born in Vienna in 1913, he was forced to pursue a career abroad, holding posts as lecturer at the universities of Caen and Toulouse; serving as head of the 'Bureau de l'Edition et des Lettres' at the French embassy in West Germany; and holding numerous visiting appointments: at the universities of Mainz, Jena, Dakar, Otago at Dunedin (New Zealand), and the University of California at Santa Barbara. Among many publications are *Gedanken über Dichter und Dichtungen*, Bern, 1982, and *Georg Büchner*, Frankfurt/M, 1985.

WALTER R. WEITZMANN was born in Vienna in 1926 and spent his childhood in the third district. His family fled from Vienna when he was twelve and made their way via Italy and Albania to Massachusetts. He graduated from Columbia University in history after the war, at the same time playing a leading role in the socialist youth movement. He held a Fulbright fellowship in West Germany in 1955-6, and revisited Vienna en route to the Hungarian revolution. He has been Visiting Professor at the University of Cornell and is currently Professor of History at the State University College in Potsdam, New York. Recent research activities have been focussed on Jewish archival material in Vienna and Israel resulting in several specialist publications. He is working on a study of Rabbi Josef Bloch.

ROBERT S. WISTRICH was born in the Soviet Union in 1945. He was educated at Queens' College, Cambridge, and at London University, where he received his doctorate in 1974. For seven years he edited the London-based journal, the *Wiener Library Bulletin*, specializing in Nazism, antisemitism, the Arab-Israeli conflict and post-war extremist movements. In 1980 he emigrated to Israel and now teaches modern European and Jewish history at the Hebrew University in Jerusalem. He has written a number of highly regarded books, including *Revolutionary Jews from Marx to Trotsky*, 1976; *Socialism and the Jews: The Dilemmas of Assimilation in Germany and Austria-Hungary*, 1982; and *Hitler's Apocalypse: Jews and the Nazi Legacy*, 1985. His history of the Jews of Vienna from 1848 to 1916 is in press.

EDITORS' INTRODUCTION:
PERSPECTIVES AND PROBLEMS

This book has as its principal concern the attempt to show how the development of political antisemitism during this century might be explored in relation to certain cultural legacies and sociological characteristics which, while not unique to Austria or Vienna, were, for reasons to be suggested, perhaps more highly developed there than elsewhere in central Europe. The volume is the product of a colloquium deliberately organized along interdisciplinary lines with contributions from political and cultural historians, sociologists and witnesses of some of the relevant historical events, coming from Austria, Israel, France, England and the United States. We hope that the intersection of approaches and interests to which this combination of concerns and origins gave rise will shed some new light on familiar historical milestones and archetypes in the history of central European culture and antisemitism. We also hope that, while our primary intention is to present new studies and findings for the student of this subject and period, we have ensured that sufficient factual information is included, particularly in the earlier chapters, to enable the non-specialist to grasp the underlying sequence of developments.

Inevitably in a collective project such as this, important events and issues have had to be omitted or lightly passed over. But these studies do not, of course, stand alone. The present volume is only one additional building block in an edifice of research and conceptual analysis dating back many years. As early as 1893, the Viennese literary activist Hermann Bahr was conducting extensive interviews with a galaxy of leading European thinkers and public figures of the day, soliciting their personal views on the already contentious issue of *Der Antisemitismus*. About the same time Marxists, including the

Viennese-based Social Democrats, were evolving the theory – still widely held today, even by non-Marxists – that the disturbing new use of antisemitism for the purpose of winning elections and gaining party adherents was to be regarded as a byproduct of the social conflicts created by the upheavals generated by liberal capitalism; that is, by the encroachment of large-scale industry and competitive (in the Viennese case, semi-competitive) market principles in the social and political as well as the economic sphere. The Marxist interpretation of political antisemitism as a type of false class consciousness which exploits traditional feudal stereotypes of the heartless Jewish moneylender in order to assign all the blame for the evils of capitalism to the Jews, bears such a close logical resemblance to the Freudian concepts of mechanisms of psychological projection and displaced aggression, that the eventual eclectic combination of elements from the Marxist with the Freudian paradigm in the work of Erich Fromm, Theodor Adorno and other members of the Frankfurt School – spanning the period from Weimar Germany and the rise of Nazism to post-Second World War America and beyond – seems in retrospect not only a logical, but an inevitable, conceptual progression. By the time that Peter Pulzer published his classic, and still essential, *The Rise of Political Anti-Semitism in Germany and Austria* in 1964 he had available a set of more or less already generic insights which he employed in a versatile manner in the interpretation of the psychological, cultural and economic aspects of antisemitism.

Antisemitism has loomed so large in Austrian and Viennese political history over the past century that its social and cultural ramifications have been ubiquitous and deep. The unparalleled influence of the cultural historian Carl Schorske in recent years, however, has not rested chiefly on his analysis of antisemitism but rather on his attempt to achieve a holistic yet intimate portrait of Viennese culture and society during the period coinciding with the high-point of political antisemitism in the city before 1914. The international acclaim which greeted the publication of his collected essays in 1980, *Fin-de-Siècle Vienna: Politics and Culture*, included a public ceremony in Vienna where he was held up as an example to Austrian scholars by Chancellor Bruno Kreisky. This high distinction was, for many admiring fellow scholars in the English-speaking world, merely a belated tribute to the stimulation and inspiration which Schorske's separately-published essays over the previous fifteen years had already conferred on those who, like several contributors to this volume, followed his footsteps to the archives, libraries and museums in the quest of Freud's, Wittgenstein's or Herzl's Vienna. As must come to pass, however, the research and ongoing scholarship which he helped to set in motion have continued, with the consequence that there has now begun to appear a new generation of criticism and research, accompanied by stirrings of discontent with what are regarded as Schorske's leaps of interpretation or thinly-supported phenomenological procedures. Examples of this admiring, but critical, tendency will be found below.

A third component in our exploration of Viennese antisemitism, largely ignored until the present, is the study of the origins and social composition of the Viennese Jewish community itself. Several of our chapters attempt to delineate major internal features of that community. Although Austrian scholars have produced valuable historical studies of the Jews in Austria, there has been no attempt to supplement the accounts of the earlier histories by writers like Tietze with modern systematic accounts of Viennese Jewry in the present century. Thus the studies reported here have had to rely mainly on original digging into archival and other primary sources with the result that they may appear to the non-specialist as narrowly-focussed and, in the first two chapters, overly statistical. The excellent study by Marsha L. Rozenblit, *The Jews of Vienna 1867-1914*, published in 1983, overlaps with that of several contributors to this volume, but with some contradictory results and interpretive differences on the question of Jewish assimilation in Vienna which remain unresolved.

The intersection, and the conscious attempt to try to link up studies of Viennese antisemitism with the city's cultural history and its Jewish social history constitute, then, the major objective of the first seven chapters of this book, those covering the closing years of the Habsburg era to the First World War. The emphasis in the chapters dealing with the subsequent periods concentrate on the development of Viennese antisemitism itself up to the Holocaust and beyond. Thus, we have followed, as far as possible, a chronological organization for the volume. Without attempting to provide an exhaustive set of thematic cross-references to the various individual approaches represented here, it may assist the reader to anticipate briefly some of the major issues and relationships.

The introductory chapter by Ivar Oxaal has as its primary aim the provision of a preparatory overview of the history, origins, location and other sociological features of Viennese Jews in the immediate pre-First World War society. As the author points out, a clearer picture of the actual structure of the Viennese community should help to dispel the hazy and impressionistic generalizations about that community, and Viennese antisemitism, which historians have frequently had to fall back on in the absence of reliable data. An issue which arises from Oxaal's re-analysis of Viennese occupational statistics for 1910 is to what extent the untypical pattern of Jewish occupations and economic status gave support to the antisemitic 'Socialism of Fools' in the Vienna of Karl Lueger and the young Adolf Hitler, whose shadow, of course, falls over the subsequent history of antisemitism throughout Europe. A continuing dialogue with Pulzer's pioneering work on this issue is explicitly indicated here, while the concern shown with the long-term historical dimension of antisemitism, in relation to the precarious and marginal position of Jews in Vienna over the centuries, can be read as a case study of the broader themes in Jewish history explored by Hannah Arendt in *The Origins of Totalitarianism* and other writings.

Steven Beller's contribution in the second chapter is also based on quantitative research, in this case aimed at discovering the degree to which the creators and publics of Viennese bourgeois culture in the terminal Habsburg era could be identified as coming from Jewish backgrounds. Beller's starting point is a sense of unease over what he regards as Schorske's reluctance to credit the Jewish presence in Vienna with any particular significance – except to serve as the butt of antisemitism. He is also concerned with the lack of specificity in Schorske's use of the term 'liberal bourgeoisie'. If Viennese culture was, as Schorske had argued, to an important extent a product of the failure of that class to gain social and political ascendancy, would it not be important to ask – given the admitted salience of antisemitism – to what extent that bourgeoisie was in fact Jewish? The answers to this apparently simple question were not easy to come by, but Beller supplies the first rigorous attempt to arrive at an approximation of the actual situation. He does not attempt here to go beyond indicating the degree to which the *personnel* of the Viennese cultural explosion were of Jewish descent. He raises, but does not have the scope here to answer, the equally interesting question of whether Jewish ethnic origins played a significant role in determining the *style* and *content* of Viennese culture – a charge laid against the Jews by the antisemites who raged against the *verjudung* of the Viennese press, theatre, literature, music, and cultural life generally, as a phenomenon involving both alien personnel and content.

Exploration of this problem is continued in the following chapter by Michael Pollak, but from a different approach. Pollak regards Schorske's attribution of central features of Viennese culture to the psychological consequences of the failure of liberalism as but a special case in a much wider historical process. Pollak shows that it is possible to deduce the wide variety of forms – literary, artistic, intellectual, political – of the Viennese *fin-de-siècle* from a consideration of the impact of a collapse of confidence in the future of the multinational Habsburg empire itself. This loss of confidence spawned new political movements like Pangermanism and Catholic, Christian Social antisemitism which intensified the pressures on the assimilating Jewish bourgeoisie and forced the population into warring camps, out of which arose collective crises of personal identities – of which the Jewish variants were perhaps the most acute, but not unique, manifestations. These conflicts, mediated through the personal experiences structured by the macro-political situation then found expression in the wide range of cultural and political tendencies – aestheticism, psychoanalysis, Austro-Marxism, Zionism – which gave Viennese bourgeois culture its distinctive concerns and flavour. It will be recognized that this dynamic, multi-level situational analysis represents a far cry from the tendency of either antisemites or some cultural historians simply to identify in an *ad hoc* manner 'Jewish' ethnic traits in the work of cultural innovators of this period.

Chapter 4 by Allan Janik, focussing on a critique of the Jewish self-hatred hypothesis, represents a personal protest against what the author regards as the over-reliance on psychological interpretations of Viennese culture. For Janik, whose co-authorship of *Wittgenstein's Vienna* produced a durable classic in the history of philosophy, neither Freud nor Schorske, nor even Pollak, are completely satisfactory guides to features of Viennese cultural life in the late Habsburg era. His basic concern is to argue that reductionist historical models of creative activity are, if not illegitimate in principle, nevertheless dangerous and difficult to substantiate empirically. He argues that modes of explanation of Viennese culture stressing psycho-pathological causal influences cannot be demonstrated even with reference to that Viennese almost universally styled as a textbook case of Jewish self-hatred, Otto Weininger. Weininger, Janik insists – in a polemic directed mainly at Peter Gay's interpretation of the Viennese thinker as a self-hating Jew in *Freud, Jews and Other Germans* – must be understood, at least in part, in terms of the scientific paradigms fashionable in his own time; and in terms of his, admittedly muddled, attempts to employ typologies based on race and gender to convey more general concepts. Janik is also concerned to remind the reader of the origins of the concept of 'Jewish self-hatred' in the racist writings of Theodor Lessing, and attempts to show how the implications of its use by the pioneering social psychologist Kurt Lewin indicates how it might be more legitimately employed, although he remains clearly dubious of the tendency to attribute unique psychological dilemmas to the interpretation of the situation of Jews in general, and Viennese Jews in particular.

Chapters 5 and 6 both directly address, again for the late Habsburg period, the issue of what has sometimes been referred to as the 'endemic' character of antisemitism in Austria. Sigurd Paul Scheichl, approaching the problem from the standpoint of the literary historian, and as a leading interpreter of the great Viennese satirist Karl Kraus, argues for the need to distinguish between different types and degrees of anti-Jewish sentiment. Not everyone who uttered anti-Jewish attitudes were dyed-in-the-wool antisemites. The real antisemites were those supporters of von Schönerer and Lueger who advocated institutionalized discrimination and racism, and should be distinguished from intellectuals whose expressed enmity toward Jews was part of an anti-Liberal backlash, or the expression of the everyday interethnic hostilities of the multinational society. Scheichl urges that it is unfair to include those who, like Weininger and Kraus, utilized anti-Jewish imagery, *Judenfeindschaft*, as a part of their critique of modern Viennese society, in the same category with the real political forerunners of the Nazis. Scheichl's essay is an undisguised apologia which poses the critical, complex and unresolved issue in Austrian historiography of the responsibility which may have to be assigned for the victory of antisemitism during the 1930s to the uncritical resort to anti-Jewish language and imagery – indistinguishable from that employed by the malevolent political antisemites – by the pre-First World War generation of Viennese intellectuals, many of whom happened to be Jewish.

At the outset of his paper Scheichl suggests that the habitual anti-Jewish rhetoric of the Viennese socialists should not be mistaken for genuine antisemitism. Despite the overlapping vocabularies of abuse, the *Arbeiter-Zeitung* was politically poles apart from the antisemitic press such as the *Reichspost*. This brings his analysis, as he is aware, on to that historical terrain which Robert Wistrich has made his own in a series of major studies. Scheichl observes that Wistrich also has recognized the need to distinguish between degrees and types of anti-Jewish attitudes and behaviour but feels that the latter scholar has, in his previous work, emphasized the similarities between the Social Democrats and the antisemitic movements rather than the gulf in the political objectives which separated them. In chapter 6, however, Wistrich provides a concise account of the way he sees the relationship between the Viennese Social Democrats and antisemitism, which indicates that he regards the primary issue not so much one of the degree of anti-Jewish motivation as the actual consequences of the opportunistic policy of the Social Democratic leaders, including assimilated Jews like Otto Bauer and Victor Adler, to attempt to outdo even the Christian Social Party in pandering to the traditional anti-Jewish reflexes of the masses. What was even worse, perhaps, was the fact that the exploitation of antisemitism by the socialists derived from a presumably infallible Marxist theoretical analysis concerning the inevitability of the collapse of capitalism, and with it antisemitism, and hence it was not only permissible but even imperative to play the antisemitic game for political purposes because to do so would hasten the day when the primary cause of antisemitism, the class struggle under capitalism, would come to an abrupt end. In this process the felt need to distance the largely Jewish-descended leadership from the charge that they were soft on Jewish capitalism undoubtedly played a subsidiary role, as did the tendency toward social and psychological distanciation by the assimilationist leaders from the growing numbers of uncouth, and much-reviled, Ostjuden who were increasingly prominent in the city's more ghettoized districts. In any case, the net result of socialist policy on the Jewish Question, Wistrich concludes, was to make antisemitism even more respectable.

Meanwhile, as Walter Weitzmann shows in chapter 7, the conservative stance maintained by the leaders of the organized Jewish religious congregation in Vienna, the Israelitische Kultusgemeinde, ensured that no major assault on antisemitism would arise from that quarter. Regarding the emperor as the ultimate, and indeed proven, protector of their major rights in civil society; and viewing the official state ideology of multinationalism as highly compatible with the preservation of Jewish religion and culture, observant middle-class Jews could acquiesce in the policy of maintaining a low profile for the Kultusgemeinde in external politics, directing most of their energies to the internal life and politics of the community. A notable exception to this tendency was the famous rabbi from the Viennese suburb of Floridsdorf, Josef Bloch, who, from his seat in the Reichsrat and by means of his own weekly newspaper, waged a one-man crusade against antisemitism and related evils. Weitzmann reveals, however, that not even Rabbi Bloch was receptive to the appeals of political Zionism launched by the Viennese writer Theodor Herzl. The attempt made by Herzl and his band of Zionist followers to wrest control of the Kultusgemeinde through partici-pation in its periodic elections came to naught in the pre-1914 period. Only after the destruction of the monarchy and the upheavals of the First World War, including the temporary influx of Galician *Ostjuden* as war refugees into Vienna, did the Kultusgemeinde acquire a pro-Zionist Chief Rabbi and a greater involvement in the menacing political struggles of the interwar period.

Writers on Austrian antisemitism appear divided in their assess-ment of whether the First World War represents such a radical fracture in Austrian consciousness that the increasingly acute manifestations of this ideology during the interwar period should be regarded as a phenomenon which is essentially discontinuous with the Habsburg variants. As will be seen, Bernd Marin's history of Austrian antisemitism in chapter 12 is at pains to periodize the setting and functions of antisemitism in various epochs. The consensus emerging out of the colloquium on which this volume is based, however, seemed to side strongly with the view that developments in the German-speaking Austrian rump of the dismantled empire, and most particularly developments in the capital city itself, were highly continuous with the prewar situation, involving strong continuities in political culture, parties and person-nel. In chapter 8, Bruce Pauley traces both some of those continuities and the unique developments arising out of the crises of the First Republic. Christian Social antisemitism continued as a major force as part of the increasingly ferocious struggle between the Right and Left, fanned by the flames of economic crisis and the promotion of antisemitism to the status of government policy in Nazi Germany.

For our colloquium Richard Thieberger provided a rich and fascinating account of what it was like to come to intellectual maturity as an assimilated Viennese Jew during the postwar era, an account which is reproduced in chapter 9 and which provides at least some insight into the commitment of young Jews to cultural creativity in interwar Vienna, despite the protracted crisis which threatened the very survival of the Austrian polity and the first manifestations of state-sanctioned antisemitism. The tragic *dénouement* of that long process for the Viennese population has often been portrayed as the consequence of the takeover of the country by the invading German Nazis, leading to the *Anschluss* of 1938. But the reconstruction of subsequent events in Austria provided by Gerhard Botz in chapter 10 suggests a very different and, for the historical reputation of Vienna, sinister and horrific scenario. The major emphasis of Botz's account of policies toward the Jews after the German invasion is that it was the Viennese themselves who spontaneously, and with great enthusiasm, initiated the most brutal assaults on Jews, and Jewish assets, to such an extent that the occupying authorities were obliged, in the interests of 'law and order', to rein in their Viennese colleagues – before, that is, they themselves applied elsewhere the lessons learned in Vienna: mass expropriation of Jewish homes and capital in order to fund the 'socialist' welfare programmes of National Socialism, which in Vienna had enhanced the standard of living of tens of thousands of righteous citizens.

There is a sour, but none the less fortunate, irony to be found in the fact that the precocious talent for Jewish persecution in Vienna meant that the majority of the Jewish population were forced to take flight before the remorseless and unconditional policy of mass extermination came into effect in 1942. An immense literature exists on the various avenues of escape taken by Jews before the Holocaust consumed the majority of the remainder, but our colloquium yielded the remarkable case of the Viennese Jews who fled to the Orient, to Shanghai. Françoise Kreissler's account of that distant refuge for 'Wiener Juden' provides ample testimony to the resilience and courage of the far-flung Viennese Diaspora, members of whom have remained creative and prominent to the present writing.

Our colloquium concludes with two highly contrasting chapters which aim to provide a degree of theoretical summation and, indeed, personal catharsis. The theoretical summation is provided by Bernd Marin in chapter 12. Marin has conducted both pioneering empirical studies into the continuing antisemitic attitudes which Viennese and Austrians generally continue to hold, even after the Holocaust, and has developed a comprehensive theoretical and historical interpretation of the total process which we have been considering in these pages. His chapter will, we believe, provide that level of theoretical grasp, however conditional, which the subject deserves. His debt to the earlier studies of antisemitism by members of the Frankfurt School and their successors in the United States and central Europe is manifest. At the same time, he provides a contemporary social-scientific updating of antisemitism in the Second Republic. It has been regarded as a sad and shocking fact by many observers that Vienna and Austria, for reasons cogently objectified and analysed by Marin, have managed, in the main – despite some worthy projects in public education – both to avoid and evade their complicity in the tragic events of the Nazi era. The skeletons mouldering in the family closet have, however, a persistent tendency to wreak revenge on the complacent present. The election in 1986 to the Presidency of the Austrian Republic of the former Secretary-General of the United Nations, Dr Kurt Waldheim, despite, or perhaps even partially because of, revelations concerning his formerly concealed service with the German army in the Balkans during the Second World War, and his physical proximity to the mass deportation of Jews from Salonika in northern Greece, was only the most publicized of the numerous 'affairs' concerning the Nazi past of Austria which displayed the Austrian talent for selective historical recall analysed by Bernd Marin.

The editors have felt it appropriate, however, to leave the last word to a survivor of Viennese and Nazi antisemitism, George Clare, a writer of rare honesty and spirit whose best-selling family history and autobiography *Last Waltz in Vienna*, covering three generations of Viennese Jews, has provided mere academic scholars with much understanding and guidance into the history of Jewish life in Vienna before the Holocaust. Despite having himself been forced to take flight from the city at the time of the Nazi takeover, and the subsequent transport of both his parents to the Auschwitz gas chambers, Clare miraculously retains a hope – 'faith' would be too strong a term – shared by many who often despair about the city's future, that the miasmic legacies of antisemitisms past and present can be dispelled and that this still great and beautiful city will recover a measure of its ancient intellectual and artistic prominence, along with its traditional glamour and sophistication. To that end we dedicate this colloquium.

CHAPTER 1

The Jews of young Hitler's Vienna: Historical and sociological aspects

Ivar Oxaal

No historical fact about Vienna is more trite, or more devastating in its imputed consequences, than the biographical datum that Adolf Hitler spent the most formative years of his youth in the Habsburg capital. His own version of that period of his life – arriving from his hometown of Linz when he was eighteen in 1907, and departing for Munich in 1913 – has formed the basis of innumerable interpretations of his behaviour as Führer. The most persistent query about the impact of his sojourn in Vienna has centred on whether the Nazi persecution, and eventual mass murder, of European Jewry had as its originating cause the violent antisemitism which the lonely and frustrated architectural student acquired at that time. This has certainly been a widely held conception of Hitler's personal development, supported by his account of the Vienna years in *Mein Kampf*. Robert Wistrich has written a penetrating reconstruction of Hitler's place within that conflictual political ethos, arguing that the architect of the Holocaust – for Hitler was, in his view, nothing less – can be clearly perceived to be acting out the Manichean attitudes and intentions of the young antisemite in Vienna:

> Indeed the origins of Nazism would be incomprehensible without taking account of the youthful experiences of its founder in early twentieth-century Vienna, sickened as he was 'by the conglomeration of races which the capital showed me, repelled by the whole mixture of Czechs, Poles, Hungarians, Ruthenians, Serbs and Croats, and everywhere the eternal mushroom [*Spaltpilz*] of humanity – Jews and more Jews.'[1]

Other historians, however, have questioned the importance of antisemitism as a primary determinant of Hitler's concerns once in power, and a major debate has developed among scholars over whether the 'Final Solution' was an intentional product of long-term Nazi planning, or an emergent consequence of a series of improvisational responses to unforeseen situations arising after the invasions of Poland and the Soviet Union. In an attempt to summarize and adjudicate this and other major controversies about the nature of *The Nazi Dictatorship*, Ian Kershaw concludes that Hitler himself took little part in the overt formulation of anti-Jewish policies either in the 1930s or in the decisions associated with the introduction of the programme of mass extermination: 'His major role consisted of setting the vicious tone within which the persecution took place and providing the sanction and legitimacy of initiatives which came mainly from others.' But he also states: 'Without Hitler's fanatical will to destroy Jewry, which crystallized only by 1941 into a realizable aim to exterminate physically the Jews of Europe, the Holocaust would almost certainly not have come about.'[2] Thus whatever general explanations may be given for the rise of Nazism – the crisis of capitalism, the threat of Bolshevism, the weakness of democratic institutions and traditions, the existence of widespread antisemitism, or a variety of historical contingencies – the stark fact would remain that the primary, if not sufficient, cause of the Holocaust was, on this reading, the evil fixation of a single powerful individual, facilitated by the enthusiastic commitment, or acquiescence, of the necessary apparatus of henchmen, cadres and implicated populations.

If the emphasis placed on the Führer's violent, racial antisemitism in the interpretation of the genesis of the Holocaust is essentially correct, then the search for causal explanations leads back to the biographical conundrum of the various psychological traits, personal experiences and environmental influences which somehow combined to induce the young Hitler to conceive of his demoniac mission. The available historical evidence, or lack of same, has permitted a wide range of more or less empirically-grounded interpretation, but two main avenues of explanation, the psychological and cultural, are present in most accounts. The psychological approaches to Hitler's underlying motivation require no elaboration here: he has been regarded as simply an evil madman whose intervention in world history is ultimately inexplicable or, among the more complex approaches, as a Freudian specimen whose hatred of Jews can be rationally reconstructed according to clinical insights into psychopathology. The psychological dimension, although tending to be highly speculative, is a necessary 'intervening variable' in order to construct a full account of the process in question, but psychological analysis by itself cannot account for the targeting of the victims of destructively aggressive feelings and actions. To be socially expressed, or even personally meaningful, the destructive impulse must be channelled and realized within a specific historical-cultural context; in this case, the pre-existing 'forms of life' constituting the cultural complex of European antisemitism.

The extremism of Hitler's personality and the fanaticism of his anti-Habsburg, anti-Jewish utterances, combined with the paranoia and sadistic absurdism with which he expressed his adherence to the metaphysics of race, has suggested to some present-day Viennese, of my acquaintance at least, that the young Hitler was merely a politically and socially marginal psychopath – a wild, isolated and ultimately pathetic figure on the outer fringe of late Habsburg political culture. Had not Viennese antisemitism been pragmatically contained and exploited for constructive ends by the great mayor, Dr Karl Lueger, during Hitler's stay in the city? Would it not be unjust even to consider Hitler as a product of the city which he came passionately to hate? Such objections are understandable and even valid up to a point, for it is clear that Hitler's chief preoccupation was not with Vienna itself but with the decadent, multiracial empire of which it was the centre. His was not a parochial, municipal antisemitism but something far more grandiose; the Jewish menace was mainly regarded as an obstacle to that total reconstruction of central Europe which was required in order that the genius of a united German *Volk*, for centuries frustrated by the selfish dynastic policies of the Habsburgs, could finally achieve historical realization.[3] To this might be added the observation that in both the desire to make a contribution to German nationalism, and in the vehemence of his racially-based antisemitism, he was emulating the culture hero of many young Germans, Richard Wagner, who was no Viennese.

It would clearly be artificial and invalid to attempt to view the development of anti-Jewish ideologies in Vienna, and the antisemitic influences impinging on the young Hitler, in total isolation from historical and contemporary developments elsewhere in Austria, the Habsburg empire or all of Europe. Nevertheless, it was in Vienna, 'the hardest, though most thorough, school of my life', as he later called it, where Hitler arrived at his life-long *Weltanschauung*. Without wishing to suggest that he was either a representative or an

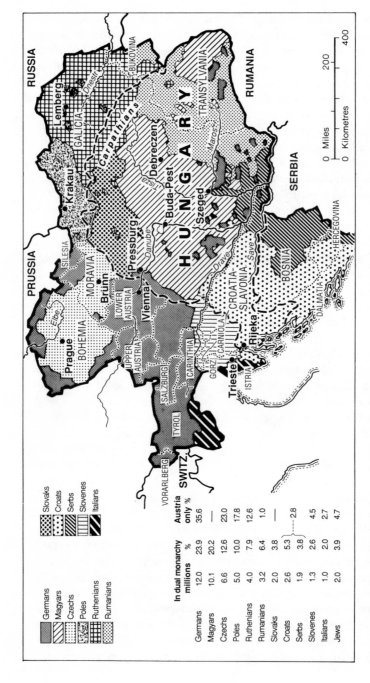

Map 1: *Nationalities of the Habsburg Empire in 1910: 1.3 million Jews lived in the Austrian portion of the Dual Monarchy (located to the west and north of the broken line from Rijeka to Bukovina). Two-thirds of these Jews, 871,906, were distributed throughout Galicia, chiefly in villages and small market towns, representing 10 per cent of the total population of the province.*

inevitable product of that environment, it will, I believe, assist in understanding how such an individual became an historical *possibility* if we look more closely at the specific cultural background, and the contemporary Viennese society, which awaited his arrival. Only the barest historical outline and sociological highlights can be presented here, nor will any comprehensive and definitive results be claimed; but it is hoped that this brief introduction to Hitler's Vienna will also assist in providing basic landmarks which may be useful as background for some of the subsequent chapters of this colloquium.

The confrontation between the city of Vienna and its Jewish inhabitants has its origins, of course, in that peculiar, widespread feature of European feudalism in which a corporate self-reproducing religious-ethnic minority was excluded from agriculture and charged with the task of fulfilling economic functions – prohibited on theological grounds to Christians – which were at once essential to the conduct of trade, and often to the ambitions, or even survival, of a particular ruler. The inherent instability of this arrangement, and the personal and collective danger in which it frequently placed the religious minority, punctuates the history of many parts of central Europe, not least of all Vienna. The expansion of trade and a money economy in the later middle ages led to the establishment, mainly through migration of Jews from Germany, of a number of Jewish traders and small communities in the towns and villages of the later Austrian crownlands, with permanent settlement by Jews in Vienna taking place during the final decades of the twelfth century. By 1196 they were sufficiently numerous in the city that sixteen of their number could be murdered by Crusaders, including Schlom (Solomon), mintmaster and financial adviser to the Babenburg Duke.[4] The desire of his successor Leopold VI (1198-1230) to develop Vienna as a centre for trade, however, ensured the growth of the Viennese Jewish community, with invitations to settle being issued to traders as far afield as Flanders. By 1204 the community possessed two rabbis and would become, like nearby Wiener Neustadt, a centre of Jewish scholarship. Mention is made in the records as early as 1235 of the Jew Teka (Tecanus) living in Vienna and acting as state banker. The community expanded to establish the institutions ensuring religious self-sufficiency: synagogue, school (*schola Judaeorum*), women's bath (*mikwah*), slaughter house (*beth mitbachia*), bakery, hospital, welfare facilities, and its own cemetery outside the city walls near the Kärntnertor. The Jewish quarter was concentrated near the central and expansive Hoher Markt and comprised some seventy, mainly two-storied, buildings in which resided from one to three families, with a total population by the latter half of the thirteenth century of around 1,000 persons. During this period they were permitted to employ Christian servants and were placed under no special restrictions concerning the ownership of property.

Meanwhile, Rudolph of Habsburg, the strongest feudalist in southwest Germany, was elected German emperor in 1273, and eventually managed to wrest the duchy of Austria away from Ottakar II in 1282, proclaiming the acquired territories, including Vienna, as hereditary possessions of the House of Habsburg, which indeed they remained in a remarkable and unbroken chain of dynastic succession lasting until 1918. During the early centuries of the Habsburg reign, however, Vienna had more the character of an eastern frontier city, a walled fortress town serving as a bastion against the Turks, than the luxurious imperial *Residenzstadt* and *Kaiserstadt* it would only fully become after the defeat of the Turks toward the end of the seventeenth century.[5]

In Vienna, as elsewhere in Christian Europe, the treatment of the Jewish inhabitants varied greatly depending on the attitude and circumstances of the current local ruler. The Viennese Jews, like most other Austrian communities, were fortunate to have been spared the mass executions which the hysteria associated with the Black Death plague years of 1348-9 visited on Jewish communities elsewhere. When the burghers of nearby Krems burned Jews in their own homes, Albrecht II sent in troops to arrest the perpetrators and hanged three of them. But by the end of the century anti-Jewish sentiment was also manifest in Vienna, and in 1406 a fire which destroyed the synagogue became the occasion for attacks on Jewish homes. To these internal frictions were added the conflicts and religious persecution of the early Reformation. The political and religious wars of the early fifteenth century associated with the upsurge of Czech nationalism and incipient Protestantism following the martyrdom of John Hus – burned at the stake in 1415 – resulted in 'a furious German crusade against heresy and heretics in Bohemia which caused widespread devastation'.[6] These conflicts had dire consequences for Jews in the Austrian lands. In 1420, Archduke Albert V ordered their total expulsion. According to some historians, chronic indebtedness to Jewish moneylenders as a consequence of the Hussite wars, and heightened religious fanaticism, were the chief reasons for the action. Poorer Jews were set adrift *en masse* in the Danube. The wealthier were imprisoned in Vienna, held without charge, then accused of collaboration with the Hussites and later with the more standard crime of desecration of the Christian Eucharist. Many of the Jews imprisoned in the synagogue committed suicide and the remaining 120 women and 92 men were burned alive outside the city walls on 12 March 1421. This scene was witnessed, it is reported, by 'einer johlenden Menschenmenge', a howling mob.[7]

> All the property of the Jews passed into the hands of the Archduke. The stones of the synagogue were used in building the university. Some Jews escaped to Bohemia; a very few managed to maintain an illegal existence in Austria. The proud Vienna community numbering between 1,400 and 1,600 existed no longer and the city became known in Jewish tradition as 'Ir ha-Damim' ('The City of Blood').[8]

Just seventeen years after this initial holocaust Christian physicians are recorded as complaining about Jews illegally practising medicine in the city. But only a few Jewish families were readmitted and lived in Vienna until late in the sixteenth century. Not that the city was free from religious persecution in the meanwhile as the Catholic rulers attempted to roll back the advances of Protestantism. In 1527 an edict by Ferdinand I prohibited Protestants from setting up businesses in Vienna and in 1551 Jesuits were summoned to lead the Viennese Counter-Reformation. During these internal crusades some 23 Anabaptists were put to death by burning, beheading or drowning in the city.[9] Towards the end of the century a group of exclusively wealthy Jews, the 'befreite Hofjudenschaft', responsible only to the emperor, was established and assumed an important position during the reign of Ferdinand II at the outbreak of the Thirty Years' War (1618), functioning as financial backers, military suppliers and monetary authorities. Ferdinand was not particularly well-disposed toward Jews, but he took care to protect their freedom of movement so long as they could readily furnish him with large sums of cash for special requirements over and above the exactions of *Schutzgeld* – literally 'protection money' – which were the customary prerogative of princes in return for granting rights of residence and business to Jews. When Jewish resources appeared to be exhausted, they were threatened with expulsion, but in response to entreaties, in 1624 Ferdinand instead ordered his council of war to find a location outside of Vienna to which the Jews could be transferred. This break with the former practice of allowing Jews to settle along certain streets within the city walls, like other corporate groups or occupations, was perhaps partly a result of the emperor's desire to adhere to the fashion, originating in Venice and Rome, of confining Jewish residents within a walled 'Ghetto'.[10] The location which quickly seems to have recommended itself lay immediately outside the city walls, but across a side channel of the Danube, the Donau canal. The isolation afforded was not very great since the area was apparently readily accessible over a timber-pile bridge to one of the main city gates, the Rothe Turm. (Map 2, although depicting a much later historical period, indicates the approximate position of the largely unwalled 'Unteren Werd', 'lower island', ghetto originally located to the left of Taborstrasse.) The area, which was then owned by the city hospital, was not regarded as particularly healthy and was sparsely settled; but protests at this incursion made by the fishermen along the canal were overruled.

The renewed patent of toleration which Ferdinand II issued in December of 1624, although it limited their presence within the city walls to daylight hours only, could be said to have conferred additional freedom and security on Vienna's hard-pressed Jewish residents who were now to be allowed to own their own houses and gardens. After further petitioning they were permitted to sell goods within the city and to operate some 70 shops and businesses there. They were forbidden to engage in agricultural pursuits on the nearby fields, but they could visit markets in the countryside and practise artisan trades. In 1632 they were authorized to establish their own civil court and prison on the model of the *Judenstadt* in Prague. This spatial segregation did not satisfy the city authorities of Vienna, however, who petitioned Ferdinand III, on his accession in 1637, to expel Jews from the vicinity, based on the traditional charges of their having poisoned the wells and desecrated the sacraments. This demand was not acceded to, but led to the concession that Jews were banned for three years from trading in the city.

By 1669 the Unteren Werd settlement had grown to an estimated 3,000 inhabitants, with three synagogues, a large hospital and, almost unique for the period, an annual budget for cleaning the district. The community was no longer characterized exclusively by a wealthy Jewish elite, but appears to have developed as a diversified and thriving satellite of the central city. In addition to its symbiotic relationship with the majority community it required its own artisans and traders – goldsmiths, tailors, shoemakers, horsetraders and innkeepers (the latter officially prohibited from serving Christians). Jewish physicians remained on call for wealthy Christians. Outsiders could be admitted, as when the community received refugees from the Cossack uprising against Polish rule in the Ukraine, led by Bogdan Chmielnicki in 1648-9, in which an estimated 100,000 Jews were massacred. The refugees enriched the Viennese community with the great tradition of Talmudic scholarship existing in the Polish lands.[11]

Incidents, however, continued to endanger the security of the new settlement. In 1642 a converted Jew about to be hanged in Hoher Markt in the inner city threw down the crucifix which the condemned were required to hold and ground it under foot. This enraged the Christian onlookers, who assaulted the Jews present and plundered the ghetto. Seven years later an altercation between some students from the city and the Jewish watchman on the canal bridge led to a student assault on the ghetto which caused the community to employ a small army of guards. These were not difficult to recruit since the end of the Thirty Years' War had deposited many professional soldiers among the 7,000 beggars then extant among Vienna's 130,000 inhabitants. In 1665 a Viennese woman was found murdered in the ghetto, where she had gone to pawn a silver watch. At first Jews were suspected, but were released when her husband was charged with the crime. But, when a rumour spread that the Jews were the real culprits after all, and had bribed the magistrate, the ghetto was stormed yet again, requiring hundreds of musketeers to quell the riot.

Further incidents – an accidental fire at the Hofburg, the royal palace, in 1665, which was blamed on Jews; renewed student rioting in 1668; a miscarriage by the empress (a daughter of King Philip of Spain) – led Leopold I to appoint a commission of enquiry headed by the vigorously anti-Jewish bishop of Wiener Neustadt. The commission evaluated the financial, religious and moral aspects of the Jewish presence and ruled against their continued toleration. A new petition from the Bürgermeister and city council called for expulsion, but, anticipating financial embarrassment to the royal exchequer, went so far as to offer to pay the annual 10,000 Gulden *Schutzgeld* obtained from the Jews. A biographer of Leopold writes:

Although the court and city lived within the same walls, they were different worlds which seldom came together. The merchants of Vienna, jealous of their various commercial rights and yet dependent on the court for much of their business, had long resented the presence among them of a prosperous Jewish community which had, in their eyes, no reason to share the city's wealth. Here, as in the Imperial cities of Germany, the Jews and their quarter of the city were technically the property of the emperor, a legal device dating back to the Middle Ages, intended originally to protect the financially useful Jewish communities from periodic outbreaks of violence against them by their Christian neighbors. . . .

There had been many petitions by the 'Good Christian' merchants of Vienna against the Jews, but the emperor's law protected them until July 1670 when Leopold signed an agreement with the city council. The city of Vienna bought the Jewish quarter from the emperor for 100,000 Gulden, and in return for the right to expel its inhabitants promised to cover all their debts up to 10,000 Gulden and to build a church on the site of the old synagogue . . . . It seems . . . likely, however, that [for Leopold] this was as much a financial transaction as an act of religious fervour.[12]

The Jewish community had managed to obtain intercessions with the emperor from Queen Christina of Sweden, and even from the Pope himself, but to no avail; this 'last expulsion', as Viennese histories optimistically dubbed it until 1938, went ahead in stages until all the Jews in Vienna and lower Austria had been set on the road. Although wealthier Jews would emigrate as far as Germany, most of the estimated 500 families appear to have found refuge in the areas of toleration much closer to Vienna. Some went to Bohemia, others to towns like Nikolsburg in Moravia, to Pressburg and the nearby Esterhazy estates in western Hungary. The burghers of Vienna did not hesitate to take full possession of Unteren Werd, renaming the area Leopoldstadt after the enlightened emperor and reconsecrating one of the synagogues as parish church in August 1670. Nine years later the plague struck Vienna with great force, and the most popular preacher of the day, Abraham a Sancta Clara, charged the Jews, along with witches and gravediggers, of having intentionally brought about the disaster. Next to Satan, he argued, Christians have no worse enemies than the Jews. As Robert A. Kann writes:

It should be carefully noted that Abraham a Sancta Clara's anti-Jewish campaign did not precede but followed the great expulsion of the Jews in 1669-70, which had taken place against the advice of several of the emperor's responsible political councillors. Abraham's diatribes against the Jews were spoken in a city without a single permanent Jewish inhabitant. Perhaps they may be regarded as a belated justification of a policy which, at least from the economic viewpoint, was soon enough to be regarded as grossly mistaken.[13]

In fact, imperial dependence on the commercial and executive skills of Jews had continued almost without a break with the appointment, in 1672, of Samuel Oppenheimer from southwest Germany as provisioner of the imperial army, in which capacity he played a key role in enabling Vienna finally to repel the Turkish threat by breaking the epic siege of 1683. He was succeeded by his nephew, the scholarly Samuel Wertheimer, who had engaged in Talmudic studies in Worms and Frankfurt, and who soon gained the emperor's favour, effectively becoming court banker and financial adviser – the wealthiest and most esteemed Court Jew of his era.[14] Wertheimer also played a leading role in Jewish affairs. Appointed chief rabbi of the collective Jewry within the emperor's domains, he earned the informal title 'Prince of the Land of Israel' through his supervision of all Jewish donations to Jews in the Holy Land. He even succeeded in having a libellous anti-Jewish book, *Entdecktes Judentum* ('Judaism Exposed') by Johann Eisenmenger, banned throughout the Reich.[15] The re-establishment of a small number of wealthy Jewish families in the *Residenzstadt* met with a predictable response from the Viennese burghers who petitioned for their renewed expulsion at the accession of Karl VI in 1712, charging that some 4,000 'accursed and depraved' ('verfluchte und lasterhafte') Jews were now in the city. This figure must have been greatly exaggerated, but it is possible that some hinterland Jews were gaining temporary access to the city through negotiations with the custodians of influx control at the city gates – a practice which is known to have been fairly routine in the nineteenth century before freedom of movement was introduced. In reply to the expulsion demand of 1712, the government, which in the end would reassert its traditional right to retain Jews in its service, asked the petitioners how it was intended to make good the financial loss to the treasury which a mass deportation would entail?[16]

Although imperial mercantile pragmatism would allow the formation, in 1736, of a recognized congregation of Sephardic Jews from Turkey active in the coffee and tobacco trade, the right of official recognition and the construction of a synagogue would continue to be denied to the Ashkenazim for another century. Conditions for Viennese Jews during the eighteenth century continued to be marked by all sorts of harassment and restrictions, ranging from the prohibition on direct ownership of real property to the requirement that they remain indoors until late morning on Sundays and holidays. There were even proposals to re-ghettoize them, but Leopoldstadt was understandably not receptive. These restrictions reached their greatest intensity in the *Judenordnungen* promulgated by the empress Maria Theresia in the 1750s and 1760s. Greater limitations were to be placed on the number and economic activities of Jews; sons of tolerated fathers were no longer to be granted automatic rights of residence; servants and other employees were forbidden to keep their families with them in Vienna; and, as a remnant of the *Kleiderordnungen* of previous centuries, which had prescribed distinctive forms of clothing, headgear, or badges, for Jews, husbands and widowers were now ordered to cultivate distinctive, easily-recognized beards.[17] The highly insular, strictly Catholic, Maria Theresia, regarded Jews from the standpoint of medieval Christianity, attempting to segregate them as far as possible from contact with Christians, especially her own person. She minimized the distasteful contact required when granting an audience to hear a Jewish petitioner by having a folding screen placed between the supplicant and herself. In denying one such petition, requesting leave for a Jew to extend his stay in Vienna, the empress wrote: 'I know of no more troublesome pestilence for the state than this nation which through fraud, usury, and financial manipulations reduces people to beggary, and who resort to such evil business which other, more honourable, men would abhor.'[18]

Historic changes in the view taken of Jews by the state were about to be introduced, however, during the reign of Joseph II whose *Toleranzpatent* of 1782, while by no means conferring an emancipated status or civil equality on the Jews of the Habsburg domains, at least recognized them as having citizenship responsibilities, if not equal rights. One of the leading Viennese historians of this transitional period, Wolfgang Häusler, has suggested that the relative economic backwardness of the Habsburg empire ensured that it would lag behind developments in western Europe, particularly in the wake of the French revolution, which led to the emancipation of the Jews proclaimed by Napoleon. The continuation of the old doctrine of toleration in its Josephinist form, rather than a breakthrough to full emancipation, had, Häusler suggests, 'its basis in the qualitative difference between bourgeois revolution and enlightened absolutism'.[19] Josephinist Jewish policy did not envisage any expansion in the numbers of Jews in Vienna, but it was openly predicated on the idea that Jews would generate greater economic benefits if their status as a feudal, closed commercial caste was reduced through enforced state education, the adoption of German surnames, and the diversification of their occupational profile. The extensive pamphlet literature of this period contains expressions of apprehension, as to where the new winds of change might lead, from both culturally conservative Jews and anxious Christian traders and artisans.[20]

The vistas of Josephinian social engineering were not limited to the few hundred Jews in Vienna, nor to the scattered small communities dotted across Bohemia, Moravia, the Slovak lands, and Hungary. An enormous challenge to modernization presented itself in the recently acquired province of Galicia where a full quarter of a million Jews were spread through towns and villages across the length and breadth of the Polish lands in the west to the Ruthenian-dominated areas of eastern Galicia. Josephinian doctrine held that these 'Ostjuden' in particular must be 'productivized', weaned away from their traditional penchant for petty trading, innkeeping and money-lending to virtuous *Urproduktion*, primary production, particularly on the land. In charge of the required educational reforms was placed Herz Homberg, a devotee of *Haskalah*, a disciple of Moses Mendelssohn and an enthusiastic supporter of the Josephinist proposals. The magnitude of the task, however, coupled with the evasions and non-cooperation of the Jewish masses, who preferred their traditional lifestyles, brought these efforts to nought.[21] These 'Ostjuden' would continue to worry the Viennese, introducing a new basis for demographic and cultural paranoia.

The emergence of Habsburg Jews into full, or nearly full, civil equality would not occur until after the 1848-9 revolution in Vienna which, despite years of reversals, halting progress towards liberal reforms followed by further renewed backsliding, by the late 1860s placed Jews on a formal, legal standing equal to Christians except in the appointment to high state office. The social transition was a gradual one; even though the Viennese Jews of the post-Congress of

Vienna period continued to be bound by many of the old *de jure* restrictions, a new spirit, and new social types, were appearing during the *Biedermeier* era. Already a Jewish intellectual hostess like Fanny von Arnstein had appeared to provide a salon glamour to the cultural life of the capital, and the ennoblement, without conversion to Christianity, of the leading figures in a number of Jewish private banks, notably the Rothschilds, conferred a new respectability and security on the Jewish elite. 'Jewish bankers', writes Robert Wistrich in his masterful analysis of this period, 'utilizing their international connections with relatives and business associates were a crucial motor of the industrialization in Austria-Hungary.'[22] And though limited in number, Jewish members of the newly-emergent bourgeois intelligentsia would play a leading role in the 1848-9 Viennese revolution, indicating a qualitative advance in the level of civic involvement over the total exclusion and self-imposed inhibitions of the past. Official statistics from the census of 1857, before the Liberal revolutionary demands had been finally conceded, reveal the existence of a much larger, occupationally diverse, and residentially integrated and dispersed Jewish community than would be expected considering the lingering effects of feudal restrictions, and the limitations of the Josephinist legacy.

In her pioneering monograph, *The Jews of Vienna 1867-1914: Assimilation and Identity*, the author, Marsha L. Rozenblit, who throughout the study emphasizes the distinctiveness of the Viennese Jews from the remainder of the population, insists that 'The Vienna Jews lived with other Jews. The creation of Jewish neighborhoods in the city served to separate Jews from gentiles and instill more deeply the perception – among Jews and non-Jews alike – that Jews formed a distinct group.'[23] There is undoubtedly a large measure of validity in this generalization. One of the consequences of Jewish residential concentration, moreover, was to reinforce, within the continuous stream of new emigrants, a sense of ethnic *Gemeinschaft* in the rapidly growing big city where Jews numbered some 6,000, out of half a million, inhabitants in 1857; 72,543 out of 726,105 in 1880; 146,926 out of 1,674,957 in 1900; and 175,318 out of 2,031,498 (8.6 per cent) in Hitler's *Weltstadt* of 1910. Spatial proximity of Jews facilitated religious, social and economic activities and linkages and produced concentrations of Jews in a number of state schools; which, in turn, caused acculturation to the new environment to take on a collective, group character as hinterland Jews were transformed into

Viennese – but together. Rozenblit is right to emphasize this duality of the process, because the impression often gained from cultural histories and biographies – a major instance is analysed by Steven Beller in chapter 2 – is of a Jewish community characterized solely by its high degree of assimilation. Nevertheless, Rozenblit's study often exhibits a gratuitous tendency to view the situation from a diametrically opposite perspective, emphasizing only the retention of Jewish solidarity and uniqueness while minimizing, or dismissing, those dimensions where the data on Jewish and non-Jewish patterns deserve a less categorical treatment.

To take the question of patterns of residential separation and integration: the Jews of Vienna during the half century of internal migration before 1914 certainly lived among other Jews – but many of them lived in close proximity to non-Jews as well. As we have seen, the formal experiment in ghettoization had ended with the expulsion of 1670; thereafter Jews were not successfully subjected to rigid residential controls. The informal expansion in their numbers in the early nineteenth century resulted in an unplanned patchwork within which Jews were fairly widely dispersed. They had resettled, on a non-ghettoized basis, in Leopoldstadt but were also distributed within the city walls, where the central synagogue, built in 1826, was located, as were the palaces of the Rothschilds and other wealthy Jews. Statistics from the 1857 census – taken just before the demolition of the city walls to make way for the Ringstrasse at the dawn of the Liberal era – suggest Jewish residential patterns which might today be regarded as examples of integrated, multiracial housing.

In his study of the position of Jews as depicted in the 1857 census, Peter Schmidtbauer found that the majority of them were cohabiting in apartment buildings also occupied by Christians. In a sample of 163 buildings in the inner city and Leopoldstadt, he found that half of the Jews in the sample were distributed throughout 137 buildings in all of which they formed a minority of tenants. On the other hand, a much more compact, ghettoized situation existed in the remaining buildings sampled. For example, No. 4 Donau Strasse along the canal front in Leopoldstadt (see Map 2) by itself housed 286 of the city's six thousand Jews.[24] The Viennese pattern stands in sharp contrast to that experienced by the Jews of Prague later in the nineteenth century: even after dispersion out of the old *Judenstadt* Prague Jews were almost totally segregated, not by neighbourhoods, which were often mixed, but by individual apartment blocks.[25]

About one in ten of the Jewish households contained in Schmidtbauer's sample from 1857 lived as sub-tenants in the same apartments with Christians – an indication of both poverty and the desperate housing shortage which existed in the city. Such intimate contact was not the norm, but it was not uncommon. At No. 1 Donau Strasse, for example, the household of the Jewish widow from Moravia contained not only three Jewish lodgers, students from Hungary, but also a Catholic maid, aged twenty-four. Down the road at No. 3 Donau Strasse lived the son of a Jewish landlord from Turkey along with – according to the manuscript census – his Catholic mistress, while employing a Jewish cook from Bohemia and lodging a Jewish widow from Turkey along with her two sons. Around the corner on Kleine Ankergasse 5 young Jewish washing maids from Bohemia, Moravia and Hungary were employed in a laundry along with 7 Christian girls and 3 Christian men. The permutations of such contacts which, although perhaps not the norm appear to be almost infinite, provide insight into how the workplace and living conditions could structure potentially intimate, primary group relationships between Jew and Christian resulting in at least a partial reduction in group boundaries. However, since most of the manuscript censuses on individual households and work-shops are no longer available for the remainder of the pre-1914 era, an accurate, comprehensive assessment of later trends is not possible. And the omission from published census material of the place of birth of the steady stream of Jewish migrants to the *Residenzstadt* would mean that not just later historians but contemporary Viennese themselves had only an impressionistic sense of who these Jews were, where they came from, and how many 'Ostjuden' had invaded the capital. Hitler provides an interesting illustration of how the muddled, pseudo-social observations of the antisemites could confuse the actual situation and exploit these fears:

> Preoccupied by the abundance of my impressions in the architectural field, oppressed by the hardship of my own lot, I gained at first no insight into the inner stratification of the people of this gigantic city. Notwithstanding that Vienna in those days counted nearly two hundred thousand Jews among its two million inhabitants, *I did not see them.* [emphasis added]

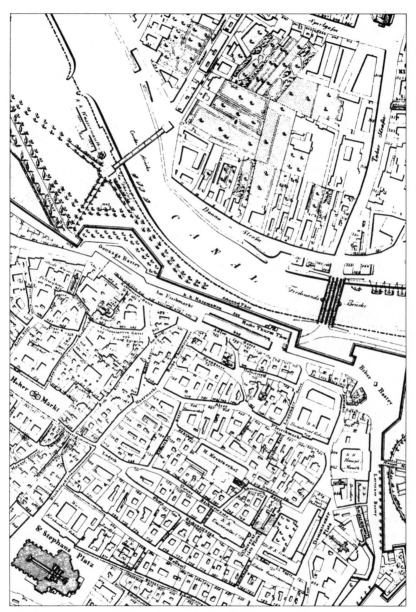

Map 2 *Parts of central Vienna and Leopoldstadt between construction of central synagogue (1826) on Seittenstaettengasse, left-centre, and the demolition of the city walls (1859)*

Apparently loath to admit, at that juncture in his narrative, that he had not been struck right away by Jewish racial features, he goes on to explain how, after his autoconversion to antisemitism, they began to appear everywhere:

> Wherever I went I began to see Jews, and the more I saw, the more sharply they became distinguished in my eyes from the rest of humanity. Particularly the inner city, and the districts north of the Danube canal swarmed with a people which even outwardly had lost all resemblance to Germans.[26]

This was a tricky way of attempting to make amends to the reader for his earlier lack of racial awareness, because he knew, having himself lived in a men's hostel north of the canal on Meldemann-strasse from December 1909, that the Brigittenau district contained the major concentration of the highly visible, impoverished, Jews from Galicia. The majority of Viennese Jews would have continued to defy his powers of observation because they would have had the same acculturated, westernized and germanized characteristics as the Jews of his native Linz, of whom he had earlier written: 'In the course of centuries their outward appearance had become European-ized and had taken on a human look; in fact I even took them for Germans.'[27]

It is possible to estimate, from the birth and marriage records of the Viennese Jewish *Kultusgemeinde*, the relative proportions of Galician Jews, Jewish migrants from other regions and native-born Viennese Jews. These sources indicate that perhaps one out of every four Jews resident in the capital during Hitler's sojourn had arrived there at some stage in his or her life from Galicia – not over 40,000, or 2 per cent of the city's total population. It appears that two of every four had either been born in the city itself, or had emigrated there from Bohemia or Moravia; and the odds were that the fourth had been born in Hungary, although he may have also come from another European country. In other words, about three-quarters of the Viennese Jewish population around the turn of the century originated from areas where they could be assumed to have had a primary exposure to western, and mainly German culture. Indeed, this would hold true for many of the Galician migrants since a number of them originated from the larger trading towns like Lemberg and Krakau where the Jewish enlightenment had taken root. Moreover, the tendency toward residential dispersion established at the outset of the modern period was well advanced by 1910, as is shown on the schematic Vienna city Map 3 indicating the percentage of Jews resident in each city district. Bearing in mind that Jews at this time were 8.6 per cent of the total Viennese population, it can be seen that the earlier mixed pattern of concentration combined with a considerable degree of dispersion persisted on a district basis – although, with some clustering of Jewish settlement within districts, and the operation of district synagogues and other Jewish organizations, the social and cultural effects of this spatial distribution on the weakening of ethnic bonds were probably greatly lessened in many instances.

The pattern of residential dispersion was not, of course, identical for all types of Jews. Degree of affluence, which in turn tended to be correlated with region of origin, meant that – as depicted in Maps 3a and 3b – the longer established Viennese-born Jews, in sharp contrast to the Galician-born, were far more likely to be found in such districts as the elite 19th 'villa district' of Döbling, or the solid bourgeois districts around the Ringstrasse like Mariahilf, Neubau, Josfstadt, Alsergrund, or within the inner city itself. If Döbling was the haven of the Viennese-born Jewish bourgeoisie and nobility, Brigittenau, the 20th district, in which the majority of Jewish residents came from Galicia was, as previously noted, the home of a high proportion of 'Ostjuden'. The overall situation was not as highly polarized as this comparison suggests, however; Jews of all origins and social classes continued to live in Leopoldstadt in particular which retained its character as reception area and core Jewish district. Moreover, there was a substantial degree of intermarriage taking place between Jewish men and women born in various parts of the empire. Birds of a feather flocked together, but many sought to cross over regional boundaries, whether facilitated by old family connections or accidental encounters. Most Galician men who were wed in Vienna married Galician-born women in 1910; but 1 in 5 married Viennese-born women, and 1 in 7 found mates from Bohemia or Moravia. Half the Hungarian grooms took Viennese-born brides, as did 4 out of every 10 Jewish bridegrooms from the Czech lands who were married in Vienna that year. Not that the core of Viennese families was in danger of dissolving within a generation: 6 out of 10 marriages involving Viennese-born Jewish males in 1910 were with Viennese-born brides.

Mixed marriages involving non-Jewish partners were also not a rarity in Vienna by 1910. The precise rates cannot be calculated

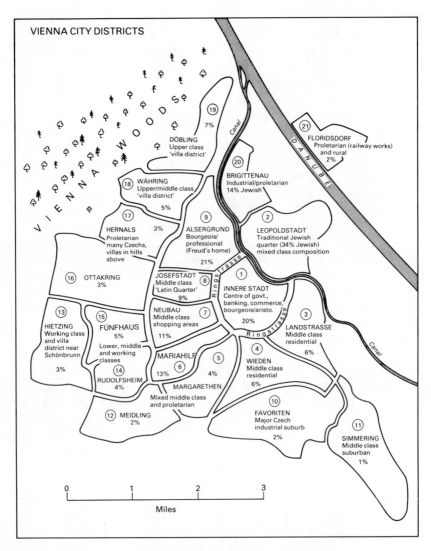

Map 3 *Vienna City Districts with notation on socio-economic images.*
Percentages indicate proportion of Jews in the total population of each district
in 1910

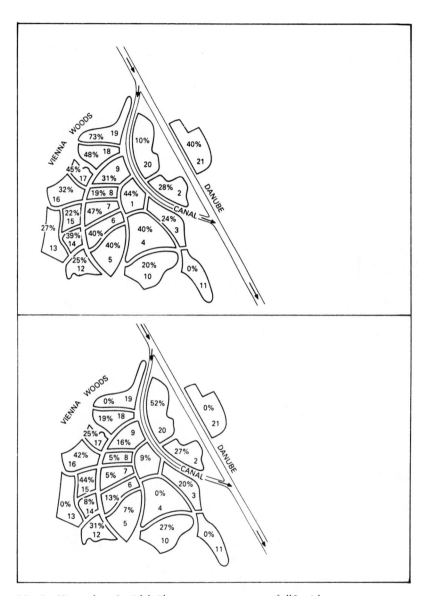

Map 3a *Vienna-born Jewish bridegrooms, as percentage of all Jewish bridegrooms resident in each city district in 1910*

Map 3b *Galicia-born Jewish bridegrooms, as percentage of all Jewish bridegrooms resident in each city district in 1910*

because such marriages do not appear in the Jewish marriage records in cases where the Jewish partner left Judaism prior to marrying a non-Jewish spouse. In 1910 Jewish conversions of all types – Catholic, Protestant, *konfessionslos* (non-denominational) – numbered 512, equally divided between men and women, the vast majority single and of marriageable age. The Jewish marriage registers themselves record that 64 out of 946 Jewish brides married non-Jewish men (legally required to be *konfessionslos*), while 91 out of 972 Jewish men married *konfessionslos* women. In her discussion of these statistics Rozenblit, while acknowledging that mixed ex-Jewish-gentile marriages must be concealed in the 512 Jewish conversions, prefers to stress a lower estimate of mixed marriages of under 10 per cent obtained from the Jewish records alone.[28] No convincing reasons are given, however, for not also including the other type of mixed marriage – where the Jewish partner departs from Judaism altogether prior to marriage. If only 1 in 5 of the conversions are assumed to have been directly associated with plans to marry a gentile, together with the marriages involving one non-Jewish partner, they produce the kind of ratio, 1 in 7, or even higher, then obtaining among the Jews of Berlin. This is a fate from which Rozenblit seeks to protect her *Wiener Juden* but, within a confusing array of arguments, she is obliged to concede the possibility that 'a great many intermarrying Jews in Vienna disappeared into the Christian or *konfessionslos* categories.'[29]

Although the number of conversions in a year were minuscule in comparison to the total size of the Jewish community – 512 out of 175,000 in 1910 – they did accumulate over a generation or more, creating an indistinct class of semi-Jews or Jews who, although regarding themselves as totally assimilated, Christian or secularized, would still be regarded by others as remaining 'essentially' Jewish. The social, cultural, intellectual and psychological ambiguities of Viennese Jewish assimilation are discussed elsewhere in this volume; here it may simply be noted that before the First World War ex-Jews of some description probably numbered about 10 per cent of the officially registered Jewish population, perhaps around 20,000 as a rough estimate. Many of them, however, would retain their ties of family and friendship with unconverted Jews – as Zionists and the orthodox noted with asperity in the Jewish press. Also the rate of intermarriage, while not on a scale to pose a serious threat to the Jewish community as a whole, was sufficiently frequent, and concentrated particularly among Viennese-born offspring, to be regarded as a fairly common, if deviant, occurrence in some Jewish family circles and milieux.

In his classic 1964 work on the origins of political antisemitism in Central Europe, Peter Pulzer began with a statistical excursion aiming to demonstrate the over-representation of Jews in many professional roles, banking, commerce and industry. The reader might have been forgiven for anticipating that Pulzer was engaged in an exercise aiming to prove that economic competition between Jews and gentiles, or even the resentment of non-Jews at Jewish cultural and economic hegemony, was a fundamental, objective cause of antisemitism. But this was not his intention; rather, he suggested that the objective economic facts were less important than the distorted and paranoid interpretations placed on them by the antisemites. The Jew of the convinced antisemite, he argued, was simply a scapegoat for the fears, hatreds and prejudices which have their origins within the antisemite himself. The role of objective facts, in this model of antisemitism, was to supply support for 'the plot-monger's explanations [which] would not be nearly so persuasive if they did not bear *some relation* to ascertainable fact and a hard core of genuine evidence' [emphasis added].[30] This formulation is appropriate for situations, like Nazi Germany, in which political paranoia distorts the Jewish presence to such an extent that it bears a minimal relation to the actual situation; but is it not less salient for Habsburg Vienna, where at least some of the major 'accusations' against Jews – precisely their over-representation in the professions, banking, commerce, etc. – were to a considerable extent true? Debate about causes must not obscure the fact that the Jews, as Jews, had no case to answer; they were only one, exceptionally successful, segment in the development of European capitalist society – evidently culturally better prepared to compete both in commerce and through achievement in the education-based meritocracy. The Viennese Marxists like Victor Adler and Otto Bauer were perfectly aware of this, but typically failed to challenge the popular perception held in Vienna and Central Europe – conveniently forgetting that capitalism had reached its apogee in Protestant Britain and America – that the destructive amoralism of the capitalist market economy and Jewish wickedness exercised through their financial power were one and the same. It was a perception conditioned by the conscious or implicit historical legacy of 700 years of economic competition and conflict, one mass execution, religious discrimination, grudging 'toleration' of a limited Jewish presence, expulsions and ostracism. Furthermore, it was a perception supported by the appearance of some striking continuities with the feudal era, such as the emperor Franz Josef's apparent dependence on the Jewish financial barons, and the protection he bestowed on his Jewish subjects. The ancient conflicts between the emperor and court on the one hand, and the burghers of Vienna on the other, were restaged just before the turn of the century, in the era of mass municipal politics, with the repeated attempt of the emperor to block the installation of the elected mayor of Vienna, Dr Karl Lueger, whose attacks on the Jews featured prominently in his Christian Social rhetoric. That Jews were by now an integral part of the Viennese economy, however, and not just an appendage of the imperial court, was demonstrated when Lueger himself, with his famous catch-phrase 'I decide who is a Jew' ('Wer ein Jud ist, bestim ich'), assumed the role of Jewish patron, successfully co-opting Jewish financiers in support of his ambitious scheme for urban modernization. It was an example of political opportunism which, as is well known, repelled the youthful Hitler even as he admired, and learned from, Lueger's exploitation of anti-Jewish sentiment in mobilizing mass support.

Rozenblit devoted a chapter of her study to an attempt to demonstrate that a major avenue of Jewish social mobility was through the virtual monopoly they managed to establish over private – as opposed to civil service – employment in salaried, clerical, white-collar jobs. If true, this would be another example of Jewish over-representation, with a vengeance:

> The rush of Jews into clerical, managerial and sales positions did not parallel any similar growth in the percentage of business employees in the Viennese work force as a whole in the decades before World War I. Jews transformed themselves in the urban environment but that transformation did not lead to the growing similarity of Jewish and gentile occupational distribution. Jewish change only led to continued Jewish distinctiveness.[31]

She further suggests that

> Between 1890 and 1910 the percentage of *Angestellte* [salaried employees] in the Viennese work force remained constant at 12-14% of the entire work force, including Jews. Most Viennese *Angestellte* worked for the imperial and municipal civil service, while most Jewish employees worked as clerks, salesmen or

managers in the business world. . . . Salaried white-collar
employment had become a Jewish profession.[32]

If these statements were true, and Jews were actually totally
outstripping other Viennese in obtaining private white-collar employment, then the direct economic-competition model of antisemitism
would appear to have occupied even greater salience in the Viennese
case, and the role of paranoia further reduced. But without wishing
to minimize Rozenblit's general point of inter- and intra-sectorial
ethnic segmentation in Viennese employment – aspects of which are
further explored by Beller in the following chapter – the above
assertions about the exclusively Jewish nature of the private
Angestellten are demonstrably erroneous, apparently based on a
misunderstanding of how the official occupational statistics were
organized.[33] At any rate, Table 1.1 and facing Figure 1.1, as
derived from the occupational census of 1910, provide a broad
overview, for the private sector only, of the distribution of Jewish
and Catholic males in the Viennese workforce. It will be noted from
the table that Catholics and Jews have almost an exactly reverse ratio
of employment in industry versus trade – two-thirds of the Catholics
are in industry, two-thirds of the Jews in trade – and that while 76.4
per cent of all Catholics are classified as workers (Arbeiter) only 30.8
per cent of the Jews are so classified. Two out of three Jews were
either self-employed (at some high or low level) or worked as salaried
employees. In the sense of over-representation as salaried employees
then, Rozenblit's point appears valid – only 9.3 per cent of all male
Catholic workers were employed as Angestellte in the private sector.

However, to focus solely on the proportionality dimension –
although an important and valid aspect of a minority's employment
pattern – may distort the overall context in which the comparison in
terms of absolute numbers is also essential. Figure 1.1 reveals that
despite the high degree of divergence in the status and industrial
concentration of Jews and Catholics, the latter were so far more
numerous in the workforce of those two predominant sectors –
481,266 compared with only 51,106 Jews – that even a low
percentage of Catholic recruitment as salaried employees in both
industry and trade meant that they actually greatly outnumbered
Jews in those occupational statuses, including self-employment,
which were components of the anti-Jewish stereotype. Moreover, the
table also suggests areas of overlap between Catholic and Jewish
employment – 1 out of every 7 Jews was classified as an industrial

Table 1.1. *Employment of Catholic and Jewish males in Vienna by economic sector and occupational status in 1910*

| | Catholic occupational statuses | | | |
	Self-employed	Salaried employee	Worker*	Totals by sector
Industry	41,453	17,596	266,690	325,739
	8.6	3.7	55.4	67.7
Trade and transport	27,381	27,096	101,050	155,527
	5.7	5.6	21.0	32.3
Totals by status	68,834	44,692	367,740	481,266
	14.3	9.3	76.4	100.0%

| | Jewish occupational statuses | | | |
	Self-employed	Salaried employee	Worker*	Totals by sector
Industry	5,464	5,455	7,337	18,256
	10.7	10.6	14.4	35.7
Trade and transport	12,975	11,479	8,396	32,850
	25.4	22.5	16.4	64.3
Totals by status	18,439	16,934	15,733	51,106
	36.1	33.1	30.8	100.0%

*Includes day labourers and apprentices;
family helpers are not included in this table.

Totals for other Viennese industrial sectors: Civil service, military, free professions, no occupation – Catholics 123,666, Jews 14,086; Agriculture – Catholics 6,686, Jews 116

Source: *Berufsstatistik nach den Ergebnissen der Volkszählung vom 31 Dezember 1910, 3. Band, 1. Heft (Neue Folge) Oesterreichische Statistik*, Vienna, 1916, p. 132

Arbeiter, possibly even a member of the socialist movement.

But the dominant contrast in Table 1 must be the finding that, excluding public employees, 3 out of every 4 Catholic men in Vienna at this time were ostensibly members of the artisan and proletariat workforce, while the great majority of Jews were traders, merchants, self-employed capitalists of some degree, or else members of the salariate. It is difficult to resist the hypothesis that a general awareness in the huge Catholic working class of this broad contrast in economic status, and often job security, between themselves and the Jewish minority would have reinforced

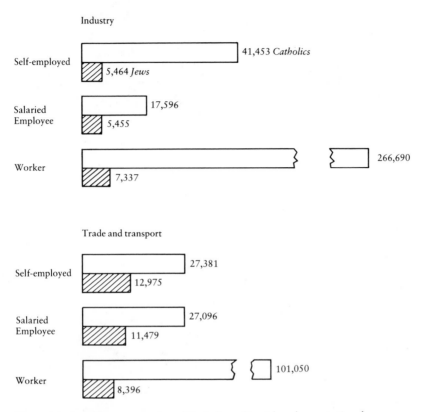

Figure 1.1 *Graphic representation of Catholic and Jewish male occupational statistics presented in Table 1.1*

traditional prejudices against the Jews, independent of the degree of direct economic contact or competition, and independent too, perhaps, of the outcry of antisemitic agitators about the number of Jews in banking, journalism and medicine. If such resentments were pervasive in the Catholic working class – which was, after all, the Social Democrats' main constituency – they would help to explain the feeble and ambiguous opposition to antisemitism on the part of the socialists which Wistrich has exposed.[34] It is manifest from these figures, as has long been impressionistically recognized, that the Jews of young Hitler's Vienna constituted, in the main, a predominantly bourgeois, petty bourgeois and white-collar minority – within or alongside the middle strata of Viennese society – in a predominantly artisan and increasingly proletarian city. The weakness of liberal social values and institutions in the population at large ensured that the transition from the feudal to the capitalist era would remain charged with the dangers and anxieties which had threatened Viennese Jews over the centuries.

CHAPTER 2

CLASS, CULTURE AND THE JEWS OF VIENNA, 1900

Steven Beller

Around the turn of the century a fundamental change occurred in western culture. The new culture broke the bonds with the past and became, in a word, modern. Many cultural historians are now coming to see Vienna, and its central European setting, as one of the prime sources of this change. This claim is open to question. Paris or even Berlin could be seen as more important in this transformation. It was just that, especially in the case of Paris, the change to modernism took place decades before that in Vienna. Yet there is no denying that Vienna did produce some of the more important contributions to our modern culture. Freud's psychoanalysis, and the linguistic and analytic philosophy associated with Wittgenstein and the Vienna Circle, stand out as particularly important. In music there was, of course, Mahler and Schoenberg, in art Klimt, Kokoschka and Schiele, in architecture Otto Wagner and Adolf Loos. In the world of literature there was a huge galaxy of talent, from Hofmannsthal and Schnitzler to Kraus, Canetti and Broch. Vienna was a fount of new ideas around 1900.

This fact has given rise to the subject in cultural history of '*fin-de-siècle* Vienna'. The idea that Vienna was the nodal point of cultural transformation goes back at least to Hermann Broch's brilliant study *Hofmannsthal und seine Zeit*.[19] In recent years, however, it has centred on American research, above all that of Carl Schorske. Schorske offers what is essentially a class explanation of the cultural events, in terms of a declining liberal bourgeoisie. He basically argues that the liberal bourgeoisie were never able to create a style of their own in Viennese society, due to the weakness of their position in that society. They therefore adopted that of their social betters, and became absorbed in the traditional, aristocratic, Baroque culture of feeling, *Gefühlskultur*, which was, according to Schorske, the antithesis of the usual liberal, northern belief in Law and Science:

> Two basic social facts distinguish the Austrian from the French and English bourgeoisie: it did not succeed either in destroying or in fully fusing with the aristocracy; and because of its weakness it remained both dependent upon and deeply loyal to the emperor as a remote but necessary father-protector.[2]

When, therefore, the liberal bourgeoisie, after a brief period of ascendancy in Austria, lost power from the 1880s onward, instead of reacting politically they, or their sons, retreated into aesthetics, the temple of art. Or alternatively, they retreated into the parallel world of the psyche, and psychoanalysis, which appears for Schorske to be more or less the same thing as aesthetics:

> By the end of the century, the function of art for Viennese middle-class society had altered, and in this change politics played a crucial part. If the Viennese burghers had begun by supporting the temple of art as a surrogate form of assimilation into the aristocracy, they ended by finding in it an escape, a refuge from the unpleasant world of increasingly threatening political reality. In 1899 the critic Karl Kraus identified the widened interest in and the commercialization of literature as a political product, a product of 'recent years which have seen the sphere of action of Viennese liberalism constricted to the parquets of theaters on opening night.'. . . Elsewhere in Europe, art for art's sake implied the withdrawal of its devotees from a social class; in Vienna alone it claimed the allegiance of virtually a whole class, of which the artists were a part. The life of art became a substitute for the life of action. Indeed, as civic action proved increasingly futile, art became almost a religion, the source of meaning and the food of the soul.[3]

This argument, the Schorskean thesis, provides a neat explanation of many phenomena, and doubtless contains much truth. Yet there are many problems with it, not least of which is the vagueness of Schorske's definition of the 'liberal bourgeoisie'. Although the central group in his schema, Schorske never really tells us who they were. Perhaps this is an unfair demand on what is essentially a collection of essays on cultural not social history. Nevertheless, if we are to take

Schorske's whole approach seriously, then we must know more about this 'liberal bourgeoisie', for Schorske does not do this for us.

Schorske's interpretation is not by any means the only theory about Vienna's fecundity at the turn of the century. Other accounts stress religious and ethnic factors which Schorske tends to play down or avoid. There is a long tradition, most recently exemplified by George Steiner, of talking about Viennese culture as if it were more or less a product of the Jewish community alone.[4] Stefan Zweig, for example, wrote in his memoirs, *Die Welt von Gestern*, that nine-tenths of Viennese culture in the pre-1914 era had depended on Jews.[5] Yet when one looks at Vienna at that time this seems impossible. Jews made up only about 10 per cent of the population. The obvious response to such figures is that it must have been impossible for such a small minority to run the high culture of the vast majority for them. This has been the line taken by most of current research, which has tended to play down the role of Jewish influence as the product of either antisemitic or semitophile prejudice and, almost as a matter of principle, irrelevant. The Jews could not have been so important as they and their enemies made out – so the Schorskean argument implies – and even if they were over-represented in the culture, they were only following the bourgeois cultural trends of their non-Jewish equivalents, so the Jewish aspect is irrelevant to understanding the culture. Writes Schorske:

> In Austria, where higher culture was so greatly prized as a mark of status by the liberal, urban middle class, the Jews of that class merely shared the prevalent values, holding them perhaps more intensely, because the taint of trade had stained their lives more deeply.[6]

> The failure to acquire a monopoly of power left the bourgeoisie always something of an outsider, seeking integration with the aristocracy. The numerous and prosperous Jewish element in Vienna, with its strong assimilationist thrust, *only strengthened this trend.*[7]

Steiner and writers like him, however, see the Jewish heritage as a vital part of the intellectual make-up of even the most assimilated central European cultural figures of Jewish descent. Clearly, some well-grounded evidence is long overdue in order to test these conflicting and impressionistic hypotheses. One of the ways in which this can be done is to attempt to discover just how large the Jewish presence actually was in the major cultural movements in Vienna around 1900.

This involves counting heads. It is a moot point which heads to count. However, the politics of who is Jewish and who not should not be allowed, in my opinion, to influence the historian's approach to this vexed question. For the historian studying the entry of the Jews into western culture during the period of assimilation, the process of conversion and assimilation must be regarded as part of the *Jewish* phenomenon, even if it produces people who are ostensibly not Jewish. Hofmannsthal and Wittgenstein, therefore, though not Jewish by religion and only partly so by descent, should figure in a study of the type undertaken here, if only at the margin, for they were both products of the assimilationary process, and conscious of it.[8] This inclusion of people as Jewish only because of their descent, and not their religious belief, is not therefore in any sense 'racist', but based on the assumption that, no matter what attitude an individual takes to his past it will have a significant bearing on the way he behaves. This study therefore adopts an inclusive approach, counting all those individuals in the cultural groups who were of at least partly Jewish descent as Jewish.

When we look at the lists of the various cultural groups we can begin to see what commentators such as Zweig and Steiner are getting at. All the regular members of the fledgling psychoanalytic movement in Vienna until 1906 were Jewish.[9] In philosophy Wittgenstein and Karl Popper were of Jewish descent. Logical Positivism originated in the Vienna Circle, a list of whose members in the pamphlet *Wissenschaftliche Weltauffassung* shows 8 out of the 14 listed to be Jewish.[10] In socialist political thought Karl Renner was most remarkable for the fact that he was the only major Austro-Marxist theorist who was not Jewish, compared to Otto Bauer, Max Adler, Rudolf Hilferding and the rest.[11] The major theoretical opposition to the Austro-Marxists, from within the liberal camp, came from the now famous Austrian school of economic theory. This school had been non-Jewish to start with. None of the founding members − Carl Menger, Boehm-Bawerk, Friedrich von Wieser − were Jewish.[12] By the interwar years, however, the tradition was being continued mainly by Ludwig von Mises, who was Jewish. His seminar, which produced such theorists as Hayek, was largely Jewish, to the extent of 23 out of 29 participants.[13]

In literature, a Jewish predominance had arisen much earlier. In

1891 Arthur Schnitzler drew up a list of the individuals whom he considered part of the new literary movement which would later be known as *Jung-Wien*. Of the 23 individuals listed 16, or 70 per cent, were Jewish.[14] The musical revolution in Vienna was originated by three figures initially: Gustav Mahler, Arnold Schoenberg and his brother-in-law Alexander Zemlinksy. All three were Jewish. It should be added, however, that Schoenberg's most famous pupils, Berg and Webern, were not Jewish.[15] This serves as a salutary reminder that not all of Viennese high culture was created by Jews. This was even more the case in the fields of art and architecture. There were very few Jews who were actual artists or architects, although there were some of major importance such as Richard Gerstl, Schoenberg's painting instructor, and the architect Oskar Strnad.[16] Where Jews seem to have made their mark in these fields it was not as creators, but as patrons and propagandists. Hence it was Fritz Wärndorfer, the son of a Jewish cotton merchant, who provided most of the capital for the *Wiener Werkstätte*. Ludwig Hevesi, the art critic who invented the Secessionist slogan 'To the time its art, To art its freedom', was also Jewish, as was another of the leading supporters of the movement, the salon hostess Berta Zuckerkandl. At least one historian of the Secession has asserted that Jews made up the great majority of the movement's patrons.[17]

In other words, at the strategic points of Viennese modernism there was a very large Jewish presence indeed, including not only the major figures cited above but a host of minor ones, with Jewish participation greater in some fields than in others but so strong that overall one might perhaps talk of a Jewish preponderance, and in certain fields of a Jewish predominance. Yet we are left with the problem of where this massive proportion could have come from when Jews made up only about 10 per cent of the city's total population. The obvious way of attempting to find an answer is to go back to the original problem identified in the above discussion of Schorske's interpretation: the question of the composition of the liberal bourgeoisie.

So what made up the core of the 'liberal bourgeoisie'? In attempting to define the 'liberal' component of the Viennese bourgeoisie we must bear in mind the major political fact that Liberalism as an organized political-ideological tendency in Vienna was swept from power in the crucial 1895 elections to the city council by the antisemitic Christian Social party with the assistance of bourgeois voters – furthermore, by the votes of members of the bourgeois intelligentsia. This is well shown by John Boyer's excellent study of the social background to the Christian Socials' success, *Political Radicalism in Late Imperial Vienna*.[18] Boyer has shown that large sectors of what should have been Schorske's 'liberal bourgeoisie' actually voted for Liberalism's foes. We know that this must have occurred because of the structure of the electoral system.

The Viennese electoral system of 1895 was divided into three curiae, or electoral colleges. The curiae were divided according to several criteria of which the level of income and property tax was only one. Thus the first curia consisted mainly of the highest taxpayers but also many middling landlords, due to the system of assessing tax for a landlord on the basis of the sum of all tax paid by tenants in the property. The bottom curia, the third, was made up mainly of the lower-middle-class artisanry. It was the second curia, however, which proved to be the most important in the elections of 1895. Middling taxpayers were included here, but the main constituents in most districts appear to have been the groups of officials and teachers given the vote not on the basis of taxes but as the presumably loyal intellectual class of the Liberal establishment. In fact the second curia became known as the *Wahlkörper der Intelligenz* – roughly translated as the curia of the intelligentsia, though the latter word is not to be confused with its Russian connotations.[19]

Until 1895 the Liberals had always been able to win because of the solid support of the first and second curiae, while the most populous curia, the third, had become virtually solid for the antisemites. Therefore, Karl Lueger's victory in 1895 must have been caused by the desertion of the Liberals by the voters of the second curia – the intelligentsia. This is apparently what happened. The 'betrayal' was openly recognized at the time. The major organ of the Liberals, the *Neue Freie Presse*, reported how officials were coming straight from their offices in their uniforms and voting for the anti-Liberals. It even printed a letter from Kronawetter, the old left-radical Democrat in which he stated: 'The swing of opinion among our lower-middle classes, officials and teachers is a complete puzzle to me.'[20]

The core of the old Liberal intelligentsia, the officials and teachers, was voting in a majority, and, it would seem, a large one, for the Christian Socials, and cannot therefore really be included as a constituent of that '*liberal* bourgeoisie' which was defeated by the rise of mass politics. This brings us to the question of just how we are to define operationally Schorske's 'liberal bourgeoisie'. Any classification of economic and social groups according to political loyalties is to a certain extent arbitrary because individuals' class backgrounds do not always correspond to their most likely and appropriate political affiliations or voting patterns. There will always be exceptions, and major ones, to the correlations between economic classes and political behaviour. Thus, while most of the aristocracy in Austria was conservative, if not reactionary, it is also true that there was a sizeable number of liberal and progressive individuals from an aristocratic background, such as Ferdinand von Andrian Werburg. More significantly for this study, while it may have been true that most of the officialdom changed sides in the decisive elections of 1895, it has been argued that the most significant part of officialdom concerned with cultural life, the high bureaucracy, continued to vote against the antisemitic Christian Socials and for the Liberals. Nevertheless there are large difficulties in including the high bureaucracy as part of Schorske's class of alienated liberal bourgeoisie. First, in the most elementary way, they cannot be seen as being alienated from power, as they continued to direct policy, especially so in an era of *Beamtenministerien*. Second, the style of the bureaucracy was not that of western liberalism, but rather of administrative rationality subject to the will of the Habsburg dynasty. It was not bound to liberal ideology, but had higher and older loyalties. Administrative Josephinism was always above politics, and tended to social and cultural conservatism.[21] While, no doubt, there were some bureaucrats who were genuinely liberal in the western sense, and also interested in avant-garde culture, it is to be doubted whether they were very numerous, or very significant in the high bureaucracy.

Similar arguments, coupled with what we know about voting behaviour in 1895, can be used to exclude many other supposedly bourgeois occupational groups from the 'liberal' sector. There is evidence, for instance, that many white-collar workers, *Privatbeamten*, and railway officials were voting for the Christian Socials by 1895, or were explicitly antisemitic in their occupational organizations. The artisanry had been against the Liberals, as champions of anti-Guild reforms, more or less from the start. Landowners, and those involved in agriculture would never be central to a 'liberal bourgeoisie'; and urban landlords, the *Hausbesitzer*, were, according to Boyer, increasingly coming over to the Christian Social side. However, it is not clear which way such occupations as *Apotheker* or *Ingenieur* would have voted, or what their political and cultural style was.[22] The negative evidence from the elections of 1895 strongly suggests that teachers were not dependable Liberal adherents although, as with the higher reaches of the bureaucracy, the upper echelons of the teaching profession, especially university professors, retained their loyalty to the Liberals. Because of the ambiguous use of the term 'professor', however, it was not possible to distinguish this sub-group of the teaching profession in the quantitative analysis below. But, on the whole, the category of teachers cannot be included in our working definition of Vienna's liberal bourgeoisie.

It should be made clear that, given the above description of the various occupational groups, my chosen division of occupations cannot be regarded as exhaustive, but rather a rough picture of the core of the liberal bourgeois sector within Viennese society. This turns out to be very much the capitalist occupational groups of commercial independents and semi-independents, industrial independents, financiers and rentiers, with the added section of what in Marxist terms might be called the 'superstructural appendages' of the capitalist class, the free professional classes of lawyers, doctors and journalists. These groups, after all, are usually regarded as the liberal bourgeoisie, partly because of their relative freedom from state control compared to such groups as officials and teachers. No doubt there were members of these groups who voted for the Christian Socials, especially in the non-Jewish group, but I think it is safe to say that, in contrast to the other groups discussed, groups in my chosen list were generally liberal in political and cultural terms. They represent the bulk of the Viennese 'liberal bourgeoisie' and have been identified by an asterisk in the list of fifteen occupational categories shown in Table 2.1 on pages 50–1.

Having delineated what we take to have been the economic groups which composed the core of the liberal bourgeoisie, we can now return to our question about the magnitude of the Jewish presence in this sector. In many of the constituent groups it was very high. Well over half of the journalists in the press club *Concordia* in 1909 were of Jewish descent. Jews also appear by religion to have made up over half the physicians and lawyers in Vienna around 1890.[23] Nevertheless, other figures for other groups point to a different picture. As shown in the preceding chapter, the census figures of 1910 indicate that Jewish men represent only about one-third of the total number of males self-employed in the trade and transport sector; a figure which, though very considerable, and a three-fold over-representation of Jews as a proportion of all independent men in this sector, is still far from any sort of Jewish numerical predominance. A numerical predominance, however, is, as we have seen, what Jewish individuals represented in the cultural elite. To be sure, the global census figures, by failing to specify actual occupations, may be rather misleading. But they are surely not so misleading as to allow for the possibility that they mask a Jewish numerical predominance in the total commercial, independent sector – the core of our definition of the liberal bourgeoisie – commensurate with that of which we have direct evidence from our empirical analysis of the cultural elite. These census data therefore appear to exclude an explanation of Jewish cultural predominance based on a simple demographic extrapolation from their overall distribution in the Viennese economic and class structure.

If, however, we look more closely at one of the preconditions for membership of the cultural elite, that of being 'educated', the view obtained of the interaction of social and cultural factors brings us much nearer to an understanding of how it was that Jews played such a major role in the development of Vienna's modern high culture. The key institutions which we must examine are Vienna's central *Gymnasien*. The *Gymnasium* was designed as the elite form of secondary education in Austria. It was not by any means the only form of secondary education, however; there were other forms, such as the *Realschule*, which provided a more vocational curriculum, the *Bürgerschule* which offered a more rudimentary education, and the various specialist schools for the arts and crafts. There were, in addition, schools of *Gymnasium* standard which, though outside of Vienna, were nevertheless frequented by Viennese boys. The most famous of these was the school of the Jesuit monastery of Kalksburg. The military academy of Wiener Neustadt might also be mentioned. Most of these schools, however, were marginal, for various reasons, when it comes to discussing the liberal, modernist wing of the cultural elite. Kalksburg, for instance, virtually disqualifies itself by definition. It can hardly have been a fortress of the 'liberal bourgeoisie' and the same can be said of the military academy.

The *Realschule* cannot be easily excluded as a source of 'liberal bourgeois' forms of education: Broch, Berg and Schoenberg went through this type of schooling. Yet it is plain that the *Gymnasium* was the central educational institution at the secondary level for the cultural elite, or those aspiring to enter it. The *Gymnasium* was, until 1904, the only form of school, graduation from which entitled the student to enter university. Moreover, it was the only curriculum which included Latin and Greek, both necessary prerequisites of a man of culture in late nineteenth-century European civilization. The superiority of the *Gymnasium* over the *Realschule* in the eyes of the cultural elite is illustrated by one of the exceptions who went to *Realschule*: the writer Hermann Broch was forced to go to *Realschule* against his will, for, in order to pursue the intellectual career to which he aspired, it was regarded as imperative to go to *Gymnasium*. Broch's emergence as a major intellectual figure was the result of his struggle against the severe disadvantage which going to *Realschule* had meant for him.[24] It was thus the *Gymnasium* which was the breeding ground for the cultural and intellectual elite.

There were eleven *Gymnasien* in the central nine districts of Vienna producing graduates (*Maturanten*) by 1910. In 1870 there had been only four: the *Akademisches*, *Piaristen-* and *Schotten-gymnasien*, and the *Theresianum*. These were followed by the *Mariahilfer-* and *Sperlgymnasien*, founded as twin schools in 1864. In 1869 the *Landstrassergymnasium* was founded, then the *Wasa-* (1871), *Franz-Josephs-* (1872), *Sophien-* (1877) and *Elisabeths-gymnasien* (1878).[25]

More or less complete records exist for eight of these schools, and for one other in part. Records from the other two were lost or destroyed during the Second World War which prevents our obtaining a complete picture of the social characteristics of *Gymnasium* graduates. These omissions are not a serious drawback for our analysis, however, since one of the schools without records was the *Theresianum*, which was specifically designed for the aristocracy or the monarchy and therefore not particularly relevant in our quest for the liberal bourgeoisie; the other school without records was the youngest, the *Elisabethsgymnasium* with, therefore, the smallest number of graduates – only 4 per cent of the total of all graduates from the central *Gymnasien* in Vienna during the years of our survey, 1870-1910.[26] It was also geographically the furthest from the centre, and therefore marginal, in an area which was not noted for large concentrations of the occupational groups which I have defined as 'liberal bourgeoisie'.

We already know, from readily accessible published sources, that Jews represented about one third of Vienna's *Gymnasiasten* from around 1880 onwards, compared with their approximately 10 per cent distribution in the city's total population.[27] Much more information of sociological importance can be obtained from the school records themselves. These come in two main forms: *Maturaprotokolle* (examination records), and *Hauptkataloge* (records for each class, in the following analysis for the eighth, final class). Both records give the following background data for each student: religion, *Stand* (occupational title) of the father, and the geographical origin of the student. It is thus possible to make a detailed analysis of the distribution of students' religious affiliations in relation to fathers' occupations, religion and geographical origins, and even religion and occupation for a given region of origin. A sample was taken from this primary source consisting of all the members of every fifth annual graduating class, in 1870, 1875, and so on until 1910. This produced a total sample of 1,810 cases, the proportion of Jews in the sample being 723 or 40 per cent, including a few students from prominent families known to have converted from Judaism. Deducting the latter from the sample, the proportion of Jewish students becomes 39.1 per cent as against the total figures from published sources of 38.8 per cent, thus indicating the highly-representative nature of our data.[28]

Turning to Table 2.1, we can now see the distribution of the *Gymnasium* graduates' religious background (including the cases of converted Jews, where known) in relation to the occupational status of the fathers. This shows us some striking features about Vienna's educated elite and the ethnic background of those occupations which I have identified as the core of the liberal bourgeoisie. Jewish fathers make up 318 out of a total of 391 merchants and commercial semi-independents – over 80 per cent – with sons graduating from the *Gymnasien* during the late Habsburg period. They comprise around 60 per cent of the financiers and industrialists, and very large minorities, in each case approaching one-half, in the liberal professions – lawyers, physicians, journalists and the like. If all the occupational categories constituting our operational model of the liberal bourgeoisie are added together – the fathers in commerce, finance, industry, law, medicine, journalism and living as *rentier* – then, as shown in Table 2.1, Jews constituted 547 out of the 838 cases in these categories, 65.3 per cent of the total, very nearly a 2:1 ratio against the combined numbers of Catholics, Protestants and other religious groups.

This overall ratio is, of course, based on data from a sample stretching back to 1870. If the figures for the later sample years of 1900, 1905 and 1910 are taken together, then the Jewish presence in the key occupational categories of the liberal bourgeoisie becomes

Table 2.1 Religious affiliation and father's occupation of graduates of Viennese Gymnasien for sample years 1870 - 1910

Student's Religion

Father's Occupation	Jewish	Catholic	Protestant	Other	Total numbers	Total percentages	Jewish per cent	Catholic per cent	Protestant per cent	Other per cent
1 Commerce*	318	53	16	4	391	21.6	81.3	13.6	4.1	1.0 (100.%)
2 Finance*	34	17	6	1	57	3.1	59.6	29.8	10.5	
3 Industry*	68	37	11		117	6.5	58.1	31.6	9.4	0.9
4 Handicrafts (Kleingewerbe)	19	96	2	1	117	6.5	16.2	82.1	1.7	
5 Public employee (Beamte)	23	297	12	3	335	18.5	6.9	88.7	3.6	0.9
6 Private employee (Privatbeamte)	62	112	12	2	188	10.4	33.0	59.6	6.4	1.1
7 Railway employee	14	52	2		68	3.8	20.6	76.5	2.9	
8 Lawyer*	37	49	3	1	90	5.0	41.1	54.4	3.3	1.1
9 Physician*	44	38	7	1	90	5.0	48.9	42.2	7.8	1.1
10 Journalist*	7	10			17	0.9	41.2	58.8		
11 Teacher	34	87	13		134	7.4	25.4	64.9	9.7	

12 Other professions (Apotheker, etc.)	16	29	12	2	59	3.3	27.1	49.2	20.3	3.4
13 Landlord (Hausbesitzer)	6	14	1		21	1.2	28.6	66.7	4.8	
14 Agriculture	2	47	1		50	2.8	4.0	94.0	2.0	
15 Private income* (Privatier)	39	33	2	2	76	4.2	51.3	43.4	2.6	2.6
TOTALS	723	971	100	16	1,810	100.0	39.9	53.6	5.5	0.9
*'Liberal bourgeois' sector totals	547	237	45	9	838	46.3	65.3	28.3	5.4	1.1
Non-liberal sector totals	176	734	55	7	972	53.7	18.1	75.5	5.7	0.7

even greater. For this era Jews make up, as before, 81 per cent of the commercial group. They comprise 71 per cent of the financiers, 63 per cent of the industrialists, which combined represents only a slight rise in the 'capitalist' sector. However, they are now 65 per cent of the lawyers, 59 per cent of the physicians and one-half of the journalists. Only among the *rentiers* is there a slight drop in the proportion of Jews to 46 per cent. If the fathers' occupations for all categories of our liberal bourgeoisie are combined then it appears that Jews in the period 1900-10 comprised *71 per cent* of that socio-economic group. In contrast, the equivalent figure for the sample years spanning 1870-80 was only 58 per cent. The Jewish presence in the liberal bourgeois sector – judging by the social characteristics of our *Gymnasien* sample – appears to have been getting ever larger as the new century dawned. It thus appears that, following Schorske's portrayal of Viennese culture, and Boyer's account of the defectors from the Liberal camp, it is not really surprising to find that Vienna's cultural personnel – outside the graphic arts – was largely Jewish because so was the social base, defined as educated, liberal and bourgeois. If you were a member of this group the likelihood was that you came from a Jewish background.

This is not the end of the story, however. We also know the regional origins of the students and therefore can build up a picture of the immigration patterns of the cultural elite. About one-third of all the *Maturanten*, the graduates of the *Gymnasien* in our sample, were born outside Vienna. The distribution of their origin enables us to put what we know about individual cases in perspective. Schnitzler's father, for instance, came from Hungary, as did Theodor Herzl. Joseph Roth came from Galicia. From a wider range of individual biographies, however, it appears that the Bohemian crownlands – Bohemia, Moravia and Silesia – formed the region from which most of the elite came. Victor Adler, Karl Kraus, Hans Kelsen, Gustav Mahler, and Sigmund Freud were all born there – in fact they were all the sons of Jewish merchants or industrialists in the region.[29] Our data confirm this impression: almost one-half of all Jewish immigrant graduates, 48 per cent, were born in the Bohemian crownlands compared to 15 per cent for Hungary and 19 per cent for Galicia. Added to this is the fact that Jews far outweigh the rest in the group of immigrants from northern and eastern regions generally. Jewish graduates form one-half of all immigrants from the Bohemian crownlands, just under two-thirds of the Hungarian-born, and almost 90 per cent of Galician immigrants. Taken together Jews account for 57 per cent of all immigrant graduates from the northern and eastern regions of the empire. Catholic immigration, on the other hand, was concentrated in the hereditary lands, today's Austria, and there was very little immigration from the southern parts of the monarchy. A further consideration is that Jews made up two-thirds of the immigrants from Russia, the Balkans and Turkey. As far as the Viennese educated elite was concerned, then – confirming the widespread image of Jews in general as a supra-national element in the monarchy – it was the Jews who provided most of the immigration from the parts of the empire outside the Alpine lands around the capital city.

The distribution of religion against occupation within the key group born in the Bohemian crownlands provides us with a partial answer to another important question concerning the background of the liberal bourgeoisie. If, as it appears, an origin in a Bohemian liberal bourgeois, especially commercial or industrial, family was especially significant in the Jewish part of the cultural elite, it also looks as if this background was, on individual biographical evidence, more or less an exclusively Jewish one. Put another way: is it a mere coincidence that most of the famous figures from a Bohemian liberal bourgeois background were Jewish, or was it the case that this background in Vienna's educated elite was more or less a Jewish monopoly, a Jewish experience, without a proper non-Jewish parallel? Our data show the latter hypothesis is correct. It will be recalled that Jewish graduates comprised about one-half of the students originating in the Bohemian crownlands. According to the figures from the *Gymnasien* data Jews accounted for 85 per cent of the merchants' sons, 82 per cent of those in the combined capitalist group of commerce, finance and industry, and 77 *per cent* of the 'liberal bourgeois' sector as a whole originating in the Bohemian crownlands, a proportion even higher than for the total sample.

If, then, the reason why Jewish individuals were so prevalent in the groups at the most strategic points in Vienna's modern high cultural elite is that Jews were also predominant in the educated elite as a whole, was there, in addition, a specifically 'Jewish' aspect to all of this? First, was the Jewishness of this elite merely accidental, or was it part of the cause of the Jewish predominance? It seems to me that the answer to this quetion has to be to recognize some sort of influence from the Jewish tradition, if only to explain the large disparity between the proportion of Jews in the sector of commercial independents – only about one-third of the total, albeit over-represented – and the huge presence of Jewish merchants' sons in the *Gymnasien*. Some room, surely, must be made here for the old idea that the Jewish religious tradition, although increasingly secularized, puts a great emphasis on education. Far from being a function solely of their class position, the large Jewish presence in the liberal bourgeoisie's educated elite (and hence the cultural elite) looks as if it must have also depended on a wish to see one's son acquire the highest and most prestigious form of secondary education available to a much greater extent than prevailed among Catholic merchants. Second, there is the equally interesting question of whether the Jewish ethnic background of those in the educated elite was merely incidental, with little or no effect on the way they thought or acted and not making them different from their less numerous, but existent, non-Jewish colleagues with the same 'liberal bourgeois' background. The answer to such a complex question, involving individual and collective assessments of the process of assimilation among Viennese Jews, is beyond the scope of the present chapter.[30] Yet, what I can do here is to suggest that further evidence collected from the *Gymnasien* data regarding career choice and achievement indicates that there was indeed a substantial difference, sociologically, between Jewish and non-Jewish members of the group coming from a liberal bourgeois background.

This additional evidence comes from the annual reports (*Jahresberichte*) of the schools, which show the career choices of *Gymnasium* graduates, and, in special cases for two of the schools, the achieved careers of former pupils. Used in conjunction with the other records, we can compare the distributions for Jews and non-Jews of careers for sons of fathers in the same occupational group, or groupings. For example, we can find out the proportion of the sons of Jewish and non-Jewish merchants who became law students. The sample base for the following results is approximately two-thirds of the total sample analysed in Table 2.1, with a total proportion of Jews of 40 per cent, almost identical to the original figure. The results of career choice, as indicated by the courses of study pursued in higher education, show quite clear, indeed basic, differences between Jewish and non-Jewish behaviour. Jewish graduates with fathers in the commerce sector opted for the faculties of law and medicine at exactly the same rate of 33 per cent for each whereas non-Jews with fathers in commerce opted for law at nearly a five-fold rate over medicine, 53 per cent for law as compared to only 11 per cent for the latter. In the 'liberal bourgeois' sector as a whole, as defined above, the disparity is a little lessened, but not much. Among Jews in this category 37 per cent opt for law, against 29 per cent for medicine; among non-Jews, on the other hand, 55 per cent opt for law and only 14 per cent for medicine – a discrepancy of 41 per cent. What is more, this disparity is almost exactly the same for the occupational categories not included in the liberal bourgeois sector: there law leads medicine among Jews by 7 per cent, but among non-Jews by 38 per cent. With respect to these major professional career lines Jews follow Jewish patterns, non-Jews, non-Jewish ones, regardless of class or occupational grouping. Why this was so is an open question. It could be argued that law, as the subject which led on to a bureaucratic career, would not have attracted Jews as much as other groups, since Jews were effectively barred from the bureaucracy unless they converted. It could equally be argued that medicine, having an ages-old tradition of the Jewish physician, was especially attractive to Jews in a way it was not for non-Jews. The main point, however, is that while over 60 per cent of both Jewish and non-Jewish students opt for a career in one of these professions the cleavage between law and medicine is structured along ethnic, rather than class, divisions.

The direct evidence for the distribution of actually attained careers tells a similar story. Admittedly the data are rather sparse, comprising the lists of ex-pupils for a certain run of years in two schools, the *Mariahilfer-* and *Wasagymnasien*. These give a sample totalling 676, which is not large enough to use the figures it produces with too much confidence. Nevertheless, the results from the two schools are fairly obvious, and, within limits, consistent. This is particularly so for the differences between the proportion of those who become civil servants and those going into the liberal professions. In the *Mariahilfergymnasium* only 8 per cent of Jews became civil servants, but fully 33 per cent of non-Jews did so. In the *Wasagymnasium*, 7 per cent of Jews, but 35 per cent of non-Jews, became civil service officials. The figures for those entering the liberal professions – becoming lawyers, doctors and journalists – represent what amounts to a mirror-image of this relationship: in the *Mariahilfergymnasium*, 59 per cent of Jews from the 'liberal bourgeois' sector enter a liberal profession, but only 33 per cent of their non-Jewish equivalents. In the *Wasagymnasium* the corresponding figures are 59 per cent of Jews and 41 per cent of non-Jews.

Moreover, this masks the fact that non-Jewish ex-pupils who are sons of lawyers or physicians are following their fathers' careers and are thus not being socially mobile. If the capitalist sector of fathers' occupations is viewed alone, without the liberal professions and private income categories – that is, with only the categories of commerce, finance and industry – then the differences between the proportions of Jews and non-Jews entering the liberal professions become even greater. In the *Mariahilfergymnasium* it is 60 per cent of the Jews, against 25 per cent of the non-Jews; in the *Wasagymnasium* 64 against 29 per cent. There are thus marked differences between Jewish and non-Jewish groups *within* the 'liberal bourgeois' sector when it comes to the *type* of social mobility they achieve.

The result of this for the liberal professions in Vienna was to be fairly dramatic. Though Jews make up only 30 per cent of the two ex-pupils lists combined, they comprise slightly over half of all those who become lawyers or physicians. This contrasts with the fact that in the samples' distribution of occupations of the fathers, Jews comprise only 28 per cent of lawyers and physicians. Similarly, although Jewish fathers in this sample comprise only 53 per cent of the 'liberal bourgeois' sector, 65 per cent of the sons who originated in that sector, and who went on to become lawyers and physicians, were Jewish. That is to say, even in a sample which seems to have under-represented the total proportion of Jewish fathers in the 'liberal bourgeoisie', according to findings cited earlier, produces nigh on two-thirds of the students emanating from that background who actually became doctors or lawyers. It is thus somewhat understandable that contemporaries referred to the liberal wing of the professional, intellectual classes as a more or less Jewish group.

As has been briefly mentioned with regard to career choice, the question of why there should be this basic difference between Jews and non-Jews in the strategies and achievement of social mobility remains an open one. On the one hand it is true that Jews were effectively barred from the highest reaches of the state bureaucracy, but it may also have been the case, as Peter Pulzer has suggested, that Jews tended to choose careers where they could retain a certain degree of independence, for traditionally Jewish reasons: hence entering the liberal professions or at least the educated elite.[31] This process needs to be further explored for the Viennese case. However, so far as the present discussion is concerned, what is important is that there was a distinctive Jewish pattern of professional career choice which differed markedly from that of the remainder of the 'liberal bourgeoisie' – what there was of it. This suggests that Jews were not merely 'liberal bourgeois' but constituted a different liberal bourgeoisie to the non-Jewish members of that group in Vienna.

The effect of all this on our understanding of Viennese culture and its origins can be illustrated by the case of Freud. If we were to ask the question of whether Freud is to be defined as an Austrian, or an Austrian Jew, then the statistics presented here show fairly clearly that, in numerical terms, the latter option would have to be taken, for he shared his background almost exclusively with Jews. He attended the *Sperlgymnasium* in Vienna's second district, Leopold-stadt, which had a studentship which was 75 per cent Jewish over the period 1870-1910. He was born a merchant's son in the Bohemian crownlands; 85 per cent of the Viennese *Gymnasiasten* with this background were Jewish. At his school, according to data in my sample, 97 per cent of merchants' sons were Jewish, and of those pupils born in the Bohemian crownlands, 73 per cent were Jewish. In my sample for the *Sperlgymnasium*, the ten individuals with Freud's background of being the son of a merchant born in Bohemia were all Jewish – although because of the small size of the sample general conclusions cannot be drawn from this. He chose to do medicine at university; 78 per cent of the 'liberal bourgeois' sector – into which Freud had, of course, been born – among *Maturanten* who opted to study medicine were Jewish. A staggering 93 per cent – 76 Jews as opposed to only 5 non-Jews – of the merchants' sons in the *Gymnasien* sample who chose medicine were Jewish. He went on to become a practising physician. Even when under-represented, as we have just seen, Jews comprised 65 per cent of all former *Gymnasiasten* from a liberal bourgeois background who went on to be doctors and lawyers. If physicians are taken alone, then this figure becomes 69 per cent.

While these figures, showing the typicality of Freud's career in relation to the wider sociological parameters which we have been investigating, should not be taken as an adequate representation of the total picture, I think they do indicate an important historical circumstance: Freud, at least, could hardly have been anything else but Jewish, in the Viennese context. It should be noted that Freud is in many ways an extreme case, and that if we subjected notable personalities such as Karl Kraus or Arthur Schnitzler to the same statistical comparison, then the Jewish contextual determinants would appear to be less. Yet they would not be all that much weaker: it still appears true to say that the social background of the cultural elite of *fin-de-siècle* Vienna was one shared to an almost exclusive degree by persons from a Jewish background.

Whether or not there was a 'Jewish tradition' or a 'Jewish influence' – and I would suggest that there was – the virtual monopoly on certain key backgrounds, as described above, would have made the Jews a special case in the Viennese context, regardless. Quite what this all signified for the culture of Vienna is a question still to be answered. What I think can be said is that the evidence collected here suggests that there is a real question to answer: without some kind of attempt to understand the Jewish aspect of *fin-de-siècle* Vienna in all its complexity no comprehensive understanding of that culture as a whole is possible.

CHAPTER 3

CULTURAL INNOVATION AND SOCIAL IDENTITY IN *FIN-DE-SIÈCLE* VIENNA

Michael Pollak

How can one explain the extraordinary flowering of creative life in the high culture of Vienna which is observed in so many domains in the *fin-de-siècle* period? And how is it that Jews played such a crucial role in this cultural renaissance? These are two questions to which I will attempt to formulate a tentative reply. Steven Beller's analysis in the preceding chapter has indicated the extent to which Jews came to occupy a strategic role within Vienna's *Bildungsbürgertum*, the educated elite, but I want to go beyond the sociological dimension, important though it is, to explore the relationship between historical developments on the level of the decline of entire polities and the social-psychological impact which this process had in restructuring the expectations and sense of social identity, and security, of entire social groups – and the implications of all this for their intellectual and artistic orientations.

Let us first briefly review the social changes which underpinned this transformation of Vienna from a cosy, secure and well ordered imperial capital, with a reputation for excellence in music and pleasant living, to the image of an abrasive and innovative centre of central European culture which the names of Kraus, Schoenberg, Kokoschka, Freud and Wittgenstein conjure up.

Here, in Vienna, were concentrated the dynamic consequences produced by the chaotic liberation of the forces of production which Liberalism, numbering the young emperor Franz Joseph among its acolytes, had brought to bear on the quieter, and still persistent, style of the Biedermeyer ethos. Associated with this classical sea-change of modern history, there occurred a gradual, but progressive, relaxation of the restrictions on freedom of mobility, both geographical and social. It is perhaps not altogether surprising to note that the Jews, formerly the most confined and excluded subjects of the Habsburg empire, would be among those who would take the greatest, and most enthusiastic, advantage of the opportunities which the Liberal era presaged.

This great historical migration within the Habsburg lands was not, of course, simply a matter of individual choice but had a collective character affecting tens of thousands of Jews in the hinterland, hoping for a better life in the great and beautiful capital city. The Jews arriving from different parts of the empire exhibit patterns of behaviour common to migrant ethnic minorities everywhere. They tend to settle in the same urban districts and seek out employment in the most open, rapidly-developing sectors. And, although their internal migration coincides with that of other groups, particularly the Czechs, a common regional origin does not, by virtue of their former social and cultural segregation in the provinces, lead to regional ties in Vienna, but rather to specifically ethnic ones. In the same way, differentiation, although not absolute, appears amongst the establishments of secondary education, some more than others, in the frequency with which they attract Jewish students. The rate of conversions and mixed marriages, although high in comparison with other European cities, remains low and in no way portends overall group disintegration.[1]

The assimilation that accompanied this social mobility has been described as a 'rationalisation and secularisation of Jewish life which led to the substitution of secular Judaism for religious Judaism'.[2] The assimilationist tendency was conspicuous as one went up the social ladder, whilst the majority of the recent arrivals from Galicia remained attached to orthodox religious rites. In a country that knew no separation between church and state and in which certain religions enjoyed officially recognized status, religious creed was an important criterion of the social identity of each and every individual. The decreasing influence of an omnipresent Catholicism in public life and the secularization of minority religions favoured, but only for a very short period in Austria, the unity of the liberal bourgeoisie, with its common denominator the belief in the superiority of Germanic culture over the cultures of the other nationalities.

It is my thesis that the imminent disintegration of the empire and the rise of centrifugal tendencies drained this common denominator of its credibility; and that the questioning of the very existence of the multi-national state entailed, in turn, a reappraisal of the frames of reference of cultural identity for each of the different social groups, forcing them to re-examine their traditions and origins, and the relationships established with all the other groups. At the end of the century it is not only the Jewish identity that is problematic but also the identity of non-Jews. This convergence of a feeling of crisis, both in the external world and within the individual and collective consciousness, took the most acute forms where the conflict between groups and these distinctive pressures were strongest — at the top of the social ladder. Let us attempt to reconstruct this relationship between the political crisis and its social and cultural consequences.

From its creation in 1804 the great dates of the Austrian empire can be read as signs presaging its decomposition. In spite of the victorious outcome of the Napoleonic wars the latter none the less brought to light the fragility of this multinational country and the increasing national aspirations. At the same time, the disappearance in 1806 of the Holy Roman Empire placed Austria in competition with Prussia for hegemony in Germany. The proclamation of a Hungarian constitution made the bourgeois revolution of 1848 a national revolution as well, endangering the unity of the empire. In 1866 the defeat at the hands of the Prussians at Sadowa and the founding of the Dualist regime firmly confirms the division of the empire between Austria and Hungary, and at the same time its loss of influence in Germany. Also, in spite of considerable economic growth during the second half of the nineteenth century, the external pressures and the internal centrifugal forces escalate right up to the eve of the First World War, one of the consequences of which is the final dissolution of the multinational empire.

In this context the situation of the rising Jewish bourgeoisie is very different in Hungary and Austria. In Hungary the co-existence within the nationalist liberal regime (1867-1918) of the non-Jewish elites and the rising Jewish bourgeoisie with its assimilationist ideal[3] was facilitated by a project for the unity of a national state that the disappearance of the dual monarchy did not deeply affect. In contrast, in Austria, the presentiment of the decomposition of the empire was a contributory factor, as early as 1870, to the questioning of loyalty to the dynasty and favoured the emergence of a Pan-German nationalism, transforming the Germanic component from 'a cementing force capable of culturally building up our country . . . into a force for internal decomposition'.[4]

Following the model of the 1848 revolution, one again finds side by side at the beginning of the 1870s Jews and non-Jews in the same national liberal student organizations (*Burschenschaften*) that oppose Pan-Germanism to national and dynastic loyalty. In these student associations opposed to Catholic and loyalist corporations can be found Victor Adler, Sigmund Freud, Gustav Mahler, then later Theodor Herzl, side by side with Engelbert Pernersdorfer and Hermann Bahr – all united in their admiration of the supposedly superior Germanic culture.[5] At the beginning of the 1870s there can be seen rubbing shoulders the future founders and leaders of the Social Democracy, of Zionism, of Pan-German nationalism along with the cultural innovators of the end of the century. This pro-German enthusiasm of the 1870s is surprising for two reasons: its effervescent character and its short-lived existence.

In the middle of the 1880s, at the time when the liberal movement is breaking up, it becomes apparent in the intellectual and university world that Pan-German nationalism is also one of the mainstays of antisemitism. The festival of 1883 held to commemorate the death of Richard Wagner, and organized by the German students of Vienna, is transformed into a political demonstration which, with its pro-Prussian and antisemitic overtones, constitutes an outright challenge to the very existence of the multinational state.[6] Propagated initially only by the Pan-German movement of Georg von Schönerer – which indeed scored some electoral victories without ever becoming a mass movement – antisemitism is quickly adopted for its own use by political Catholicism, then in the throes of a total mutation. The Christian Social movement had its origins in the alliance between the federalist reformers of neo-absolutism, who lost power in 1859, and the social-Catholic reformers grouped around Freiherr von Vogelsang. The Christian Social movement changes, as early as the end of the 1880s, into a popular party which can rely on a dense and decentralized network of communication and professional associations, and in Vienna, on the far-reaching charisma of its leader Karl Lueger.[7] With the transformation of the Christian Social movement antisemitism gains access to a large public that the Pan-German party, limited to a bourgeois public, would never have been able to reach. Better equipped to formulate projects in line with the specifically Austrian and therefore Catholic traditions, the Christian Social movement can present its antisemitism against the background of a 'glorious' history in which Austria plays the role of principal defender of the Christian faith against all its enemies. Using in its propaganda all the manifestations of the upward mobility of the

Jewish bourgeoisie; using also as a pretext the Jewish origins of certain leaders of the rising Social Democrats, the Christian Social movement could rely on a very heterogeneous social base. Even before 1900 there occurred in Austria the formation of a political antisemitism as the lowest common denominator of mutual interest for large sectors of society. This Christian Social antisemitism united a weakened aristocracy and large masses of the petty-bourgeoisie in a defensive struggle against 'Jewish big capital'. At the same time, this antisemitism was also used against the Marxist Social Democrats – presumably directed by 'Jewish leaders'.

As early as 1897 the voting power of the Christian Social movement forced the emperor to withdraw the veto which had prevented Karl Lueger from becoming mayor of Vienna. From then on, religious creed and cultural roots became unavoidable questions. These attributes are obviously part of each individual's legacy and make-up in all times and places, but they achieved an acute salience in the period under consideration. To be or not to be a Jew, as well as the religious, cultural and racial standards alleged to justify such a classification, became matters of such importance that there was little or no chance of evading classification. At this stage the individual's social identity became entangled in a complex process of individual and collective struggle directed at achieving advantageous social positioning, while at the same time arriving at a definition of oneself *vis-à-vis* the various traditions and groups which constituted Viennese society. Self-definition in its various forms on the part of a particular group, as well as group reactions to social labelling employed by others, coalesces to the point where historical analysis sometimes becomes problematic.

The end of liberalism and the growth of antisemitism were felt most poignantly by those whose status was directly threatened by the disintegration of the Habsburg state: the Jews, defined by the very official history of the monarchy published in 1883 as a 'people', but with no recognition of their qualities as a nation.[8] If the empire were to disintegrate, the Jews, according to this definition, would be the only people within the monarchy unable to claim a territory for itself. Without this anxiety being openly voiced at the time, the end of the empire, prefigured by the collapse of liberalism, nevertheless threatened not only the social identity but the very physical integrity of the Jews.[9]

The extremely rapid shifts of ideological and political allegiances was even more evident in the Viennese press than at the level of governmental politics where it was contained by electoral laws. The circulation of the important traditionally liberal and *Kaisertreu* newspapers in which the assimilationist Jewish bourgeoisie could recognize itself (*Presse, Neue Freie Presse, Fremdenblatt*), stagnated at around 60,000 copies. The Pan-German press (*Deutsches Volksblatt, Ostdeutsche Rundschau*) grew in strength up to 1900, its most successful year, when more than 50,000 copies were printed, then fell back to 35,000 around 1910. On the other hand, the organ of the Christian-Social movement, the *Reichspost*, increased rapidly from some 6,000 to 25,000 copies between 1900 and 1905, while the Social Democrats' *Arbeiter-Zeitung* doubled in the same period from 24,000 to 54,000 copies.[10]

In certain vital respects this complete reshuffle of the political and ideological terrain both foreshadowed and prepared the way for the emergence of the configuration that was to become characteristic of German-speaking Austria after the dissolution of the multinational state. Already we can discern a situation in which a bloc defining itself primarily in spiritual and religious terms confronts another defining itself in terms of social class. Moreover, this polarization placed the Jewish bourgeoisie, such an important component in Viennese high society, in the acute dilemma of being unable to continue along the established nineteenth-century assimilationist road by means of the secularization of Jewish lifestyles, without overt denial of creed nor rupture with their own community. The rise of the Christian Social movement decisively reinforced religion both as a criterion for determining the social status and identity of the individual and as a criterion limiting access to certain governing positions. Furthermore, to compound their exposed position, Social Democracy, on the other hand, demanded in effect that the Jewish bourgeoisie deny their class origins.

In the light of these developments, it is not surprising to discover that the reformulation of Jewish identity – an indissolubly intellectual as well as organizational process – was carried out at the same time as, and in reaction to, these profound transformations in the world of non-Jews. The result was an unprecedented proliferation of Jewish associative life at the end of the century, but also internal tensions between the advocates of the old assimilationist model on the one hand, versus the 'Jewish nationalists' and Zionists on the other.[11] The creation in 1880 of the Österreichische-Israelitische Union, an organization of defence against antisemitism, marked the conversion of the old liberals to support for a policy of Jewish self-organization within the framework of the institutions of the empire. There was a very quick reaction to this tactical shift – whose aim was to maintain the essence of the former assimilationist model – from the Zionists and 'nationalists' who demanded complete recognition of a Jewish nation on an equal footing with the other nationalities that made up the monarchy. At the same time groups of orthodox Jews succeeded in making themselves more influential in organizing the religious life of the rising number of Jews from the east. Thus, as among Catholics, in the Jewish group also, at the end of the century, religion was again gaining ground as a primary criterion of identity.

In reply to the attack by antisemitism and to the dangers inherent in the dissolution of the multinational state, the reorganization of Jewish life and the projects aimed at redefinition of the collective identity followed the same pattern as the political evolution in the non-Jewish sphere: a renewed emphasis on the religious dimension on the one hand and a nationalist retreat on the other. Although they remained in a minority in the successive elections for control of the Israelitische Kulturgemeinde, the nationalists and Zionists from 1902 managed to gain between 25 and 45 per cent of the votes cast, with electoral participation nonetheless rarely going beyond 30 per cent of those registered to vote (see Table 7.1 in Walter Weitzmann's discussion of this point in chapter 7 below). Under the stress of perpetual tensions, multinational Austria seemed to proceed from a state of harmony to one of anxiety, even in the eyes of the Jews, this so-called *Staatsvolk* par excellence. In a confused and strained political and intellectual climate there developed a search for identity and authenticity, a retreat into oneself and one's origins as a sort of ultimate place of refuge.

This polarization of social life based on the criterion of religious creed recalls, in addition to the limits of assimilation, the limits of all secularization in a society not accompanied by the institution of a clear separation between church and state and the secularization of public life. It is from this angle that one could perhaps put forward certain hypotheses about the rapid increase in conversions during the period. These occurred not so much to the advantage of the Catholic church in its position as state religion, conversion to which might be expected to have given optimal importance to the specific advantages that denial of a Jewish identity procures in an antisemitic society. In fact, conversions were fairly equally shared between Catholicism, Protestantism, and the non-denominational, *konfessionslos*, category.[12] Not only did this last category procure few advantages for those converted but may even have led to social isolation in a society where organizations based on religion provided an important part of the educational, health and social services. In certain cases the conversion to Protestantism could indicate a particularly ostentatious assimilation not so much to a sociological majority but to the ideal of German culture full of future promise rather than to an Austria in its death throes. But Protestant conversion could also, as could the conversion to a non-denominational status, betray the choice of a 'lesser evil', of a 'smaller obstacle' or of a refusal to be classified; a refusal, that is, to give religion a paramount function in the definition of the social identity of each and every individual.

The individual's refusal to grant to religion the power it exercised socially is also evident in the perfectly opportunistic choice of religion in relation to the stage reached in the Jewish apostate's professional career. Thus the rate of reconversions to the Jewish religion is particularly high amongst those who, following intellectual careers or employed in administration, found that antisemitic barriers prevented their advancement despite conversion. As progress in a career is limited in time the average time-lapse between conversion and a return to Judaism was, in a number of cases cited by Rozenblit, hardly more than two to five years at the end of the century.[13]

If one can delineate the political reorientation of the period, the emerging of new tensions, and, correlatively, the elaboration of new definitions of Jewish and non-Jewish collective identities as a process started off by the acceleration of the centrifugal forces of the empire, and of the foreboding over its decomposition, one can also observe individual refusals to conform to these transformations. Recognizing this leads us to reformulate the question of the crucial role of Jews in the cultural renaissance of *fin-de-siècle* Vienna. The new political organizations and their collective identities come from an attempt at realignment whose objective is the affirmation and protection of the group. At the same time there can be found among the cultural innovators a high proportion of people from families who have followed the same spatial and social trajectory. These Jewish families coming from the provinces most clearly represent the model of social ascent that the multinational monarchy offered. The rise typically begins with small provincial trading at the beginning of the nineteenth century, progressively scaling the heights to important trade or banking activities in the capital, and in later generations to the liberal professions and intellectual careers with, as supreme reward, admission into the 'second society' (*Zweite Gesellschaft*), a term which in Viennese society signifies the intermediary social stratum between the bourgeoisie and the lower aristocracy. Without wishing to adopt a purely reductionist approach to their intellectual projects, may we not post the question of the latter's role in the process of attempting to redefine their social identity? Even by explicitly opposing this process, they refer to it, and by doing so they participate in the collective task of political transformation and redefinition of the group identities in Austria at the end of the nineteenth century.

Throughout the nineteenth century, the term 'assimilation' was synonymous with adherence to German culture. Some Jewish intellectuals who had often been the staunchest defenders of German culture and whose attitude was now rendered problematic by antisemitism, were faced at the end of the century with an intricate problem of identity. To the difficult problem of coping with a dual identity, both Austrian and German, was now added that of Jewish identity, and both intellectual and political projects bear the stamp of this difficulty. For want of a common perspective, a multitude of perspectives are put forward. The experience of a wounded, insecure, threatened and ambiguous identity gives rise to a multitude of projects intended to counteract the threat. The starting point of such projects lies in a multiplicity of the differing contemporary cultural heritages: liberalism, religion, Marxism, and the optimistic 'scientism' of the nineteenth century.

One can observe basically two modes according to which stabilization of identity was attempted. First, political involvement such as with Austro-Marxism or Zionism provided alternative attachments for the declining identification with Austrian nationality or loyalty to the monarchy. Second, aesthetic and psychological projects had the effect of stabilizing the self by displacing altogether the criteria of identity from the social and particular group level, putting in their place a primary concern with the inner self and a critical awareness of the self.

Breaking with the nationalists of Georg von Schönerer on the question of antisemitism, a certain number of the intellectuals of Jewish origin, the most committed politically, were inevitably drawn into identifying with the budding Social Democracy in which they often held positions of responsibility at the side of the founder of the party, Victor Adler. The latter was a forerunner of that type of former intellectual turned political leader which is so widespread in the history of Austrian socialism. The Austro-Marxist tradition is, in reality, the result of this organic link between two movements: that of the working class, and that of identity-seeking intellectuals produced by the – often Jewish – upper classes. Therein too lies the reason why the Austrian Social Democracy always posed as the heir to certain liberal intellectual values. It evolved as a tradition which enabled intellectuals of Jewish origin to preserve unimpaired certain elements of the heritage encompassing both the former liberalism and impetus towards assimilation.

Diametrically opposed to a perspective which would integrate the project of Jewish emancipation into a revolutionary transformation of society – and which thereby would project the solution of the problem of being a Jew into the future – Zionism reversed the logic of the antisemitic stigma. Rather than react to the attacks defensively by minimizing the distinctiveness of Jewishness by denying it, or by denouncing it as prejudice, Zionism endowed it with positive value, encouraging a pride that allowed positive identification with a heritage and a socially-despised group, while also providing a basis for group defence by means of collective mobilization. Likewise, Zionism sparked off a complete revolution within Judaism, a complete reappraisal of the criteria of Jewish identity. As Herzl stated: 'In my view, the Jewish question is neither a social question nor a religious question ... I see it rather as a national question which, if it is to receive a solution, must be examined in terms of politics.'[14]

Yet another response was perhaps the sublimation of the problem in scientific terms. It enabled some Jews to get over an experience of truncated identity while safeguarding the liberal heritage. That is the road chosen by Sigmund Freud. His personal experience as the son of a modest Jewish Moravian family who rose to a professorship at the university of Vienna is, I would venture, at the root of, and is reflected in, the procedures of psychoanalytical interpretation. This personal trajectory is also the subject of *The Interpretation of Dreams.*[15]

In the cases of Austro-Marxism and Zionism, the intellectual project went hand in hand with organizational undertakings which provided a multitude of individuals with a stabilization of their sense of identity, either by providing them with careers in a genuinely alternative society – which is what the Social Democratic party had become – or by a Zionist promise of a 'radiant prospect of honour, freedom and happiness . . . to our bold spirited youth to which all careers are already closed'.[16] Even in the field of psychoanalysis the intellectual project received the support of organizational work intended to provide the doctrine with continuity and institutional permanence. The difficulties and resistance encountered by psycho-analysis, and by Freud personally, at the time, were in truth also due to his Jewish origin, an origin shared by the majority of his early disciples.[17] To counter the hostility met in an academic and social context strongly marked by antisemitism, it was necessary to 'stick together' and to be able to rely on the unfailing cohesion of the group. Consequently, the first Viennese society of psychoanalysis, founded in 1908, functioned organizationally like a sect.

Beyond the organizational work that accompanied their intellec-tual projects, the founders of political Zionism, Theodor Herzl, of the Austrian Social Democracy, Victor Adler, and the psychoanalytical movement, Sigmund Freud, have a common biographical preoccu-pation which is perceptible in their style of argument and their rhetoric. All three succeeded in converting their personal destinies into political resources and into justifications for mobilization. The political writings and speeches of Theodor Herzl indefatigably recall his experience as a writer and intellectual rejected because of his Jewish origins. Presenting his own case as a model for identification and an exemplary cause for others, Herzl offered himself as a spokesman and managed to solve his own personal problem of identity through collective action. The mobilization to which he gave initial impetus was then able to grow beyond his wildest expectations because, over and beyond a political programme, it offered millions of people a means to solve a common identity problem by retrieving their pride politically.

Victor Adler, who became a convert to Protestantism so that his children should not have to suffer the consequences of non-denominational, *konfessionslos*, status at school,[18] often referred in his speeches to relations between intellectuals and the working class. Not only did he offer Jewish intellectuals a chance (without explicitly stating it in these terms) to integrate hopes of assimilation into a revolutionary project, but, citing cultural work as one of the primary tasks of the movement, and by offering himself as an example, Adler also defined a positive role for the Jewish intelligentsia and institutionalized within the party a degree of autonomy for cultural activities rare in the political praxis of working-class organizations.

One of the books that played a key role in the constitution of

psychoanalysis, *The Interpretation of Dreams*, has an autobiographi-
cal nature which is utterly alien to academic tradition. The analysis it
provides of Freud's relationship with his father, with politics and
with the world of German-speaking academics must have evoked
similar experiences in the minds of a good many of his disciples. By
re-establishing his own sense of identity, Freud, too, offers himself as
a model for identification. By imitating him or by following
unconditionally in his footsteps his disciples were able to cope with
their own identity problem. The new truth, the scientific cause to be
defended, provided this circle of analysts with a sense of their own
future, with a mission, in a word, with a sense of identity during an
unsettled period.

Zionism, Austro-Marxism or psychoanalysis are not, of course, as
previously noted, phenomena which can be reduced to the
stabilization of a Jewish identity, or more particularly that of
intellectuals, yet it is an aspect which is essential to the understanding
of the reception they received, even though their following ranged
well beyond a strictly Jewish public. It could even be advanced that
Austro-Marxism and psychoanalysis, both of which were working
towards a secularization of the world, could provide a rallying point
for both Jews and non-Jews who rebelled against the prevailing
tendency to assign social identities on the basis of religious affiliation.

In another field central to cultural renewal, that of literature, we find
intellectual effort directed far less toward sweeping social reorganization. Rather, the latter is restricted to redefinition of the role of the
writer and to a progressive dissociation between the literary
techniques of the orthodox artist on the one hand, and the writer-
cum-journalist on the other. This work of redefinition of the artist's
identity can be found not only in private correspondence but also in
the published works of the writers who belonged to the *Jung-Wien*
group. Here again, the intellectual project, principally the quest for
aesthetic purity, was, as it were, determined on a higher level by the
problem of national identity; by the link between the literary project
and cultural traditions.[19]

The families of the writers of *Jung-Wien* belonged to the most
loyalist strata of Viennese high society. Profoundly affected by the
financial crisis of 1873, by the conflicts of nationality and by the
nascent working-class movement which attracted certain of their
sons, these 'good families' tried their utmost to perpetuate their
social position. Far from rebelling, their writer-sons sought a new

meaning to their lives at a moment when all political pursuits appeared to be in vain.

This disillusionment with politics assumed forms which were inseparable from the greater or lesser degrees of Jewishness of the various members of the group. Tenuous or almost non-existent in the families of Schnitzler and of Kraus, religious traditions left their stamp on the youth of a writer like Richard Beer-Hofmann. The assimilation of the forebears of Hofmannsthal, elevated to the ranks of the aristocracy as early as the end of the eighteenth century, was fortified by marriages outside the Jewish community. The mother of Leopold Andrian, herself the daughter of the composer Meyerbeer, was of Jewish origin. Only a few of the older writers of the *Jung-Wien* group personally shared the Germanic enthusiasm of the 1870s. It seems highly significant that the two most conspicuous exceptions, Hermann Bahr, one of the few non-Jews in the group, and Theodor Herzl, both felt excluded, or at the very least rejected, from good Viennese society because of their provincial origins. At the end of the 1870s, committed as he was to Germanic ideals, the German-speaking, Hungarian-born Herzl was able to voice a feeling of cultural superiority with regard to Hungary where his family had always opposed assimilation via magyarization, and to challenge the *Kaisertreu* Jewish upper classes of Vienna from whose ranks he remained excluded. Later, under the impact of the growing antisemitic movement, Herzl, the marginal character of Viennese high society, was to elaborate his Zionist project.

Hermann Bahr's own political commitment, likewise, cannot be dissociated from his personal fortunes – those of a provincial who blamed all the social obstacles he encountered in Vienna on the exclusiveness of a Viennese high society which should be destroyed along with Austria by union with the German Reich. After his relegation from the university of Vienna in 1883, and his long exile in the provinces – in Graz, Cernowitz, then in Berlin – Hermann Bahr was able to reconcile himself with his homeland and to re-establish relations which secured him an undisputed position as cultural and literary go-between. In 1895, well after his escapades as a nationalist and antisemitic student, he married a young Jewish actress, in spite of his family's opposition to such a '*mésalliance*'. As early as 1892 he was the first to emphasize the patriotic feelings expressed in the *Jung-Wien* literature.[20]

But on what basis could anyone, particularly artists, aspire to be Austrian patriots in 1890? The answer, I think, lies in recognizing that the creation of a specifically Austrian cultural identity arose from the process of attempting to resolve the contradictions of a wounded identity in the realm of literature and the arts.

The paradoxical convergence of a patriotic revival and aestheticism is largely due precisely to the impossibility of founding an Austrian sense of national identity on historical arguments. Making of aesthetic excellence a criterion of Austrian patriotism answered the needs of artists who, torn as they were between conflicting criteria of German, Austrian or Jewish orientations, could thus dissolve the problem of dual identity posed by the role of the artist and the political fact of belonging to a national entity.

But aestheticism hardly managed to hide the anxiety and the difficulties of living without a secure national and cultural identity. Thus almost all the conflicts which broke out within the inner circle of the 'true artists' which emerged from the *Jung-Wien* arose from diverging interpretations of national identity. Hofmannsthal's position of authority, and his growing success on the German market, enabled him to refuse any national label and to refer to artistic purity as the sole support for an artist's legitimate identity. Even before the war this stance enabled Hofmannsthal to avoid having to opt for an Austrian patriotism which was explicitly opposed to the German tradition and which would undoubtedly have reduced his chances on the German market. A conflict between Hofmannsthal and Leopold Andrian, another member of the group and Hofmannsthal's close friend, on the subject of the collaboration with the literary review, *Pan*, published in Germany, anticipated the latter's voluntary retirement from a literary career. Andrian had insisted on withholding collaboration on a special issue on Vienna which would have placed the latter among the lesser ranking centres of German literature.[21] From 1900 onwards Andrian chose to turn to more useful pursuits than literature: he opted for the diplomatic service.

When, in 1908, Arthur Schnitzler made antisemitism a theme of his novel *Der Weg ins Freie*, Hugo von Hofmannsthal expressed his dismay to him and informed Beer-Hofmann of his disappointment on reading a work so lacking in aesthetics. In fact he reacted as if the articulation of the theme in itself were an infringement of the sanctity of the artist's *raison d'être*. Because Schnitzler's attitude challenged his own political conception of a specifically Austrian identity,[22] Andrian professed himself to be shocked by the book, 'the most personal of my creations' according to Schnitzler.[23] This difference of views led to an estrangement. As from 1910 the two friends of long standing hardly saw each other any more and their regular exchange of correspondence came to an end.

The difficulties which came to light over the same period between Beer-Hofmann and Hofmannsthal arose from a problem of a similar nature. Beer-Hofmann, who retained and practised the religion of his forefathers, from 1900 adopted Jewish mythology as a source of inspiration. After his play *Jaakobs Traum* had been performed, Hofmannsthal voiced very clearly one of the factors which entailed a loosening of their ties after 1910: 'It is a matter of chauvinism and national pride. To echo what a solitary Pharisee might say, I see only as the root of all evils.'[24] The 'Austrian myth'[25] created in this literature remained a key factor of Austrian cultural awareness as distinct from German identity, and one to which the different Austrian political families[26] progressively adhered to.

After this cursory review of creative projects in three such different fields as politics, psychoanalysis and the literature of *Jung-Wien*, we can return to the two questions put at the start of this paper. As Steven Beller has shown, it is hardly surprising that, quantitatively speaking, Jews should have played a paramount role in Viennese intellectual life at the end of the century. This was a result of very specific means of access to new status available to Jews under the monarchy throughout the second half of the nineteenth century. For a very short period, the prevailing liberalism in politics had minimized the importance of religion among the current criteria of social identity in Austrian and Viennese society. But by the end of the century this criterion, though subject to alterations, was restored to its dominant role. The redefinition of the political scene was achieved through reformulating collective identities on the basis of national, class, but also religious criteria. The renewal of the activity of voluntary associations and the politicization of Catholic thought are evidence of this, as is the evolution that can be seen in the Jewish group.

The process of redefinition can most clearly be observed in the intellectual and artistic spheres. Lack of prospects for the future left the way open for a multitude of projects which all had in common the proposing of collective or individual means of providing stability for a much-jeopardized sense of identity. It was perhaps the highly concentrated, simultaneous, nature of the structural changes – the coincidence of a crisis of political survival with a crisis in the most intimate feelings about the self – which created an aura of acute insecurity within the intellectual circles of the Viennese upper class and entailed a breach with the patterns and beliefs of the past. Paradoxically, it was precisely 'modernity' which characterized many of the attempts to restore a climate of security.

Within the Viennese context, projects as diverse as Austro-Marxism, psychoanalysis, Zionism, but also a form of aesthetic patriotism, were produced within relatively confined milieux of intellectuals, many of whom were acquainted with one another, consorted with one another, and who often entertained lasting bonds of friendship. But within these small milieux the internalization of constraints could lead to the rejection of any sort of allegiances, to social isolation and to that psychological self-rejection so often mentioned in literature concerning the period. The cultural innovations we have briefly surveyed were a response to an existential need to redefine, and to establish new relationships between diverging traditions. In the construction of these intellectual projects there is another feature which is characteristic of Viennese culture: this lies in the fact that the redefinition of identities and of group connections follows a logic of combining elements previously held separate in traditions which seldom offered any common meeting ground.[27] Simultaneously, some Viennese Jewish intellectuals revolutionized and politicized Jewish thought, while others in the cultural field were able – in their intellectual and artistic creations – to retrieve the role of intermediary between separate national and cultural traditions, which had long been that of the Jewish upper class in economic life.[28] Little wonder, then, that the effects of this cultural renaissance ranged well beyond the limits of the Jewish community of Vienna and that it is commonly considered to be one of the mainsprings of modern culture.

CHAPTER 4

VIENNESE CULTURE AND THE JEWISH SELF-HATRED HYPOTHESIS: A CRITIQUE

Allan Janik

As colleagues have already indicated in the preceeding pages, the question of the extent and nature of Jewish participation in the creative cultural movements of Vienna at the turn of the century suggests a highly variegated, complex process requiring further basic research into the Viennese social structure and its cultural dynamics. In the present essay I hope to make a contribution to the preliminary tasks of methodological critique and conceptual clarification by challenging the tendency to frame interpretations of the intellectual contributions made by men of Jewish background (however remote and attenuated) as the expression of some sort of underlying, Jewish-related, neurotic complaint. Among the explanatory mechanisms so employed is the notion that a neurotic condition of varying severity labelled *Jewish self-hatred* was a pervasive stimulus in the work of some important artists and intellectuals of the period. The main objective of the following discussion will be to challenge the validity of this concept even when applied to the thinker who nearly everyone has taken to represent the very archetype of the self-hating Viennese Jewish intellectual: Otto Weininger.

The Jewish self-hatred model should not, in my opinion, be viewed as an isolated, radical quirk in the conceptual approach taken by many writers to Vienna at the turn of the century. Whether or not employed by a particular analyst, it clearly is a member of that family of images and vocabularies which have been marshalled to explain the worrisome, even repellent, anti-liberal and anti-modernist currents of the Viennese *fin de siècle*. On this reading, the failure of liberalism, the withdrawal into aestheticism, subjectivism, the analysis of dreams rather than harsh external realities, represent — along with such notions as Jewish self-hatred — not only a form of decadence but a type of dangerous cultural pathology presaging, perhaps, the eventual triumph of Nazism. I have taken issue elsewhere with this anti-anti-modernist critique of Viennese cultural life[1] – what was so marvellous, after all, about the intense overcrowding, squalor, exploitation and mass insecurity which accompanied the halting introduction of capitalist modernization in Vienna? That the assimilating Jewish population was caught up in this social convulsion is an important datum in the social history of the city; but it is one of the merits of Frederick Morton's lively, and aptly named, survey of the events of 1889 in Vienna, *A Nervous Splendor*, to have pointed out that the only figure of note in the city's cultural life, in that year of the Meyerling tragedy, entirely free from tormenting self-doubts was Johannes Brahms. Even the immensely successful Johann Strauss was insecure – not to mention the cases of Bruckner, Hugo Wolf, Crown Prince Rudolf and, yes, Jews like Arthur Schnitzler and Sigmund Freud.[2]

If, as I am suggesting, there is an obvious danger in interpreting the psychological stress experienced by Jewish intellectuals as a totally unique phenomenon, then similarly there is a danger in regarding Viennese cultural life during this period – including its major inputs from persons of Jewish background – as totally distinctive and discontinuous from the city's older cultural traditions. I have criticized Carl Schorske in particular for failing to relate the culture of Vienna's *fin de siècle* to its rich traditional, historical contexts and thereby running the risk of attributing to an all-pervasive late ninteenth-century 'failure of Liberalism' a causal specificity with regard to cultural phenomena which it may not fully deserve[3] – although, as Steven Beller has correctly noted, Schorske eschews a uniquely Jewish dimension in his interpretation of the period.

I believe that in order to understand the origins of some of the most salient intellectual attitudes and styles of the late Habsburg era we may have to look further back into the city's cultural history. For example, I have argued, following suggestions put forward by the late Robert Kann, that one of the leitmotifs of the *fin de siècle*, the fierce moralizing and condemnation of Viennese architectural ornamentation inaugurated by Adolf Loos – and the closely linked demand for integrity and clarity in the work of Karl Kraus, Arnold Schoenberg and Ludwig Wittgenstein – can be read as latter-day expressions of the style of public criticism established in Vienna by the late seventeenth-century court preacher, Abraham a Sancta Clara. These formative years of Viennese culture followed the forced re-

Catholicization of the city, which had gone over to Protestantism at the onset of the Reformation; and the distinctively Counter-Reformation styles of the Baroque and Mannerism, with their stress on ornamentation, soon became symbols of Habsburg authority. Thus the Baroque established a hegemonic standard of public taste but at the same time provided an aesthetic target for later social criticism. Meanwhile, the imperial theatre provided Vienna with its first taste of secular culture and furnished the meeting place for the aristocracy and the new, rising bourgeois class, so anxious to imitate the luxurious aristocratic lifestyle. It was a growing concern for this pursuit of luxury which evoked a moral response in the form of a kind of theatrical religiosity in the sermons of Abraham a Sancta Clara.

> Abraham effectively turned the charm of secular culture, its theatricality, against itself in hilariously devastating sermons which castigated the worldliness of the Viennese for some forty years from the 1660s onwards. Abraham is a particularly important figure for our story for he marks the beginning of the Viennese rhetorical tradition as well as a mode of social criticism. Abraham's rhetoric foreshadows Lueger in its exploitation of local idiom, its wit and emotional appeal but also Karl Kraus in its resourceful efforts to turn the tables on the corrupt – although it must be hastily added that Kraus's values were hardly Abraham's. . . . By considering Abraham we begin to see how Viennese moral fervor could take such unusual forms as, say, a theory of harmony with Schoenberg or a book of highly technical aphorisms which tried to get clear about what it is you cannot say with Wittgenstein; [and] it helps to explain how Lueger and Kraus, for all their differences, both manifest a single aspect of the Viennese cultural heritage.[4]

The foregoing analysis, extracted from an essay in which I attempted to account for the wider historical bases of cultural creativity in Vienna, is reproduced here as only one example of how an exploration of Vienna's pre-Liberal cultural traditions may turn up some surprising continuities influencing both the *Problemstellungen* and style of the late Habsburg years. Many other, less historically remote, influences could of course be cited. There is, however, no intention here to rule out of consideration the causal significance of explanatory models applied specifically to the Viennese *fin de siècle*, including those which posit the supposed traumas and frustrations of individuals, classes, generations or ethnic groups. The main test to be applied to such hypotheses and concepts is simply to raise the questions 'does it make sense?' and 'how good is the evidence?'. In the case of the Jewish self-hatred hypothesis as applied to Otto Weininger I am afraid the answers are not very supportive.

I wouldn't join any club that would have me as a member.
— Groucho Marx

What is self-hatred? Many writers about central European Jewry seem to think they know since the term, as I have already suggested, is liberally invoked throughout the literature. However, from the way it is used I am inclined to think that these writers, like St Augustine confronted with the question 'what is time?', know what self-hatred is only until somebody asks them. In the usages that I am familiar with the term is used principally to explain away a Jew's rejection of Judaism. Recent research challenging the validity of the similar idea of 'negative self-image' among blacks has drawn attention to the suspect methodologies of studies which have employed this concept in Britain.[5] This should alert us to the dubious facility with which even distinguished writers about the Jewish case have ideologically conjured with this notion. I find the claim that Weininger's animosity toward Jews can be simply explained by his self-hatred perplexing both on account of the scanty reliable information about Weininger's life, and because it is typical of the way the term gets invoked in explanations in the history of ideas.

Let me begin with an anecdote which exemplifies the way the concept has been used in practice.

In the spring of 1984 a senior history major at one of the major Ivy League Universities presented a thesis on Weininger to the department for honours.[6] For the most part his examiners were puzzled why somebody should waste the time involved in writing a thesis on a figure whom a distinguished historian had identified as a self-hater. In short, the whole project seemed to them less than worthless. This was by no means the sole incident which drew my attention to what I take to be the problematic character of self-hatred, but it well illustrates what I find questionable about the concept, namely, the idea that to call someone a self-hater is at once to describe and judge him in a way that closes a discussion. Since I learned from Karl Popper to suspect such closure moves, and since I learned from Alasdair MacIntyre to ask not what does our conceptual apparatus in social science reveal about social phenomena, but what it *conceals* about them, I am convinced that this is *just* the sort of move to question in social explanations. So, I want to ask why it is that identifying somebody as a self-hater is a sufficient condition for dismissing him in the history of ideas? My intuition from the start was that it was not. The criticism of the thesis on Weininger just mentioned provides a clear example of why. Let me explain.

Weininger was dismissed on the basis of Peter Gay's allegation that he was a self-hater, if not, indeed, *the* self-hater. But why does Gay say what he does about Weininger and self-hatred? What are his sources? To ask these questions is to undertake an interesting expedition into the archaeology of a concept, for what we discover are distinct but not separate 'levels' of concepts built upon the foundations (ruins?) of other concepts. In his *Freud, Jews and Other Germans*, and especially in the essay 'Hermann Levi: A Study in Service and Self-Hatred', Gay describes the phenomenon as 'the frantic urge to escape the burden of Jewishness not merely by renouncing but by denouncing Judaism; it is a term which collects a complex of feelings under a single rubric.'[7] To analyse this complex Gay has recourse to the work of Theodor Lessing, who coined the term in his book of that name in 1930, as well as Kurt Lewin's 'Self-Hatred Among Jews', which he rightly describes as 'one of the few attempts to deal scientifically (if briefly) with the question'. In addition he cites some psychoanalytic observations of Rudolph M. Loewenstein and Freud's notion of the Oedipus Complex, which he takes to be the key to the mechanism of 'unconcious punishment'. Gay's primary example of self-hatred is, of course, Otto Weininger.

Of Weininger Gay says the following:

His life and work provided spectacular evidence for the terrifying power of *Selbsthass*. In 1903, he published the book *Geschlecht und Charakter*, on which his problematic immortality rests; four months later he committed suicide in the house in which Beethoven had died – a melodramatic end to an (at least inwardly) melodramatic life. In his book, which an oddly assorted collection of misogynists and antisemites found congenial and quotable, Weininger postulated a sharp contrast between males and females, and between 'Aryans' and Jews. It was a seductively simple system, with a false lucidity . . . woman, representing sensuality, is ethically infinitely inferior to man; the Jew's embodying skepticism and the spirit of imitation, is equally inferior to the Aryan . . . by converting to Protestantism, Weininger had expected to make himself into an Aryan: his definition of Judaism was not a racial one. But evidently fearing the sinister influence of woman within him, and recognizing his ineradicable Jewishness, Weininger eradicated his two linked problems by shooting himself.[8]

In what follows I shall have a good deal to say about: (1) this 'oddly assorted collection of misogynists and antisemites', who constituted his readership; (2) the 'seductively simple' character of Weininger's argument; (3) the 'evident' character of Weininger's fears about himself; and (4) Weininger's 'indelible' Jewishness. However, my discussion of these details of Gay's exemplification of self-hatred in Weininger will have to be put off till after we take a look at the concept itself.

I chose to begin with the anecdote from the Ivy League history department because it well illustrates how scholars have a way of accepting a congenial opinion from a distinguished colleague less than critically. There is nothing particularly strange about that; however, it is at odds with good scholarship; for it distracts them from *der Sache selbst*. Thus, if unlike the Ivy League historians, we inquire into the sources upon which Gay's views of Weininger rest, we discover that we are on less firm ground and, generally, in a more complex situation than Gay imagines. My point, then, is that the reasoning upon which the explanatory power of the concept rests is effectively buried under several 'layers' of scholarship. My contention is that 'excavating' this concept will help to explain how what I allege to be its misuse originates in less than conscious ways. As we have seen, Gay's principal sources are Lessing and Lewin. My claim is that the reasoning of the former is wholly objectionable on account of its explicitly racist character, and that Lewin's excellent discussion has wholly different aims, and, therefore, a wholly different significance, than Gay's own.

The simple fact about Theodor Lessing's account of Weininger in *Der Jüdische Selbsthass* is that it is based upon a racism which is just as crude as anything that the most vulgar Nazi ideologues might have asserted. For Lessing Weininger's problem was rooted in hatred for his blood: 'Weininger hated his blood and his blood was Jewish blood.'[9] For Lessing Weininger is a paradigm case of self-hatred precisely because he tried to reject not simply a social role but a biologically determined identity. The impossibility of doing so determined his frustration and ultimately his drive to self-destruction. Lessing's own murder at the hands of the Nazis has tended to obscure his own racism and, thus, the fascist foundations of his concept of self-hatred. However, his racism did not go unnoticed by Nazi thinkers such as Alexander Centgraff.[10] This does not pass entirely without comment by Gay, who describes Lessing's book as 'part diagnosis and part display of a distasteful masochism',[11] but he fails to appreciate how Lessing's racism thoroughly tinges the book's main point, the very concept he would adopt from Lessing to explain Weininger – ironically, in a way that Weininger's work itself, as Gay admits, is *not* racist.[12] For Lessing's argument to work the Nazi picture of Judaism as ineradicably rooted in biology, or something very like it, must be the case. Now, presumably Gay does not want to endorse the metaphysical notion that there are races which can be identified on the basis of their biological characteristics. However, if he does not, he is obliged to give us another account of Jewish identity, one which avoids the pitfalls of Lessing's racism. Gay is aware of this and, indeed, rests his case upon Kurt Lewin's classic, 'Self-Hatred among Jews', of 1941.[13] Yet, in doing so *he fails to observe that Lewin's intention was never to provide a model for explanation in the history of ideas.* Lewin's aims were quite different and it is precisely these differences which are crucial for understanding how the concept should and should not be employed.

In a mere fourteen pages Lewin developed a sophisticated, theoretical account of the dynamics of self-hatred as it results from pressures an individual feels to free himself from Jewish – or Black – identity, yet finds himself constrained in these efforts by society at large. Caught in the middle, his life is shot through with tension between the centrifugal and centripetal forces acting upon him, which tension expresses itself as aggression against his Jewish identity. Several things are worth reflecting upon with respect to this position. First, Lewin distinguished sharply between group and individual self-hatred. By the former, he understood such phenomena as the German or Austrian Jews' dislike for their east European co-religionists – so trenchantly depicted recently in the novels of Aaron Apelfeld; by the latter, the animosity of the individual Jew, 'directed against the group, against a particular fraction of the Jews, against his own family, or against himself. It may be directed against Jewish institutions, Jewish mannerisms, Jewish language or Jewish ideals.'[14] It is the latter which principally concerned him. Second, Lewin presented a model of group dynamics which would explain why a Jew or a Black might assume such an attitude, but it is important to point out that this model is merely a conceptual scheme. Lewin offers no empirical evidence which would confirm the value of his model. Third, this is, doubtless, tied to the fact that his paper is addressed to members of the Jewish community. In fact, his analysis is in aid of exhorting the Jewish community to make an understanding of the problems of maintaining a Jewish identity in secular society an integral part of Jewish education. Thus, Lewin could assume that his American audience was sufficiently familiar with the phenomenon he describes *not* to require further empirical evidence. Peter Gay, on the other hand, takes the concept to have explanatory power in a wholly secular 'civil' context – a basic shift which is, from Lewin's perspective, dubious. This brings us to the fourth significant characteristic of Lewin's paper, and one which is crucial for determining the explanatory value of self-hatred in the history of ideas: the difficulty of identifying self-hatred. '*In most cases*', Lewin writes, '*expression of self-hatred . . . is so blended with other motives that it is difficult to decide in any particular case whether or not self-hatred is involved.*'[15] If this is right, the burden of proof that Weininger offered 'spectacular evidence for the terrifying power of *Selbsthass*' lies clearly with Gay. On Lewin's account, we are obliged to demonstrate that self-hatred is operative in a given case and this is far from being a mere matter of classification of behaviour or substantive assertion. This brings us back to Gay's caricature of Weininger.

If Gay's approach to Weininger illustrates a problem with respect to the employment of the concept of self-hatred in the history of ideas, it is one involving a peculiar type of reductionism to which liberal historiography is prone.[16] The sort of reductionism to which I am referring is present explicitly or implicitly, in varying degrees, in the work of such writers as Paul Giniewski, William Johnston, George Mosse, Jacques LeRider and even Michael Pollak as well as many others. It consists of dismissing Weininger as a thinker on the basis of a superficial knowledge of his texts and his problems, and then explaining away what they at best partially understand in terms of some sort of psychopathology. Since I have argued at length elsewhere that psychoanalysis is largely irrelevant in the history of ideas, and that such an approach fails to do justice to the complexity of Weininger's thought – that it wrenches Weininger out of the contexts of the debates in which he saw himself as participating, and that our knowledge of his biography simply does not permit such psycho-pathological speculations – I shall not repeat those arguments here.[17] But I want to point out the following in response to Gay.

Apart from the antisemites and misogynists who read Weininger with enthusiasm, we have to explain why it was that some of the greatest minds of the century read him with equal enthusiasm: Karl Kraus, Georg Trakl, Ludwig Wittgenstein, Hans Kelsen, Karl Popper and a host of others. Note: this is *not* to say that they endorsed every word he wrote, far from it, but they found him sufficiently important and stimulating that he simply cannot be dismissed without the *close* reading of his text that the tactic of deeming him a self-hater would seem to preclude.

Moreover, Weininger's 'seductive simplicity' is something that has been read into a highly complex – and confused – argument in *Geschlecht und Charakter*. Paradoxically, most of the problems surrounding Weininger arise because the very complexity of his argument invites grotesque over-simplification on the part of superficial critics. However, it is also noteworthy that most of the enthusiasm, or, indeed, revulsion which has arisen in the wake of Weininger's work, as Gerald Stieg has pointed out,[18] is not traceable to *Geschlecht und Charakter* but to the posthumous *Über die letzten Dinge*, which Weininger obviously did not publish himself, and, indeed, may not have intended for publication. Weininger can certainly be read as a *terrible simplificateur* – he may even seem to invite such a reading – but his argument is far from simple. People who so read him, however, tend to emphasize his views about the inferiority of women and Jews and either to omit or dismiss what is in fact the book's main claim, that the male and the 'Aryan' have a moral obligation *not to mistreat* the female and the Jew, even if the female, for example, desires such mistreatment in the form of debasement through sexual union. This position may be bizarre but it is not simple.

We know almost nothing for certain about Weininger's inner life. He was a very private person. Accounts of his inner life tend to be based upon his posthumous writings and/or upon highly speculative psychoanalytical accounts of it. Interestingly, an unsympathetic critic, who endorses the latter approach, has provided compelling reasons for rejecting the former.[19] Weininger certainly did have a very precarious mental balance and feared for his ability to be moral (i.e. chaste). However, it is far from being 'evident' that he had doubts about his Jewish identity precisely because *it is less than clear that he had a Jewish identity in the first place*. I am very puzzled about what Peter Gay thinks is *indelible* about Weininger's Jewishness. It is wholly unclear what he is endorsing here. This last point brings me to something central to the whole discussion of self-hatred.

It is clear that there is such a phenomenon as rejection of one's heritage, and no less clear that this is fundamentally a problem of identity; what is not clear, however, is just what constitutes identity. This has been particularly vexing for Jews who no longer profess Jewish religious beliefs and who, nevertheless, are forced to retain some sort of Jewish identity on account of antisemitism. French Jews, it would appear, walked into a trap in admitting under such circumstances that their Jewishness consisted of belonging to a 'race'.[20] This, they thought, in a period deeply under the sway of a popularized and debased 'Darwinism', would give them a curious kind of equality with members of other 'races'. We forget at our peril in thinking of the *fin de siècle* that racial explanations for character traits were part and parcel of a certain type of *enlightened*, eugenically-oriented social reform in the work of figures as diverse as Francis Galton (Darwin's cousin), Herbert Spencer, Cesare Lombroso, Ernst Haeckel and Emma Goldmann. Be that as it may, the notion of an 'indelible' Jewish identity such as Gay appeals to would seem to be a vestige of such a belief or some secularized version of the Biblical conception of Judaism. In either case such a concept of identity would be metaphysical; in no case would it be of value in social science. To put the point another way, would we want to speak of other sorts of identity, say, Polish or Irish, as 'indelible'? I doubt it. That Darwin's theories rightly understood undermined the notion that there are 'races' within the species *Homo sapiens*, on the one hand, and the theological notion of Jewish identity, on the other, is simply irrelevant to secular discussion, it has no 'civil status', if you like. For this reason I take the differences between Lewin and Gay to be of the utmost importance. What Lewin said about self-hatred was addressed to the American Jewish community in which such a theological belief plays a legitimate role; what Gay says is not; but, nevertheless, seems to smuggle in a whole lot of covert theological baggage in secularized form.

My aim till now has been to identify what I take to be a piece of covert metaphysics parading as social science. Social science has no room for identifying one group differently from another except on empirical grounds. My point is that there seems to be a tendency in the United States, and to some extent elsewhere, to discuss Jewish problems, especially those bearing upon identity, in ways that we do not normally talk about parallel identity problems in other groups (with the possible exception, as noted above, of Blacks). The point is that there are indeed other groups, notably American Chinese, among whom rejection of the Chinese heritage has been common.[21] My question – and I emphasize that I take this to be an open question – is *do we want to describe this as self-hatred?* I suggest that if we do not, we ought not to speak of self-hatred in other contexts either. I take it to be an important clue that we for the most part do not use the term in other similar contexts when we in fact could. In a slightly different vein, it would seem that a significant proportion of American women, especially in the Bible Belt, defend on the basis of tradition and religion a family structure which seems to frustrate and exploit them systematically. I do not recall hearing the term self-hatred applied here. It is just this failure to apply the term here that I take to be suggestive. I further suggest that to term such a defence of a seemingly oppressive social structure as self-hatred, a description which those so described would in fact reject, indicates that the imputation of a charge of self-hatred is a *political* evaluation of a situation. I think that this too tells us something very important about the concept in question. In any case, examples could be multiplied. Mexicans, for example, joke that lack of identity is the defining characteristic of Mexican identity.[22] Moreover, most of the ideas associated with self-hatred – such as deep concern and high value being placed upon European, as opposed to Indian, physical features – are present here, but the term self-hatred is not typically invoked. The reason that I think it is not is because it is so *vague* as to be less than illuminating. Still less, I think, would we want to describe, say, Thorstein Veblen's diatribes against American education as self-hatred. In contexts other than the Jewish one, in short, the term seems to be highly dispensable. Yet, it remains typical that a recent book critical of the theocratic tendencies in Israeli politics was greeted with charges of self-hatred.[23] The point is that, once more, this seems to be a way of rejecting an argument without examining its merits. Those who invoke the concept of self-hatred often seem to want to put something *beyond criticism* and, therefore, employ the concept of self-hatred as a kind of *ad hominem* response to criticism.

But let me shift to a more positive side of my argument; for my aim has not been merely to be nihilistic, but rather to induce a healthy scepticism with respect to the use of the concept self-hatred. A good starting point here is Wittgenstein's admonition not to look for *one* thing corresponding to a word, but to pay attention to the variety of phenomena we designate with it. How many *different* things does self-hatred refer to? I do not propose to be able to answer that question in the brief space available to me, but to suggest how scholars might profitably begin to analyse – break down – the question of self-hatred into manageable components, such that we might attain a deeper understanding of what Lewin has rightly identified as important with respect to the problem of members of minorities who seek alternative identities; while avoiding the kinds of pitfalls which I have suggested that its application presents.

Self-hatred, which as Lewin pointed out has 'almost an endless variety of forms',[24] seems to refer to at least four distinct *classes* of phenomena. Self-hatred functions in (1) sociological, (2) psychological, (3) metaphysical explanations of identity crises as well as (4) in explanations of any and all hostility to Judaism on the part of Jewish intellectuals in the history of ideas. Lewin helped to provide the basis for an important subject in sociological approaches to American race relations over a generation. This tradition of social analysis was admirably summarized by Simpson and Yinger in successive editions of their classic textbook *Racial and Cultural Minorities*. In their analysis of the ways in which minority groups come to accept the stereotypes which persecuting majorities project upon them, they point out:

> Those of high status define one's group as inferior; one experiences discrimination because of group membership; yet the attitudes of the majority prevent one from leaving the group. Those who try to solve this problem by accepting the definitions of the dominant group are caught in a difficult situation as long as prejudice continues.[25]

Thus, at a certain point in American history, ghetto Blacks – and, indeed, often the urban poor generally – came to believe that they were intellectually inferior because their teachers assumed that they were and treated them on that basis. It is beyond question that this is a frequently occurring social phenomenon deserving the fullest possible study. What is less than clear is whether it should be called self-hatred; for it is in fact a specific instance of how those in authority create social stereotypes through acting upon stereotypical assumptions.[26]

In the second, psychological sense, there can be no question that individuals suffer enormously as they struggle to cast off unwanted identity. It is very odd, however, to describe the resentment they can feel for the rejected group self-hatred; for in at least one construal of the situation a self in the sense of identification with the original group is precisely what is *lacking* in the alleged self-hater. Here it is important to point out that identity is one of those things that a person has or not (except when identity is metaphysically conceived), or, to put the matter differently, our beliefs about our identity constitute our identity. I take the basic problem with respect to the concept of self-hatred as it is frequently employed to be that it covertly posits such a metaphysical notion of identity, or, at least, encourages us to misconstrue identity along these lines. Invoking self-hatred tempts us to assume without any special empirical justification that all members of a group share the *same* identity. However, this is precisely what we should suspect as wanting with respect to someone who wants to move from one group to another. It seems that the desire to make such a move presupposes just the *lack* of identity which self-hatred rules out. It is a lack of identity which prompts the Jew to want to assimilate in the first place.

If nothing else is certain, we can be fairly confident that the concept of self-hatred is a red herring in the history of ideas because it diverts our attention from evaluating the *merits* of claims such as those of a Weininger by focussing judgment upon the substance of the claims rather than the evidence and reasoning upon which they rest. In effect, it is little more than a way of saying that the commentator finds his ideas repulsive. My suggestion is that there is a good deal more merit in refuting repugnant views than in confining them to the realm of the unspeakable. It seems to me that the real target in Jewish discussions of self-hatred is often assimilation which continues to be a ticklish subject in many Jewish quarters. This may be with good reason in those precincts. However, it does not mean that such discussions carry weight extramurally, as it were. But this would merit a separate study. Let me close by re-stating what I take to be the merits of my critique.

In the history of ideas self-hatred obscures as much – or more – than it illuminates. Its use has involved a pernicious tendency to evaluate beliefs on the basis of their substance alone and not upon the reasoning upon which they are based. Thus, in the case of

Weininger, commentators like Gay have formed their evaluations of a complex thesis about social reform, determinism, the constitution of social convention (curiously close to Sartre), moral duty and the like, on the basis of Weininger's animosity towards Jews alone. Indeed, even the latter is wholly ambiguous. What Weininger means by 'Jew' is first and foremost an Ideal Type, which he would have done better to describe as the Conformist. Weininger hopelessly confuses his own argument by insisting that conformity is most predominant among Jews. In this he merely follows H.S. Chamberlain. In fact, this is the weakest and most poorly developed section of his book. To evaluate the book on the basis of the chapter on Judaism alone is to obscure the fact that he worked well within the mainstream of programme for social reform, which programme based their analyses of deviance upon genetic determinism. Comparisons with Freud obscure this point because Freud was in fact criticizing just such assumptions at the time Weininger wrote, but *from without*. It was only much later that the superiority of Freud's (still flawed) perspective on the subjects Weininger wanted to illuminate became clear. However, by this time Weininger was more than fifteen years dead. Weininger was much closer to Havelock Ellis, Magnus Hirschfeld and, above all, Cesare Lombroso than he was to Freud. Far too many commentators have failed to realize this, i.e. to see that nearly all that we tend to find obnoxious in his thought was commonplace in the social reform programme, biology and sexology of his day. To approach Weininger as merely a self-hater is to provide one more reason for ignoring the actual context in which he worked. It is in terms of the latter alone that we can come to appreciate his occasional insights and the many genuine flaws in his thinking in such a way that they cease to be threatening, titillating or scandalous. To have analysed Weininger in the fashion I suggest is to see him as the historical curiosity that he is. My objection to considering him as a self-hater is that such a tactic systematically misunderstands his texts and prevents us from rationally, theoretically, freeing ourselves of his particular mode of foolishness once and for all. Speculative psychobiography is no substitute for critique. But Weininger is only one of many instances of the obfuscatory power of the self-hatred hypothesis. Since I am convinced that this subject is crucial for any assessment of the contribution of the Viennese Jews to their culture and to ours, I offer this analysis as a preliminary methodological critique of a stock concept which, I believe, mystifies and prevents accurate assessment of our subject.[27]

THE CONTEXTS AND NUANCES OF ANTI-JEWISH LANGUAGE: WERE ALL THE 'ANTISEMITES' ANTISEMITES?

Sigurd Paul Scheichl

Whoever is familiar with Austrian politics in the last quarter of the nineteenth century will not be astonished at reading the following sentences from the editorial of a Viennese newspaper. The article deals with the Dreyfus affair:

> The entire banking and investment gang, more or less Jewish, fights for Dreyfus and hopes to advance its unjust cause by winning Dreyfus's just cause. When Dreyfus is found innocent, they expect to be acquitted of the crimes of usury and exploitation. The courageous and high-minded attack of Zola is followed by the suspect band of vicious and greedy Jewish parasites, who hope for their personal whitewash and for the opportunity to commit further crimes as a result of this affair.

> Das ganze Gelichter von der mehr oder weniger jüdischen Finanz kämpft mit für Dreyfus und hofft, mit dieser guten Sache seine schlechte Sache zu retten, und erwartet, wenn die Unschuld von Dreyfus erwiesen wäre, von den Verbrechen des Wuchers und der Ausbeutung freigesprochen zu werden . . . hinter [Zolas kühnem und edlem] Angriff marschiert die ganze verdächtige Bande der jüdischen Schmarotzer, und gierig erwartend tuckisch, daß irgendeine persönliche Reinwaschung für sie herausspringe und Gelegenheit zu neuer Missethat gebe.[1]

'Gelichter von der mehr oder weniger jüdischen Finanz', 'jüdische Schmarotzer' – this is the language typical of the period, the language of Schönerer and Lueger, which was to become the language of Hitler.

There are, however, some inconsistencies in this article. On the one hand, it attacks the predominantly Jewish world of finance, which is backing Dreyfus, on the other hand it calls Dreyfus's most ardent defender, Zola, 'kühn', courageous, and 'edel', high-minded, and even speaks of the Dreyfus case as a 'gute Sache', a just cause. The article, then, both uses the vocabulary of antisemites and sides with the Jew, whom it apparently considers innocent; this is an attitude that could hardly be expected of a truly antisemitic newspaper.

Other parts of the article are even more confusing, e.g.:

The great gangs of exploiters try to let loose the demon of racial hatred and hope to defeat republican democracy by using antisemitic demagogy.

[Die großen Ausbeutercliquen] versuchen, die Bestie des Rassen-hasses zu entfesseln, und wollen mit Hilfe der antisemitischen Demagogie die republikanische . . . Demokratie überwinden.[2]

How can one and the same article at once attack 'Rassenhaß' and 'antisemitische Demagogie' and turn against 'jüdische Finanz' and 'jüdische Schmarotzer'?

The moment has come to name the newspaper this article is from: it is the Social Democratic *Arbeiter-Zeitung*, whose editors, Victor Adler and Friedrich Austerlitz, were both of Jewish origin. This paper certainly was in a difficult situation, particularly as far as the Dreyfus case was concerned.[3] Of course, it wanted to write against the reactionary groups that were responsible for the condemnation of Dreyfus; but writing against these 'forces of suppression'[4] meant more or less writing for the 'forces of exploitation',[5] for banking and industry, the *milieu* to which Dreyfus belonged and which supported him. Nevertheless, the attribute 'Jewish' could have been dropped in either passage without really changing the meaning.

The fact that it has not been dropped seems to indicate that such discriminatory vocabulary was used much more loosely in this period than today, even by people who were political adversaries of both Lueger and Schönerer. We have no reason to think that anything the *Arbeiter-Zeitung* published on the Dreyfus affair was in favour of antisemitism; but in order not to be confounded with the *bourgeois* liberal, predominantly Jewish press the workers' daily felt it to be necessary to attack Dreyfus's allies and made use of the widespread antisemitic prejudice,[6] in spite of the great number of its Jewish contributors. To us, the generation after Auschwitz, allusions of this kind must appear at best as frivolous, if not as criminal.

Nevertheless, the *Arbeiter-Zeitung* was anything but an antisemitic paper. This becomes quite clear when we compare it to newspapers that had an explicit antisemitic programme. Their articles on the Dreyfus affair are very different indeed. They do not hesitate to slander Dreyfus personally in enumerating some of his real or invented love affairs and in remarking:

> So this is the true image of the Jewish hero whom our Jewish hack-writers want to make the delight of the whole civilized world. Indeed, those who espouse the cause of this creature are worthy of him.

> So sieht also der jüdische Held aus, für den sich die ganze civilisierte Welt begeistern soll, wenn es nach dem Willen unserer Schmocks ginge. Wahrlich, die sich dieses Subjectes annehmen, sind seiner würdig.[7]

These papers ask for political action:

> Will the conclusion be drawn? Will the French army and the French civil service be purged of the great number of Jews who have sneaked into the most important positions?

> Wird man die Consequenz . . . ziehen un das französische Heer sowie die französische Verwaltung von den massenhaft zu den wichtigsten Posten emporgeschlichenen Juden säubern?[8]

And they generalize:

> Dreyfus is a Jew. So there are enough reasons to distrust him and to believe that he rather than a Frenchman proud of his nation has committed high treason.

> Dreyfus ist ein Jude. Es gibt also genug Gründe, ihm von vorneherein mit Mißtrauen zu begegnen und einen Hochverrath eher zuzumuthen [!], als einem Franzosen mit ausgeprägtem Nationalgefühl.[9]

The spectres of 'internationales Judentum', international Jewry, of 'internationale Judenpresse', international Jewish press,[10] and of a world-wide pro-Dreyfus conspiracy based on 'Israels Geld', the money of Israel, i.e., the Jews,[11] particularly haunt the *Reichspost*, a Christian-Social daily. This newspaper, which was very close to the Catholic church, combined antisemitic agitation with a violent dislike of everything modern. So it writes about Zola:

> For the Jewish press, Zola is the foremost novelist of our time, because his novels reek of the depravity that is the pleasure of literary Jews.

> Zola ist ja der Judenpresse der erste . . . Romancier der Gegenwart, . . . weil seine Romane jenen Gifthauch des Lasters athmen, in welchem den Literaturjuden wohl ist.[12]

These examples should make sufficiently clear the difference between the *Arbeiter-Zeitung* and the truly antisemitic press. The Social Democrats' criticism of French antisemitism is inconceivable in the context of the *Reichspost* or the *Deutsches Volksblatt*. If the adjective 'Jewish' could be (and should have been) missing in the *Arbeiter-Zeitung*, it is the main point of the attack in the antisemitic newspapers.

This difference is what the following pages will be about. The *Arbeiter-Zeitung* is against parasites (capitalists), including 'Jewish parasites', because they are parasites; the *Reichspost* is against 'international Jewry', because it is 'Jewry'. Now I am far from defending the *Arbeiter-Zeitung*'s frivolous use of 'Jewish' in an attack like this, but we cannot fail to observe the difference between such regrettable rhetorical concessions to a widespread prejudice and a political programme based on this and only on this prejudice, even if this programme, as is the case with Lueger, has not been executed. This is not a difference of degree, but, in a moral sense, a difference of quality, and I wonder whether this difference is not obfuscated if we call both attitudes towards Jews 'antisemitic', if we speak of Weininger as if he had been a disciple of Schönerer, perhaps even if we identify the thought of Houston Stewart Chamberlain with that of, let us say, Lanz von Liebenfels.

On another level, Robert S. Wistrich seems to see this problem, when he makes a difference between what he resents as 'antisemites' in the Austrian Social Democratic Party and the 'Jew-baiters'[13] such as Schneider and Vergani. But on the whole his excellent and well-documented study does not insist sufficiently on this difference. The book suffers from a point of view that pays much more attention to what Austrian Social Democracy and Austrian Social Democrats had in common with the antisemitic movements around 1900 than to what was different between them. Certainly, one must endorse Wistrich's judgment on a very strange article by Friedrich Austerlitz: 'The spectacle of a Jewish Marxist intellectual upholding the prejudices of the ignorant rabble in such uncritical language makes curious reading today.'[14] But it is just as important to keep in mind that – in Wistrich's own words – the programme of Lueger was 'a programme of racial discrimination which no Social Democrat would have actually approved'.[15]

If I insist on making a difference of quality between anti-Jewish prejudices on the one hand, antisemitic political programmes on the other, I do of course not wish to excuse those prejudices nor to extenuate the responsibility of the persons who gave voice to them. Nobody who spoke or wrote against Jews as Jews is free of guilt. But many of those who were guilty of this prejudice were far from having any intention to persecute Jews.

But before turning to this problem, we should analyse more 'antisemitic' materials. I do not intend to deal in detail with Austrian Social Democracy, and indeed I could hardly add anything to the results of Wistrich, even if my approach is different from his.[16] I should like, however, to quote one source he has not used, the autobiography of the Belgian Social Democrat de Man. De Man, who lived in Vienna in 1907 and 1908, speaks about anti-Jewish prejudices uttered by socialist leaders in private. The fact that a majority of leading Social Democratic intellectuals were of Jewish origin is said to have provoked dissensions of several kinds. 'The non-Jewish party leaders, such as Karl Renner and Schuhmeier, were quite explicit on these conflicts in private talks.'[17]

But these prejudices remained an affair of private talks, and they never became a political programme. They have left their traces in the agitation of the *Arbeiter-Zeitung* or the *Volkstribüne*, which tried to use the widespread Viennese antisemitism for the aims of their party,[18] but the exclusion of Jews from public life had never been one of these aims. Wistrich, although critical of some of Schuhmeier's positions, recognizes his 'willingness to confront anti-Semitism directly', and calls him 'a defender of the Jewish proletariat in Austria'.[19] This difference between private prejudice and public attitude must be insisted upon.

It cannot be ruled out, however, that the success of the National

Socialists with former Austrian Social Democrats, limited as it was, after 1934[20] may be explained with surviving prejudices of this kind. The same may be true even for the period after 1945, when Austrian Social Democrats were less than zealous to arrange the return of Jewish refugees to Vienna.[21] These questions cannot be analysed in detail here, although it is important to mention such possible negative consequences even of personal prejudice.

This is not the place either to discuss the origins of this prejudice against Jews, which is one level of anti-Jewish feeling. Another level is a direct consequence of the socio-economic development of the second half of the nineteenth century, which led conservatives like Karl von Vogelsang to identify 'Jewry with all the evils of secular modernity'.[22] Many of the public statements hostile to Jews can be reduced to this type of conservative *Kulturkritik* in one of its many forms. The 'anti-liberal backlash',[23] particularly strong in Vienna, and the identification of many influential Jews with the Austrian Liberals, the philosemitic attitude of Austrian Liberalism made it difficult for Austrian intellectuals to be critical of Liberalism without being critical of Jews. 'A temporary convergence of radical and conservative critiques of the dominant liberal-capitalist order'[24] found its expression in a hostility towards (liberal and rich) Jews common to the Christian-Social Party, to the followers of Schönerer, to conservatives and to independent intellectuals like Karl Kraus. They all identified Jews with the new forms of economy they rejected: some of them identified them also with other 'modern' ideas they did not exactly cherish. Notably, criticism of the Jewish role in the press seems to have been frequent in Vienna.[25]

Some of these enemies of modern times and, by consequence, of the Viennese Jews, made a political programme out of this hostility, notably Lueger and Schönerer. With others, e.g. with Kraus and Weininger, this hostility is not a political programme but certainly more than mere personal prejudice. It is part of their, basically conservative, *Kulturkritik*; it is part of their rhetoric against the modern age, but they do not call for any political or social change to the disadvantage of the Jews. Weininger, for instance, insists upon his not wishing to pave the way for any persecution of Jews[26] and writes explicitly: 'It is not the boycott of Jews that is advocated in this book nor their expulsion nor their exclusion from office.'[27] We know that, nevertheless, Weininger's writings would later be used to justify antisemitic persecutions; but in spite of that there is no reason to doubt the subjective honesty of his words.

So we have three different hostile positions towards Jews between about 1870 and 1938. Hostile remarks against Jews may be due to a mere personal prejudice, or to a critical, more or less conservative, attitude towards the 'modern age', or to somebody's allegiance to one of the antisemitic mass movements and their ideology of racism. All three positions exist at the same time, and somebody who had personal prejudices against Jews or was convinced of the positions of *Kulturkritik* need not have become an antisemite in the political sense, although it was not unlikely that he became one.

It might be possible for social scientists to develop a scale in order to measure more precisely the degree of hostility towards Jews. In fact, the mere occurrence of the words 'Jude' on the one hand, 'Judentum' on the other in a given text might be an indicator of a lower or higher degree of dislike for Jews. As a literary historian, I do not feel capable of developing such an instrument for the analysis and evaluation of texts of the past. Thus, I shall limit this paper to the presentation of some examples for the three positions of prejudice, *Kulturkritik* and full-fledged racist antisemitism.

My second example, after the Austrian Social Democrats, are the ill-famed students' fraternities. A recent study about this important multiplier of antisemitism[28] proves that prejudice can develop rather fast into political action. In 1863 one of these fraternities, the Vienna *Burschenschaft Silesia*, admitted three Jewish students as members; in the discussion about this admission, however, some of the older members seem to have expressed their fear, 'daß durch eine Mehraufnahme von Israeliten die Silesia zu einer Judenverbindung werde'[29] (that by admitting more Jewish members the *Burschenschaft Silesia* might become a Jewish fraternity). Apparently, hostility towards Jews was not yet a principle of this *Burschenschaft* – otherwise the Jewish members would not have been admitted – but the prejudice against Jews was already strong enough to create the idea of restricting the number of Jewish members. Whatever reservations some members of some *Verbindungen*[30] may have held towards the admission of Jews, it is nevertheless a fact that very many of them had a considerable amount of Jewish *Bundesbrüder* (members), and Theodor Herzl joined the *Burschenschaft Albia* as late as in 1880.

In a second period of university antisemitism the so-called *national* (i.e. Pan-German) fraternities of Vienna completely stopped the admission of Jewish members around 1880; most of them even excluded their Jewish alumni.[31] The exact reasons for this rapid development are not yet quite clear. One must certainly consider the very high percentage of Jewish students in the Vienna universities, particularly in some of their schools (law, medicine). Hein also mentions the role of the clergy in secondary education, the Catholic press, notably Vogelsang's *Vaterland*, and anti-Jewish motifs in successful novels of the time (e.g. by Freytag and Raabe) as possible reasons for this change of attitude towards Jews.[32] If these influences were really so strong, it would be possible to draw a parallel between the move of the fraternities towards antisemitism and the anti-Jewish position of *Kulturkritik*. Of course, one also has to consider the influence of everyday politics on the Viennese students.[33] Not before 1885 did Georg von Schönerer, in close contact with many of the fraternities, add a twelfth point to his *Linzer Programm* of 1882, which had hitherto not been antisemitic: 'In order to carry out these reforms it will be indispensable to abolish the Jewish influence in all spheres of life.'[34] This claim, which is antisemitic in the most narrow political sense of the word, became part of the fraternities' political programme; some of them had explicitly advocated such measures even before this change in the *Linzer Programm*, as early as in January 1884.[35]

The climax of this evolution was the so-called *Waidhofener Prinzip*, which decided that members of the *national* fraternities had to refuse duelling with Jews. Duels being very important for the social reputation in this period, the non-admission to this way of defending one's 'honour' was indeed a giant step towards socially isolating Jews and Jewish members of the professions. The *Burschenschaft Silesia*, who, by the way, still had Jewish alumni,[36] gave as a reason for its adherence to the *Waidhofener Prinzip*, 'daß man eine unsere nationale Existenz und die germanische Moral gefährdende Rasse isolieren müsse'[37] (that it was necessary to isolate a race so dangerous for our existence as a nation and for Teutonic morality). This statement seems particularly significant both because it speaks of a Jewish 'race' and because it postulates a particular 'Teutonic morality'; it thus shows quite clearly the features of racist ideology.

One must add that this turning towards political antisemitism was not inevitable. Hein mentions in some detail the Prague *Burschenschaft Alemannia*[38] and the Vienna *Corps Marchia*,[39] which continued to admit Jewish members in spite of external and internal pressures to become 'Aryan'. Other *Verbindungen* did exclude their Jewish members but did not sign the *Waidhofener Prinzip*.

Although I do not yet want to draw conclusions I should like to say here that the development of a vast majority of Austrian *Verbindungen* from the prejudice to the *Waidhofener Prinzip* seems to be symptomatic for several reasons. It is a good example for the spring-tide character of antisemitism around 1880 (and, as in the last-mentioned cases, an example for the possibility to resist it); it shows quite clearly the different stages of hostility towards Jews; and it makes clear the close link between these stages. If I insist on the difference between a personal prejudice against Jews and the antisemitism of the *Waidhofener Prinzip*, I do not at all mean that the prejudice is inoffensive; the development of the Austrian students' fraternities proves the contrary: this prejudice could (and can) turn very rapidly into an extremely aggressive antisemitism.

My third example is a private correspondence from the last quarter of the nineteenth century,[40] which shows various degrees of hostility towards Jews, from prejudice to explicit racial antisemitism. The correspondents were the Tyrolean poet Adolf Pichler (1819-1900), professor of geology at the university of Innsbruck, and the famous historian of English literature, Alois Brandl (1855-1940), a native of Innsbruck, who received his academic training at the university of Vienna and very soon became a professor of English literature at Prague, later on at Göttingen, Strasbourg and Berlin. Neither Brandl nor Pichler is very important in the intellectual history of the nineteenth century, but they may well be representative of Austrian *bourgeois* intellectuals of the time, with a liberal background, but tending more and more towards German nationalism. Their correspondence has a very personal character; very often it is an exchange of literary ideas but political remarks are by no means infrequent. So these letters may give a good idea what men of this background really thought about the 'Jewish question'.

Pichler, who had fought in the Vienna revolution of 1848, was still in contact with another liberal of that heroic age, the Vienna Jewish writer Ludwig August Frankl (1810-94), to whom he sent his young Innsbruck friend when Brandl enrolled in Vienna.

Brandl's first remarks about Jews – he may not have known any before coming to Vienna – are made when he tells about a visit at Frankl's. He is very respectful of the old writer, particularly of his 'riesige literarische Welterfahrung' (his tremendous experience of the literary world, letter 12 of 11 February 1878). In spite of his respect, this very letter also bears traces of Brandl's personal prejudices against Jews. He mentions an 'orientalisch leidenschaftlichen Ausbruch' (outburst of oriental passion) of Frankl's hatred; he also talks about Frankl's thriftiness that alone can explain how the old writer can live 'in diesen niedrigen, engen düstern, stinkenden Zimmern seines Judentempels' (in these low, narrow, gloomy, foul-smelling rooms of his Jewish temple). In fact, Frankl was the secretary of the *Kultusgemeinde*, the Vienna Jewish community.

The following lines from Brandl's subsequent letter make it likely that the observations he made in Frankl's family were the observations he wanted to make because they corresponded to his prejudice:

> With Frankl and in literary circles I often observe with respect the vigorous sense of family that has made the Jewish people keep together since the Tower of Babylon. But the sense of humanitarianism is unknown to the Hebrews; for them it is a mere word that they use like paper money without believing in it.[41] (Letter 14, February 1878)

The generalizations go far beyond what Brandl can have observed in only one visit; they go far beyond the expression of personal antipathy too. Nevertheless, Brandl continued to frequent the Frankl family and other Jews.

Many of Brandl's remarks on Jews resemble those on Frankl. Often he does not even express an opinion but just mentions the Jewish origin of the person he writes about, even if this origin is of no consequence (e.g. letters 19 of 1 June 1878, and 28 of 27 December 1878; as late as in letter 367 of 26 December 1896, he writes about Ludwig Fulda: 'Er ist Judaicus' – he is Jewish – and about his wife's 'gleiche Herkunft' – the same origin of his wife).[42] Such remarks may even be positive. So he writes about baptized Jews of Prague that they 'über ... die gesamte Judenschaft lachen, und unter mancherlei harmlosen, orientalisch nuancierten Schwächen einen guten Kern verraten' (letter 148 of 18 December 1884; that they laugh at Jewry as a whole and are good at heart in spite of some inoffensive half-oriental foibles). This letter also indicates that Brandl believed in the possibility of the assimilation of the Jews. On the other hand, one must insist on the fact that this letter on converted Jews shows that Brandl adhered to a more or less racist definition of 'Jew'; earlier he had written: 'Der Jude ist mir gewiß nicht wegen seiner Religion unangenehm' (letter 19 of 1 June 1878; I certainly do not dislike the Jew because of his religion).

It is also part and parcel of his prejudice against Jews, when Brandl observes that he was the only Christian at a *soirée* in the Schottenring palace of an apparently Jewish banker. The remark also seems to imply criticism of the increasing role of Jews in Vienna's high society.

Apparently, Brandl's remarks on Jews are more than the expression of a certain social antipathy against strangers. The young scholar gives a negative judgment on the role of Jews in several spheres of public life. He approaches the *Kulturkritik*'s image of what is Jewish when he writes that in German literature witticisms are the province of the Jews, or when he speaks about the Jewish influence in Vienna's literary life: 'denn heute sieht es auf dem Wiener Parnassus aus wie im Tale Josaphat' (letter 81 of 19 March 1881; today Vienna's Mount Parnassus resembles the valley of Jehoshaphat). He still speaks of a 'Jubelgeheul der jüdischen Presse' (cries of triumph of the Jewish press) in 1895, and the occasion for this remark is interesting: Brandl expects this 'Jubelgeheul' to greet the publication of a popular book on Shakespeare by Georg Brandes, a Jewish critic, which was to be a rival of Brandl's own book on the same subject (letter 337 of 11 March 1895). And in a global statement on Austrian politics, on the dangers for the 'German character of Austria', Brandl writes ironically as late as on 24 March 1897: 'wir haben es weit gebracht, durch die Wiener und Juden!' (how successful we have been, thanks to the Viennese and the Jews!). Judgments like this leave no doubt as to Brandl's conviction of the Jews being dangerous, of the necessity to distrust them, to fear their sense of solidarity, which makes Brandl think of all kinds of coterie and nepotism.

About half of Brandl's comments on Jews are to be found in the early part of the correspondence (until 1881), in his Vienna years. This is certainly the period in which the ambitious (and perhaps slightly opportunistic) young man is particularly respectful of Pichler, who was a well-known personality, and in which Pichler's influence on Brandl is particularly strong.

His most radical statement on Jews is to be found in one of these early letters: 'Über den Juden bin ich mir klar: ich hasse alle jene, die sich noch als Nation fühlen' (letter 42 of 7 June 1879; I've made up my mind about the Jew: I hate all those who still feel as a nation). Even in this – isolated – remark Brandl does not really cross the borderline towards political antisemitism, since he avoids all racist vocabulary and apparently does not envisage any 'solution' of the 'Jewish question'; implicitly, he even accepts assimilation, i.e., the possibility of Jews not feeling as a (Jewish) nation. Nevertheless this sentence, using the generalizing singular 'der Jude' so typical of antisemitic rhetoric, is proof of the deep roots of Brandl's anti-Jewish prejudice.

In subsequent letters, however, Brandl never made similar statements. On the contrary. He is obviously taken aback by the Russian pogroms, when he writes to Pichler in 1881: 'Was denken Sie von den Judenverfolgungen in Rußland? Sie werfen jedenfalls Klarheit auf die Antisemitenbewegung' (letter 86 of 19 May 1881; What do you think about the persecutions of the Jews in Russia? In any case, they teach us what we have to think about the antisemitic movement). That Brandl has learned the lesson of the pogroms, which made him see the ultimate consequence of his own prejudice, may be concluded from the fact that he did not respond to Pichler's answer, who had half defended the pogroms (letter 87 of 1 June 1881; see below).[43] In fact, from now on he hardly ever reacts to the antisemitic remarks of Pichler from Innsbruck, which become increasingly frequent after 1881.

So we can observe a certain development of Brandl's views. He becomes older and more mature – and more independent of Pichler. Moreover, antisemitism in the 1880s became more radical and thus somewhat revolting to persons of Brandl's social position. He also left Vienna in 1884 and Austria in 1888; so he lived far from the Vienna atmosphere with its large Jewish influence and the rising radicalism of antisemites. Finally, there may have been private reasons for the more or less slight change in Brandl's attitude towards Jews. Certainly, he never explicitly disavowed antisemitism (at least not in these letters), but on the whole the letters do not allow to speak of his 'unconcealed sympathy'[44] for antisemitism, either.

Adolf Pichler was much more radical than Brandl, and although he had little or no contact with Jews in Innsbruck, he mentions the problem more frequently than his younger friend. The unpleasant humour of his coarse remarks on 'Jewesses', which nevertheless also show his prejudices, are not worth detailed analysis. Pichler also uses jokingly Yiddish words when he alludes to Jews, a stylistic feature characteristic of his dislike of Jews. So he writes: 'Grüßen Sie mir Frankulos und bleiben Sie koscher' (letter 82 of 24 March 1881; My greetings to the Frankulos[45] – and stay kosher!).

Just as Pichler's prejudice seems to be stronger than Brandl's, his attitude also shows more clearly the features of *Kulturkritik*. His relative lack of success as a writer may have contributed to his opinion of Jewish domination in literary life and of a particularly Jewish, successful conception of art. Art by Jews is for him superficial and commercialized:

> I've heard some pieces by Rubinstein. Technical virtuosity, obtrusive, everything just pasted on the surface, nothing coming from inside, nothing but Jewish merchandise. How different was the appeal of Palestrina's *missa brevis* on Sunday: everything simple; simple and great, nothing but the theme.[46] (Letter 178, 10 April 1886)

In 1881 Pichler had made a similar judgment on Heine (letter 87; see below). It is interesting that Brandl's opinions on the art of Ludwig August Frankl are very similar, though Brandl avoids the generalizations of Pichler and pays more attention to the particular situation:

> An enviable, abundant imagination flares in *uncanny* splendour but it does not touch the heart with a pure and holy flame. If this imagination would be matched with your *thought*, only then I should be satisfied by the 'Tropischen Könige'. I cannot feel sympathy [for Frankl].[47] (Letter 15, 21 February 1878)

Pichler, less interested in economics than in literature, nevertheless also insists on the too great impact of Jews on Austrian economy:

> What do people in Vienna say about Rothschild who just shakes his *Beikeles* and makes totter the Mount Olympus of Austrian government bonds? A sublime spectacle, isn't it?[48] (Letter 109, 28 January 1882)

The name of Rothschild as well as the word 'Beikeles'[49] are typical clichés of the language of the antisemites.

Pichler is close to them in more than his language. Thus, he writes on the occasion of the *Antisemitismusstreit* provoked by Treitschke:[50]

> The Jews are like scabies; it is not a fight between religion and religion but between race and race, and even the ancient heathens have been aware of that.[51] (Letter 67, 26 January 1880)

And even of his old acquaintance Frankl he says:

> The humanitarianism of Frankl is not real humanitarianism. All his bequests are for Jews. And I just want to say that Vienna or Berlin alone have as many Jewish inhabitants as all of France or of Great Britain, and you can find examples concerning Jewish profiteering just everywhere.[52] (Letter 68, 18 February 1880)

A very important document is Pichler's answer to Brandl's dismayed question about his opinion on the Russian pogroms:

> The Russians have been unjust, but what has happened to the Jews has been just. The reaction against this race, which is not a people but co-operates everywhere in the exploitation of others, will become even more radical. The Germans cannot tolerate forever that the Jews empty their pockets but shit into their hearts and heads. No nation would be as apathetic when their literature is turned into Jewish literature, but then the Germans are not a nation. Look at the British, French, Italians, Spanish: there, the Jews are at best tolerated but nowhere is their influence dominant. And this happens even though they are superficial and without substance, not excepting the disgusting Heine. Heine does not owe his success to what is true and beautiful in his works but to his superficial and trivial witticisms – and of course to Jewish publicity, which again needs a Messiah. I know a few excellent Jews, but I do not like the Jews.[53] (Letter 87, 1 June 1881)

This is the language, these are the ideas of Austrian political antisemitism. At least indirectly Pichler here asks for the exclusion of Jews from German cultural life. In another letter (of 1895) to another friend Pichler even uses one of the metaphors typical of the most brutal forms of Jew-baiting: 'You know that I do not dislike the Jew as an individual, but it is high time to invent a bug-destroyer against *the* Jews.'[54]

There can be no doubt that Pichler is beyond the threshold of personal prejudice, also beyond the threshold of a *Kulturkritik* for whom the Jews were a metaphor for the dangers of modernity, were 'hostages of civilisation',[55] even though, for example, his judgments on Heine and Rubinstein show parallels to the opinions of those foes of liberalism. Pichler uses the vocabulary of the antisemitic mass movements and is not far from approving their strategies. I should, however, admit that he hardly ever mentions the political parties in question. There are very few remarks on Lueger and Schönerer in his letters – but there can be hardly any doubt that Pichler was at least potentially a voter for the latter.

Pichler is not important enough to warrant an exact analysis of the reasons for his antisemitic position. It certainly has to do with the disillusionments of the old liberals of 1848, many of whom could only with difficulty accept the development of Austria under liberal influence.

In the light of his letters one cannot quote without irony a polemical poem on Pichler's 80th anniversary. The major conservative argument against the formerly liberal writer Pichler, who is here depicted as a traitor to truly Tyrolean values, is epitomized in the line:

For eighty years you have been a slave of the Jewish cause.

Doch du warst achtzig Jahre Judenknecht.[56]

The mere fact that Pichler did not quite fit into the conservative image of the Tyrol was sufficient to attack him – as a philosemite. This line shows how easily conservatives identified liberalism and Jews, regardless of any facts.

It is necessary to insist on the private character of these letters. Pichler's and Brandl's prejudices, their 'antisemitism', were a private matter for them, and neither of them seems to have been ready to militate in favour of antisemitism or to be active in public antisemitic propaganda, at least in this period of their lives. And I should also add that the remarks analysed in this paper do not make up a major part of the correspondence: the 'Jewish question' is not one of its major topics.

Pichler and Brandl have been looked at in some detail not because they are so important in the intellectual life of the period, but rather because they may be fairly close to average intellectuals of the time. That is why they are symptomatic, the changing Brandl perhaps even more so than the blunt Pichler. They are symptomatic because they feel the need to discuss the problem of the relations with Jews, because they share the prejudices of their contemporaries and because they finally draw different conclusions from their situation: Brandl, in Germany, just does not care very much about the problem any longer, Pichler, in Austria, becomes more and more radical. They are symptomatic, too, because Brandl's development shows that the road from personal prejudice to public hatred was not irreversible; the evidence of these letters would hardly permit one to call Brandl an antisemite in the late 1890s, even if his old prejudices turn up again once in a while. On the other hand, he does not seem to have resented in the slightest Pichler's attacks on Jews; at best, he does not react to them but he certainly never writes a word of disapproval. Antisemitism, thus, was something quite respectable in Austria around 1900.

There are more prominent enemies of the Jews in Austrian cultural life than Brandl and Pichler. Although there is not enough space for other case studies I shall mention some interesting examples that have in part been treated elsewhere.

Whoever knows that Marie von Ebner-Eschenbach cordially detested Lueger and militated against antisemitism in the 1890s will be surprised to read her early book *Aus Franzensbad* (1858).[57] At least two passages of these inoffensive satirical letters[58] draw a rather negative picture of the exterior and of the manners of Jewish guests in the Bohemian spa of Franzensbad. Ebner-Eschenbach, who even imitates the Jews' bad German, is not at all aggressive, but when she puts 'diese "Herrschaften"' (these 'ladies' and 'gentlemen') — an upstart Jewish family — under quotation marks and contrasts them with plain-looking 'wirkliche große Herrschaften'[59] (real ladies and gentlemen), she shows that at least in 1858 she shared some of the social prejudices against Jews. Her later attitude proves again that this prejudice need not have inevitably ended in the ranks of the antisemitic mass movements.

Weininger,[60] Kraus[61] and the writers around the review *Der Brenner* (1910-54)[62] are well-known examples for intellectuals close to *Kulturkritik*, whose positions have often been described as 'antisemitic'.[63] The present writer, as indicated in the foregoing citations, has made a detailed study of Kraus's frequent attacks on Jews. There is no doubt that Kraus has more in common with the antisemites than he should have had, but on the other hand one must not fail to observe the differences.

Apparently, the identification of liberalism and economic modernization in Austria with the Jews was so strong that any anti-liberal position could not but become a partly anti-Jewish position, all the more so when criticism of the liberal press was involved. In this sense, Kraus's so-called 'antisemitism' shows close parallels to the elements of antisemitic rhetoric in the Social Democratic press, and both Kraus and Austrian Social Democracy have some positions in common with the Christian-Social party and even with Schönerer. A sentence of Weininger sums up precisely the reasons for which these writers were critical of Jews: '*Jüdisch* ist der *Geist der Modernität*, von wo man ihn betrachte'[64] (the spirit of the modern age is Jewish, from wherever one looks at it).

Turning against modernity, as Weininger and Kraus did, meant turning against Jews in Austria of 1900. As to Kraus, one has to keep in mind that for him the most negative element in modern society was the press. Since the role of Jewish journalists was enormous in Austria,[65] Kraus's criticism of the press (which, of course, also included the non-Jewish press in spite of its lack of importance) received almost automatically an anti-Jewish flavour. Other aspects of public life and culture in Austria that were attacked by Kraus also had a strong Jewish element, and when Kraus interpreted the civilization of pre-1914 Austria as characterized by the loss of traditional values, he explained this loss by the Jews' loss of faith: they were a 'Menschenart . . ., feind ihrem und jedem Glauben'[66] (a kind of people hostile to their own and to every other faith).

Although thus rooted in *Kulturkritik* (rather than in political antisemitism), Kraus's polemics use a rhetorical language that comes once in a while fairly close to the vocabulary of antisemites. In a particular context he even speaks of 'Rasse',[67] even though he did not believe in this notion;[68] he uses words like 'Nebbichs'[69] and describes the triumphant 'Lord of the hyaenas', the lord of the war profiteers as a typical Jew. (More exactly, he uses the traits of Moriz Benedikt, the most influential of Vienna's Jewish journalists, in stressing his typically Jewish features.)[70] This symbolic character of *Die letzten Tage der Menschheit* even praises the triumph of the new – implicitly Jewish – values over the old Christian world, a triumph that Kraus believed to be completed by the First World War.

Nevertheless, it is only part of the picture if one concentrates on Weininger's and Kraus's 'antisemitism', as close as particularly Kraus may seem to this attitude in some parts of his writings. Too many features characteristic of antisemitism are absent from their work to make such an identification possible. These writers were against any persecution of Jews – I have quoted Weininger on this subject – they refused all theories of race, they maintained cordial personal contacts with Jews, and they insisted on the non-political character of their criticism of Jews.

Moreover, both Kraus and *Der Brenner* found a new and very positive relationship to Jews, when these were menaced by National Socialism. *Der Brenner* turns towards the Bible and insists on the brotherhood between Christians and the chosen people;[71] one of the most important contributors to the review in these years, Paula Schlier, reminds her readers of the fact that Jesus was a Jew physically.[72] Both personal prejudices against Jews (which may have survived in private remarks) and *Kulturkritik* were subordinated to this attempt at a religious reconciliation with the Jews.

Kraus first reacted to the rise of a manifestly dangerous antisemitism in Germany by changing allusions to Jewish names in texts he read in public lectures in Germany.[73] Anti-Jewish generalizations are less frequent in his work after 1918,[74] anyhow.

But Kraus also found a more personal way of showing his increasing doubts about the consequences of his anti-Jewish attitude (which he never did give up entirely). There is a letter from him to Sidonie Nádherný from March 1929, which rebukes his friend because she has apparently used the words 'herausfordernd jüdisches Gesicht' (provocatively Jewish face) for Georg Knepler, who then accompanied Kraus's lectures on the piano.[75] Kraus makes Sidonie Nádherný understand that by using such words she approaches the attitude 'aus dem solche Formulierungen kommen' (which gives rise to such words), i.e. political antisemitism, with which she should have nothing in common. Here he expresses clearly his contempt for antisemitism (as he does, of course, also in *Die Fackel*), and even protests against personal prejudice.[76]

In 1934, he even publicly acknowledges his admiration for certain features of Jewish tradition and his personal indebtedness to some of these traditions.[77]

The material briefly presented here shows the existence of a 'climate of general intolerance'[78] in Austria that reaches far beyond the activities of antisemitic movements, though these movements could not have succeeded without such a climate. The omnipresence of hostility towards Jews can perhaps only be truly understood if private, literary and journalistic documents are studied rather than political statements. From documents of this kind one can also learn that negative opinions on Jews did not exclude contacts between Jews and their enemies, that in spite of this climate of intolerance hatred was apparently not characteristic of everyday relations between people. Brandl wrote disparaging letters about Frankl – and continued to see him (as Pichler may have continued to write to Frankl). This would not have been possible if antisemitism had been a dogma for all those who had prejudices against Jews or who resented modernity and the Jews with it.

A precise image of this climate of intolerance against Jews must be a multi-layered image. It must take into account the nuances between the attitudes of, let us say, the *Arbeiter-Zeitung*, Weininger and Lueger; one must not forget either that it was possible to admire Jews and nevertheless partake in this intolerance against Jews in general.

Contemporaries were quite conscious of these nuances within 'antisemitism' or these different 'antisemitisms'. So Engelbert Pernerstorfer (?) wrote in an article of 1904:

> Of course nobody can be blamed for not feeling a particular
> sympathy towards Jews: one cannot force anybody to love or to
> hate. Such a personal antisemitism of feeling is a matter of private
> life, and everybody is entitled to it as to disliking stammerers or
> bald-headed men. But there is a very long way from such attitudes
> to the political antisemitism of our days, which is by no means
> acceptable or even tolerable.[79]

A fairly unimportant Innsbruck review, *Der Widerhall*, makes a similar distinction in 1919: 'Individual antisemitism of feeling is a matter of course. Political antisemitism is an idiocy.'[80] The editor of this review, by the way, was a Jewish journalist, Otto König.

And finally a rather pathetic example, pathetic because of its date, 1931, when a prelate, one Monsignore Kolb, a partisan of Catholic Austrian fascism, tried to make a distinction between 'his' justified antisemitism, the antisemitism of *Kulturkritik*, and the unjustified antisemitism of National Socialism:

> *I am an old antisemite myself.* I should wish that the cultural
> antisemitism, of which I have always been a partisan, become the
> general outlook of Catholic politicians. It is not the antisemitism of
> violence and pogroms that can help us but the cultural
> antisemitism that fights against Jewish cultural inflation in all
> spheres.[81]

In 1931, Kolb, whose statement seems to have been meant in a political sense, should have known that the time for making distinctions between good and bad antisemitism was definitely gone. Nevertheless, the point he tries to make is not quite unimportant: it is the difference between dislike and murder.

Of course, there is no such thing as a 'good' antisemitism. Our generation knows that we must not tolerate any hostility towards Jews (or any other minorities): neither prejudice nor *Kulturkritik* nor racial hatred. Auschwitz has finally made us recognize the common features of all hostility towards Jews, and we know that the antisemitic mass movements would not have been possible without personal prejudice and without the theories of *Kulturkritik*. It cannot be excluded that Weininger and Kraus had a part in making political antisemitism respectable for those antisemites who were capable of reading these authors. And it is obvious that for the Austrian *bourgeoisie*, always respectful of the academic world, scholars such as Pichler and Brandl (and too many others) contributed to the legitimization of its prejudices.[82]

But although it is an important rule of hermeneutics to evaluate texts of the past by a set of values of our time – and this rule is all the more important when the texts concern a problem like antisemitism – we have nevertheless also to ask the question: 'In short, is it fair to see in [Adler, Pernerstorfer, Kraus, Weininger] a harbinger of the twentieth-century politics of the "Radical Right"?'[83] Is it fair not to ask what people have thought in their time but only what has become of their thought in our time? Or: Is antipathy towards a group of people identical with murder, because murder has been a (theoretical, then practical) consequence of this antipathy?

We have to ask both questions. The question what has become of anti-Jewish thinking in our time must always be kept in mind if we do not want to whitewash doubtful positions of the past. It is all the more important to keep this question in mind because insisting on different types of 'antisemitism' might be understood as an attempt to find respectable ancestors for antisemitism or even to excuse this ideology.

This is, of course, not the intention of this chapter. But on the other hand we cannot properly understand the situation of the Jews in Austria if we do not ask the other question, if we label any nasty remark on Jews as 'antisemitic' in the narrow sense of the term. This would necessarily give the impression that Austerlitz or Weininger had the same part in preparing Auschwitz as had Lueger, who himself was certainly not an antisemite of the National Socialist type.[84] Brandl's attitude is not identical with that of Pichler; the

Burschenschaft Silesia of 1863 has, in this respect, little in common with the *Burschenschaft Silesia* of 1895; Kraus is not Goebbels. We are confronted with different degrees of hostility against Jews, some of them acceptable for the contemporaries under the relatively peaceful conditions of constitutional Austria around 1900, the others even then an offence to the idea of humanity. These differences are part of the multi-layered social reality of the period, and we may even fail to grasp correctly a text of this time if we focus only on the rather global concept of antisemitism, where we should rather ask whether the author is, for example, an anti-liberal using antisemitic rhetoric or whether he is indeed a partisan of racism.

> Whatever importance [Christian-Social and other] influences may have had on the ideological origins of National Socialism, it is no less essential to distinguish between different epochs, particularly with respect to the 'Jewish question'. In this context it is salutary to recall that: Luegerite antisemitism operated within the framework of a conciliatory, supranational Habsburg dynasty which was not hostile to Jews; *mass* violence within this political system was rare; and economic life was not yet caught up in the disastrous cycles of depression, inflation, and mass unemployment of the post-1918 era. Most importantly, the inviolate character of the *Rechtsstaat* and of a political culture based on law still existed.[85]

Perhaps it would help to distinguish between the different attitudes of that period if we used different words. I have elsewhere tried to use the terms *Judenfeindschaft* (hostility against Jews) and *Antisemitismus*, the one for the critical identification of Jews with modernity (for which there are, after all, some historic reasons), while *Antisemitismus* is characterized by a programme of specific political and social measures against Jews, by the use of the pseudo-scientific (then perhaps scientific) notion of 'race' and by the tendency towards a mass movement.[86]

This attempt to make a difference between *Judenfeindschaft* and *Antisemitismus* has been called 'sophistic',[87] without really discussing my arguments. I am nevertheless ready to accept this criticism, if we regard the problem from the point of view of our time. But if we wish to study the 'exceedingly complex defense mechanism against unwarranted social change',[88] which antisemitism in Austria was, as a complex phenomenon of *its own time*, we must not identify all aspects of this mechanism with the subsequent antisemitism of violence and murder.[89] Brandl, Weininger, Kraus, even Pichler and Lueger, can justly be blamed for many errors but they cannot be blamed for a historical development that made 'the conditions in the first Austrian Republic, as in Weimar Germany, ... vastly different from anything that they could have imagined'.[90] And they cannot even be blamed for not being able to imagine such future developments in a country whose Jews were, at least in the western parts of the state, sufficiently protected against all but verbal attacks.

There is no such thing as an innocent hostility against minorities. But what has turned out an objective contribution to National Socialism – which could choose among many sources[91] – should not always be understood as subjective guilt.

Colin Walker has written on *Judith und Holofernes* by Nestroy:

> It is difficult to deal dispassionately with manifestations of antisemitism in an earlier age. All roads seem to lead to Auschwitz. Obviously it would be quite wrong to consider Nestroy's play in the light of the crimes of our century.[92]

Perhaps a model of different degrees and types of hostility against Jews can help to solve this difficulty. And a more precise image of the different sources of modern antisemitism may even help to combat antisemitism and hostility against minorities more effectively, e.g. by showing what can become of a seemingly only private prejudice. It would indeed be sophistic if I were only interested in being fair to the past and not convinced that combating such developments today is also an important task of historical and literary scholarship.[93]

CHAPTER 6

SOCIAL DEMOCRACY, ANTISEMITISM AND THE JEWS OF VIENNA

Robert S. Wistrich

In the famous passage on the Galician *Ostjuden* who settled in Vienna's second district, the Leopoldstadt, during and after the First World War, the novelist Joseph Roth observed:

> It is frightfully difficult to be an *Ostjude*; and there is no harder fate than that of alien Eastern european Jews in Vienna. For the Christian Socials they're Jews; for the German nationalists they are Semites. For the Social Democrats they are unproductive elements.[1]

Both the Christian Socials and the German Nationalists, as Roth pointed out, included antisemitism as an important part of their programme. The Social Democrats, on the other hand, 'furchten den Ruf einer "jüdischen" Partei' – feared being labelled as a 'Jewish party'.[2] This perceptive summing up of the situation in the 1920s is no less valid for the late Habsburg period, as I have endeavoured to show elsewhere.[3] The Social Democrats of Habsburg Austria, influenced as they were by classic leftist prejudices against both Jews and Judaism, remained entangled in a defensive and largely futile war to prove that they were not a *Judenschutztruppe* – a 'Jewish protective guard'. Given this premise, they could scarcely wage an effective battle against militant political antisemitism. The fact that the Austrian Social Democrats did eventually take a stand against the Catholic and Pan-German varieties of antisemitism which exercised such an influence in nineteenth- and twentieth-century Austria, should not obscure the extent to which the party leadership itself flirted with, and even contributed to, the growth of the phenomenon.

The discussion of socialist and Marxist attitudes to antisemitism (whether in Austria or elsewhere) has often been confused by the erroneous and illogical assumption that left-wing parties are immunized against racial, religious or ethnic prejudice.[4] The theory and above all the *praxis* of the Austrian workers' movement is a good illustration of how unfounded is this assumption when examined in the light of concrete historical situations. Not only was the labour movement far from immune to the cultural and political antisemitism that began to pervade broad strata of German-Austrian society from the early 1880s onward, but it was from the outset permeated with prejudices against Jews.[5] This was as true at the mass level as it was in the upper reaches of the Austrian party. The major difference was that in contrast to the German Nationalists or the Christian-Socials this 'socialist' antisemitism was never really activated or used as a major strategic weapon in politics. It did not feature in official party platforms nor was there any intention of deliberately and actively discriminating against Austrian Jews, though calls to limit their presence and influence within the Socialist Party were heard on several occasions:[6] the main expression of socialist antisemitism lay, however, in the highly ambivalent stance adopted towards the rise of a populist and remarkably successful *Antisemitenbewegung* in Vienna after 1890. The seeds of the failure adequately to resist and combat the propaganda of this movement are already apparent in a letter of Karl Kautsky from Vienna in 1884 where he complains: 'We are having great trouble in preventing our people from fraternizing with the Anti-Semites. The Anti-Semites are now our most dangerous opponents, because their appearance is oppositional and democratic, thus appealing to the workers' instincts.'[7]

Kautsky as a Marxist naturally attributed the impact of these early antisemitic appeals to the Austrian workers of von Schönerer's *Deutsch-nationale* to the *kleinbürgerlich* character of the Viennese population.[8] His Austro-Marxist pupils, like socialist theoreticians in other European countries, continually sought to explain antisemitism at this time in purely socio-economic terms as a reaction of *déclassé* petit-bourgeois strata to the impact of large-scale capitalist methods of production.[9] This explanation has admittedly a certain validity for Vienna where the artisanal character of local industry and the crisis of the craftsmen was indeed central to the *origins* of the antisemitic movement in the 1880s. Moreover it is also true that at least in the early phases of industrialization in Austria there was less of a clear dividing line between the lower *Bürgertum* and the proletariat, so that typical antisemitic stereotypes might in the early 1880s more easily have infiltrated the nascent working class.[10] Nevertheless the classic Marxist schema, according to which antisemitism (to quote Engels's letter of 1890 to an Austrian correspondent) is exclusively a reaction of 'medieval, declining strata against modern society',[11] is only partially applicable to Austria or to other European societies in the late nineteenth century. Furthermore, as the record of the Austrian Socialists was to show, such views, while ostensibly intended to demonstrate and warn against the 'reactionary' character of antisemitism, proved quite insufficient to guarantee the immunization of the labour movement against ethnic prejudices.[12] The Marxist assumption that modern capitalism must inexorably lead to the disappearance of the pre-modern, pre-industrial lower middle strata in the population and thereby to the collapse of the antisemitic movement was also to prove illusory, especially in the Central European context. This was, moreover, a decidedly flimsy basis on which to wage a successful resistance to antisemitic demagogy. Its only practical result was the propagation of a new Marxist dogma in the 1890s to the effect that historical development would inevitably drive the antisemitic *Kleinbürgertum* into the arms of the only truly consistent anti-capitalist party, the Social Democrats.[13]

In their reliance on this rather mechanistic and fatalist concept of historical development, the Austro-Marxist theoreticians were not essentially different from their colleagues in most other European social democratic parties. However, the social, economic and political context in which they operated was substantially different and it is this which perhaps explains why the concessions they made to antisemitic terminology and attitudes appear to be greater than one would have a right to expect. In the first place the Jewish problem in Vienna had become more acute by the 1890s than elsewhere in western or central Europe, though parallel developments did occur all over the Continent. Between 1869 and 1880 the Jewish population had risen from 40,227 (6.10 per cent of the total population) to 72,588 (10.06 per cent). By 1910 there were, as already shown in chapter 1, 175,818 Jews (8.63 per cent) in Vienna where 50 years earlier there had been only 6,217 (2.16 per cent) – a stupendous rate of growth which, when related to the occupational structure of Viennese Jewry and the historic traditions of Judeophobia in Catholic Austria, make the rise of political antisemitism seem less than surprising. Moreover, from the socialist standpoint the economic structure of Viennese Jewry, and in particular its crucial role in banking, industrial capitalism, commerce, department stores, the liberal press and the free professions, did not make the Jewish community appear as the natural ally of a proletarian movement.[14] Even among the poorer Jews of the Leopoldstadt, who had immigrated after 1860 from Hungary, Galicia or Moravia, there were serious social and cultural obstacles to Jewish participation in the labour movement. Most of the immigrant Jews of lower status were not genuine proletarians and very few were factory workers.[15] They did not live in the typical proletarian quarters of Ottakring, Hernals or Favoriten, and a far greater proportion of Jews than gentiles, even at the lowest levels of society, were independent *Selbstständig*.[16] Even more significant, the poorer Jews were far from assimilated, retaining in many cases their distinctive language (Yiddish), their dress, mannerisms, mores and exotic religious customs. At the turn of the century with the increased immigration to Vienna of the more traditionalist and orthodox *Ostjuden* from Galicia, the cultural gap between this Jewish sector and modern Social Democracy appeared almost unbridgeable. The rise of Jewish nationalism in *fin-de-siècle* Vienna was a further factor alienating another important section of the Jewish population from the Austrian Social Democrats who were totally unsympathetic to either Zionism (or even to the more modest claims for Jewish cultural-national autonomy) in Galicia and Bukowina.[17]

On the other hand, by the end of the nineteenth century, there were also the first clear signs of active Jewish participation in the Austrian labour movement. The most striking feature of this new trend was the role played by a growing section of the Jewish intelligentsia in the leadership of the Social Democratic party, in the party press and in its myriad cultural, youth and sport organizations. This intelligentsia was already thoroughly Germanized and identified itself with the zeal of neophytes both with the national and social objectives of the pan-Austrian labour movement.[18] Along with this assimilated stratum of middle-class intellectual Jews, there was also a palpable drift towards social democracy among the new class of commercial employees (*Handelsangestellten*), who constituted a significant proportion of Vienna Jews by the turn of the century.[19] A small nationally-minded sector among these commercial employees also became attracted to labour Zionism after 1900 though not to an independent 'Bundist' Jewish workers' movement which had no cultural or socio-economic base under Viennese conditions. The Poale-Zion organizations in Austria before 1914, it should however be noted, recommended voting for the Social Democrats wherever

Jewish national candidates were not available.[20] After the First World War the drift of Vienna Jews towards the Social Democrats, which had occurred before 1914 only among specific and restricted circles of intellectual Jewry, became a flood and as a result the image of 'Red Vienna' literally fused in antisemitic circles with that of 'Jewish' subversion.[21] Both Jews and Marxists were alleged to be bent on the systematic destruction of traditional Catholic society and culture.

Figure 6.1 *Antisemitic cartoon (1922) depicts a Jewish capitalist and a Jewish Marxist, arms linked, attempting to fool a militant antisemitic worker*

The seeds of this post-war clerical and fascist propaganda against 'Red Vienna' can be found however in the late Habsburg period. It was no accident, for example, that the young Adolf Hitler explicitly related his hatred of Jews and Social Democrats to his experiences in turn-of-the-century Vienna. The fear and anxiety induced by the *Judensozi* (the so-called 'Jewish' Social Democrats) was rooted in the class distinctions that continued to pervade gentile Austrian society and exacerbated by the impact of the *Christlichsozial* agitation after 1900. Having finally conquered the city of Vienna in 1897, that Catholic populist party under the leadership of Karl Lueger turned the burden of its propaganda against its newest and most dangerous rival, the rising Social Democratic Party. Christian Socialism sought at the turn of the century to become *the* party of the Viennese German bourgeoisie and the supreme defender of *Mittelstand* interests against the 'Red Menace'. Karl Lueger, who in the 1890s had so successfully united the middle and lower *Bürgertum* against the decaying liberal order in the name of traditional ideals of Austrian *Bürger* culture, now found a new rallying-cry in the crusade against Social Democracy.[22]

The 'Red Fear' and the 'Jewish Question' merged in the propaganda of Lueger's movement from the moment it had achieved office. Anti-intellectualism, *Mittelstand* phobias concerning prolet-arization, anxiety over socialist atheism, and petty-bourgeois fears of Jewish competition were cleverly exploited by the *Christlich-Soziale* to mobilize their bourgeois clientele. It was from this agitation, which was the first systematically to synthesize hatred of Socialists and Jews, that Hitler picked up his hysterical anti-intellectualism as well as his fateful identification of Marxism with Jewry.[23] Further-more, it was in Vienna that he 'discovered' the decisive role which Jewish intellectuals played in the Marxist parties and the roots of what he subsequently convinced himself was a satanic conspiracy against the German *Volk*. 'The names of the Austerlitzes, Davids, Adlers, Ellenbogens, etc.', he histrionically recalled in *Mein Kampf*, 'will remain forever engraven in my memory.'[24]

Hitler's assumptions, which ultimately led to the mass murder of European Jewry, were of course utterly remote from the actual theories of Austro-Marxism and from the *praxis* of the Social Democratic movement in Austria-Hungary. Not only did Hitler completely ignore the pronounced German character of the Austrian Socialist party (and its strong emotional attachment to the idea of *Anschluss*) but he clearly knew nothing whatsoever about the outlook and attitudes of the Jewish intellectuals prominent in the labour movement.[25]

Far from favouring 'Jewish' interests or identifying themselves with other Jews, whether in ethnic, religious or class terms, the so-called 'Jewish' leadership of the Austrian Social Democracy bent over backwards to *dissociate* themselves from their former co-religionists. In order perhaps to refute the antisemitic attacks on their leadership, they indulged in strategies either of avoidance, trivialization of antisemitism, or even sophisticated justifications which only revealed the extent of their alienation from Jewry. The founder and leader of the Socialist party in the Habsburg empire, Victor Adler, son of a wealthy Jewish family from Prague, a fervent German nationalist in his younger days and a convert (to Protestantism) at the age of twenty-six, set the tone on this as on other major issues. Adler resolved his own personal 'Jewish question' by adopting an official policy of 'neutrality' on all problems involving conflicts between philo- and antisemites. In practice, under Viennese conditions of the 1880s and 1890s this meant favouring the antisemites as against their liberal 'philosemitic' opponents. Otto Bauer, who belonged to the younger generation of Austro-Marxists, later continued this policy, writing in 1910 that 'Marx's essay on the Jewish question (of 1844) already differentiated us sharply from liberal philosemitism'.[26]

The reluctance of the Social Democrats to recognize the specificity of the 'Jewish question', especially in its national dimension, reflected two distinct traditions – that of the liberal assimilationist Jewish bourgeoisie and that of Marxist ideology – which came together in a common antipathy to feudal-clerical antisemitism, to the *Ostjuden* and to Zionism. At the 1897 Party Congress which found itself dragged, as a result of Lueger's triumph in Vienna, into an unexpectedly frank discussion of both anti- and philosemitism, it was interestingly enough a rank-and-file socialist Jew from Moravia, Jakob Brod, who challenged Victor Adler's policy of indifference to antisemitism, as one of the causes of the Social Democratic defeats in the recent Reichsrat elections:

> Until now the tactical line of the party has been to prevent under any circumstances the suspicion from arising that the party is Judaized. The aim was simply to demonstrate that we are not lackeys of the Jews. But I say to you that even if we live a hundred years, we will never convince the petty-bourgeoisie. What have the comrades in the party leadership done to convince the unenlight-

ened elements that aside from the Jewish bourgeoisie there is also a Jewish proletariat? In Vienna the terms 'Jew' and capitalist are synonymous. I have never known it to be mentioned in the *Arbeiter-Zeitung* or in any meeting (shout: Oho!) — wait till you know what I wish to say — I mean that the Jewish proletariat is the most oppressed, miserable and backward of all (shout: But yes!).[27]

Brod's criticisms, which were angrily rebuffed at the Congress, pointed to one of the fundamental weaknesses in Viennese socialist efforts to counter antisemitic demagogy. The Socialists, instead of emphasizing the class-differentiation within Austrian Jewry, frequently equated capitalism and Jewry along the familiar lines of Christian-social ideology. Since the 'Jewish spirit' (*Judengeist*) according to Marx as well as Baron von Vogelsang (Lueger's spiritual godfather) was identical with the 'spirit of capitalism', it followed that a consistent antisemite should ultimately wish to join the only party which was determined in both theory *and* practice to eliminate capitalism as a whole and with it the basis for the separate economic existence of Jewry. In this way the Austrian Social Democrats both implicitly and explicitly could and did appeal to an antisemitic mass constituency, seeking to present themselves as the most rigorous adversaries of both 'Jewish' and 'Gentile' capital.

This indirect use of antisemitic rhetoric under a Marxist veil to undermine the Christian Social adversaries of the labour movement was a dangerous game to play. It immediately differentiated the socialist party from the Liberals, who in spite of their own equivocacy on the 'Jewish question' never adopted such dubious tactics. It should moreover be remembered that until the crushing Liberal defeat in Vienna in 1897 the socialists had concentrated most of their fire against the Liberals as the 'class enemy' and even expressed open sympathy with Lueger's successful crusade against Austro-liberalism.[28] The Social Democrats had frequently denounced the Viennese 'Jew-press' (*Judenpresse*) — itself a classic antisemitic expression — as the bastion of liberal capitalist opinion and above all for opposing the demands of the workers for universal suffrage. In the eyes of Victor Adler and his colleagues the *Neue Freie Presse* and the capitalist Jewry it represented was and remained a more dangerous enemy of the labour movement than the rowdy antisemitic petty-bourgeois (*Kleinbürgertum*) of Vienna.[29] Hence the Marxist insistence on equating the so-called dangers of 'philosemitism' (i.e. the defence of 'capitalist' Jewry) with those of antisemitism and the actual practice of striking harder at the former. As Jakob Brod put it at the 1897 Party Congress: ' "If now and then Comrade Dr Adler dealt the antisemites a blow, he made quite certain that the Liberals also came in for similar treatment" (Cries of: Quite right!).'[30] The party leadership, including Adler, Pernerstorfer and Franz Schuhmeier, rejected this critique even though politically the Liberals were by 1897 clearly a spent force and the real obstacle and danger to the workers' movement came from Lueger's cohorts.

Schuhmeier none the less declared: 'Indeed the Liberals are simply waiting for the moment when we make the antisemites the sole object of our attack, to re-establish themselves.'[31] Adler himself reaffirmed that: 'We have always said: Let the Christian Socials work, for in the last analysis they are working for us. I still think so today.'[32] With regard to the Jews, Adler sarcastically asserted: 'The special feature of the Jewish question as it manifests itself here in Vienna is that the capitalist bourgeoisie has a Jewish complexion. That the Jews must suffer this is sad. But we are also tired of always finding Jews in our soup.'[33]

Adler's strategy cannot, however, be explained away as a natural reaction to the predominantly bourgeois ethos of Viennese Jewry (somewhat exaggerated by the Social Democrats) or to its socio-economic influence. From a Marxist viewpoint it would have been more logical for the labour movement to favour an alliance with progressive Austro-liberal elements (among whom the Jews were well represented) against the feudal-aristocratic ruling classes of Austria-Hungary. But the Social Democrats preferred to exploit the profound unpopularity of the Liberals for their own purposes and they obviously calculated that defence of the Jews was not a vote-catching cause in Vienna. Moreover, if the Marxist assumption, that Austrian antisemitism was no more than a temporary phenomenon of *Mittelstand* protest doomed to disappear, was correct, there was indeed reason to welcome the Christian-Social victory over liberalism and wait patiently to inherit the Promised Land once the *Kleinbürger* awoke from his illusions.

The positive fruits of this strategy would become apparent after the First World War, once a truly democratic suffrage permitted the working masses fully to assert their voting power in Vienna. In the meantime, during the Lueger era (1897-1910) the socialists, as the leading opposition to the ruling Christian Social administration of Vienna, continued to demonstrate their ambiguity on the 'Jewish question'. The main thrust of their policy and propaganda on this issue was to paint Lueger and his colleagues as hypocritical 'lackeys of the Jews' (*Judenknechte*) who did business with rich Jews and cynically hoodwinked the 'fools of Vienna' (i.e. the antisemites) who had put them in power.[34] Lueger was pictured as the Roman Catholic protector of Rothschild and Gutmann, the Jewish barons of high finance and industry. Not the Social Democrats but the *Christlich-Soziale* were the real *Judenschutztruppe*. As for the Jews of Vienna, they still controlled the metropolitan liberal press, the banks, big industry, the universities, the arts and sciences, if one was to believe the Viennese *Arbeiter-Zeitung*. The socialist central organ excelled in turning antisemitic demagogy on its head: 'If there is anyone to whom one can apply the word "judaized" it is to the Viennese mayor.'[35] The point that its editor, Friedrich Austerlitz (himself a Jew), wished to make with this kind of witticism was that never had Jewish millionaires prospered as much as under Lueger's rule – a classic example of what Hitler later also condemned as Christian Social 'sham-antisemitism' (*Scheinantisemitismus*) in his *Mein Kampf*.

Socialist use or misuse of this type of rhetoric was doubtless intended dialectically to unmask Christian hypocrisy by the use of familiar antisemitic terminology – to expose thereby the gap between words and deeds, theory and practice that typified Christian Social rule. Unfortunately, the result was that antisemitic stereotypes of radical provenance which equated 'capitalist' and 'Jew' received a new kind of respectability and legitimacy precisely because they were used by those who claimed that they were actually fighting against antisemitism. In the context of *fin-de-siècle* Vienna, far from immunizing the workers against Judeophobic prejudices, the Austrian Social Democrats tended therefore to reinforce their potency in the mistaken belief that equivocation and ridicule would ultimately work to their advantage.

CHAPTER 7

The politics of the Viennese Jewish community, 1890-1914

Walter R. Weitzmann

The Jews of Vienna formed a large and relatively successful community, the largest such community in western Europe. Its population had grown at an unprecedented pace which contributed to its problems and explains, in part, the conflicts that arose within it and the manner of their resolution. Like most urban centres and like most Jewish communities, it had grown less through natural increase than through immigration. Unlike other European and American communities, however, the influx into Vienna was the result of internal migration from the Austrian provinces.[1] The newcomers were, on the whole, German-speaking Austrian citizens, whose acculturation and integration into the metropolis of Vienna and, just as importantly, into the Jewish community that received them was assumed to be a necessary and natural process. The increasing stream of immigrants after 1880 posed severe problems of integration to the assimilationist, affluent, and seemingly secure and confident Jewish community whose institutions of integration and self-governance had developed under very different conditions.

The subject of this essay will be the conflict generated by the need to cope with the internal dynamic of growth, on the one hand, and the external threat posed to the established Jewish community by the new mass politics of antisemitic parties. The focus of the essay will be on the *Israelitische Kultusgemeinde*, the semi-legal institution chartered by the Austrian state to represent the Jews of Vienna.

By the law of 21 March 1890, the state 'regulated' the affairs of its Jewish citizens, recognizing the *Kultusgemeinde* as a semi-legal corporation representing Vienna's Jewry, charging it with the tasks necessary to provide for the religious needs of its members, and granting it the right to collect revenues in the form of taxes and fees from its members to meet its obligations.[2] Disagreements over the obligation by the IKG to provide religious facilities for the orthodox minority, and the insistence of the Sephardic community to remain autonomous, delayed the adoption of new statutes until the end of 1896.[3] The new by-laws defined the tasks of the *Kultusgemeinde* to be essentially religious and cultural: specifically to build and maintain synagogues, to employ and supervise the *Gemeinde* rabbis, to provide for and supervise the religious education of its youth, to assure the provision of kosher food and the availability of a ritual bath, to maintain a Jewish cemetery for its dead, and, lastly, to provide for the needy, the sick, and the old within the limits of its financial means.

The policies of the *Kultusgemeinde* were to be decided by a governing board (the Vorstand) of 24 (later 36) members, elected in a three-year rotation by the eligible, tax-paying, voters of the *Kultusgemeinde*. The actual decision-making authority, however, was the executive committee (Vertreter-Kollegium) composed of the presidium – the president, and two vice-presidents – and eight members of the board, elected by the larger board plenum. Although it was to be a self-governing body, as a semi-legal corporation the IKG was accountable to and functioned in an administrative capacity to the state, keeping the birth, marriage and death records of the Jewish inhabitants of Vienna and having corporate rights similar to those of Austrian hamlets or towns without autonomous charters. Seen from the point of view of the state, the IKG served as an agency of government. From the point of view of the Jewish community the IKG served as an agency ministering to its religious and charitable needs, and was expected to manage the conflicts that the different religious and social attitudes within Vienna's Jewry would inevitably produce. This dual role had posed no difficulty in the past. But in an era of increasing disagreement over the scope of *Kultusgemeinde* tasks and their costs, conservatives tended to emphasize the restrictive role imposed by the state and the limited financial means available, while reformers stressed the needs of a changing Jewish community.[4]

Since all resident Jews automatically belonged to the *Kultusgemeinde* the IKG can be seen as a microcosm of Jewish life in Vienna. In reality, there were in Vienna thousands of non-practising Jews who accepted their designation as Jews but lacked any sense of Jewish self-identity. If they attended services, it was usually on the High Holy Days only, and although most of them did not sever their connections to Judaism by converting to Christianity and tended, in their social contacts, to consort almost exclusively with other Jews, they remained outside the many Jewish cultural, charitable, social and political organizations that provided the substructure of interests represented by and reflected in the leadership of the IKG. Though they were required to pay IKG taxes if they were affluent enough, they grumbled about the amount they had to pay and lacked sufficient interest to vote in *Kultusgemeinde* elections.

On the other side were the many 'Ostjuden', Jews from Galicia or the ultra-orthodox communities of eastern and northeastern Hungary, who wished to maintain their traditional ways of behaviour, dress and religious practice and who were not easily integrated into the mainstream of the *Kultusgemeinde* structure. Since many of them were too poor to be taxpayers and voters, they stood outside the IKG, silent members of the community at large, a potential source of political mobilization, but remaining without much influence in community affairs.

The core of Vienna's Jews, those who were conscious of their Jewish heritage and wished to practise it, maintain it, and transmit it were, however, represented in and by the *Kultusgemeinde*. Although there were other, voluntary, secular, Jewish organizations in Vienna like the *Israelitische Allianz*, the *B'nai B'rith* and the *Österreichisch-Israelitische Union*, each of these represented only a fraction of the active, self-conscious Jews of Vienna. Although the leadership of all these organizations tended to overlap, the only collective, legitimate voice of the community was that of the *Israelitische Kultusgemeinde*.[5]

The *Israelitische Kultusgemeinde* did not come into being until after the revolution of 1848. Although the Austrian government had dealt with Vienna's Jews through a group of 'Vertreter', it had steadfastly refused to recognize the existence of an organized, self-governing community.[6] After emancipation, the IKG finally received a provisional set of statutes in 1852, and a permanent constitution in 1867. Its spokesmen included the cream of Jewish society. But in the 1890s, the wealthy, and often ennobled, financiers and industrialists withdrew from personal leadership and involvement in IKG affairs, concentrating their efforts on business affairs and participation in 'non-denominational' activities. They continued to support the Jewish community with bequests and endowments, although their critics charged that they gave as much to endow non-Jewish charities as to Jewish ones. Their tax contribution to the IKG was generally low, given their small numbers and the low maximum set by the by-laws. To attract their wealth and interest and keep them involved in Jewish community affairs was one of the main aims of the IKG board. When the *Kultusgemeinde* expanded its board from 24 to 36 members in 1900, it gave those taxpayers paying 200 Kronen or more a separate curia with 12 seats and allowed them to vote in the regular curia as well. This gave some 600-1,000 IKG members control of more than ⅓ of the board seats, the political price paid for keeping their gifts and endowments flowing.[7] Indeed, the income from taxes made up only one-half of IKG expenditures, the shortfall being met by other revenues derived from burial, marriage and baptism fees, the renting of temple seats and the income from endowments and charities. Taxpayers were ranked in four classes, the minimum tax being 20 Kronen (10 Gulden in the pre-1892 currency), and the maximum, 6,000 Kronen. Few paid at the upper level. In 1895, out of the Jewish population of 135,000 barely 12,000 paid community taxes and because of the three-year residence requirement even fewer could vote. Of these, only 210 paid taxes higher than 150 Kronen, the majority being in the 20 to 50 Kronen category.[8] By 1912, when the maximum ceiling was raised to 12,000 Kronen and when, as the result of improved assessment procedures, increased affluence and inflation, the number of taxpayers had risen to 25,000 out of a population of about 180,000, only 1,100 of them were in the privileged voter category.[9]

Contemporaries attest to the general assimilationist tendency among Viennese Jews. The mainstream of the *Kultusgemeinde* certainly was assimilationist, if by that one means the adoption of the lifestyle of the non-Jewish majority and the reform of religious practices to make them more adaptable to modern life and to the norms of behaviour current in the country of which they were citizens.[10] This desire to acculturate was true not only of Jews native to Vienna – by 1910 close to 40 per cent of the population of marriageable age had been born in Vienna – but also of many native Galicians, not all of whom were ultra-orthodox or estranged from modern, western, ways. Many of them married native Jewish brides, studied at Vienna's university, and were integrated into the assimilated structure of Viennese Jewish society without too much difficulty.[11] There was, however, an increasing number among them who maintained their traditional way of life, and who, in appearance or behaviour, were perceived by native Jews to reflect negatively on them. These were the 'Ostjuden' for whom the assimilated majority of the IKG leadership had little sympathy. Acculturation and adaptation to a 'western', i.e. Viennese, lifestyle was expected, Shtetl ways in business or religion openly discouraged.

The Viennese Jewish community was known for its willingness and ability to compromise on matters that threatened to split other communities apart. In Germany acrimonious debates raged over the preservation or reform of traditional religious rites and practices, splitting rabbinical congresses. In Hungary in the 1860s, the orthodox, with the support of the government, seceded from the liberal, 'neologian' majority, and formed a separate religious community.[12] In Vienna, no such breach occurred. Here, under the leadership of J.N. Mannheimer, Vienna's chief rabbi in the Biedermeier period, the religious rites were reformed in a way that pleased both reformers and conservatives. Known as the Vienna rite, it retained the practice of conducting services in Hebrew, provided for sermons in the German language, but stopped short of allowing the use of the organ. Mannheimer's cantor, Sulzer, not only supervised the training of a choir but wrote a great deal of music to accompany the new service.[13] To please their stricter co-religionists within the community, a synagogue for the observance of the Polish rite was established. But this orthodox synagogue, which was as much influenced by native orthodox desires as those of 'Polish' descent, was very different from the orthodox 'shul' found in the Galician or Hungarian hinterlands. Its house rules, for example, prohibited the chaotic praying style that both reformers and orthodox, assimilated to Vienna's society, found undignified and disruptive of orderly worship.[14] Mannheimer's reforms avoided incipient conflict at a time when assimilation was taken to be the undisputed means of integration and acculturation, and when the Josephinian notion that Jews must deserve their emancipation by showing their willingness to shed their more backward ways was accepted even by Vienna's Jewish leadership. That was certainly how Adolf Jellinek, Mannheimer's successor, viewed the reforms which he extolled as a gateway to emancipation:

Without them [wrote Jellinek] we should still have the notorious Jew-schools with their disorderly noise and their tasteless sing-song. . . . We should still stand as beggars outside the palaces of our law-givers, feeling refreshed and blessed by the smiles of their doorkeepers; we should still be speaking an idiom that has become the laughing stock of the whole world.[15]

But the Mannheimer compromise, and indeed, the ability to bridge the gulfs separating the diverse religious views, broke down as the ethnic and social composition of Vienna's Jewry changed. As the number of poorer, ultra-orthodox Jews from Galicia or from the northeastern, Carpathian hinterlands of Hungary increased, it was much more difficult to integrate them into the existing Jewish community structure. They tended to ignore the 'synagogue house rules' established early in the century to assure the 'dignity' of services and preferred to continue to pray in their accustomed, more or less disorganized fashion which embarrassed more assimilated Jews. Two generations after Mannheimer's reforms, IKG board members were still complaining about their noisy and undisciplined behaviour.[16] Community rabbis were known to make deprecatory remarks about 'Ostjuden' and prominent Jewish intellectuals, like the philologist Ludwig Gomperz, felt no affinity with the 'Ostjuden' they encountered.[17]

In the decades following the 1848 revolution, new arguments over religious rites broke out, fostered by conservatives who tried to divide the community as had happened in Hungary. Though they had the support of Graf Thun, the Minister of Religion and Education, because he believed that orthodox Jews were politically more reliable subjects than reformed Jews, many of whom had been active in the revolution, they failed in the attempt to split the community.[18] Throughout the 1860s and 1870s, the amount of support the IKG was to give ultra-orthodox congregations was heatedly debated. In the 1890s, a number of orthodox synagogues petitioned the government and held up the approval of the new IKG statutes for six years, until the assimilationist majority agreed to promise to provide to the best of its ability for the religious needs of all religious currents in Vienna.[19] But although the orthodox groups felt continually disadvantaged, they remained in a minority. Their opposition to the assimilationist leadership of the IKG was never enough to threaten the latter's hegemony.

The notables in the Jewish community who participated in community organizations and synagogue affairs naturally reflected the values of the society to which they had acculturated. They wore the proper clothes, were impeccably groomed, spoke German with a Viennese lilt and grace and wrote it with grammatical precision. If their wealth conferred power within and beyond the Jewish community, their assimilated manners and their education brought them status in both worlds. They saw it as a Jewish duty to be active in Jewish community affairs but, during Vienna's liberal era, often devoted as much or more time to municipal affairs and to Austrian liberal politics. Like most liberals they accepted as natural the existing limited suffrage prevailing in Austrian elections and feared its extension as a threat to their hegemony and to the values to which they subscribed. They were charitable to the poor, of both Jewish and Christian profession, but had no wish to see them enter either the meeting halls of the IKG board or the parliaments of Austria. In the *Reichsrath*, the Austrian parliament, the few Jews who held seats saw themselves as representatives of their political club and not as representatives of a Jewish constituency. They rarely addressed Jewish issues, engaged in no debate when antisemitic speakers raised the so-called Jewish question, and stayed away from parliament on days when such embarrassing topics were discussed.[20]

Until the 1880s there was no voice that spoke forcefully for a greater activism against the growing threat of antisemitic agitation and for a greater effort to broaden the narrow focus and concerns of the IKG establishment. With the election in 1883 of the Galician-born, German-educated Rabbi Josef Bloch to the *Reichsrath* from the Galician district of Kolomea, the inchoate movement to reform the *Kultusgemeinde* and to revitalize the apathetic Jewish community by uniting it against the external threat of antisemitism gained an effective spokesman.[21] Unlike other Jewish members of the *Reichsrath*, Bloch rarely spoke on matters of general politics. When antisemites charged Jews with being too wealthy, he produced figures to show the abject poverty of the great mass of Jews; when they misquoted the Talmud alleging it to contain maxims for commercial crooked-ness and for anti-Christian hostility, Bloch destroyed their unlettered arguments. He took on the worst of the antisemitic demagogues like Ernst Schneider and did not shy away from debating even the legendary Karl Lueger.[22] As a member of the Polish Club which supported the conservative government of Taaffe, Bloch was not, as were most Jewish politicians, tied to the German Liberal party. In 1884 he launched his own weekly paper, the *Oesterreichische Wochenschrift*, which soon rivalled the semi-official *Die Neuzeit* and *Die Wahrheit* in readership, and for the next forty years became the organ of those Jews who wished a stronger expression of Jewish identity but remained within the tradition of moderate religious reform and outside the movement of Jewish nationalism.

Bloch's militant defence of Jewish interests, his refusal to let antisemitic charges stand unanswered, his insistence that Jews must confront antisemitism and not bury their head in the sand, and his support of the conservative Taaffe regime, made him extremely unpopular with the liberal and assimilationist elites of the IKG leadership. They viewed him with hostility and suspicion as a potential leader of the 'little man' who reflected the concerns of those Galician-born Jews who admired Bloch's courage and cared little for the politics of Liberalism which many of the IKG notables uncritically supported. When Taaffe proposed the creation of a chair of Hebrew Studies and recommended Bloch to fill it, the IKG notables, afraid of the visibility and vulnerability the creation of a chair of Jewish studies would entail, intervened to prevent his appointment.[23]

Bloch believed in making the *Kultusgemeinde* more responsive to the concerns of Vienna's increasingly heterogeneous Jewish population and in making the IKG board more representative of the increasingly diverse interests it was meant to serve. But he rejected the idea of democratizing its decision-making processes. Like other adherents of the liberal values of 1848, he rejected and was afraid of mass politics; he himself had been elected by fewer than 2,200 voters in his district. He saw his own role, in the many Jewish organizations in which he was active, as a mediator of conflict and a creator of consensus. Predictably, he praised Heinrich Klinger, president of the IKG until 1903, a master at mediating between the vested interests represented by the board. It was under Klinger's reign that the first reforms of the IKG structure were voted. In a compromise revision of the statutes, the board allowed for a voluntary contribution of 10 Kronen which would allow those who took advantage of it to vote in IKG elections. But it also created the upper curia for the well-to-do which increased the power of the notables. This coupling of concessions to the upper strata of the community while diffusing the vociferous demand to widen the tax and suffrage structure of the IKG, appealed to Bloch. It suggested the creation of a new consensus, the cementing of a harmony of interests that would strengthen, not divide the community. A more far-reaching reform, in Bloch's view, would have politicized the *Kultusgemeinde* and threatened to fracture what was already becoming a brittle structure.[24]

His background and temperament disposed Bloch to uphold the idea of unity created from diversity, and to distrust all nationalisms whether they were German, Czech, Hungarian or Jewish. Influenced by the ideas of Adolf Fischhoff, the Jewish physician-leader of the revolution of 1848, Bloch developed the notion of a multinational state in which Austria's diverse nationalities could live together in mutual tolerance under the benevolent umbrella provided by the monarchy. Jews, Bloch thought, were best off in a state where national conflicts were muted; they had everything to lose in an atmosphere of nationalist fervour which would trap them in a vice of ethnic hostilities in which they inevitably would become political scapegoats.[25] Although he showed great sympathy to the idea of a revival of Jewish identity, and in the 1890s opened the pages of his weekly to Herzl and, later, to those of his followers who had abandoned political Zionism, his initial interest in Zionism quickly gave way to hostility when he realized that it aimed at much more than revitalizing a passive Jewish community or instilling in it a greater Jewish spirit. In Herzl, and his weekly newspaper, *Die Welt*, he saw a competitor to his own journalistic enterprise. In Herzl's uncouth and radical successors, he saw a divisive force in the Jewish community, whose disregard for accepted codes of civility and whose ruthless attacks on the very groups on the *Kultusgemeinde* board on whom Bloch counted to achieve reform, repelled him.[26]

Bloch did not like the 'politics in a new key'. In community affairs, he was increasingly pushed from the position of reformer to that of defender of the status quo. Bloch also believed and had argued forcefully for an all-Austrian organization of Jews which would transcend the atomistic provincialism of the 427 *Kultusgemeinden* of Cisleithanian Austria, and would be able to speak with one voice for all Austrian Jews.[27] In time such a *Gemeindebund* was created, but it remained impotent, hampered by its narrow definition of purpose and its lack of will.

In the meantime Bloch urged the creation of a Jewish civic association (*Bürgerklub*) which would prod the Jewish bourgeoisie of Vienna into political and civic action. Out of his 1884 proposal grew the *Oesterreichisch-Israelitische Union* (OIU), founded in 1886. Its leadership and much of its membership included liberal Jewish professors, politicians, businessmen and lawyers concerned with the deterioration of *de facto* Jewish rights amidst the growth of antisemitism, and with the inactive attitude of *attentisme* exhibited by the IKG leadership. The purpose of the OIU as stated in its statutes was to further Jewish education, history and culture, which they thought the IKG was sorely neglecting.[28] Its main offices were in Vienna but as the organization grew it not only added a legal bureau for the defence against antisemitism to its roster of activities, but also organized reading circles and branches in the provinces of Bohemia and, to a lesser extent, Galicia. At the turn of the century, the dominant figure in the OIU was Sigmund Mayer, a self-made textile merchant who tried to apply to municipal Jewish community politics the techniques of rationalization and organization that had served him so well in his business.[29] As early as 1898, Mayer had complained at an OIU meeting that the IKG board suffered from 'a surfeit of Gemüthlichkeit and a corresponding lack of vigor'.[30] With Bloch's help and the tacit acquiescence of the IKG leadership, who in traditional fashion tried to co-opt and integrate this incipient opposition, the OIU added to its functions the organizing of a nominating committee charged with drawing a balanced slate of candidates for the biannual election to fill the vacant posts on the rotating IKG board.

Neither the opposition mounted by Bloch nor by the assimilationist leaders of the OIU resulted in a meaningful reform of the IKG. Their vision of what the Kultusgemeinde should be was not essentially different from that of its founders and leaders. At election meetings, their leaders spoke of 'allowing a fresh breeze to blow through the IKG offices', of 'bringing in new blood'. Indeed, one of the functions of the OIU-sponsored Wahlcomité was to solicit new names to be added to the list of IKG board incumbents. In that sense, this nominating committee of notables became a useful mechanism for the replacement of the old elite with new blood drawn generally from the same vein. On the whole it probably did better in balancing out the diverse interests that had to be represented than the incumbent board or its presidium could have done. But the reform programme accompanying their proposed slate of candidates never went beyond pious generalities. More importantly, their 'programme' was only an expression of the committee that wrote it, it was in no way binding on the candidates they nominated. By common consent, and following the liberal view of indirect, or 'virtual' representation, the elected candidates were responsible only to their conscience, their re-election assured by their inclusion in a common, unity slate.[31]

In so far as there was dissent, it was not united. Dr Alfred Stern, once suspected of being 'oppositional' himself, but now the autocratic leader of the entrenched powers,[32] was quite right when in 1900 he said, 'While there are always differences of opinion, no opposition party exists on the IKG board.'[33] Stern admitted that there were disagreements over religious practices between those who preferred stricter forms of observance and those who leaned in a more liberal direction. He also mentioned differences over whether the construction of a new palatial temple should have precedence over other priorities. Some thought a new ritual bath was more important than a nursing home for the aged. Others believed that renewed interest in things Jewish must come from inner conviction, involving the younger generation, and not through outward show. Stern even admitted to a strong movement to revise the IKG statutes, including its tax/suffrage system, a movement to which he said he stood in firm opposition. But disagreements, he continued, need not make for factionalism. To polarize these differences would introduce a mood of negativity, create factionalism within the board and politicize the purely administrative functions of the *Kultusgemeinde*.[34]

Stern's list of differences was rather narrow and reflects more his view of acceptable dissent than the deeper issues that underlay them. What was viewed by Stern as minor disagreements on isolated issues were actually the symptoms of a deeper malaise within the community at large. Stern and his fellow board members thought they could bridge these disagreements by skilful coalition building, without fundamentally restructuring the political and administrative structure of the IKG or revising their limited view of the *Kultusgemeinde*'s functions. They hardly dealt with the deeper and more trenchant issues that reflected the changes that had taken place within Viennese Jewry. In a community increasingly heterogeneous in composition and increasingly more stratified in wealth and income, in which the poorer segments were less willing and able to integrate and assimilate, the old, creaky IKG structure and the liberal assumptions under which it operated came increasingly under attack from within the IKG establishment as well as from the new nationalist/Zionist opposition.

Looming large among these issues was the fiscal problem which the growth in numbers had imposed on the community. Whereas the tax base of the IKG had remained relatively stable, at least until the upper ceiling of taxes was raised, the growing expenditures created the ever-present threat of a deficit.[35]

While income from endowments and revenues (burial services, temple seat rentals, matriculation fees) brought in annual surpluses, social expenditures experienced staggering increases, foremost among them the expenditures for poor relief. The Jewish tradition of providing for one's poor was, of course, very strong. Municipal poor relief was abysmal and needy Jews had to rely mostly on the generosity of their more affluent co-religionists. This was especially so for those immigrants who had not yet achieved legal Viennese resident status (*Heimatrecht*), which was a prerequisite for receiving poor relief, and thus were shut out altogether from public aid.[36] To alleviate the need, scores of Jewish organizations and hundreds of private individuals dispensed aid to a growing number of indigent Jews. Amidst this confusion, a poor but enterprising Jew could make the rounds, from agency to agency, collecting as much as his persuasive powers could get him. This system rewarded persistence more than need, allowing some to collect multiple hand-outs while others went without relief.

Beginning with the 1890s, attempts were made to regularize poor relief and avoid such chaotic distribution. In 1907, after long discussions, the Central Office for Jewish Poor Relief was founded. Its task was not to dispense funds, but to act as a central clearing house to whom all agencies and individuals giving aid would send the names of their clients and the amounts given. There was thus created a central registry, a rationalization of practice and a check on abuse. Its first annual report, representing only one-third of the agencies dispensing aid, showed that 13,000 individuals were being supported. The number of Jewish poor was therefore fairly large. At a conservative estimate, adding in persons not captured by the first year's activities or supported by the municipal dole, and assuming that many of the recipients were heads of families, there must have been at least 25,000-30,000 Jews who received some form of assistance in the years before the First World War.[37]

The IKG was, of course, involved in all aspects of poor relief. The president, through the executive committee, had available a sum of money which he used to support the needy widows or dependants of deceased IKG taxpayers. The IKG supported *Armenanstalt* paid out to the general poor moneys in the form of regular, quarterly payments or one-time hand-outs. In addition to the funds dispensed directly, the IKG budget contained various items earmarked for the relief of the institutionalized aged, poor, sick, and orphaned. Some of these moneys went to institutions in the form of subsidies, others supported foundations established by bequests and endowments like the Hospital and the Home for the Aged.[38]

In the debate about poor relief, the fiscal conservatives on the board argued that the IKG should stick primarily to its 'Kultus' functions and leave charity in private hands. The *Kultusgemeinde* should be just that, one spokesman said, not a welfare institution. They urged that the municipality be encouraged to be more charitable to its Jewish residents and encouraged Jews who met the residency requirements to apply for the Viennese *Heimatrecht* and thus become eligible for relief. Some board members believed that the rich were not being charitable enough in supporting their poorer brothers. Others believed that the support of charitable enterprises and institutions of social welfare should come before the building of new, palatial temples to serve the representational needs of the Jewish bourgeoïsie.[39]

The struggle for a slice of the IKG budget raged on other fronts as well. The district synagogue societies, some of which had difficulty supporting themselves from the dues of their small membership, rarely exceeding 300, required large subsidies to help them maintain their temples and pay off construction debts.[40] The district synagogue associations helped to lift an otherwise unbearable burden from the shoulders of the *Kultusgemeinde*. Without them, the IKG would have had to build and maintain temples and rabbis in those districts where no IKG temples existed. This system was both a source of conflict and a bond tying temple societies and other subsidized institutions to the IKG. For while the temple societies tried to increase their influence on the board to assure themselves of building loans, subsidies and a share of the fees connected with performing marriages and 'baptisms', they became also more dependent upon the goodwill of the IKG presidium, whose decisions in these matters were rarely challenged. While there were always some temple societies who felt disadvantaged, it proved impossible to weld them into a permanent opposition.

The mainstream district temple societies had another vital interest to preserve. They often stood in conflict with the smaller irregular congregations usually of an orthodox persuasion. Vigorously opposed to the proliferation of these so-called *minyanim*, they prodded the IKG to limit their numbers and prohibit their establishment in the vicinity of district synagogues. To the temple associations, the *minyanim* were both competitors for rentable temple seats and a public embarrassment to the image of Jewish harmony and decorum they wished to project.[41]

The question of decorum was a recurrent issue in IKG board discussions. The religious apathy of many Viennese Jews meant that during the week, and even on the Sabbath, the community synagogues were attended only by the few regular members. But on the High Holy Days there was never enough space for those Jews who attended services only on these occasions. To accommodate them, the IKG rented space in hotels or concert halls, and allowed, as well, the establishment of temporary, store-front prayer rooms. Often arguments over the practice of selling more tickets than there was space, or over the inadequacies of the services offered, created public disturbances that ended up in the police courts. At a time when antisemitic feeling ran high, the IKG notables on the board felt more anxious than ever to proceed against such undignified behaviour. As Alfred Stern put it, in a discussion of such an incident:

> Given today's mentality, we have a major interest in seeing that religious services are conducted with dignity and decorum. We cannot afford in today's Vienna to have all sorts of excesses occurring in the streets.[42]

These issues created conflict but no permanent opposition to the prevailing leadership. They related to the claims of diverse, but vested interests within the Jewish community. Their resolution did not depend on major reforms such as a widening of the suffrage might have brought. The spokesmen of these particularist interests represented institutions that did not, on the whole, represent either the Jewish masses or the non-practising Jews outside the structure of community institutions. Moreover, because the claims advanced were for particular attention, an astute politician like Alfred Stern could keep them from coalescing into a serious, organized challenge to the status quo.

The eternal threat posed by the growing political and social antisemitism, on the other hand, touched many more Jews. Its origins coincided with economic stagnation and, indeed, was a consequence of the long depression that had begun in the great crash of 1873 and stretched into the 1890s. For the more affluent Jews of Vienna, their human dignity was at threat; for the poorer Jews, economic survival was affected, as they seemed more than ever excluded from the shrinking economy of Vienna's trades and crafts. In Vienna, as was the case throughout the monarchy, the Jewish community was put on the defensive, as Lueger's Christian Socials took over the governments of Vienna and of Lower Austria, nationalist antisemites took over the Liberal party, and Vienna's Democrats were reduced to the handful of forty-eighters like Ferdinand Kronawetter whose support came almost exclusively from Jewish voters. Progressively isolated, without political allies, the IKG tried to adjust to Karl Lueger's reign, perceiving his antisemitic rhetoric to be an opportunistic device to gain votes. Lueger himself maintained cordial relations with individual Jews and was thought by many to be a restraining force on the more radical, racist antisemites in his party.[43]

Occasionally, the IKG's leaders would protest specific discriminatory actions to the higher provincial or imperial officials, relying on the goodwill of the ministerial bureaucracy to protect them against the populist, antisemitic upswell from below. But the defence of Jewish rights required greater vigilance than the IKG was willing or able to give it. Barely represented in the Municipal Council and its committees, and aware of their impotence, Jewish magistrates sometimes stayed away from meetings when antisemitic resolutions were tabled. During the summer months, when the Jewish bourgeoisie went on *Sommerfrische*, spending the entire season at mountain spas or lake resorts, all vigilance ceased. On one occasion, a school ordinance that would have created separate classes for gentiles and Jews almost passed without dissent because the Jewish member of the municipal school commission, having been absent, took no preventive action.[44]

This particular instance illuminated the need to rethink the efficacy of older methods to avert anti-Jewish actions. In the past the political influence of notables within the community had sufficed to meet the threat of hostile legislation. Now even the civil rights of Jews, which until recently had seemed a permanent acquisition, were suddenly vulnerable and tenuous. The attacks of the antisemites not only revealed to many assimilated, non-participating Jews their non-elective affinity with other Jews, but also suggested the need to become more self-conscious in defence of their rights. Jewish nationalists argued for a change of tactics; Zionists for a change in strategy. Both called for the mobilization of the Jewish 'people' to band together, to claim nationality rights in the multi-national state of Austria, and to create for themselves a *Kultusgemeinde* that would reflect not only the religious identity of Viennese Jewry but their national character as a 'people'.

'Every pogrom', Lucy Dawidowicz wrote in one of her essays, 'became a catalyst of Jewish identity.'[45] This was certainly true of Vienna's Jews, though we must not exaggerate the depth of feeling that was stirred or the numbers who were so affected. Many Viennese Jews were not personally affected. Most Viennese Jews, even the most assimilated, had few close social or personal contacts with non-Jews. The social antisemitism they encountered offended their sense of self-worth but was not perceived to be a serious threat to their physical or economic existence. Ironically, the very fact that

Viennese society kept them at a distance cushioned the perception and the impact of the antisemitic threat. As long as antisemitism remained at the level of insult, many Viennese Jews tried to ignore it or await its passing. Yet Bloch's *Oesterreichische Wochenschrift* had taught the Jewish community to react to words as well as physical acts. It had become a rallying ground for the defence of Jewish rights and Bloch did not cease to point out that Lueger's antisemitism hurt the Jewish lower classes more than it did the rich. In time the words of the antisemitic agitators would have a far more dangerous effect. They poisoned the atmosphere and created a milieu in which Viennese Jewry became ever more isolated from gentile society and thrown increasingly on its own resources.

In the early years of the twentieth century, Bloch's paper had been joined by others more strident in extolling Vienna's Jews to unite and fight. Herzl's *Die Welt*, and after his death, the *Jüdische Zeitung*, the *National-Zeitung*, and the *Neue National-Zeitung*, all reflected a new sense of Jewish nationalism or Zionism. Ironically, it was the sons of the Jewish bourgeoisie, students at the university of Vienna, who had been the first to express the new militancy. They were in the exposed trenches of racial warfare, and, unlike their elders, regularly faced physical violence from German nationalist students who attacked them with clubs while denying them the right to challenge them to a duel. Reading the Jewish press, one is struck by the increasing violence reported against Jewish students and even, in admittedly isolated cases, against innocent Jewish passengers of public conveyances or frequenters of Prater restaurants and suburban wine gardens. Only the blind and the deaf could fail to note an ominous change in the atmosphere, a chilling decline in civility, a more open expression of hitherto latent anti-Jewish *ressentiment*.[46]

The response of the *Kultusgemeinde* to these attacks was so restrained it failed even to satisfy moderates like Moritz Güdemann, Vienna's chief rabbi and foremost intellectual opponent of Herzl's Zionism. Two events especially roused the consciousness of Vienna's Jews and showed the impotence of the IKG in the face of international and domestic provocation. In 1905 and 1906 a series of pogroms in Russia stirred the conscience of the world. In reaction to the Tsar's October Manifesto, reactionaries led by the infamous Black Hundreds stirred up anti-Jewish riots. In December 1905, Karl Lueger made one of his most intemperate attacks on the Jews. Concerned with the growth of Social Democracy and their campaign for universal suffrage, he struck against the weaker enemy, the Jews of Vienna. Lueger warned them that the fate that had befallen their co-religionists in Russia might also await them, if they continued to support the subversive Social Democrats. This was too much even for those notables who had continued to do business with Lueger and had believed his antisemitic opportunism to be on the wane. The IKG passed a resolution demanding that Lueger retract his hidden call for a pogrom, but urged no other action. Lueger responded by calling for an economic boycott of Jewish shops. The clear signal that what was happening abroad could easily spill over into Austria produced a relatively mild protest but was not translated into more vigorous action.[47]

The appalling toll of the Russian pogroms created widespread public sentiment for public action. This was not a matter of confronting a popular mayor but protesting the actions of a foreign government unable to protect its Jewish subjects against the actions of mobs incited by reactionary political and government officials. For liberal and enlightened Jews, the issue was untroubled by conflicts of patriotism. It involved applying universally accepted standards of behaviour to the retrogressive actions of a backward, autocratic regime. In Stern's absence the IKG Executive Committee declared a day of mourning and ordered all community temples to hold services for the pogrom victims. It also passed a resolution of protest to be signed by all Austrian *Kultusgemeinden* and asked the leaders of the major Jewish communities throughout the world to join in a common effort to persuade their governments to intercede with the Russian government on behalf of the Jews in Russia.[48] More significantly, they voted to endorse a mass meeting of protest which the nationalist student corporations of Vienna had organized. As soon as Stern heard of this action he wrote a letter from his sickbed, insisting that the IKG board rescind the endorsement of the mass protest meeting. He found it unacceptable to join a venture controlled by student radicals that might lead to unpredictable actions and even end up in a demonstration before the Ministry of Foreign Affairs. The board yielded to Stern's authority and rejected the recommendations of the executive. It is indicative of the unwillingness of the board members to exert a collective will of their own that Stern, until his overthrow in 1918, was generally able to impose his iron will upon the restless but listless board. But while Stern's authority prevailed, that of the *Kultusgemeinde* declined.[49]

ALFRED STERN (1830-1918)
President of the *Israelitische Kultusgemeinde*, Vienna

No other issue of the time caused as much furore as the case of Theodor von Taussig, a privileged member of the IKG board and the director of the Austrian *Boden-Creditanstalt*, one of the half-dozen or so great banking establishments of Austria.[50] When it was revealed that the *Boden-Creditanstalt* had been instrumental in procuring a large loan to the Russian government at the very time of Jewish persecution, public reaction in the Jewish community, encouraged by the nationalist and Zionist press, forced Taussig to resign his seat on the IKG board. Under great public pressure, the board faced a conflict of loyalties between person and issue and, perhaps predictably but surely foolishly, chose to support Taussig. Although a number of board members, including the president, Alfred Stern, were glad to see Taussig resign, the majority voted a resolution praising his contribution to Jewish life and asking him to reconsider his resignation. In the long debate on the issue the majority argued that as the responsible director of an Austrian bank, Taussig carried responsibilities which he could not slough off merely because they conflicted with his feelings as a Jew. Some even argued that Taussig had done a service for Russian Jews since the Tsarist government would have retaliated against them had the loan failed. The minority conceded that Taussig might have made the only choice possible but argued that he had an obligation to accept the consequences of his choice and that this meant resigning his seat on the board.[51]

In the sixty years of its existence as a semi-legal corporation, the *Kultusgemeinde* had seen conflicts develop that revolved in the main around the issue of religious observance, the size of the tax bite put on its members, and the access to revenues to be dispensed. On the whole the conflicts had been muted and kept within the bounds of the interest groups and concerned religious associations and temple societies that composed the IKG active constituency. Mild reforms had been urged on a leadership that seemed to grow somewhat stale and immobile, and some reforms had in time been passed, filtered through the smaller groups of IKG insiders. The result had been meagre. The tax base remained narrow and left the great majority of households outside the self-governing structures of the *Kultus-gemeinde*. As reward for accepting a higher tax burden, the rich notables were given a third of the expanded board seats and the vote in determining the rest. Tax assessments had been improved by charging district commissions with the task of making assessments of those who lived in the district. But the reforms stopped at an acceptable threshold of maintaining the elitist, notable structure of the decision-making bodies and restricting the 'tasks' of the *Kultusgemeinde* to the narrowly defined functions of providing for the religious and educational welfare of the Jewish residents of Vienna.

The opposition that coalesced around the Zionist movement in the 1890s demanded a much more radical set of structural changes which grew out of a very different vision of what the *Kultusgemeinde* ought to be. Theodor Herzl and Max Nordau had called upon their followers to 'conquer the *Kultusgemeinde*'. What Herzl really meant by this is not clear. His diaries seem to show that he was more intent upon using the radicalism of his student followers as means to 'épater les bourgeois' or to force concessions from the IKG leaders, than in launching an all-out campaign to dispossess them.[52] Until Herzl's premature death in 1904, Vienna was the centre of the world Zionist movement. It concentrated on creating a press, an international organization, and a broader base for its movement. The early leaders of Vienna's Zionists thought of themselves as notables, able on their own to negotiate with others of similar rank and position. They looked upon Herzl as a charismatic leader whose autocratic manner they accepted because he made few demands on them. They did not think of themselves as radicals overthrowing the existing structures by ruthless and unceasing agitation from below. They wanted recognition for the nationalist/Zionist position in the councils of the IKG, not a total replacement of what they considered a valuable resource of the Jewish community. Neither Herzl nor his companions were organizers of masses, nor were they ready to surrender their independence and sometimes excessive self-esteem to the sort of party discipline which the younger generation of Zionists, after Herzl's death, insisted upon.[53]

Vienna's Zionists believed that the *Kultusgemeinde* should become a true *Volksgemeinde* − creator and servant of a revitalized national Jewish existence. Its main tasks should be to stimulate the awareness of Jewish nationality among all members of the community. The *Kultusgemeinde* should collect the 'shekel', the contribution the Zionists asked of supporters to finance their political goals. It should offer lectures in the history of the Jewish people, organize labour exchanges for the unemployed Jews, decentralize its operations to give more responsibility and autonomy to the districts, and democratize its suffrage and tax structure. Although the Zionists were quite willing to make tactical alliances with all disaffected groups, the disgruntled *minyanim* for example, they were mostly secular in their outlook. They viewed Jews as neither a religious denomination nor a mere '*Stamm*', but rather as a people with not only a history but also a political and territorial future. Until the goal of political Zionism was reached, defined as the establishment of a Jewish homeland/state in Palestine, there was work to be done in the 'host' countries of the diaspora. The debate over what this involved often divided the early Zionist movement, between those who thought that preparation for the final goal meant primarily a cultural awakening of the Jewish people, and those who thought more in concrete political terms. In Vienna the advocates of '*Gegenwartsarbeit*' – political and educational activity within the framework of '*goluth*' existence – were in the majority. This made them not only pleaders for the ideas of a Jewish homeland, but, more troubling for the Jewish establishment, into an independent Jewish political force, pressing for the election of Jewish nationalist candidates and the restructuring of Jewish community life, working for the recognition of a Jewish nationality in the distribution of *Reichsrath* seats in the debates on Austrian suffrage reform, and calling for the re-education of the Jewish people in the direction of Jewish autonomy within the host country.[54]

This insistence on struggle within the diaspora brought the Zionists into irrevocable conflict with the *Kultusgemeinde*. Reformers and early sympathizers like Bloch could accept and even approve of their aim of revitalizing the community and furthering a greater sense of Jewish identity, but they balked at transforming the *Kultusgemeinde* into a *Volksgemeinde*, by which the Zionists meant a centre for the re-education of the Jewish people and for the expression of Jewish nationality. This would not only create conflict with the state authorities but also exacerbate conflicts within the Jewish community. Nor could they accept the Zionist-nationalist view that the Jews were a people and should strive for political autonomy within the Habsburg state. They feared that the Zionists were reversing the gains of decades of struggle for emancipation and integration of Austrian Jews into the monarchy as full-fledged citizens. They viewed the Zionist demand for separateness as having the effect of 're-ghettoizing' Austrian Jewry. They were especially appalled when Zionists commented favourably on antisemitic schemes to separate Jewish and gentile children in the public schools, or when Zionists invited Werner Sombart, the author of the controversial *The Jews and Modern Capitalism*, to Vienna to propound his theory of Jewish separateness and peculiarity.[55]

But it was not only their goals, but the means they used to make themselves heard that frightened and repelled the community leaders and former supporters of their cause. To Bloch and Mayer, Stern and Güdemann, their intolerant radicalism that permitted no compromise, and their failure to distinguish between the common external enemy and the IKG leadership, was insufferable. Indeed, Bloch accused the student radicals of the early Zionist movement of aiding the Lueger antisemites.[56]

As the more intransigent and most active militants took over the leadership of the Vienna Zionist organization, they turned against Herzl's former companions whose style of civility they saw as abject surrender or as personal ambition. Oskar Marmorek, who had once thought he would succeed Herzl in the leadership of the Zionist movement, was one of the first to fall before the onslaught of the Young Turks in Vienna's Zionist movement. Marmorek tried both to co-operate with the *Kultusgemeinde* and remain loyal to the Zionist cause to which Herzl had recruited him. In this he had the support of the *Aktions Komité* who refused to finance an electoral battle against the IKG. When the nominating committee in 1904 proposed a united ticket that would include some opposition candidates, and offered Marmorek a seat on the board, he accepted in order to avoid the acrimony of what would have been a losing campaign and to use the IKG board as a forum for the Zionist reform proposals. He believed, as was typical of the generation that shared the values of the liberal era, that it was better to have a Zionist on the board than to build a radical opposition outside it. For this he was excoriated by the Vienna organization that had by then been taken over by the student activists. Led by Adolf Böhm, their fiery leader, they carried a vote of non-confidence against Oskar Marmorek and eventually preferred charges against him with the Cologne *Aktions Komité*.[57] In August 1908, Max Nordau, to whom Marmorek had appealed, wrote him a letter expressing his sympathy and support:

> I have not hesitated to express my indignation to Wolffsohn and Alex [Oskar's brother] regarding the intrigues of the Vienna Jews. . . . The knaves [*Buben*] who have inflicted their ruthlessness upon you have grown up in a Christian-Social atmosphere and, as is so often our Jewish way, have absorbed all the mannerisms and methods of the antisemites in the suburbs, just as many of our Russian brothers have adopted the style of the Black Hundreds. You have distanced yourself from the mob. That is all you could do and that is what you did.[58]

The conviction held by the younger Zionist that the Zionist movement must organize itself as a disciplined party to win control of the community alienated not only the established leadership but also Herzl's companions many of whom, after his death, retired from the Viennese Zionist organization. Their list of names is impressive: Heinrich York-Steiner, Oskar Marmorek, Leopold Kahn, Leon Kellner, S.R. Landau, S. Krenberger, J. Upremny, Nathan Birnbaum, and many others of lesser renown. The new Zionist leadership showed a remarkable talent for alienating even its occasional allies, the orthodox opposition to the IKG. One of their leaders, Adolf Böhm, flaunted community opinion by refusing to have his newly born son circumcised, believing that Zionism was not a religious but a national cause.[59] Student corporations alienated religious community leaders by scheduling nationalist activities on Saturday, and Zionist leaders attacked a community rabbi, arousing the fury of a number of Galician Jews who defended him.[60] Somewhat ruefully, Isidor Schalit, himself one of the radical leaders and for a while head of the Austrian Zionist organization, looked back upon his youthful days and wrote, 'We lacked Herzl's circumspection and foresight. We were young men unconcerned about defeat. We wished to do battle, whatever the odds.'[61]

Committed to an entirely different vision of the role that the *Kultusgemeinden* should play, and dominated, in Vienna, by a group of militant leaders hardly out of the school room, Vienna's Zionists rejected the liberal and tolerant politics that strove for harmony and compromise and instead practised what Carl Schorske has so aptly characterized as 'politics in a new key'.[62] Not bound to traditions, unconnected to other community leaders by personal ties and business connections, imbued with their inviolability and unconcerned with personal fates, they demanded discipline from their members and leaders and were always ready to attack without regard to outcome. In many ways they copied the tactics and style of the politics of the streets that had taken over Vienna's municipality, just as the consensus politicians of the community had exhibited the style of notable politics of the liberal era.

There were, of course, major differences between the mass parties of the Social Democrats and Christian Socials and the 'cadre' organization of the Zionists. The former were much more successful at organizing their members and voters on a permanent basis. As mass parties they reflected either the class interests of their members, as with the Socialists, or their common fears, anxieties and resentments, as with the Christian Socials. The pre-First World War Viennese Zionists were a group of motivated individuals without solid organizational roots in the Jewish community, though they tried hard to diversify. In 1909 a Jewish athletic club, the *Hakoah*, was formed; after the war it would become a highly successful soccer club able to compete with world-class teams.[63] Many districts had a Zionist club, women's groups were being organized, and Labour Zionism, in the form of *Poale Zion*, was beginning to take root. But although the Zionists were beginning to attract to their ranks able organizers like Robert Stricker, Jakob Ehrlich and Desider Friedmann, their organizational network remained weak and their small membership was dominated by the affiliated student corporations.[64] When the Galician Zionists withdrew from the Cisleithanian organization to form their own group, the Viennese leadership found itself in control over the least numerous segment of Austrian Jewry, the district of 'Western Austria'. Lacking masses to lead, the leaders exhibited the symptoms often found in sectarian groups. They began to bicker among themselves. Their organization, having no permanent paid staff, was characterized by rapid turnover of membership and leadership. This was partly because of the predominance of present or former students in the movement and partly because the activity of sectarian politics burned out its practitioners after a short time of service.[65]

What bound the Zionists together was their ideology: that Jews were a people whose vital existence could not be defined in religious terms, that this concept of nationality transcended class and other divisions within Jewry and bound together all Jews who committed and submitted themselves to their national destiny, a national homeland in Palestine. What divided them was the interminable debate about 'minimalist' and 'maximalist' programmes, about the nature of work in the diaspora, cultural versus political, the flexibility of permissible tactics, and the forms that party discipline and organization should take. Even in the *Reichsrath*, the four Jewish nationalist candidates who had been elected in the wake of the suffrage reform of 1907, and had formed a separate Jewish faction, began fighting among themselves. What had promised to be an opportunity to present within the parliament a unified, Jewish position turned instead into an embarrassing fiasco. The 'Jewish Club' in the national parliament proved to be as self-destructive as the Zionist organization outside it. In 1911 all except the relative outsider Benno Straucher, who had a political base of his own as president of the Czernowitz *Kultusgemeinde*, lost their seats. One of them, Arthur Mahler, left the nationalist movement with great bitterness to take up a career as art historian.[66]

Before the First World War, Vienna's Zionists proved incapable of converting the growing dissatisfaction with the status quo into a movement that could mount a serious challenge to the established IKG leadership. Their failure was assured by their own incapacities, but was also the result of the environment in which they operated. The highpoint of the awareness of Jewish identity in Vienna had been reached in 1906 and thence was on the wane. As the Social Democrats began to gain and the Christian Socials to lose support, traditional attitudes of apathy and lassitude re-emerged. A great many Jews would have agreed with a contemporary assessment by Richard Charmatz that antisemitism, by 1907, had begun to decline in Vienna. As for the Zionists they de-emphasized the 'struggle' for universal rights, believing this to be no more than tilting at windmills.[67]

Even if their leaders had been more adept at organizing than at in-fighting, more successful in creating permanent coalitions of under-represented constituencies, rather than alienating them, the obstacles to transforming the IKG would still have defeated their efforts. In 1912, a new leadership emerging from the chaotic early days of the movement gave up the tactic of uncompromising opposition and came to an agreement with the IKG establishment. Prodded by the Zionist *Aktions Komité* in Cologne, which had for some time looked askance at the Viennese radicals, they dropped their attempt to conquer the *Kultusgemeinde* from without, gave up the unequal electoral battle, and agreed to a united ticket which allotted them two seats on the board.[68]

For a century the Jewish community had been led by its successful, assimilated and politically astute economic elite. Its governing machinery had been designed to serve a more or less homogeneous population of a few thousand. By 1914 it was showing the strains of having to cope with the problems of a community, almost 200,000 strong, divided in wealth and belief, and restive under the patriarchal rule of its notables. There were, as we have seen, numerous issues that generated conflict, and yet dissent remained muted or frag-mented. Despite the evident failure of the traditional methods of integration and mediation to function as before, and despite the sense of threat that the hostility of the gentile community engendered, neither the moderate opposition nor the Jewish nationalists were able to bring about the changes that would have accomplished what both of them sought in different ways: a revitalization of the Jewish community at large and their more active participation in *Kultus-gemeinde* affairs.

The reasons why neither moderate nor radical reform succeeded in their goals lie primarily in the general apathy of Vienna's Jews toward Jewish community affairs. This permitted the continuation of a system by which the function of the *Kultusgemeinde* was defined as purely administrative, and its governance placed in the hands of a small group of men whose wealth or prestige derived from their leadership position in the district synagogues, or in the network of prestigious Jewish organizations, seemed to entitle them to represent Vienna's Jewry.

In 1910 the Jewish population of Vienna was 175,000 souls. Of these 25,000 were assessed for IKG taxes. But no more than half of these were actually entitled to vote in 1910. To become a duly registered voter, one had to have paid IKG taxes for three consecutive years; female taxpayers were ineligible to vote. After the close election of 1906 Stern ruled that only those members would be registered to vote who had paid their entire year's dues to date on which voting rolls were prepared. This disenfranchised almost 5,000 voters who had fallen into the habit of delaying their tax payments until the very end of the year. In 1912, after this odious restriction was removed, the ratio of taxpayers to voters improved but the proportion of adult Jews who had the vote was still anachronistically low at a time when even Austria had accepted universal manhood suffrage.

The prevailing apathy among the enfranchised Jewish bourgeoisie reduced participation in elections even further. Rarely did more than $\frac{2}{5}$ of those entitled to vote actually do so. Even in bitterly contested elections, the turn-out was low. In 1906 when the Zionist-led opposition managed to garner 44 per cent of the vote only 27.5 per cent of those eligible cast a vote. In 1908 Stern reduced the number of voters by his strict interpretation of the voting regulations to avoid a possible defeat. He need not have worried. Despite the reduction in the number of eligible voters, the turn-out was greater than ever before, both in percentage terms and absolute numbers. Voters turned out in great numbers to show their support for the official list; the Zionist vote sank to a disappointing 23 per cent. There was little doubt that the majority of the community voters supported the established leadership. As Table 7.1 makes clear, the entrenched

Table 7.1 *Elections to the governing board of the* Israelitische Kultusgemeinde *in Vienna, 1900 - 20*

Year	Eligible voters[a]	Votes cast[b]	Votes cast % of elig.	Official list highest vote[b]	% of votes cast	Opposition highest vote[c]	% of votes cast
1900	13,000	3,150	24	1,913	61	1,407	45
1902	13,111	4,735	36	3,398	72	1,414	30
1904	14,521	1,668		no contest			
1906	16,032	4,416	28	2,414	55	1,962	44
1908	11,137	4,997	45	3,961	79	1,139	23
1910	12,228	4,446	36	3,031	68	1,582	35
1912	18,289	1,960		no contest			
1920	19,303	10,553	55	5,912	56	3,714	35

Source: [a] *Tätigkeitsbericht, 1912-1924,* Tabelle XIV; *Verzeichnis der im Wiener Gemeindegebiet wohnhaften Wähler, AW/50,1;* [b] *AW/50-56;* [c] this includes votes achieved by a coalition of oppositional parties, led by the Zionists. Although there was an official list, and sometimes one or more opposition lists, votes were cast for individuals. The 'highest vote' category in each instance reflects the number of votes cast for the top vote getter on each list.

incumbents reacted to each threat to their hegemony by successfully rallying the conservative forces of the community to their support. After the 1910 victory over the Zionist opposition, the IKG board rescinded the restrictive 1908 ruling and restored the formerly disenfranchised to the rolls, a sure sign that the IKG establishment felt safe again.

The history of electoral struggle shows that a radical opposition had no chance of taking power in the pre-war Jewish community. What needs to be explained, however, is why the moderate reformers failed so dismally to develop an alternative to the reigning group. Over the period of its existence, the leadership of the *Oesterreichisch-Israelitische Union* often differed with the IKG board and its president over what needed to be done. When, in 1900, a second curia for the wealthy was established, the OIU came out against the change. But what they objected to was not some means to give the rich preferred status, but the specific formulations, especially the clause that gave them a double vote, in their own curia and in the general curia as well. When one of its leaders sent a sharp memorandum to the IKG board objecting to its failure to honour their election promises of reform, he was rejected by the OIU executive and subsequently resigned his position. When the issue of reform of the by-laws came up again in 1908 and 1909, the OIU demanded that the IKG board publicly declare that within a specified timespan they would put the promised reforms on the agenda Stern refused, although he had been urged to do so by the leaders of the *Allianz* and *B'nai B'rith* who believed that such a promise was a cheap price to pay for maintaining harmony. Rebuffed, the OIU did not put up a slate of opposition, reform candidates; rather in a huff, it withdrew from the election and remained aloof. Yet its membership turned out to vote so that if the OIU executive had intended to boycott the elections of 1908, their membership certainly did not get the message.

Had the OIU been resolute in their declarations of reform, and had they been able to mobilize their membership to follow their call, they could have easily taken control of the IKG board over a six-year period. In 1905, the OIU had 2,500 members in Vienna, almost all of them eligible to vote. Had they wanted to or been able to convert these numbers into political power, they could have achieved their professed goals. They did not do so because, like Josef Bloch, its leadership thought that open confrontation, challenging the leadership of the IKG in contested elections, would produce, at best, a Pyrrhic victory. It certainly would have meant splitting the organizations that were reflected in the IKG power structure. It would have violated the tradition of harmony and compromise. It would have polarized and politicized the community. It would have been unthinkable.[69]

Unlike the OIU, the Zionists had the will to power, but not the troops. Unlike Herzl and his companions, the new leadership was quite willing to risk winning the *Gemeinde* and lose the support of the established institutions, but they did not have the means to accomplish their aims. Their membership was too low, too young, and too poor seriously to challenge the IKG at the ballot box. In 1908 there were barely 800 members in Vienna; in 1913 there were only 1,500 members in the district, of whom at least one-third were students. Occasionally, the Zionists were able to make alliances with disgruntled but marginal groups within the community network. They supported the struggle of the *minyanim* and their spokesman, Zipser, was a main speaker for their opposition ticket in 1908. But they were not, on the whole, comfortable with the more orthodox Jews, nor were the latter with the Zionists. In any case, no lasting coalition emerged. Many of their allies had by then disassociated themselves from their tactics of constant confrontation. Moreover, the Jewish *Mittelstand*, whom the Zionists claimed to represent, were vastly under-represented in the voting lists of the IKG. As Table 7.2

Table 7.2 *Voter participation in elections to the governing board by city district, 1910, 1912*

District	Jewish population 1910	Eligible voters, 1910	Eligible voters, 1912	% of pop. 1910	% of pop. 1912
1	10,807	1,999	2,464	18.5	22.8
2, 20	70,923	3,096	4,788	4.4	6.8
3, 11	10,389	768	1,385	7.4	13.3
4, 5	10,895	814	1,269	7.4	11.6
6, 7	16,348	1,636	2,464	10.0	15.1
8, 9	26,323	2,033	3,431	7.7	13.0
12–15	11,249	681	1,004	6.0	8.9
16, 17	7,950	407	566	5.1	7.1
18, 19	7,839	729	1,081	9.3	13.8
21	1,767	99	180	5.6	10.3

Source: Jahrbuch der Stadt Wien, 'Ergebnisse der Volkszählung 1910', Beilage; *Tätigkeitsbericht, 1912–1924*, Tabelle XIV; *Jüdische Zeitung*, Nr 42 (29 October 1912), p. 20.

illustrates, the districts with the heaviest Jewish population had the lowest percentage of eligible voters. Even if one accepts the most generous combination, a comparison of the eligible voters with the Jewish population as of 1910, rather than 1912, one finds that in the combined districts (2 and 20) of Leopoldstadt and Brigittenau, only 6.8 per cent of its 70,923 Jews had the vote. On the other hand 22.8 per cent of the Jews residing in the Inner City were eligible, and the districts where many Jewish professionals lived, like the 9th, or where middle-class shop-keepers resided, like districts 6 and 7, also had a relatively high percentage of eligibles, as did, of course, the villa district where the rich who preferred not to live on the *Ringstrasse* built their villas. (See Map 3, p. 30.)

Successful reform, therefore, had to come from within the establishment, for without a revision of the suffrage that would enfranchise the poorer segments of the population, there was no likelihood of basic change. But the tacit rules of consensus politics and the many diverse and vested interests represented on the board made the incumbents unlikely leaders of an internal revolt. The candidates who represented temple societies, or the architects who were on the look-out for contracts, the 200 IKG *Beamten*, tenured officials to whom the by-laws gave the vote, or those who kept their seat for representational purposes, anxious to grace their successful careers with some measure of community service, could always be relied on to rally to the establishment. Yet there were signs, toward the end of our period, that even these men were becoming restive. Although they did not implement the reforms necessary to move the IKG into the twentieth century, they would move the presidium in directions that pointed to the future. The district commissions were given some tasks that had been centralized before, including the assessment of the taxes within each district. The IKG began to support projects in Palestine, and the tax ceiling was raised in 1912 to 12,000 Kronen, and within another year, to 20,000 Kronen.

But further reform was successfully stopped by the iron resistance of the aging president, Alfred Stern, who used the immense powers of the presidential office and his personal authority to block or reverse any movement of rebellion. Whereas Heinrich Klinger had used his powers gently, seeking consensus and compromise with all groups, Stern ruled with an iron hand. When he was away, the board liked to move timidly toward reform. But from sickbed or vacation spot, Stern ultimately restored his authority. And most of the time, as in the case of the pogrom action, or when a revision of the statutes threatened, he succeeded. On one occasion, when the board in his absence voted a resolution he opposed, he rescinded their action by a suspensive veto which he converted into a permanent one. To make the board pliable to his will he often threatened resignation. That this threat had so much weight shows to what extent the IKG establishment was afraid of public confrontations. As long as Stern was in office, he had little difficulty in maintaining his autocratic authority.[70]

It would take the breakdown of political order and a revolutionary act to change the structure of the IKG. In November 1918, in a dramatic re-enactment of the events in Russia, the Zionists and their nationalist allies, acting in the name of the newly created Jewish national council, marched into the meeting halls of the *Kultusgemeinde* and, using the presence of 50,000 Galician refugees who had crowded into Vienna during the war as a threat, forced the board to accede to their demands for a radical revision of the existing by-laws. Alfred Stern resigned − perhaps abdicated would be a better term − and a commission equally composed of IKG board members committed to reform and representatives of the *Nationalrat* was charged with drawing up a new set of statutes. Even before this event, H.P. Chajes, a highly respected scholar sympathetic to the

Zionist cause, had been appointed to replace the ailing chief rabbi Güdemann.[71] It would take another fourteen years and the misery of inter-war conditions to propel the Zionists to power in the *Kultusgemeinde*. For the elections of 1920, the diverse factions in the community organized themselves along party lines, taking advantage of the newly instituted system of proportional representation. Although the assimilationists were in the majority, with the orthodox party far behind, the Zionists emerged as formidable challengers. With the revision of the tax provisions, lowering the minimum tax to what would have been 8-10 Kronen in pre-war currency, the long struggle for broadening the *Gemeinde* base was over. The number of taxpayers, and of eligible voters, almost doubled. After a brief period of electoral co-operation in the elections of 1924, the conflict resumed. In 1932, in the last election before the *Anschluss*, the Zionists gained a plurality of the votes and a majority of board seats and elected Desider Friedmann as IKG president. The Zionist success did not mean that Vienna's Jews had become Zionist. Only $\frac{2}{3}$ of the eligible taxpayers had voted and a majority of them had rejected the Zionist list.[72] Vienna's Jews were as divided as ever. Assimilationist Jews were active in the Social Democratic Party, Jewish nationalists in the *Betar* and other Revisionist organizations; the orthodox showed little strength, and there was relatively little Zionist socialist activity. But within the *Kultusgemeinde* the inter-war period ended the era of notable politics. Open conflict was no longer avoided. The Jewish groupings were clearly organized into permanent factions, the political nature of the *Kultusgemeinde* was accepted, and a new kind of conflict resolution was adopted which, since it provided representation for all political currents in the community, produced greater co-operation between the parties than had ever been the case before the war.[73]

CHAPTER 8

POLITICAL ANTISEMITISM IN INTERWAR VIENNA

Bruce F. Pauley

The enormity of the crimes committed against Jews by Nazi Germany have overshadowed antisemitism in other countries prior to the implementation of the so-called Final Solution.[1] This is especially true of antisemitism in interwar Austria. Although there was little that was really new in the discussion of the 'Jewish Question' during the First Austrian Republic the country's desperate economic plight, together with the Nazi takeover in Germany, intensified the debate and made some solution to the issue seem imperative to many antisemites.

The diminutive Austrian Republic with its 6.5 million people and 32,000 square miles is a strategic country for the study of antisemitism. Here east met west and north met south, geographically, politically and culturally. The country contained almost every form of fascism from the generally pro-Italian Heimwehr (or Home Guard) to the pro-German Austrian Nazi party, and also almost every possible form of antisemitism. There was the old-fashioned and comparatively subtle cultural and religious antisemitism of many Catholics and the modern, racial and radical variety practised by the Nazis and a large number of lesser-known groups. Likewise, the Jewish population was evenly and bitterly divided between those 'westernized' Jews, who desired cultural or even social assimilation, such as were also found in Germany, Italy and France, on the one hand, and Orthodox, sometimes Yiddish-speaking, Jews and Zionists more commonly found in eastern Europe, on the other, who favoured religious or political separatism. Consequently, antisemitism was probably more intense in Austria than anywhere else in western or central Europe including pre-Nazi Germany, though in all likelihood it was less extreme than in Poland, Hungary, Rumania, or Lithuania.[2]

Both Austrian antisemitism and Jewish migration into Vienna were drastically increased as a result of the Great War of 1914-18. Now, for the first time in the modern era, antisemitism became far more *salonfähig* and was no longer the monopoly of the lunatic fringe.[3] The war was in every respect a catastrophe for both Austria as a whole and for the Jews in particular.

Ironically the monarchy's Jews enthusiastically supported the war as an opportunity to fight Tsarism and to disprove the old antisemitic charge that Jews could not make good soldiers.[4] Habsburg archdukes and senior officials in the Austro-Hungarian army did indeed recognize the bravery of Jewish soldiers,[5] and until 1916 censors prevented any antisemitic articles from appearing in Austrian newspapers.[6] Nevertheless, antisemites accused them of shirking front-line service.[7]

The attitude of even the imperial government began to change in 1918 because of the Zionists' support for the general strike in Vienna in January. Thereafter, some government officials began to believe in an international Jewish conspiracy and no longer hindered counter-revolutionary and antisemitic propaganda.[8] The antisemitic press now repeatedly charged that factory owners were profiteers, ignoring the benefits that big landowners and peasants – almost none of whom were Jewish – also derived from the war.[9]

In the meantime, a new wave of Jewish migration into Vienna was proving to be a far larger source of antisemitic agitation than real or imagined war profiteering. Soon after the war began, Galicia was overrun by Tsarist troops. Military authorities ordered the evacuation of civilians from the battle zone. The Jewish inhabitants, well aware of the antisemitic policies of the Russian government in recent decades, needed little encouragement to leave. The Russian invasion caused the greatest flight of Jewish refugees since the seventeenth century. Altogether some 340,000 refugees had already left Galicia by the end of 1915; of these, 137,000 found asylum in Vienna, where many had friends and relatives. Sixty per cent or 77,000 of the newcomers were Jewish; almost overnight Vienna's Jewish population grew by nearly 50 per cent. The refugees aggravated a severe shortage of food and fuel. The Jews among them – mostly desperately poor peddlers, artisans, and cattle dealers – arrived in the Austrian capital virtually penniless. To ward off starvation some of them resorted to crime.

Although the number of Jewish refugees in the imperial capital was never more than 125,000, some antisemitics claimed the figure was as high as 400,000. Most of the homeless Jews were returned to their native provinces as soon as they were evacuated by Russians; but 35,000 still remained in Vienna in 1918 and were reluctant to go back to their often devastated homes. By 1921, all but 26,000 had been forced to leave, and those who remained were resented more than ever by the city's long-time residents, including many acculturated Jews.[10]

The first postwar years brought still more complaints from Austrian antisemites. The Peace Treaty of St Germain, signed in September 1919, was negotiated in part by the ethnic Jew and left-wing Socialist foreign minister, Otto Bauer (although it was signed by the moderate non-Jewish chancellor Karl Renner). It imposed harsh territorial and economic terms on the already destitute country. Even more alarming to antisemites was the participation of the Social Democratic Party (SDP), with its many Jewish leaders, in the federal government until 1920. The Socialists also completely controlled the government of Vienna until the party's demise in 1934. The administration of Vienna, especially the Jewish city councillor, Hugo Breitner, was determined to implement an extensive social welfare programme paid for by steeply graduated federal income taxes, which fell most heavily on the already hard-pressed middle and upper classes. Socialism, defeat, democracy and Jewry, therefore, came to be equated in the minds of many conservative Austrians after the war.

Events outside Austria also contributed to the increase in antisemitism in the early postwar years. The Bolshevik revolutions in Russia (in 1917), and Hungary and Bavaria (both 1919) all aroused the ire of antisemites because of the prominent roles played by ethnic Jews.

The war and revolution in Austria also affected population trends. The growth and indeed the maintenance of the city's Jewish community had, during the nineteenth century, depended on immigration from the Bohemian crownland, Hungary and Galicia. With these areas now belonging to foreign countries population movement virtually ceased. The rapid increase in the city's Jewish population was now reversed. Owing to a high death rate, a low birth rate, and a few mixed marriages, the 201,513 Jews who had been counted in the census of 1923 declined to 191,481 in 1934[11] and to fewer than 170,000 by 1938, a decrease of 1.5 per cent per year for fifteen years.[12] The percentage of Jews in the city also declined from 10.8 in 1923 to 9.4 in 1934.[13] Ninety-one per cent of the Jewish population of Austria lived in the capital city whereas only about 15,000 lived in the rest of the country, or 0.64 per cent of the total provincial population.[14]

One would suppose that these statistics would have gladdened the heart of the most rabid antisemite, who could have looked forward to a 'final solution' to the 'Jewish problem' in a few generations without any recourse to expulsion or violence. No such development occurred. The main reason was that Austrian census takers recorded only the religion of the Austrian people despite efforts of antisemites to include 'race'. Consequently, antisemites imagined that there were anywhere from 300,000 to 583,000 'racial' Jews in Vienna.[15]

Often, antisemites simply ignored the statistical decline by pointing out how much greater the proportion of Jews was in Austria compared with Germany, France or Great Britain.[16] Occasionally they admitted there was a diminution in the Jewish population, but claimed this was more than offset by an increase in Jewish economic and cultural influence.[17]

There is no doubt that the cultural and economic status of the Viennese Jews was a major cause – or at least excuse – for antisemitism. Even Jews conceded that they had a great influence in the country's cultural and economic life.[18] A plethora of statistics supported this observation. By Jewish reckoning Jews in 1936 accounted for 62 per cent of the city's lawyers and dentists, 47 per cent of its physicians, over 28 per cent of its university professors, and 18 per cent of its bank directors. Ninety-four per cent of the city's advertising agencies were Jewish, as were 85 per cent of the furniture retailers, and over 70 per cent of those involved in the wine and textile trades.[19]

Jewish power in questions of public opinion was, if anything, even greater. For example, shortly before the war 123 of 174 newspaper editors were Jewish[20] and 70 per cent of the city's cinemas were owned by Jews.[21] Antisemites never tired of citing these and other statistics to 'prove' that Jews enjoyed an unfair and privileged economic and cultural status in the city. However, these figures did not by themselves adequately describe the position of Jews in Viennese society. Nor did they fully account for the sharp increase in antisemitism after the war.

Jews were concentrated in business and the so-called free professions, not because they sought to avoid manual labour more than gentiles, as antisemites charged,[22] but because for centuries prior to 1867 they had been prevented by law from owning land or holding public offices.[23] They also became self-employed because gentiles would not hire them.[24]

Antisemites usually mentioned only the fields in which Jews were over-represented, not those in which the opposite was true. Jews continued to encounter discrimination in seeking civil service positions and were under-represented in primary and secondary teaching. In 1934, of 160,696 civil servants in Austria, only about 700 were Jewish. Even the most eminent scholars could not be promoted to full professor after the war. No school directors were Jews and no Jews became judges or senior military officers during the Republic.[25] Whereas 200,000 Christians found employment with Jewish firms, very few Jews were employed by Christians. Half a million civil servants and government pensioners (1.5 million if dependants are counted) were supported in large measure by Jewish taxes.[26] One should add that no Christians were obliged to seek the services of Jewish lawyers or doctors or were forced to read Jewish-owned or -edited newspapers. They did so because they found the services superior and the prices competitive. Organized boycotts simply failed, as they did also in Nazi Germany.[27]

No statistics were ever kept on the income of Viennese Jews,[28] but it is certain that many of them, especially recent immigrants from Galicia, were poor. One clue as to their general poverty was that free burials for impoverished Jews just before and during the war outnumbered first- and second-class burials by a ratio of about ten to one.[29] In 1934, 55,000 Viennese Jews were dependent on some form of welfare from Jewish institutions.[30]

At the heart of postwar antisemitism was not just the wealth or poverty of the Viennese Jews; their domination of certain occupations was, after all, already well established in the years between 1900 and 1914, a time when antisemitism was relatively subdued. But that had been a period of rapid economic expansion when jobs were plentiful for both Jews and gentiles. By 1919, however, Vienna no longer served an empire of 54 million people, but instead a land-locked Alpine state with only 6.5 million inhabitants. The gentile-dominated civil service, which had already been far too large for the empire, was now grotesquely overstaffed. Gentiles, therefore, sought employment in the traditionally 'Jewish' fields of industry and the free professions. Industrialists, however, were also in a desperate situation having had their prewar domestic markets cut off by new high tariff barriers imposed by the Successor States.[31]

The economy of republican Austria never fully recovered its prewar status. Vienna's educational and cultural institutions – universities, libraries, theatres, opera houses, etc. – which had been subsidized by imperial revenues now had to get along on much smaller budgets. The postwar inflation, which reached its peak in Austria in 1921–2, virtually wiped out the long-accumulated savings and pensions of the thrifty. And, of course, the Great Depression, which left as many as 600,000 Austrians unemployed, simply worsened the country's economic situation and sharpened the competition for jobs still further.[32]

That antisemitism was not merely a product of terrible economic conditions, however, is proven by the history of the Austrian Social Democratic party. No class was more vulnerable to the perils of business cycles than the proletariat. And yet the Socialist party was certainly the least antisemitic of the major political parties of Austria. Consequently, it was also the party which attracted by far the largest Jewish vote. About 75 per cent of all Viennese Jews voted for the SDP[33] both because of the party's relative freedom from antisemitism and because of its welfare programme and stand on the issue of church and state. Many Jews, however, objected to the party's anti-religious, anti-Zionist and pro-assimilationist philosophy.[34]

Jews flocked to the SDP after the Liberal party, which had championed their emancipation in the 1860s, declined in the 1890s as a result of the extension of the franchise to the lower classes.[35] The founder of the SDP, Victor Adler, was a baptized Jew and many other intellectual leaders of the party were of Jewish descent; the party's newspaper editors soon became overwhelmingly Jewish, a fact which troubled even some Jewish members of the party.[36]

The prominence of Jews in the SDP's leadership made the party sensitive to the repeated antisemitic charge that it was a *Judenschutzpartei*. Moreover, because all other parties had well-developed antisemitic programmes, the SDP could take the Jewish vote for granted[37] and even indulge in some antisemitic rhetoric of its own. The Socialists tried to turn the tables on the (Catholic) Christian Social party (CSP) and the Greater German People's party (GVP) and even the National Socialist German Workers' party (NSDAP) by accusing them of being the guardians of Jewish capital.[38] Capitalists were denounced more for being Jewish than for being capitalists.[39] In some Socialist publications the dress of Orthodox Jews was ridiculed and antisemitic caricatures were used in posters. Terms like

Bankjuden, jüdische Presse, and *Börsenjuden* were frequently employed by both editors and speakers.[40] Ironically, the worst offenders were renegades who looked at their Jewish heritage with disdain. By contrast, nearly all non-Jewish leaders of the SDP stood firm against antisemitism, opposing, for example, attempts to exclude Jews from summer resorts.[41]

Although the SDP was the only Austrian party to make any attempt to fight antisemitism, and was the first party to take a stand against the Nazis, it did not have a unified programme for resisting antisemitism. The latter was considered to be no more than an anti-Socialist plot which would disappear with the complete establishment of Socialism.[42]

The Jewish policy of the Christian Socials, like that of the Socialists, was formed in all its essentials with the foundation of the party in the 1890s. It combined the traditional anti-Judaism of the Catholic church with the resentment the bourgeoisie felt toward the Industrial Revolution, which it blamed on Jewish capitalists. The overrepresentation of Jews in many commercial fields was also seen as a threat to the existence of the Catholic bourgeoisie. Like the Socialists, however, the CSP had no clear racial theory and preferred slogans and demagogy to antisemitic legislation.[43]

This demagogic tradition can be traced back to the party's founder and first great leader, Dr Karl Lueger, who was also the mayor of Vienna from 1897 until his death in 1910. Lueger resembled his contemporary, Georg von Schönerer, in exploiting antisemitic sentiments of the lower middle class; but he differed sharply from the Pan-German leader in supporting the Habsburg dynasty and the Roman Catholic church. Lueger's nonracial antisemitism made it possible for him to appoint baptized Jews to important positions. Viennese Jews made even more progress in commercial affairs during his administration than during the previous Liberal era.[44] Lueger's Jewish policy also made it possible for him to avoid conflicts with the teachings of the Roman Catholic church, which recognized baptized Jews as full-fledged Christians.

Lueger's legacy of denouncing Jews in the abstract while tolerating them in practice was carried over by the Christian Socials into the First Republic. During the first postwar election campaign in December 1918 the CSP programme called for a strong defensive fight against the 'Jewish danger' and Jews were described as *volksfremd* (foreign) even if they were assimilated. The official programme of 1926 and 1932 also called on the party to fight the 'destructive' (*zersetzende*) and revolutionary influence of the Jews in both intellectual and economic affairs.[45] The programme failed to say how this was to be done, however, or even to say who was a Jew.

To a considerable degree the party's antisemitism reflected the views of its long-time postwar leader, priest, and sometime chancellor, Dr Ignaz Seipel. Seipel denounced the notion of racial antisemitism[46] and in 1927 toned down the antisemitism of the recent party programme in order to gain the support of liberals and democrats. Moreover, he never indulged in vulgar, public antisemitic outbusts.[47] He was willing, however, to use antisemitism as a weapon against the Social Democrats and feared that Christians were threatened economically, culturally, and politically by Jews, especially those in the leadership of the SDP. Although Jews were not a separate race, a possible solution to the Jewish problem, he suggested, was that they be treated as a separate nation within Austria, a programme already advocated by the Zionists.[48]

Although the antisemitism of Seipel, and probably most members of the CSP, was nonracial and comparatively moderate, the opposite was true of the party's Christian Workers' Movement. Antisemitism was an essential part of its Linz Programme of 1926, and, along with religion, was one of the principal ways it distinguished itself from the egalitarianism of the Social Democratic party. The programme said that Austrians had the right to protect themselves in the same way that Americans did against the Chinese by treating the Jews as a national minority with their own schools, doctors and judicial system, as demanded by the Zionists. Moreover, the antisemitism of the Christian Workers' Movement was racial and not 'merely' religious.[49]

Aside from Seipel himself, Catholic clergy played an active role in the discussion about the Jewish problem. Anti-Judaism, of course, was a deeply rooted tradition within the Roman Catholic church, dating back to Antiquity and the Middle Ages and beyond. For centuries the church had held Jews collectively responsible for the murder of God.[50] The age-old antagonism between Catholics and Jews was enhanced during the First Republic by the attempt of some Jews to stop the spending of tax revenues for the construction of church buildings in Vienna. Jewish leaders in the SDP also favoured legalizing divorce.[51] Catholic clergy responded with frequent anti-Jewish attacks. One priest, Father Georg Bichlmair, the leader of the 'Paulus-Werke' for baptizing Jews, gave a lecture in Vienna in March

1936 in which he contradicted Catholic teachings about race by saying that baptized Jews should not be allowed to hold high office in the church hierarchy or the civil service up to the third generation.[52]

Even Catholic bishops did not scruple to make direct and formal pronouncements condemning the Jews. For example, only a few days before Hitler's appointment as chancellor bishop Johannes Gföllner of Linz issued a *Hirten*, (pastoral) letter, to the faithful in which he claimed that Jews had a harmful influence on almost all aspects of modern culture including law, medicine, the press, the theatre and the cinema. They were also responsible for capitalism, socialism, and communism. It was not just the right, but also the duty of Christians to stop the spread of this Jewish 'spirit'.[53] Nazis, who loved to quote from this letter, were careful to avoid mentioning that the bishop also said that it was impossible to be both a good Catholic and a Nazi. Nor could they have been pleased when later in the same year the entire Austrian episcopate denounced Gföllner's letter for arousing social hatred and conflict.[54] But four years later the Nazis' propaganda was given fresh ammunition when another Austrian bishop, Alois Hudal, wrote that Nazi nationalism and racism were compatible with Christianity as long as fundamental Christian dogmas were not violated.[55]

Catholic antisemitism could also be found in the interwar years in the *Reichspost*, the official organ of the Christian Social party. It discussed the 'Jewish problem' in all sections of the newspaper including the advertisements (none of which could be purchased by Jews). All the usual antisemitic charges could be found in the pages of the *Reichspost*: Jews were blamed for the loss of the war and were responsible for the Communist regime in Russia; Jews held too many positions at the University of Vienna, especially in the faculties of medicine and law. After the early postwar years the paper's antisemitism was tempered somewhat by its editor, Friedrich Funder. But as late as 1934, the *Reichspost* sympathized with the antisemitism in Nazi Germany, especially the boycott of Jewish businesses and the reduction of Jewish cultural influence. On the other hand, Funder, like his early hero, Karl Lueger, was never a racial antisemite and did not hesitate to associate with Jews socially. A baptized Jew for him was no longer a Jew.[56]

Despite all its antisemitic rhetoric the CSP did not implement any discriminatory legislation against the Jews in the many years it held power between 1920 and 1934, if only because the party needed the money of Jewish bankers.[57]

In the spectrum between the demagogic, but usually nonracial, antisemitism of the Social Democrats and Christian Socials, on the one hand, and the racial and sometimes violent antisemitism of the Nazis on the other, the Austrian Heimwehr (HW) or Home Guard stood squarely in the middle with one foot in both camps. The Heimwehr was a paramilitary formation which was founded shortly after the collapse of the empire in order to defend Austria's southern borders against South Slav incursions. It soon evolved, however, into a primarily anti-Socialist movement.

At the Heimwehr's height in the late 1920s, 70 per cent of its up to 400,000 active members and sympathizers were peasants, many from antisemitic areas like Styria and Carinthia. Their traditional fear of Jews was now combined with their hatred of Socialists and their distrust of the great metropolis, Vienna, which the Socialists now ruled. Heimwehr members in most other provinces, while sharing the anti-Socialism of their comrades in the south, were too Catholic to indulge in racial antisemitism. Moreover, the two wings of the movement were badly split over the issue of *Anschluss* with Germany with the Pan-German racist wing in the south and parts of Lower Austria in favour, and the Catholic wing elsewhere strongly opposed.[58]

Complicating the issue of antisemitism still further was the much needed financial support of Jewish bankers who sympathized with the HW's staunch anti-Marxism.[59] Richard Steidle, from the ultra-Catholic Tyrol, and the movement's co-leader from 1927 to 1930, said that the Heimwehr was not antisemitic, but merely opposed to Jewish Marxists. Patriotic Jews were welcome co-fighters against Marxism. But another HW member, Dr Franz Hueber, a minister of justice in the federal government and a brother-in-law of Hermann Göring, announced that Austria 'ought to be freed from this alien [Jewish] body'. As a minister he 'could not recommend that the Jews be hanged, that their windowpanes be smashed, or that their shop display windows be looted. . . . But racially impure elements ought to be removed from the public life of Austria.'[60]

Prince Ernst Rüdiger Starhemberg, the Heimwehr's sole leader (with one interruption) from September 1930 until its dissolution in 1936, could be either radical or moderate on the Jewish issue, depending on his audience. In a speech delivered to a HW crowd in 1930 he proclaimed that

The object of our movement is to create a people's state in which every *Volksgenosse* [racial comrade] will have the right to work and to bread. [The Nazis' slogan was '*Arbeit und Brot.*'] By a *Volksgenosse* I mean only one inspired by the race instinct of the Germans in whose veins German blood flows. In 'the people' I do not include those foreign, flat-footed parasites from the East who exploit us. [This was an apparent attempt to distinguish between *Ostjuden* and 'natives.']⁶¹

Starhemberg became more temperate after he joined the government as vice-chancellor in 1932, particularly when he was speaking to foreign journalists. To a French newspaper he said in March 1934 that he merely wanted to break Jewish 'predominance'.⁶² English and American reporters were told a few weeks later that it would be crazy to solve the Jewish question by force,⁶³ and a Hungarian newspaper was told at about this same time that all Jews who rejected internationalism and who were not a burden to the state were not part of a Jewish problem. The Heimwehr, he added, completely rejected Nazi racial theories.⁶⁴

The Heimwehr tried to bridge the gap between moderate, traditional, Catholic anti-Judaism, and modern, racial antisemitism. At the same time it was divided between the Catholic political camp in Austria, represented by the Christian Socials, and the German national camp, represented by the Greater German People's party, and increasingly after 1930 by the National Socialist German Workers' party.

The antisemitism of the GVP, like that of the SDP and CSP, could also be traced to the last forty years of the monarchy, and specifically to Georg von Schönerer, the first great antisemitic leader of prewar Austria. The appeal of von Schönerer's antisemitism, however, had been reduced by his linking it to a demand that the German-speaking portions of Austria be attached to the German Reich. On the other hand, his call for the elimination of Jewish influence from public life, which he added to the infamous Linz Programme of the Liberal party in 1885, was to be repeated by virtually all antisemites in postwar Austria.⁶⁵

Von Schönerer's career was cut short in 1887 when it was discovered that he was married to a woman with a Jewish ancestor. By that time he had already established a tradition within Pan-Germanism of

emotional indignation and intolerance, suspicion about the

integrity of people who did not go along with [the Pan-Germans], [and] contempt for political parties. . . . The movement's opponents – the majority of people of Schönerer's day – regarded it as a political aberration; the Pan-Germans saw themselves as the heralds of the future. History has provided sinister confirmation of the boast.[66]

During the 1920s the GVP was one of the most important heirs to Schönerer's ideas. A middle-class coalition of nationalistic groups, it favoured free trade, an *Anschluss* with Germany, and racial antisemitism. It also supported the concept of a *Volksgemeinschaft* or people's community. This idea had the dual advantage of ending the class struggle, which was advocated by Marxists, while excluding the 'parasitic' Jews, who were not ethnically Germans and who, therefore, could never be part of the *Volksgemeinschaft*.[67] According to the party's official Salzburg programme of 1920, the Jews were to be treated as a separate nation and their influence over the country's economic and public life was to be greatly reduced.[68]

Like other antisemites, the members of the GVP did not draw a sharp distinction between Jews and those people who had been affected by the 'Jewish spirit'. The Jews, they alleged, were only interested in making money and dominating the world.[69] Members of a special GVP 'Committee on Jews' disagreed only on how Jews sought world dominion. Some thought it was a well-organized conspiracy directed from New York, whereas others believed it was simply a matter of instinct.[70] Despite their efforts to combat Jewish power through the publication and distribution of leaflets and pamphlets, members of the GVP themselves admitted that they had not been very successful up to 1924, except for increasing social segregation.[71]

Another antisemitic organization which had close ties to both the GVP and NSDAP and for a time even the CSP was the 'German-Austrian Defensive League of Antisemites' or *Antisemitenbund* (AB) for short. It also resembled the HW in trying to be *überparteilich* (or nonpartisan) and in being organized around a single issue, in this case antisemitism, however, rather than anti-Marxism. The AB was founded in 1919 and flourished until 1925, during most of which time it co-operated closely with the GVP and NSDAP.[72] Thereafter, its popularity declined, as did the popularity of antisemitism in general in Austria, until a revival of both occurred with the coming of the Great Depression. The organization's official newspaper, *Der eiserne Besen,* was published weekly and reached a maximum circulation of 6,000. Membership was drawn from the entire non-Socialist camp and consisted largely of wage earners, employees and workers.[73]

The ideology of the *Antisemitenbund* was in most respects unremarkable. Like other nationalists it regarded the Jews as a race, but also said that it fought the 'Jewish spirit'. It wanted to protect 'Aryans' from the economic, social, and political influence of Jews through the legal separation of Jews and gentiles in matters of education, administration of justice, and welfare. What made it unusual was its desire to co-operate with all other antisemites, both domestic and foreign, in order better to fight the alleged world organization of Jews.[74]

The *Antisemitenbund* virtually disappeared from public view during the relatively prosperous late 1920s, and during the early 1930s it was surpassed by the far more boisterous antisemitism of the NSDAP. However, it underwent a major renaissance after the prohibition of all the political parties of Austria, beginning with the Nazis in June 1933.[75] During these years the AB led a precarious existence, however, because Austrian security forces were convinced that it was a mere cover for the illegal Austrian Nazi party. From mid-1935 until early 1937 the AB was not even allowed to hold public meetings.[76] In fact, many leading Austrian Nazis, such as the *Gauleiter* of Vienna, Leopold Tavs, did have connections with the *Antisemitenbund*.[77] Perhaps in an attempt to keep their eyes on the illegal Nazis and to distract them from more dangerous activities, the authorities permitted the AB to hold meetings, attended by large and enthusiastic crowds, during the last year of Austria's independence.[78]

The most infamous of the antisemitic organizations of Austria was without doubt the Nazi party. But once we look beyond its popular reputation we discover that its ideas and methods of propaganda were in no respect novel. It is even doubtful whether its Jewish policy prior to the *Anschluss* was any more extreme than that of the *Antisemitenbund*, the Christian Workers' Movement, or some elements of the Greater German People's party.

If it was unique in any way it was in how it combined different aspects of antisemitism from all other political parties. One could find the same anti-Jewish capitalism of the SDP,[79] the same attacks on the Jewish leadership of the SDP[80] made by the CSP and the Heimwehr, the same charges of 'Jewish materialism'[81] made by the

GVP and the AB, the same violent criticism of Jews for their supposed domination of the Viennese press and cultural life,[82] found in all the non-Jewish political groups of Austria, and the same racism as in Schönerer's Pan-Germans, the GVP, the AB, and parts of the HW.

The Nazis were more consistent in their antisemitism than their rivals. Their 'scientific' racism and aggressive opposition to Jews avoided the semi-religious, semi-racist, and basically defensive antisemitism of most Christian Socials. Unlike the Socialists they rejected all Jews, not just those who were capitalists, and unlike the HW and the CSP,[83] the Nazis did not accept money from Jewish financiers. In contrast to all their antisemitic rivals, except perhaps the *Antisemitenbund*, Nazis were not supposed to associate with even baptized Jews. Thus, the Nazis, unlike most other antisemites, could claim to be fully *kompromisslos* on the Jewish question.

Even the 'solutions' to the Jewish problem offered by the Nazis were derivative of other political groups. For example, the Nazis, like many Christian Socials, supported Zionist efforts to have Jews emigrate to Palestine or Madagascar in order to establish a state of their own.[84] A disguised Nazi newspaper, *Der Stürmer* (not to be confused with Julius Streicher's scandal sheet of the same name in Nuremberg), also warmly endorsed the idea of recognizing the Jews as a national minority with their own schools and taxes.[85] This same idea had been put forward at various times by Ignaz Seipel; a former minister of culture and leading CSP member, Emmerich Czermark; and Leopold Kunschak, the leader of the Christian Workers' Movement.[86] (It was also advocated by the Austrian Zionists, but passionately opposed by the acculturated Jews of Vienna.[87]) The idea of expelling all Jews who had immigrated to Austria since 1914, as well as making summer resorts *Judenrein*, had already been proposed by the *Antisemitenbund*.[88] The goal of complete segregation in all activities, athletic, academic and professional, carried out in Nazi Germany during the mid-1930s, had been discussed many years earlier by the GVP.[89]

Probably the favourite solution to the question advanced by nearly all antisemites, including the Nazis, bore the Latin phrase *numerus clausus*, or proportional representation. If the Jews made up only 10.8 per cent of the Viennese population in 1923 and 9.4 per cent in 1934 then they should be limited to those same ratios in such fields as commerce, law, medicine, banking and higher education. Young Nazis at the university of Vienna and other Viennese institutions of higher education, who frequently brutally attacked their fellow students of the Jewish tradition, were especially eager to limit the number of Jewish students who would soon be competing with them for employment.[90]

Interestingly enough, even the most ardent racists wanted to count only avowed religious Jews in their scheme, and not the inflated number of 'ethnic' Jews they so frequently complained about. Moreover, the ratio was to be imposed only where Jews were unusually numerous, not where they were grossly under-represented, as in the civil service, the school teaching profession, and land-owning.[91]

Only the Social Democrats opposed these solutions proposed by the Nazis and other antisemites. Officially their view was that antisemitism was simply a bourgeois prejudice which would disappear in time. Socialist (and Communist) theoreticians equated Zionism with reactionary nationalism and assumed that it was only a question of time until all Jews were fully assimilated. Thus, antisemitism would end when Jewish identity ceased.[92]

The Austrian Nazis enjoyed an inestimable advantage over their antisemitic rivals in being able to point to their brethren in Nazi Germany who were actually doing something besides talking about the Jewish problem. There Jewish influence had been eliminated from the civil service and cultural life of the country and German Jews had been deprived of their full citizenship rights. But the Nazis' Jewish policy in Germany prior to the *Anschluss* was actually moderate compared to the demands of many Austrian antisemites. Jews were not yet required to emigrate, had not been killed simply because they were Jews, and were even allowed to engage in business. *Kristallnacht* and the Holocaust were still unforeseen events of the future. Such a 'middle-of-the-road' programme was bound to appeal to a broad spectrum of antisemites, not just hard-core Nazis in Austria and other countries. Undoubtedly, this is exactly what it was intended to do. The policy also made an *Anschluss* between Germany and Austria seem all the more attractive to those Austrians who saw the Jews as the root of their misfortune.

Nazism and antisemitism grew simultaneously after the arrival of the Great Depression. The Depression, which struck Austria perhaps more ferociously than any other country in the world, led to a rapidly escalating rate of unemployment, and the collapse of

Vienna's great Rothschild banks, the *Bodencredit* and the *Creditanstalt*. One Austrian emigré reflected years later that

> these failures did more than hurt the Jewish community financially; they undermined the belief that Jews were particularly gifted, and indeed vitally needed, for the conduct of financial transactions and enterprises. Added to the substantial losses suffered by hundreds of thousands of gentile bank depositors ... the end of the myth of Jewish competence in money matters gave a renewed impetus not only to antisemitic feelings, but even more so to the idea that antisemitic actions could be taken without harm to the economy.[93]

The Nazis, in fact, made a point of this very issue in their propaganda.[94]

The growth of unemployment and antisemitism in turn gave a great boost to the Austrian Nazi party. The continuing growth in popularity of the Austrian Nazi party after 1932 persuaded the Austrian government, headed by Engelbert Dollfuss from 1932 to his assassination by Nazis in July 1934, and by Kurt von Schuschnigg thereafter until the *Anschluss* in March 1938, to compete for the support of the antisemites, or at least not to drive them all into the Nazi fold.

The issue of antisemitism appeared to be all the more acute after 1933 because of the emigration of German Jews following Hitler's *Machtergreifung*. This was, in reality, a phoney issue, Nazi claims notwithstanding; most German Jews, unable to find work in impoverished Austria, soon moved on to other countries. Whatever burden the refugees presented was imposed mainly on the already financially hard-pressed *Israelitische Kultusgemeinde* (IKG), the official communal organization for Jews in religious and cultural affairs.[95]

The Dollfuss/Schuschnigg regime hoped to lessen the Nazi appeal by showing that it too could be antisemitic. Dollfuss talked vaguely about adopting that which was 'positive and worthwhile' in the Nazi ideology. Although Dollfuss and Schuschnigg, as practising Roman Catholics and members of the now (after 1934) defunct Christian Social party, rejected racial antisemitism, they both professed to be opposed to the cultural and economic 'foreign penetration' of Jews.[96] This kind of phraseology, as we have seen, was the stock and trade not only of the Nazis, but most other antisemitic groups as well.

However, neither Dollfuss nor Schuschnigg could afford to alienate totally either the local Jewish community or the western democracies by appearing to give in to pressure from Germany. They desperately needed support wherever they could find it, and the Jews gave substantial sums of money to the Austrian government.[97] Viennese Jews, like those in Hungary at this time, found themselves in the absurd position of looking to moderate antisemites for protection against radical ones.[98]

The Austrian government protected Jews in a number of ways. Both the old constitution of 1919, and the new authoritarian constitution introduced by Dollfuss in 1934, guaranteed Jews freedom to practise their religion and equal political rights as citizens. Strangely enough, Jews were the only Austrians after 1934 who were able to have political parties and elect officers through democratic elections to the *Kultusgemeinde*.[99] Schuschnigg also prevented the Salzburg provincial parliament from enacting a law prohibiting the ritual slaughter of animals in 1937.[100] The disgustingly antisemitic newspaper, *Der Stürmer*, was eventually banned from making street sales and some issues were confiscated.[101] On a number of occasions the federal chancellor reassured both foreign and domestic Jews that Jews in Austria would not be treated like second-class citizens, as long as they took a positive attitude toward the state and respected the culture and religious values of the majority of the population.[102] A few Jews, most of them Zionists, were even appointed to high positions in the Austrian and Viennese municipal governments.

The Austrian government did not want to appear to be giving in to German pressure to persecute Jews; on the other hand, it feared that being too friendly toward them would provoke Nazis both at home and abroad and might even alienate members of its own government.[103]

The compromise Jewish policy which the Dollfuss-Schuschnigg government pursued amounted to tolerating nongovernmental antisemitism while practising only economic discrimination itself. Direct attacks on the Jews as a religious community were usually avoided. Meanwhile the Schuschnigg government quietly and gradually reduced the number of Jews in banking and the legal and medical professions to bring their numbers more into line with their proportion of Austria's total population (*numerus clausus!*).[104] Jewish doctors who worked in municipal hospitals were dismissed after the ill-fated Socialist uprising in Vienna in February 1934. Officially, these Jews lost their jobs because they were Socialists and not because they were Jews. However, 56 of the 58 physicians who were released were Jewish (defined 'racially') even though four-fifths of them had in no way been active in Social Democratic politics.[105] It hardly needs to be added that Jews continued to be almost completely excluded from other federal, provincial and municipal positions.

The role of Jews in the commercial life of Austria was left largely, but not entirely, unimpeded. Even here there were instances of large export houses discharging their Jewish employees, especially those doing business with Nazi Germany.[106] If it is admitted that Jewish commercial life was not too seriously disturbed during the Dollfuss-Schuschnigg years, the concession is less significant than it might appear. After all, Jewish businessmen in Nazi Germany were left relatively unmolested until 1938.[107]

In the realm of education, a Vienna school board ordinance in September 1934 establishing 'parallel (i.e. segregated) classes' for all non-Christian students (Jews and children without religious affiliation) could be, and was, interpreted as an antisemitic move. To be sure, the *Jüdische Presse*, the organ of Orthodox Jews, welcomed the policy as a first step toward the establishment of religious schools.[108] *Die Wahrheit*, however, representing the views of acculturated Viennese Jews, vehemently objected that the new classes would enlarge the already deep gulf between Christians and Jews.[109] Even *Die Stimme*, the mouthpiece of the Zionist faction, was not too pleased with the new ruling because it did not provide for Jewish teachers or a Jewish curriculum.[110] The Schuschnigg government blandly answered these objections by saying that it was simply trying to make religious instruction easier, in accord with Jewish desires.[111]

Probably the most common type of antisemitism during the Dollfuss-Schuschnigg years was the passive variety. For example, antisemitism was tolerated in an otherwise tightly controlled press just as long as the attacks were directed exclusively against Jews and not against the government.[112] Even a Nazi front newspaper, the *Wiener Neueste Nachrichten*, which was secretly subsidized by Germany, was allowed to continue its antisemitic diatribes.[113] The same was true of other Austrian newspapers including the semi-official *Reichspost*. Only in really extreme cases or where a paper had known connections with the Austrian Nazi party was it shut down, as was true of *Der Stürmer* in 1934.

We have already seen how a purely antisemitic organization like the *Antisemitenbund* was allowed to function right up to (and beyond) the *Anschluss*, albeit under close police surveillance. Private clubs and professional organizations continued to be allowed to exclude Jews and adopt antisemitic policies.[114]

How did the Viennese Jews respond to the increasingly threatening situation of the interwar years? In fact, their reactions were just as varied as the types of antisemitism they encountered. Not only did they differ according to particular incidents, but also according to the religious, political, social and economic background of the Jews themselves. Just as the non-Jewish Austrians were bitterly divided into Pan-German nationalists, conservative Roman Catholics, and militantly Marxist Social Democrats, so too were Jews in Vienna and the rest of Austria split into acrimonious camps. In no respect was the mythical Nazi view of Jews more absurd than in its depiction of them as monolithic world conspirators.[115] Indeed, Jews could not even agree on the most fundamental questions of survival.

Until at least 1932 most Jews were acculturated into Viennese society and considered themselves to be loyal Austrians first and Jews second. They were organized in the *Union österreichischer Juden* (Union of German-Austrian Jews). These were by far the wealthiest and best educated of the Austrian Jews and, therefore, had the most to fear from a Nazi takeover and the least to expect from a voluntary move to Palestine.

As the largest party in the *Kultusgemeinde* until 1932 the Union was able to continue its prewar policy of making formal complaints to the Austrian government over specific cases of antisemitism. With so many lawyers in their ranks the Unionists believed themselves to be particularly well qualified for this kind of action.[116]

The leaders of the IKG hoped that their grievances could be resolved through normal legal channels: police authorities, law courts, and district attorneys. Formal declarations and personal remonstrances to government officials were also employed. The results, however, were mixed.[117] Throughout the 1920s the IKG protested the vicious attacks on Jewish students made by their *völkisch* adversaries. Usually the government replied that it could not interfere with academic autonomy.[118] However, the protests of the *Kultusgemeinde* and the Union over the attempt to divide students at the University of Vienna into 'nations' did eventually result in the Austrian supreme court declaring the law unconstitutional.[119]

The Zionists, who were the principal rivals of the Unionists, hoped that withdrawal from Austrian politics and society (dissimilation), along with the building of a separate Jewish culture, would win the respect of gentiles and would lessen outbursts of antisemitism. If some such attacks still occurred the Jews could appeal to the League of Nations to enforce the minority rights provisions of the Treaty of St Germain.[120] This suggestion caused near apoplexy among Unionists, not only because it acknowledged Jews to be a separate nationality, as alleged by racial antisemites, but also because they believed (and with good reason as it turned out) that the League could not be counted on for protection.[121]

Far more militant and aggressive than either the Unionists or the Zionists was the *Bund jüdischer Frontsoldaten* (League of Jewish War Veterans). Founded in the summer of 1932, when antisemitism and the Austrian Nazi party were reaching their peak strength, the BJF was inspired both by the older and larger *Reichsbund jüdischer Frontsoldaten* in Germany and the Heimwehr in Austria.[122] Like the Heimwehr, at least in its heyday prior to 1930, the BJF was *überparteilich*. By deliberately avoiding partisan politics and emphasizing military virtues of discipline, obedience and physical fitness, it hoped to overcome the chronic divisiveness of the Jewish community in Austria. Boasting some 8,000 members by February 1934, its main goals were to support the independence of Austria and physically to protect the Jewish people against violent Nazi hooligans.[123]

Unfortunately, these were the only two things that the BJF or other Austrian Jews could agree upon. Otherwise, they were at loggerheads about dealing with the domestic and foreign peril of National Socialism. Except, perhaps, in the final emergency following the Berchtesgaden conference between Chancellor Schuschnigg and Hitler in February 1938, the greater the danger, the more the Jews fought each other, with neither Unionists nor Zionists hesitating to accuse the others of being related to the Nazis.[124]

If the Viennese Jews were bitterly divided, however, they were no more so than other Austrians, and probably somewhat less. If they failed to anticipate the Holocaust and were unable to halt the spread of Nazism, at least they understood, better than anyone else, the real threat represented by National Socialism not only to themselves, but also to the whole of western civilization.

After surveying this kaleidoscope of antisemitic parties and movements, along with the Jewish reaction to them, a number of conclusions can be drawn. Although there was never a time after 1914 when antisemitism entirely disappeared from the political scene, it was clearly stronger during times of rapid Jewish immigration, political upheaval, and economic hardship. Thus, the years 1914-18, 1919-23, and 1930-3 were periods when antisemitism flourished, whereas the fifteen years before the outbreak of the First World War and the late 1920s saw a remission of the disease.

It is also obvious by now that the vocabulary of the antisemites was interchangeable. Such words as 'parasites', *volksfremd*, *verjudung*, 'Jewish spirit', 'cancerous growth', 'destructive', and 'materialistic', just to name a few of the more polite ones, were used with equal frequency by all opponents of the Jews. By the time the Nazis inherited this vocabulary it had lost its capacity to shock or disgust.

We have also seen how antisemitism was a political tool used to reinforce other more important objectives. It was just one way that Socialists and Christian Socials had of attacking each other. For the Pan-Germans in the GVP and the NSDAP it was a way of bringing an *Anschluss* closer by undermining the integrity of the Austrian government. Because the Jewish 'problem', as defined by ardent antisemites, was essentially insoluble by any normal or civilized political action, antisemitic demands were a sure fire way of embarrassing and undermining the government.[125] For conservatives antisemitism was a useful way of denouncing anything associated with capitalism, liberalism, Socialism, democracy, or modern culture. Rather than criticizing these things on their own merits it was easier and more effective to condemn them through their association with some prominent group of Jews. For the Nazis its most important utility was in appealing to the largest possible cross-section of Austrians. It is unlikely that any other issue, even the Treaty of St Germain or unemployment, could have attracted so much popular support as antisemitism.

The eclectic nature of Nazi antisemitism lulled Austrians, both Jews and gentiles, into thinking it was no more radical than its predecessors.[126] This reasoning must have been confirmed by the seemingly 'moderate' nature of antisemitic legislation in Germany between 1933 and early 1938. Traditional antisemites could see their programme being enacted; Austrian Jews could take comfort that their co-religionists were not being forcibly expelled from Germany and were sometimes actually prospering.

Finally, although few if any Austrians could have anticipated the

Holocaust in 1938, seven decades of unceasing antisemitism obviously had a certain conditioning effect. At the very least a large number of Austrians had come to think of the Jews as being alien, overprivileged, dangerous, and not worthy of the equal rights of citizenship.

Figure 8.1 *Scare election poster of the Christian Social party in 'Red Vienna'*

CHAPTER 9

Assimilated Jewish youth and Viennese cultural life around 1930

Richard Thieberger

Born in Vienna in 1913, I left the city in 1934. In 1919 I was six years old, hence my childhood corresponded with that of the Austrian First Republic and my departure coincided with the beginning of the Schuschnigg era. I subsequently returned to Vienna for a single visit in the autumn of 1935, when I completed my doctorate. In order to explain, at the outset, my personal circumstances during the period in question it will be necessary to locate my status as a child and adolescent in relation to Viennese society. My father was born in Biala, in Silesia, and had come to settle in Vienna after finishing his secondary education in Brünn (today Brno), in Moravia. My mother's family had been a part of the Jewish bourgeoisie in the Habsburg imperial city for two generations. Her grandfather, originally the headmaster of a Jewish school in Moravia, had arrived in Vienna in 1868 and started up a small business.

Thus, my studies commenced under the new republican regime, in a city administered by the Social Democrats. Cultural life in those days breathed an air of liberation, symbolized at the outset by the triumphant reception accorded to Arthur Schnitzler's play *Professor Bernhardi* – suppressed by the censor during the monarchy – at the Vienna Volkstheater on 21 December 1918.[1] Viennese Jews could only be pleased with the advent of a political ideology which recognized their full citizenship rights. Even those nostalgic for the monarchy – and they were numerous! – quickly came to terms with the new, lawful government. But what is meant by the term 'Jews'? There certainly was an official and administrative definition: Jews were regarded as all those who belonged to the *Kultusgemeinde,* and the population census continued, as under the monarchy, to distinguish individuals according to religious confession. It should not be concluded from this, however, that all Jews inscribed in the rolls of the *Kultusgemeinde* rigorously observed the Law, that is, the prescriptions of the Torah. Far from it.

In the 'assimilated' milieux – we will explain what is meant by that term in a moment – people were satisfied with observing that which they believed was essential in the tradition: circumcision and Bar-Mitzvah for the boys, Rosh Hashana, fasting on Yom Kippur, Passover and, of course, the religious services connected with marriage and funerals. Every Jew who had not converted was buried in the Jewish cemetery. This occurred in the case of Arthur Schnitzler in 1931 although his family was by no means orthodox in religion. Even under the republic, religion retained its official character, and the rabbi had the status of an official of the civil authorities just like the Roman Catholic priest and the Protestant pastor. Religious instruction was provided in both the primary and secondary schools and Catholic and Protestant theological faculties were part of the state-run university. That is how Cardinal Innitzer attained the post of *Rektor* during my years of study at the university.

According to the official statistics, the Jewish population of Vienna comprised about 10 per cent of the total inhabitants of the city. This figure included all Jews: the orthodox and observant – with little interest in seeking out contact with members of other faiths (who would in any case not have welcomed them in their midst) – as well as the assimilated Jews who had virtually broken away from traditional Judaism. However, it should be kept in mind that the expression 'assimilated Jew' is rather vague and open to several interpretations. Might not something be said for the rigid criterion of the official definition? Why should a Jew who had opted to become a free-thinker not still remain a Jew – especially if he had not sought to deny his origins? This way of regarding the matter had nothing in common with racism. One could even go further and ask if conversion and baptism would remove from the catechumen his Jewish qualities. Certain princes of the church thought not ... however, I have no intention of launching into a theological controversy. During the years with which we are concerned, there were also Jews who did their utmost, whether among Christians or free-thinkers, to forget their origins. One can well ask, however, whether antisemitism was directed more at the Jews who remained Jews or at those who made a deliberate move into other groups.

My personal experience, and consequently the perspective of my recollections, was primarily a product of those milieux which voluntarily remained Jewish, but were also open to a range of social and cultural contacts. During my elementary and secondary schooling the fact that I was Jewish did not expose me to any social prejudice and merited no concealment on my part. It was not until I entered the university that I encountered antisemitism in its most virulent and despicable form, about which I will give some details below.

Many of the Jews of Vienna shared in the fate of the Social Democrats. The first wave of emigration from Austria, in fact, took place in the aftermath of the fire at the Palace of Justice in 1927 – provoked by the acquittal of those charged with shooting at a peaceful socialist demonstration – which led to a massive and bloody confrontation between the police, aided by the *Heimwehr*, and socialist protesters. The writer Manes Sperber made his departure at that time, although his decision to seek refuge in Berlin was perhaps not the wisest choice. The crisis associated with the Palace of Justice fire also made an indelible impression on Elias Canetti, who likewise considered leaving Vienna at that point.[2] Many Jews had an acute sense of danger, but this was not true of all: there were those who thought, during the following years, that the dangers would gradually be surmounted – even up to the final hours when Schuschnigg appeared to have coped with Hitler's demands. We now know the consequences of these sad illusions.

The liberated atmosphere of the immediate postwar period was increasingly polluted and became positively suffocating with the suppression of parliamentary democracy under Chancellor Dollfuss in 1933 and the civil war which followed in 1934. The most threatened political activists on the Left, among whom were many Jews, suddenly left Austria. It was not in 1934, however, that Vienna was to fulfil the imaginative prophecy made by Hugo Bettauer in his 1922 novel, *Die Stadt ohne Juden: Ein Roman von Übermorgen* ('The City Without Jews: A Novel of the Day After Tomorrow'). I recall, for example, that one of my older cousins, who was a deputy secretary-general of the Social Democrat trade unions, gave his full support to the policy of the vice-mayor of Vienna, Ernst Karl Winter, charged with the responsibility of winning over the workers to the Dollfuss regime. Although Winter's efforts were perfectly legitimate and consistent with his ideological outlook, the collaboration of a leader of the opposition in attaining this objective was open to criticism. Although I was not politically engaged myself, I judged my cousin's actions quite harshly and avoided meeting him after that.

But it is not my intention to pass judgment on him now, after his death; I have mentioned him only because he represented a fairly common tendency among the various groups of Austrian Jews in this period.

Turning away from politics to inspect the cultural domain we soon find that there also political developments played a dominant role, going so far as totally to overwhelm cultural life.

My high school was an experimental institution in that era of lively pedagogical reforms. It was called the *Bundes-Reform-Realgymnasium*, on Albertgasse in the eighth district. Its headmaster was a Latinist, always elegant and amiable, a Christian conservative whose politeness could never be faulted. This estimable 'Hofrat' counted among his teachers those of pro-German tendencies like the famous physicist Oswald Thomas, the creator of the Vienna Planetarium, who organized nocturnal excursions with his students in order to observe the heavens. Some students not in classes taught by Oswald Thomas were also allowed to come along on an equal basis. I was one of those. Looking back, it strikes me as improbable that I felt at ease in that company. But the nationalism of that teacher was hardly sullied by antisemitism. One day, for example, he remarked to the Jewish chaplain: 'You're a Jewish nationalist? That's splendid.' After 1945, when I wanted to find out what had become of that chaplain – who was also the rabbi of our district – the required information was supplied by none other than the former Catholic chaplain. It transpired that our rabbi had found refuge in London, where my letter reached him shortly before his death.

Our school also employed some socialist teachers, like my French instructor. He later joined the Resistance and I encountered him after the war as a headmaster. We also had a young and lively history teacher who had been discharged after the *Anschluss* because he refused to leave his wife, who happened to be Jewish. He had joined the Communist party and when I met him again years later he was the head of a department in the Ministry of Education. We were taught German for a time by a writer of dubious qualifications; originally from the Sudetenland, he was a contributor to Josef Goebbels's *Völkischer Beobachter* on the subject of the Viennese theatre. When I learned of this I approached him after class and asked him how he could do it. His reply was cynical but not at all hostile towards me. 'One has to live', he told me, 'and the miserable salary the government pays me doesn't let me live decently.' This incident had no repercussions – I continued to be one of the best students of German.

There was no cleavage among the students in our class along confessional lines of Catholic, Protestant or Jew. I was quite surprised to learn recently from an old class comrade, rediscovered in Washington, DC, that he had never felt really secure because his family had emigrated from Poland. But this anxiety was not a product specifically of the scholastic milieu; it is surely a universal problem connected with immigration from tradition-oriented societies and the encounter with modern culture.

The authorities set up student councils in several schools, not in order to take part in the administration, but to organize extra-curricular activities, each of which were to be run by a special committee. I found myself elected chairman of the literary committee (*Literaturfachgruppe der Schulgemeinde RG VIII*). Our programme envisaged lectures with discussion afterwards, literary readings and theatrical evenings. Accordingly, I proposed to one of our young teachers that he give a lecture on the theme of freedom in German literature, and he agreed. As best I can recall after fifty-six years, he spoke mainly about Schiller. We thought it was splendid. Seated beside me as chairman of the meeting was one of our teachers, present in his capacity as the representative of the staff. The first person to speak from the floor after the lecturer was my friend Fritz Hochwälder, who had left the Gymnasium after the fourth year in order to enter the family upholstery business.[3] Hochwälder, a Jew and socialist, criticized the fact that the speaker had failed to mention Büchner. Now, the adaptation of *Woyzeck* (a fragment of George Büchner's revolutionary drama) by Franz Theodor Csokor, had just recently shaken up the Viennese bourgeoisie.[4] The teacher in charge of supervising the meeting, and who happened to be an editor on the *Reichspost*, the organ of the Christian Social party, took fright and decided to dissolve the proceedings. When I was called upon the next day by the headmaster to provide an explanation, I defended the principle of maintaining contact with those comrades whose personal circumstances did not allow them to continue their studies. 'All that is fine,' he responded, 'but in no case will it be possible to invite elements foreign to our institution to your meetings because I have no means of taking action against them.' (In the original: 'Gegen schulfremde Elemente habe ich keine Disziplinarmassnahmen in der Hand.') We thereupon decided to abandon the activities of the literary committee at the school and transferred ourselves into the city under the name 'Gruppe der Jungen'. It consisted essentially, but not exclusively, of young intellectuals, the majority of them Jewish. But we were not conscious of being in a majority: for us it was simply a circle of friends with liberal ideas. No one was excluded. Everyone who wanted to join our discussions was welcome. The structure of this free association was our response to the restrictions imposed on us by the school administration. Moreover, this freelance activity was not in the least a hindrance to our regular schoolwork; on the contrary, if the press carried a report of our meetings we were likely to be congratulated by our teachers.

But our society was certainly one of the last, except for political or religious groups, to be organized in Austria under the First Republic. Intellectuals from all sides joined in our discussions. And when I had the novel idea of asking Fritz Hochwälder to adapt Schnitzler's *Reigen* as a drama for radio, the head of literature at Austrian radio, himself a Catholic poet, was present at our performance.[5] He congratulated us on the performance and expressed regrets that he was unable to invite us to give a performance over the air. The subject, it seemed, would have provoked too many protests. In addition to meetings, the founding members of our society launched a literary monthly which also, perhaps, has to be regarded as one of the last manifestations of Viennese youth refusing to conform to the on-going political compartmentalization. The title of this review was the *Literarische Monatshefte*, and it was run by two members of our group: one Jewish, Ernst Überall, and the other Catholic, Ludwig Schweinberger. To tell the truth, we were not always sure which confession our friends belonged to. Überall now lives in New York, according to recent information from mutual friends. Others among our young collaborators survived: Alfred Werner-Weintraub acquired a reputation as an art critic in New York; Thomas Otto Brand-Hirschmann,[6] half-Jewish it seems, made a career as a Germanist in higher education in the United States, and we met again some years before his death; Heinz Politzer, who achieved fame as a Germanist through his Kafka research, attained, before his death, a chair at the University of California at Berkeley.[7] I also rediscovered in New York one of our truest and most notable poets, Fritz Brainin. Another collaborator on the *Literarische Monatshefte* whose poems are engraved on our memory has survived in Vienna where she still publishes: Hertha Staub.

There were also other, less literary, journals edited by boys somewhat older than ourselves, but in regular contact with us. Their leading spirits were Erwin Barth-Wehrenalp, Wolfgang Foges and Peter Smolka. When Smolka died recently Chancellor Bruno Kreisky wrote an obituary from which I learned that the latter had also assisted in the distribution of our reviews, in his own way – by hawking them on the streets.

The epoch which I am attempting to evoke covers the years from 1928 until 1934-5. In the earlier years of this period, when we were students at the Gymnasium and carried on our cultural activities in the city, we felt ourselves to be completely free. Not a single obstacle hindered our independent activities. But all that changed in 1931 when I became a student at the university of Vienna. Antisemitism manifested itself there in the noisy presence of many youths, some of whom, from all evidence, were not actually students. Neither the university administrators nor the state authorities took the situation firmly in hand at the outset but let matters slide. On the day of my matriculation I was surprised to be handed a form by a student, which I was supposed to fill in, which contained one space for '*Volkszugehörigkeit*' – a term which is probably best translated into English as 'ethnicity', but with an implicit racial denotation. By the time I came to this heading I had already filled in my nationality, '*Staatsbürgerschaft*', and legal place of residence, '*Heimat-zuständigkeit*' as well as '*Religion*', which was common practice, since in Austria confessional identification was required at every turn. But since this was a requirement imposed on everyone, Jews never felt that it was discriminatory. As to declaring one's nationality, nothing was more commonplace; moreover, the district where you lived normally accorded you a form of local citizenship, authenticated by a certificate called a '*Heimatschein*'. So for each of these three headings I routinely filled in 'Austrian', 'Viennese' and 'Jewish'. To be honest, some had acquired the bad habit of calling themselves '*Mosaisch*' or '*Israelitisch*' in order to avoid the pejorative word '*Jude*'. The Zionists had reacted vigorously against this terminological devaluation, however, and, receptive to their argument, I perhaps on this occasion deliberately employed the adjective '*Jüdisch*'.

But what, I wondered, was the right answer for the fourth heading, that which asked for my '*Volkszugehörigkeit*'? To which 'people' did I belong? The concept of race had never seemed valid to me. The people, or *Volk*, was for me synonymous with the nation. Perhaps the course on the French Revolution given by our excellent history teacher at the Gymnasium inculcated these precepts. I had always felt myself to be a part of the Austrian people – but I thought I understood what was really meant by this new category. One had only to look at the face of the fellow who had handed me the questionnaire. In defiance of all reasonable expectations, this was no university employee but rather a young representative of one of the powerful antisemitic student organizations which the university officially permitted to monitor the registration of all new students on the spot. 'So that's the way things work here,' I said to myself. Attempting to strike a compromise between an answer which seemed to me plausible, and that which was expected by the simpleton opposite me, I wrote in the blank space 'Austrian Jew'. He thereupon took the sheet away from me and openly crossed out the adjective 'Austrian'. To him, the *Volk* to which the Austrians belonged were the Germans. But a Jew could still claim the 'nationality' of being Austrian. In 1931 no one had yet acquired the power to deny that. But an Austrian 'people' simply did not exist for the nationalist students, who would only accept under the rubric '*Volkszugehörigkeit*' answers like 'German', 'Serbian', 'Hungarian', 'Jew', or some other, on the condition that it had the connotation of 'blood'. So this was what I encountered as soon as I set foot in the hallowed sanctuary of the university of Vienna, access to which was even denied to the police.

Now and then, and with increasing frequency, the door of a lecture theatre would be abruptly thrown open from the outside, and hordes of youths armed with weapons like clubs and brass-knuckles appeared shouting 'Jews out!' I particularly remember one such interruption during a lecture in German literature by Professor Josef Nadler himself. This limited man, who was none the less well regarded in the right-wing nationalist press, would not stand for having his class interrupted. Greatly angered, he cried out to these kill-joys: 'The greatness of the German people comes from their commitment to work!' Confronted by these fine words the riff-raff provisionally retreated; but when the class was over the instructor, in his turn, withdrew, leaving the lecture hall to the Jew-hunters. If some Jewish students were unable to complete their studies at the university of Vienna during those years it was mainly by reason of the acute insecurity in this 'academic sanctuary'.

We knew that the hours between ten and noon were the most dangerous, because the most important classes were scheduled for the latter part of the morning. One day, when we were due to take a

French phonetic examination with Professor Elise Richter, we arrived at the university to discover that a fight was in progress in the university forecourt. Since it was out of the question to go there unarmed, our little group of examinees crossed the Ringstrasse to wait for our teacher's arrival on the tram. Elise Richter saw the impossibility of entering the university building and we wound up taking the semester's exam at her home. Many years later I learned that Elise Richter came from Jewish origins and that she had been dismissed from her post the day after the *Anschluss*, was barred from the library, and was eventually deported to Theresienstadt, where she died, 78 years of age. Recently, the Austrian government put up a plaque to her memory at the University of Vienna which I had the honour of dedicating.[8]

I do not know under what pretext two of my German instructors were forced into premature retirement: one of them, Robert Franz Arnold, specialized in literature, while the other, Max Hermann Jellinek, was a linguist. We were certain that their departure in 1934 was due to their Jewish origins. Some circles without doubt viewed such a background as incompatible with providing instruction in the German language and literature. Moreover, neither Jellinek nor Arnold could ever have obtained a full professorship – they only attained the status of *Extraordinarious*, roughly equivalent to a Reader in the British university system, or associate professor in the North American system. The principal chairs, at least in that discipline, were reserved for persons with an impeccable pedigree in the eyes of the responsible authorities at that time. It should be borne in mind that while Red Vienna was in the hands of the Social Democrats it was the Christian conservative Austrian government which administered the university. Thus my two professors could be simply forced out well before the arrival of Hitler in Vienna – despite the fact that professor Arnold was legally a Roman Catholic, as I learned when his widow sent me a notice of his death in 1936.

Viennese antisemitism made the university a favourite stamping ground at the beginning of the 1930s not only from a desire to prevent Jewish students from obtaining their degrees, but also because of the simple fact that the tradition of academic sanctuary gave the ringleaders shelter from the police. This situation finally so completely undermined the authority of the state that it cancelled this legal immunity. From now on the entrance of students into classrooms was tightly controlled by uniformed police; it became mandatory not only to present one's credentials as a student but to prove that one was officially enrolled in the course. In those days the report book of the student listed all the courses for which he was registered during the year, and only those who could show that they were regularly enrolled were admitted to the lecture hall.

We would soon find, however, that this belated concern with ensuring equality among students had scarcely anything to do with genuine law enforcement, but rather with the aim of imposing their own rules. There was no question of equality when it came to harvesting the fruits of our studies, at least where it concerned those who wished to pursue a teaching career. There, as in other fields, it was pointed out to us that the economic crisis obliged the government to give first thought to the plight of the native population. From 1933, if my memory is correct, a Jew was no longer able to obtain a teaching post at secondary level. The key term invoked in this connection was *bodenständig*, theoretically meaning a long-established native of a place. However, a Jew whose family had resided in Vienna for several generations was not considered, under this regime, as *bodenständig* – while a recently arrived Sudeten German was so regarded: and this several years before the *Anschluss*!

But international cultural exchanges continued and involved, in part, the sending of teaching assistants to schools in the countries with which such relations existed. Some Austrian students were thus designated for temporary working visits to France, which did not seek to exclude Jewish candidates, having come to the entirely correct conclusion that the Austrian government was antisemitic. That is how I came to arrive in France in 1934, as mentioned at the outset of this essay. It was often possible for an assistant to extend his stay after the first year, and even beyond that. This was the experience of some of my non-Jewish comrades who arrived in France at the same time that I did. As it happened, my extension was requested by the French government with some insistence since the mayor of the town where I was teaching was also the Minister of Commerce and gave strong support to my request. When I presented my request to the ministry in Vienna, however, they coldly informed me that the teaching assistants ought to return home in order to give the benefit of their knowledge of the French language to Austrian students. The functionary who came out with this argument knew perfectly well that in the adjoining department no Jew would be considered for even a probationary post in secondary education. The Chancellor responsible for this policy was Kurt Schuschnigg.

But let me conclude these fragmentary evocations of Vienna around 1930 by briefly mentioning the unforgettable impressions made on the Jewish youth of my generation by the artistic richness of Viennese life: the operas, the concerts, the theatres, the exhibitions. Often it was possible to establish direct personal contact with the artists. I mentioned above that our 'Gruppe der Jungen' welcomed certain writers; and with others we made definite contacts which have remained decisive throughout our lives. I will resist the temptation to give a long list of the names of popular and classical singers, actors and comedians who have remained idols for us, just as a Josef Kainz or a Selma Kurz were for our parents. All the same, I must mention Lotte Lehmann, the unforgettable creator of the role of the Marschallin in *Der Rosenkavalier*. She ended her career by teaching singing in California, and I was very moved when I attended a concert at the Lotte Lehmann Hall at the University of California in Santa Barbara. Needless to say, the Burgtheater made a profound impression while the Volkstheater, at that time under the direction of Rudolf Beer, a Jew, acquainted us with the contemporary repertoire and presented some of the greatest actors on tour. And the internationally-renowned Theater in der Josefstadt, under the direction of another Jew, Max Reinhardt, sparkled with incomparable productions, classic and modern, including foreign plays. . . . And on the margin of official cultural life the influence and legacy of Karl Kraus was enormous, even though we did not always share his opinions. . . .

Here I must close these recollections of my youth as an assimilated Viennese Jew. I hope that my unsystematic approach will none the less serve to provide a first-hand testimony which will give some insight into the historical processes analysed by other contributors to this colloquium.

CHAPTER 10

THE JEWS OF VIENNA FROM THE *ANSCHLUSS* TO THE HOLOCAUST

Gerhard Botz

Austria, and particularly Vienna, have managed so far to obscure their participation in the history of the Third Reich. After all, the 1943 Moscow Declaration of the Allied foreign ministers declared Austria the first victim of Hitler's aggression, and the whole self-image of the Second Republic is based on this simplification of history.

In this way their connection with, and responsibility for, the Nazi dictatorship have been completely removed from the historical consciousness of Austrians, who could logically assume that the extinction of independent statehood in 1938 was followed by a seven-year historical vacuum. Virtually none of the existing general histories of modern Austria stresses the considerable contribution to the functioning of the Third Reich of a large part of the population.[1] The major role played in the persecution and annihilation of the Jews by the Viennese – and not just party members or their 'Reich-German' superiors – would have to be singled out. I cannot present here an outline of the end of Vienna's Jews without calling attention to these facts. A change of perspective is required from one which simply regards the Jews as victims of an imported antisemitic policy arising from German National Socialism to one which also looks at the identity of persecutors and the nature of their socio-economic motives.[2]

An analysis of the socio-economic forces and the political measures accompanying the persecution of the Jews in Vienna from 1938 to 1945 also allows one to demonstrate that the sharp controversy which has sprung up recently concerning the 'Final Solution', particularly among German historians,[3] is being conducted too narrowly. In this German debate two points of view confront each other: the first argues that Hitler's personality, his actions and an early pre-determined plan of the Führer's had envisaged the 'Final Solution', which was then consistently put into practice;[4] a second, opposing view stresses the gradual, step-by-step development of the concrete measures of persecution in the Third Reich. According to Hans Mommsen,[5] the most explicit exponent of the second view, the cumulative radicalization of National Socialist anti-Jewish policy arose chiefly from the internal dynamics of the rival power centres of the Third Reich[6] and from the consequences of foreign and politico-military developments which moved towards the destruction of the Jews within the German sphere of power without direct initiatives by Hitler.

In my opinion both positions underestimate the significance of the antisemitic mobilization of considerable parts of the population in favour of Nazi measures against the Jews; both underestimate the extent to which the persecution and annihilation of the Jews satisfied immediate economic and social requirements of large groups and classes in a very concrete manner – a process of persecution which in fact acted as a surrogate for the social welfare policies the Nazis had promised their followers. The combination of antisemitic persecution and the satisfaction of material interests does not appear to me, at least in the Viennese case, to have been simply an attempt by the National Socialist regime to justify the persecution of the Jews – as Mommsen stresses to have been the case in the whole of the Third Reich – rather, material interests were one of antisemitism's most powerful motivating forces. On this factor rested the 'popular unanimity'[7] of Viennese antisemitism since the nineteenth century, which had always been more than an ideological concept of racial values concerning the depravity of the Jews. It was no coincidence that Schönerer's ideological, racial antisemitism had been denied success with Vienna's masses,[8] while Lueger's pragmatic, economic, religio-cultural-based antisemitism could be made into the integrating force of his Catholic lower-middle-class movement.[9] The precondition for this was that the Jewish part of the population was not a tiny minority, but represented a sufficiently large potential economic target, or was perceived as such by the antisemites. And, as a number of the foregoing chapters in the present volume have repeatedly indicated, this was the case in Vienna, where a pattern of relative Jewish affluence existed until the Nazi takeover. Viennese Jews were rather highly concentrated in middle-class occupations and the learned professions, as well as in capitalist circles.[10] Thus the antisemites were of the opinion, and not without some justification, that harassing the Jews could bring them collective benefits. In fact, antisemitism was to a great extent also a substitute for social policy in favour of the non-Jewish population at the cost of Jews and other persecuted minorities in Vienna and other central and east European cities.[11] It was this high economic and social status of Jews which became the theme of the Nazi persecution in Vienna after the *Anschluss*.

It was therefore not just pure demagoguery and propaganda in preparation for the persecution of the Jews when the *Völkischer Beobachter*, in its Vienna edition of 26 April 1938, wrote about the popular mood six weeks after the *Anschluss*:

By the year 1942 the Jewish element in Vienna will have to have been wiped out and made to disappear. No shop, no business will be permitted by that time to be under Jewish management, no Jew may find anywhere any opportunity to earn a living and with the exception of those streets where the old Jews and Jewesses are using up their money, the export of which is prohibited, while they wait for death, nothing of it may show itself in the city. (. . .) No one who knows Viennese opinion regarding the Jewish question will be surprised that the four years in which the economic death sentence on the Jews is to be executed seems much too long a time to them. They are puzzled by all the fuss, by the pedantic attention to the maintenance and protection of Jewish property; after all it is very simple: 'The Jew must go – and his cash must remain.' (. . .)

While in many instances National Socialism drew the attention of North-Germans to the private, almost unpolitical danger of the Jews, in Vienna, on the contrary, the Nazis professed a commitment to responsible education of the public. This posture was intended to demonstrate the blamelessness and purity of the movement – and thus to stem the exuberant local antisemitic radicalism, steering the understandably violent reactions to the Jewish excesses of a whole century into orderly channels.

This means, and let everyone take note, because Germany is a state based on the law: nothing happens in our state except by due process of law. (. . .) Here there will be no pogroms, certainly not through Mrs Hinterhuber wanting to get at Sarah Cohen, in the third courtyard, on the half-landing, by the watertap.[12]

These were the problems and perspectives of the Vienna Nazis immediately after the *Anschluss*. The measures of anti-Jewish persecution until the 'Final Solution' – 'eradication' from the economy was the metaphor used in the *Völkischer Beobachter* of April 1938 – followed by and large these basic themes. But the persecution of the Jews in Vienna presented itself in a variety of forms, depending on particular circumstances: as a groundswell of spontaneous protest, or as a response to either an attachment of traditional elites to a bureaucratic concept of 'law and order', or to the assertion of the anti-institutional radicalism of the activists of the Nazi movement, or even to the requirements of the foreign policies of the Greater German Reich.[13] Without intending to claim a teleological progress in a straight line in the 'extirpation' of Jews from Viennese society, I shall nevertheless show that the persecution of the Jews in Vienna from 1938 to 1942 moved forward in phases, with each of the various manifestations of antisemitism in Austria being built on the preceding one or at least complementary to it. One can distinguish eight distinctive stages in the progressive elimination of the Jews from Viennese society between 1938 and 1943; these eight stages were required for the progress of the Holocaust – the ultimate 'elimination' from society in the annihilation industries.

1 *Exploration of the perpetrators' emotional potential and demonstration of Jewish defencelessness.* In Vienna the *Anschluss* was immediately accompanied by events resembling pogroms, such as had not occurred until then in the 'Old Reich', that is to say in Germany before the *Anschluss* of Austria.[14] This was because the *Anschluss* was not just a transfer of power by a kind of occupation, but was at the same time an internal take-over of power by the Austrian Nazis and a popular rising. The political and social discontent that had accumulated over the years among the middle-class following of National Socialism was discharged with elemental force against the Jewish part of the population. In the foreground were symbolic acts aimed at the destruction of a sense of identity: humiliations and arrests, but also brutal physical assaults and robbery, while 'scrubbing-squads' of Jews were made to clean the streets or the quarters of the storm-troopers. Children had to deface their parents' business premises with abusive words – *Jude* was thought to be one – and strictly orthodox Jews were forced to commit acts of sacrilege. Not only Nazis but also fellow-travellers and people who cared but little about National Socialism took part in week-long raids, with or without the 'authorization' of the

NSDAP.[15] The targets of these raids were the private apartments of Jewish bankers and of members of the intelligentsia, of the Jewish middle classes as well as the tens of thousands of poverty-stricken Jews, the Jewish-owned department stores of the *Mariahilfer-Strasse* as well as the pathetic little shops in the *Leopoldstadt*.[16] Jewellery, cash, clothing, furs, carpets, works of art and furniture were carried off by the plundering mob.

The shock suffered at that time by so many Viennese Jews can still be discerned in the many novels which have attempted to come to terms with that pogrom which until then had been altogether unimaginable in a 'civilized' country.[17] The despair drove many Jews, particularly of the upper middle classes, to commit suicide – as many as 220 in March alone.[18] Every other problem aired in the correspondence columns of the *Neues Wiener Tagblatt* in the beginning of April 1938 appeared under code words, such as 'Question of Life and Death 1938', 'Kismet', 'Worried', 'What is To Be Done?', 'Desperate Wife and Mother', 'Distraught', 'Altogether in Despair', '1938', 'Unhappy', 'Question of Existence'.[19]

This pogrom-like situation might at the outset have been somewhat encouraged by the new men in power as a safety valve for the uncontrolled social revolutionary tendencies among their own followers; however, the longer the state of chaotic interventions in the economic and administrative life of Vienna continued, the higher rose the anguish of the leading Nazi functionaries. Most anxious of all was Josef Bürckel, who had been appointed Reich-Commissioner in Austria and who feared that the National Socialist 'Reconstruction' would be hindered by the chaos. Above all, Berlin had expressed concern that 'in Austria there had occurred widespread confiscations of property' which had been impossible to control.[20] Therefore measures were taken, even before the 'plebiscite' of 10 April 1938, to rein in the pogrom.[21] This led to a phase of seemingly legal actions whose function it was to prepare the further progress of anti-Jewish measures.

2 *The conceptual delineation and definition of the enemy group.* As long as it was possible for non-Jews to become victims of persecution because of the blurred outlines of both the popular and the 'scientific' idea of 'the Jew', there was no assurance that radical measures of persecution would be tolerated by the large but not actively participating parts of the population. This principle was later to become clear during the euthanasia actions. The category 'Jews' had,

of course, been definitively delineated by the Nuremberg racial laws, which were formally introduced into Austria on 20 May 1938. They stated what legally constituted being a 'Jew', the criteria being in the last resort based on religious-historical factors rather than racial-biological nations. Since Nazi genealogists made good use of the resulting boom, everyone soon knew whether or not he came under the classification of 'Jew'.

This process of authoritative definition found its clearest pre-liminary expression in the special marking of identity cards for Jews. In July and August 1938, legislation was introduced covering the entire Reich which required Jews to adopt the distinctive first names 'Israel' or 'Sarah'. The passports of Jews were also marked with a large red 'J' on the first page. From the age of about fifteen, all Jews were obliged to carry the identity card at all times; they also had to declare their Jewish identity 'unasked, and on pain of prosecution, whenever they had dealings with the civil or Party authorities'.[22] Moreover from the beginning of November 1938, all Jewish-owned shops had to display inscriptions in Hebrew lettering.

In the course of the temporary advance of traditional authoritarian-bureaucratic tendencies in the Nazi policy in Austria during the summer of 1938, this restricting categorization was the precondition for a sort of 'legal' (i.e. regulated by law) antisemitism which showed itself in the schools, the professions, and the economy. In the area of education, blow followed blow against the Jews after the plebiscite of 10 April 1938. On 24 April a *Numerus clausus* was introduced for Jewish university students (2 per cent), followed on 27 April by separation of Jewish pupils in the secondary schools and the establishment of eight purely Jewish secondary schools, and on 9 May by the same action with regards to primary, comprehensive and trade schools. By 1 July 183 Jewish teachers had been dismissed, and the number of Jewish pupils of compulsory school age diminished accordingly as many Jewish schools were closed down. From the autumn, only 1 per cent of university students were to be of Jewish descent; on 14 November they were completely excluded. Instead of the previous 6,000 secondary school pupils there were now only 500, all of them crammed into the single remaining secondary school. Altogether, approximately 16,000 pupils had been affected by the 'de-schooling' which had taken place in April. 'At first they were taught in accommodation provided by the city. At the end of the school year 1938/39 all public education of Jewish children was forbidden.'[23]

By the end of November 1938, those of mixed race were also excluded not only from the free professions, the press, literature, theatre, film, music and creative arts, but also from the professional bodies of physicians, pharmacists, lawyers and notaries public. They thereby lost to their 'Aryan' competitors their right to practise.

By these measures, which carried out earlier demands of German nationalist and Christian Social antisemitism, the social and organizational networks of Viennese Jewry were destroyed, even before the physical destruction of the Jews set in. With the loss of the multiplicity of everyday Jewish social organizations, Jewish identity also lost its social basis in Vienna. Thus, Nazism destroyed an important precondition of the cultural achievements of the Viennese Jews.

3 *Destruction of economic means of subsistence.* The same kind of 'legal' discrimination was carried through in the economic field. In the public services and in some sectors of private enterprise, Jewish employees and workers were dismissed in large numbers, which led to a temporary increase in the rate of unemployment in Vienna. In spite of that, some rabid Austrian Nazis found too slow the process which had begun in March and was to continue for several more months. According to a plan of the *Ostmark*'s economics minister, Hans Fischböck, all 200,000 of Vienna's Jews ought to relinquish their workplaces to unemployed 'Aryans' in one comprehensive action. However, in contrast to the public sector and the free professions, the governmental agencies moved in fact with some caution in relation to private enterprise. Economic considerations were decisive. Reich-Commissioner Bürckel, who, notwithstanding his wide-ranging powers regarding 'Jewish policy', was under strict instructions from Göring, proceeded from three principles. The aims were: first, to remove 'the Jew' unconditionally from the economy and finally from Austria altogether, especially from Vienna; second, 'de-judaization' was to proceed in a way which would prevent any serious damage to export or domestic trade; and, third, it was required that the 'Jewish question' be solved in a legal manner by means of severe legislation in order to preserve the economy intact.[24]

These guidelines were difficult to put into effect at first, particularly in Vienna. In contrast to the 'Old Reich', where the 'de-judaization' of the economy was dragging on, in Austria after March 1938 the 'spontaneous Aryanization' was carried out completely without any orders from above and without following rules. Looking back, Reich-Commissioner Bürckel remarked: 'The splendid history of National Socialism and the rising in Austria has had a cloud cast over it by the extent of robbery and theft which occurred in the first few weeks, which required me to take most severe action.'[25]

The extent of 'Aryanization' had become so great in Vienna that it could no longer be met by improvisations as in the 'Old Reich'. According to National Socialist estimates, of the 146,000 businesses in Vienna, 36,000 (25 per cent) had been in Jewish hands; of the capital value of these firms – 800 million *Reichsmark* – 300 million was Jewish.[26] Even after the wave of 'spontaneous Aryanization', 26,000 of these enterprises still remained. In some cases these were handed over to approximately 25,000 'Aryan administrators', which meant Nazis.[27] In others the enterprises were continued in the form of so-called 'NSBO-enterprises' (National Socialist *Betriebs-Organisation*-firms) by National Socialist co-operatives of the 'Aryan' employees, which were then put under the control of NSDAP.

To prevent senseless destruction of the economic capacity of the *Ostmark* and to mobilize for the Balkan trade which was a burning interest of Göring's, Bürckel had no choice but to legalize the system of commissars which had spontaneously emerged as a 'necessary evil', to get the policy to contain the worst excesses, and to attempt, in the months following the *Anschluss*, a half-way orderly method of 'Aryanization'. In consequence 'Aryanisation Instructions' were speeded up, dictated by events in Vienna for the whole Reich at the end of April 1938. Administrative methods developed in Austria soon became models for the 'Old Reich' as well as for the 'newly-acquired territories of the Reich'.

The Nazi party itself increased the economic dangers by making 'Aryanization' into an instrument of social and economic welfare in the hands of its members and followers – a process facilitated by the size of the Jewish economic sector in Vienna. At the same time this 'middle-class' welfare system came into conflict with the economic, and particularly macro-economic-orientated organs of the Nazi state. Most of the 'provisional managers' (*Kommissare*) were either unable or unprepared to take a long-term view of economic management, while on the other hand the 'Four-Year Plan' was directed toward economic efficiency for war. The interests of the non-Jewish middle class, moreover, favoured the liquidation of those frequently uneconomic small and medium-sized Jewish businesses, a measure which was put into effect towards the end of 1938. The Vienna Nazi leadership was thus able to justify accelerating the concentration and improvising the structure of Vienna's economy, which was limping along behind that of the 'Old Reich' anyway, even at the danger of causing bitter resentment among the 25,000 'provisional managers'.

For the Viennese Jews, 'Aryanization' meant mostly economic expropriation. The most rapid 'Aryanization' to the end of 1938 involved 'several hundred Jewish enterprises of importance for defence and economic development' – mainly large-scale enterprises – 'all well-known obviously Jewish businesses' as well as the big department stores.[28] These especially were the targets of spontaneous or orchestrated antisemitic outbursts. The very large Jewish industrial enterprises and joint stock companies were approached by the Third Reich with circumspection; the property of foreign Jews was not touched until the outbreak of war.

The radical policy of 'Aryanization', tried and carried out mostly in Vienna through a combination of spontaneous action from below and official regulation from above, earned distinction for the Austrian Minister for Economics, Labour and Finance, Dr Hans Fischböck. He had already aroused the admiration of Göring and the managers of the economy of the 'Old Reich' in the autumn. In consequence this procedure was applied to the whole of the Reich at the end of 1938. The Austrian procedure became a kind of model for the remaining parts of the Greater German Reich.

4 *Forced emigration.* After a large part of Viennese Jewry had been ruined through the destruction of their economic base, they were obliged to leave the country. But they now faced such obstacles as travel expenses, immigration quotas, fees, the limited chances of integration in other countries, and the barriers of German bureaucracy and the 'Reich-escape tax' (*Reichsfluchtsteuer*). The more successful the expropriation of the Jews became, the more difficult it became for Viennese Jews to find avenues for emigration. The Gestapo in Vienna therefore devised the following solution, as the chief of the Gestapo, Heydrich, reported after the *Kristallnacht*:

> We did it by demanding a certain sum of money through the Jewish community from the rich Jews who wanted to emigrate. With this sum, plus some payments in foreign currency a number of poor Jews could also be got out. The problem was not to get rid of the rich Jews but of the Jewish mob.[29]

The Gestapo utilized the enforced co-operation of the Jewish community organization, the *Kultusgemeinde*, a division of labour between the persecutor and persecuted which was to prove its usefulness right into the Nazi extermination camps. Eichmann had come to Vienna for this task and was to excel himself in the creation and management of the 'Central Office for Jewish Emigration in Vienna' to such an extent that it opened up a further career for him.[30] As in other areas of the anti-Jewish policy, this Central Office had grown out of the necessity of mastering the administrative problems of Nazism's Jewish policy in Vienna.

The activities of the Vienna Central Office considerably speeded up the enforced emigration of Jews, which reached its high point of almost 10,000 emigrants as early as September 1938, one month after its foundation. Between the *Anschluss* and the end of July 1938, only 18,000 Jews left Vienna as emigrants. In the three months to October 1938, however, 32,000 Jews emigrated; and by July of the next year a further 54,000 followed. On 30 November 1939 the count was 126,445 Jewish emigrants, a number which did not significantly increase later on. In addition to the profits gained through 'Aryanization', this expulsion of the Jews brought the Reich the sum of 1.6 million dollars which had been raised by Jewish immigration aid societies by the end of November 1939. After the beginning of the war Jewish emigration soon came to an end. Even so, another 24,500 Viennese Jews managed to emigrate during the Second World War.[31]

5 Radicalization and Reichs-Kristallnacht. In the late summer of 1938 the bureaucratically softened law-and-order phase of the Nazi regime in Austria was followed by a newly radicalized policy. The threatening economic and socio-political crisis brought about by the increased armaments policy urgently required further foreign policy and military expansion,[32] which went hand in hand with increasing severity of control over internal political adversaries, national minorities and Jews. The *Reichs-Kristallnacht* of 9 November 1938[33] marked the beginning of a new phase in the politics of the Third Reich. Vienna, once again in the vanguard, had already witnessed pogrom-like attacks against Jews in October.

The Vienna pogrom was probably more violent and the cause of more bloodshed, as far as the Jewish population was concerned, than that in the 'Old Reich'. Apart from the thousands of shops and dwellings demolished in Vienna, 42 synagogues and prayer rooms were burnt down, at least 27 Jews were killed and 88 were severely injured. In addition, the numbers of those who out of despair made an end to their lives rose by leaps and bounds. In Vienna 6,547 were arrested in the course of the *Judenaktion*, 3,700 of whom were taken to the concentration camp of Dachau straight away. The greater part of the concentration camp detainees were released only during the first part of 1939 on production of proof of emigration documents, or on the condition of emigration within fourteen days.[34]

The result of this 'unchaining of the lowest instincts', as the representatives of 'orderly, legal' antisemitism in the Gestapo uneasily put it,[35] brought with it in the end a speeding-up of 'Aryanization' and a radicalization of the entire anti-Jewish policy as Hitler's foreign policy moved towards the Second World War.

6 *Spatial segregation (ghettoization)*. A few days after the pogrom of November 1938, there was an intensified revival of 'spontaneous Aryanization' of houses and flats such as had occurred in the days immediately after the *Anschluss*. This time, however, the robbery of Jewish dwellings was managed from above as a means of propaganda and served as indemnification of 'comrades, men of the people, who had served the Nazi movement in especially deserving ways'.[36] To cope with this problem, which assumed immense proportions, the Vienna City Council – but not the Reich authorities or the NSDAP – devised administrative procedures and prepared a draft law to deprive Jewish tenants of protection. Of particular interest to the Nazi City Council administration – which calculated a housing shortage of about 70,000 dwellings for the total indigenous population of Vienna plus new arrivals from the Reich – were the dwellings occupied by Jews, originally also numbering 70,000 and representing approximately 10 per cent of the total housing stock of Vienna. By the end of 1938 alone, following forced emigration and 'spontaneous Aryanization', 44,000 Jewish homes had been occupied by 'Aryans', but there remained more than 26,000 dwellings to be 'Aryanized'.

Once again, a problem was tackled by the Reich authorities for the territories under their control only after the solution had presented itself in Vienna. The structure of the housing problem and the acute need for accommodation in Vienna, given the fact that Jewish property constituted a significant economic share, created in the city a special radical form of persecution of the Jews. The accommodation occupied by the Jews, and therefore at the disposal of the Nazi regime, totalled 70,000 dwellings – 6,000 more than the Social

Democrats in 'Red Vienna'[37] had managed in fifteen years of intensive building policy! The intensification of the war economy in the Third Reich and its internal supply crisis in 1939 made the procedures developed in Vienna worth copying throughout the Nazi sphere of power. I have characterized this specific substitutive form of socio-political procedure, including certain aspects of 'business Aryanization', as *negative social policy.*[38]

Complementary to the 'Aryanization' of homes was the development of semi-ghettoes in city districts along the Danube Canal, particularly in the *Leopoldstadt*. The concentration of the Viennese Jews (still numbering almost 100,000 in October 1939 and now defined as 'Jews by race' in the sense of the Nuremberg laws) in single houses, entire blocks and parts of some districts was partly a side-effect of the legal framework of the 'Aryanization procedure', and partly a deliberate policy of the Viennese Nazi district leaders. This process of relocation went on until it found its final conclusion in 1942.

This process of segregation again aroused the objections of those Nazi functionaries, party members and 'comrades' who were affected by the ghetto formation; they insistently demanded the removal of the Jews from their district, not least so as to seize for themselves the remaining, often overcrowded, Jewish homes. As early as July 1939, a plan had surfaced in Reich-Commissioner Bürckel's office to expel the remaining Viennese Jews to barracked encampments; the plan envisaged 'an intensive productive employment of the inmates'.[39] The Viennese City administration clearly had in mind two concentration camp-like labour camps in the vicinity of Vienna and by the beginning of September 1939 had prepared detailed building plans.

A change in these plans came with the outbreak of war. The planned 'overall measures' of which Heydrich informed the commanders of the *SS-Einsatzgruppen* in Hitler's name on September 1939, envisaged the early deportation of 300,000 poorer Jews from 'Greater Germany' to Poland. They also cast a glance at a 'Final Goal' (*Endziel*) which was not yet clearly defined.[40] Only after the rapid conquest of Poland made that more comprehensive solution appear realistic did the Viennese authorities abandon their plans of re-locating the Jews in a nearby vicinity. That Hitler had the 'declared intention' in supporting this re-location measure 'to cleanse the *Ostmark* of Jews as a beginning' is supported by sources.[41] A memorandum in Bürckel's staff files states: 'This re-location procedure will be concluded in three quarters of a year at the latest.

With it the Jewish problem in Vienna will have been completely solved.'[42]

It cannot be excluded, given the early date of the proposed deportation initiative in Vienna, that Viennese anti-Jewish policy had an influence on the Reich policy in this area as well. After all, Hitler may well have looked with greatest interest, as well as sense of first-hand knowledge, at that city where he had first learned of the 'Jewish problem'.[43] We see here a typical oscillation and opportunism in the anti-Jewish policy: always working toward the ultimate goal within the realm of the possible, never restricting itself to any single line of policy.

How this deportation policy was implemented in Vienna, in so far as it had not simply arisen from the pressure by the 'Aryan' Viennese, is revealed in the following citation from a report to Bürckel by a National Socialist *Ortsgruppenleiter* from a Vienna Jewish residential area (*Rossau-Alsergrund*) in 3 October 1939:

> The extent of anti-Jewish feeling in the population is beyond measure. It is entirely thanks to the exertion of all our energy that in no case have riots occurred. I am fully conscious that this cannot be carried on forever, and that it is a pretty thankless task for a political leader, you will understand. The populace constantly points to the fact that the Jews are the only ones responsible for the war, and that they ought to be dealt with accordingly. People cannot understand why Jews receive the same quantities of food-stuffs as do Aryans. They fail to understand why Jews are not conscripted for forced labour and are left to pursue their dark schemes. The population is completely convinced that the Jews know of ways and means to obtain more goods, even these days, than they are entitled to. Proof, however, is not available, since this would be the task of the police to provide, who cannot cope in our Jew-infested district. The population sees it sometimes as a sign of weakness that organs of the Party are not entitled to do away with abuses. People feel themselves severely disadvantaged, as long as 'Aryans' have to live in damp cellars while Jews are permitted to wallow in beautiful apartments. The morale of part of the population is being so thoroughly affected by their living in such close proximity with the Jews that it will not be possible for many years, in spite of great efforts, to win them over. Therefore I propose:
> 1 Either to set male Jews to work in mines or similar labour

where they can be supervised easily, and accommodate their female family members in nearby camps.

2 Or, should this not be possible, to consider their evacuation to Poland, east of the Vistula, since it is all the same whether 2.5 or 2.7 million Jews live in Poland.

3 Should this be impossible as well, then the transfer of Jews should be carried out under other considerations than hitherto. Either:
   a. to those habitations which are unhealthy (mainly cellar flats where even today Aryans have to live with their children) or
   b. into apartments exposed to the dangers of air raids (4th or 5th floor).[44]

Procurement of accommodation at the expense of the Jews, i.e. negative social policy, also played a central role in all other newly conquered territories of the Third Reich and in the 'Final Solution', though I shall not go into the question of how far this applied to Poland and Romania. It was probably less a mere instrument of rationalization and pseudo-moral legitimation than an effective moving force towards the 'Final Solution'.[45]

Until the beginning of 1942, by which time the victorious *Wehrmacht* had opened up new perspectives on Jewish transportation to bleak and unhealthy reservations (previously the French colony of Madagascar had been mooted), insurmountable obstacles had arisen due to the internally competing institutions of the Third Reich; hence the deportation of Jews did not really get under way. However, as early as October 1939 there had been two transports of Jews from Vienna to Nisko; although their continuation was prevented by Himmler 'for reasons of technical difficulties'.[46] Obviously, the pressure of events, and the requisite internal radicalization of the Third Reich in the phase of the Blitzkrieg, had not yet developed sufficiently to overcome the obstacles to such mass deportation measures.

7 *Realizing the Nazi stereotype of the 'Jew'*. The formation of ghettoes and the earlier elimination of the Jews from the economy and the rule of law had led to a further deterioration of the already intolerable situation of the Viennese Jews. In this way the National Socialist persecution policy created a multitude of Jews who corresponded to the stereotype promoted by Julius Streicher in *Der Stürmer*: filthy, down-and-out Jews who snatched greedily at any

chance of business dealings. The consequence of the persecution re-enforced the propagandistic stereotype of the 'Jews' and broke the remains of solidarity on the part of their 'Aryan' neighbours at the same time. The 'Jew' became as disgusting for the 'Aryans' as the antisemites had depicted him as being since time immemorial. For 'vermin' and 'parasites' nothing but extermination was appropriate, as *Völkisch* antisemites had already imagined several decades earlier.[47] Only in the wake of this process of de-humanizing the Jews did it become possible further to radicalize the persecution, thus making the Holocaust itself capable of realization.

There remained in Vienna at the beginning of October 1939, 66,000 so-called 'persons of Jewish faith' (*Glaubensjuden*), 39,000 persons of so-called 'Jewish race' (*Rassejuden*),[48] and approximately 13,000 foreign and stateless Jews. Their further pauperization and marginalization was once more put in motion by 'legislative measures'. As early as September 1939 a curfew was imposed and the existing limitations on access to parks and recreational facilities were tightened even further. At the beginning of January 1940 the times during which Jews, whose ration cards were marked with a 'J', could enter provision stores were limited to those when goods in demand had been sold out.

In 1942 Jews were forbidden to obtain cigars, eggs, meat, full-fat milk and white flour. After they had already been forced in 1939 to hand over all jewellery and precious metal, they were now robbed of fur and woollen clothing. Since the end of 1941 they had been excluded from all public social services, as well as from listening to the radio, use of public transport and use of the telephone. They were forbidden to leave the area of Greater Vienna without permission. The apex of social discrimination was reached with the law of September, 1941, which required the identification of Jews by a yellow Star of David – *Judenstern* – which was to be worn prominently on the left side of the chest. Without it Jews were prohibited to show themselves in public.[49]

A National Socialist report about the economic situation of Vienna's Jews in the summer of 1940 stated 'that they mostly had no income, apart from isolated cases like doctors and dental technicians who treated Jews and lawyers who represented Jews'. Of Vienna's 'Jews by faith' about 40,000 were without means. In September 1939, 35,500 persons were fed each day by the Jewish communal administration and 31,364, about one-half of the remaining 66,000, received cash grants. The budget of the Jewish community required a

monthly sum of 1.4 to 1.5 million *Reichsmark* in order to fulfil all
the tasks of social support with which it had been charged and in
order to finance emigration up to August 1939. Since these large
sums came mainly from foreign-aid committees, the start of the war
meant an almost total collapse of Jewish self-aid.

The situation of these Viennese Jews was made even more difficult
by the fact that 40 per cent of them were above 60 years of age, with
those less than 40 years old amounting to only 19 per cent. In
addition, women were overrepresented by a factor of two to one.
The preponderance of the aged and of women was a consequence of
emigration – for economically active persons, men, and middle- and
upper-class Jews emigration was less difficult – and the extremely
deteriorated conditions of life which had made the remaining
Viennese Jews into a moribund community even before their
deportation.[50]

8 *Removal and annihilation.* In June 1940 Hitler informed the new
Gauleiter and Reich-Commissioner of Vienna, Baldur von Schirach,
that it was his firm intention to remove the Jews of Vienna to the
Generalgovernement in Poland. Half a year later the Führer repeated
that 'the 60,000 Jews who still live in the *Reichsgau* Vienna are to be
despatched with all haste to the *Generalgovernement* even now in
wartime, because of the need for housing in Vienna.'[51] And in
November 1941, Hitler admonished his Reich-Commissioner of
Vienna to apply himself energetically to the deportation of all the
Jews and then to the removal of all 'Czechs and other ethnic aliens'.
That way, the dwellings of 400,000 to 500,000 people would be
made available to the 'Aryan' Viennese![52]

Thus, the systematic persecution of minorities in the Third Reich
was a calculated variable in the redistribution of economic benefits. It
seems most likely that the political process which led to the 'Final
Solution' might well have continued in the case of a German 'Final
Victory' in the war, and might also have included the Czechs and
other 'alien ethnic minorities' in the then expanded German
conquered territories. In Vienna, the appropriate administrative
organization was already in preparation; Viennese Nazis spoke in
this context of 'the expulsion and removal of the Czech minority in
Vienna'.[53] However, tactical considerations seem to have led
Himmler as early as May 1940 to postpone this other kind of 'final
solution while the war is in progress'.

Preference was to be given instead to the 'Final Solution' of the

Jewish Question. Until it was dismantled on 1 November 1942, the Viennese Jewish community administration was obliged to compile the lists for the series of transports which started in 1942. Afterwards this role was taken over by 'the Council of the Jewish Elders'. Soon 'Jewish search personnel' and 'marshals' had to drag the Jewish victims to the transports under the supervision of the SS. Initially, the arrests took place during the day. Since the 'marshals' often had to wait for hours until the Jewish victims had returned home, the arrests were soon carried out at night when the Jews were under curfew.[54]

Persons of 'mixed race' – *Mischlinge* of first and second degree – were safe from these arrests, as at first were employees and workers of the *Israelitische Kultusgemeinde*, invalided ex-servicemen, and indispensable workers; but later only those of 'mixed race' remained exempt.[55]

Petty offences, like the inadvertent covering over of the Jewish star, possession of a cigarette butt, or infringement of the curfew by a few minutes, led to immediate despatch to a staging camp. There the Jews had to hand over all their cash while awaiting the next transport and sign a document to state that they relinquished voluntarily any claim on their remaining property in favour of the Reich. Each was allowed no more than 50kg of luggage on the journey by cattle-car, the hardships of which many did not survive.

Between 15 February and 12 March 1941, five transports went to the *Generalgouvernement*; this was then discontinued because of the preparations for the attack on the Soviet Union, although only one half of the contingents originally planned had been dispatched. In Poland the Jews were dumped in little country towns, which caused an acute food shortage.[56]

Before suffering mass murder the Jews had to be moved out of sight of the 'Aryan' Viennese, so that their extermination like 'vermin' could not easily stir human compassion among their fellow Viennese. What happened to them in far-away Poland was not clearly known and did not disturb very many Viennese. The anonymization of the victims of automatic weapons and bombing raids, which enables the spatial and emotional separation of the commanders and perpetrators from the suffering and pain of the human beings attacked – thus preventing the formation of empathy which might inhibit such deeds – is certainly a precondition of modern warfare, as it was for the Nazis' 'Final Solution'.

After the attack on the Soviet Union, the SS terror organization moved on to the direct murder of the Jews. Early in the course of the accelerating 'total solution of the Jewish question in the German sphere of influence', trucks were used which had been converted into mobile gas-chambers. Later in the autumn of 1941, the SS began to put into use the gas-chambers which had been found useful in the 'euthanasia programme'.

In 1942 mass deportations set in anew, and this caused a sudden monthly lowering of the numbers of remaining Viennese Jews by 4,000 to 5,000 persons. In that year alone, 32,000 of the 43,000 Jews were deported. On 15 April 1943 there were still 7,544 Jews in Vienna. Of those, nearly 3,900 lived in 'privileged' mixed marriages and about 1,550 in 'non-privileged' ones.[57]

By the end of 1944, the Jews in Vienna were again reduced by one-quarter through the deportation of 1,646 and transfer of 249 Jews to concentration camps. Only about 5,700 Viennese Jews survived the Third Reich in Vienna. Beyond that only 2,142 survived the inferno of the annihilation camps where, including the concentration camps, approximately 65,500 Austrian Jews had met their end.[58]

According to Erika Weinzierl[59] only slightly more than 200 Jews had been hidden by non-Jewish Viennese and thereby saved. This figure is to be contrasted with another one which is based on an estimate of Simon Wiesenthal's in 1966. To quote Wiesenthal: 'At least 3 million murdered Jews have to be blamed on the Austrians who were participants in the crimes of National Socialists (as SS and concentration camp personnel).'[60]

In conclusion, the following points summarize the process of the persecution of the Jews and their elimination from Viennese society:

1 The events leading up to the destruction of the Viennese Jews must be seen as a process, but not one with a clearly-defined goal or one that moved unilinearly in a predefined political direction. Although the general direction of antisemitism was determined, it was not fixed in detail in its timing, means or degree of radicalism.

2 National Socialist anti-Jewish policy found widespread support in Vienna; it was based on anti-Jewish traditions popular since the Middle Ages.

3 The annihilation of the Viennese Jews in the Third Reich showed essentially the same dynamic of hostility towards the Jews as existed in Vienna already before 1900, as indicated in other papers in this volume. Its most powerful driving forces in the Third Reich, radiating from the regional areas, were immediate material interests.

This should not be taken to mean that the strong antisemitism of many Viennese did not also have socio-psychological, cultural or religious causes. The official and party-organized persecution of the Jews was put into effect with a thoroughness which on occasion called forth criticism from even the Gestapo and the economic and state bureaucracy. This points to the extent of the pent-up and socially explosive frustration at the root of the antisemitism of the population and the Nazis of Vienna. It also reflects the massive economic and status-anxiety of the middle layers of a society which had entered the dynamic of capitalist development, threatened by crises and in a state of rapid modernization. Antisemitism doubtless did have a strong anti-capitalist dimension.

Since the economic motives of Jew-hatred have to be reckoned the stronger, the more insecure the economic situation of a country – and the more prominent, affluent and concentrated the Jewish population – the antisemitism in Vienna was more intense than that in the Old Reich. In consequence, from 1938 on Vienna was always a few steps ahead of Germany in the process of persecution of the Jews. Not only were the comparable measures applied earlier in Vienna than in Germany, but they could also count on much broader support among the non-Jewish population. Here, the organizational instruments and procedures could be developed which would later be applied by Eichmann in the 'Final Solution'. It is not surprising, therefore, that in connection with the expulsion of the Jews from their homes, concrete plans were devised in the office of the Reich-Commissioner earlier than anywhere else in the Greater German Reich (except perhaps by Hitler and the innermost circles of the leadership) from the mass deportation and incineration in concentration camps of the entire remaining Jewish population of Vienna.

The response of the party membership to the announcement of a considerably more stringent Jewish policy immediately after the start of the war, which eventually was to bring about the deportation and annihilation of 65,000 Viennese Jews, shows that fantasies and desires in that direction had long been entertained. The 'Final Solution' had already been within the realm of the thinkable before the Nazi period and it became feasible only at the end of a politico-social-psychological process, which dehumanized step-by-step the image of the 'Jew' and weakened the still existing feelings of solidarity with the victims among the non-Jewish population. At the beginning of this process antisemitic action on such a massive scale was implausible; by the end it was a self-fulfilling prophecy.[61]

Viennese, Austrians and other members of the Hitler-Reich could therefore easily soothe their conscience when observing fragments of the monstrosity of the final consequences of Nazism's anti-Jewish policy while gaining substantial material advantages from the Jews' persecution.

CHAPTER 11

AVENUES OF ESCAPE:
THE FAR EAST

Françoise Kreissler

That central European Jews in flight from Nazi persecution would choose such a remote destination as Shanghai and the Far East as places of refuge must, at first sight, seem puzzling and even bizarre. In fact, in most instances this decision arose out of practical necessity. With its extraterritorial foreign concessions Shanghai was probably one of the only cities in the world, together with Tangier and Panama, which imposed no restrictions on its foreign immigrants other than customs control. The local authorities required no visa, and no residence or work permits. Bureaucratic obstacles to emigration like visas and affidavits were still unknown in this Chinese metropolis. Shanghai offered a last chance of escape for all those without parents or friends already residents of a foreign country, and for those who no longer wanted to wait for the much sought-after visas to Great Britain, the United States or some other country. To all these desperate persons asking for advice and help the Viennese *Kultusgemeinde* recommended that they leave for the 'open city' of Shanghai. It is clear, however, that for the vast majority of refugees Shanghai was regarded as merely an intermediate stage, a place of transit, before a subsequent remigration elsewhere. This perception of Shanghai as a place of temporary refuge explains why the central European immigrants never sought, as we shall see, to integrate themselves into Shanghai society.

The Austrians who emigrated to Shanghai generally belonged to the assimilated Jewish middle class of Vienna who had been progressively deprived, as described in the preceding chapter, of their means of subsistence in Austria, particularly after the *Kristallnacht*. Some of these emigrants had been imprisoned in the concentration camps of Dachau and Buchenwald, released on the condition that they immediately leave the country. Most of these refugees were Jewish, but a few Christian spouses followed their partners into exile.

It is difficult to establish the exact number of Austrian immigrants to Shanghai, but we would estimate a figure of about 5,000 persons, e.g., as high as one-quarter of all European emigrants in the city, the others being mostly of German and Polish origin.[1] Most of these Austrian refugees were Viennese Jews, with a trifling number of Jews from Innsbruck, Graz and the Burgenland.

Some of these immigrants left Austria during the very first weeks of the *Anschluss*, the first of them arriving in Shanghai in August of the same year.[2] But the vast majority did not decide to emigrate until after the *Kristallnacht* of November 1938. After this date, hundreds of Viennese Jews left the country weekly. By the end of 1939 most of the refugees had arrived in Shanghai; only a few succeeded in reaching the city in 1940 and 1941. After this date it became impossible to seek refuge in Shanghai because of developments in the war: the outbreak of hostilities in Europe in 1939, the imposition of restrictive regulations concerning the entrance of Jewish refugees from central Europe by the Japanese and western authorities in Shanghai, the start of the war between Germany and the Soviet Union in 1941 and, in the same year, the onset of the war in the Pacific.[3]

Most of the refugees reached China by sea, embarking from Italian ports, usually Trieste, on ships of the Italian Lloyd Triestino line. After a voyage of three to four weeks via Suez, Bombay, Colombo, Singapore and Hong Kong they arrived in Shanghai. A few emigrants departed on German ships from Hamburg, but their voyage lasted almost two months since German ships refused to pay the transit fees through the Suez Canal and had to take the long route around the Cape of Good Hope.[4] A few refugees still managed to reach China after the beginning of the war, travelling overland through Siberia after having traversed Europe from west to east. The decisive event most often precipitating the decision to leave their native land was the arrest of a relative or close friend.

On their arrival in China, the majority of the refugees entirely ignored the local political situation. For many months the Chinese and Japanese armies had confronted each other for the control of China. Except for the districts comprising the extraterritorial foreign concessions, the city of Shanghai had been occupied by the Japanese since 1937. The French and international concessions remained under western colonial jurisdiction and control, and it was there that the refugees settled – a place of apparent international accord and coexistence. They had thought they would be disembarking in a peaceful haven, but in fact they arrived in a city at war, almost entirely occupied by Japan, the ally of the Third Reich.

After a welcome by Jewish self-help organizations chiefly financed by American co-religionists, but also by the rich Sephardic Jews of Shanghai, the refugees were first housed in the rude *Heime* constructed for that purpose. Those who had sufficient financial resources quickly sought accommodation in the French concession; the less fortunate were settled in the Hongkou quarter which, although part of the international concession, was occupied by the Japanese army. Since 1937, when it had been bombed by the Japanese, Hongkou had lain in ruins, abandoned by its inhabitants. The low rent for the few remaining houses attracted the mass of the refugees to Hongkou, where they would live for some years. The relief organizations installed their headquarters in this part of the city and were in complete charge of all the needs of those who could find no housing or work.

The various groups inhabiting Shanghai adopted a wide range of attitudes towards these emigrants. For the Chinese, these few thousand refugees were but a small addition to the over two million Chinese refugees in the city, victims of the Sino-Japanese war. These central European refugees were perceived above all as Europeans, no different from other westerners already congregated in Shanghai for the most diverse reasons – reasons which the Chinese had traditionally ignored. By contrast, the reactions within the foreign communities in Shanghai were much more varied and complex. The existing Jewish communities were fearful of this mass influx of European Jews, without, however, openly expressing such feelings. Since the nineteenth century, a small but socially and economically influential Sephardic community originating in India and Iran had formed in Shanghai. Mostly British subjects, they had acquired within a few decades leading positions in the city's financial and political circles. They were willing to welcome the first European refugees, but as the figures mounted to several thousand they became apprehensive.[5] Nevertheless, the wealthiest of them continued to provide support throughout the war years, although they avoided close contact with their European co-religionists.

The other Jewish community in Shanghai consisted of the Russian Ashkenazis who were relatively recent settlers in the Chinese metropolis. From their position at the bottom of the social ladder they did not look with favour on this 'invasion' of newcomers. Having left Russia during the revolution and civil war, these Jews had experienced great difficulty in consolidating their social and economic position and now felt threatened by this new source of competition from European refugees generally better trained and skilled, and prepared for better jobs than they were able to aspire to.

In addition to these Jewish communities, Shanghai contained a long-established German enclave consisting mainly of merchants and businessmen. Although they rarely expressed enthusiasm for National Socialism, they refused to endanger, through thoughtless and rash actions, the safety of members of their families still living in Germany. The German General Consulate – the official representative of the Third Reich and National Socialism in Shanghai – exhibited a hostile attitude towards these Jewish refugees and, after the *Anschluss*, absorbed the functions of the Austrian consulate in the city as well. An antisemitic pamphlet (see Figures 11.1 and 11.2) distributed in the city during 1938–9 very probably came out of the German consulate. The edifying title of this tract was *The 'Chosen People' Have Invaded Shanghai!*, with the provocative subtitle, 'Be Prepared to Resist an Economic Invasion and Be Prepared for an Era of Crime, Sin and Intrigue'. Although the perpetrators of this pamphlet, 'the Anti-Jewish KKK', might create some confusion, the style, terminology and arguments developed in its pages were familiar enough to the refugees – referred to here as 'Semigrants' – a term which left no doubt as to the intentions and origins of the authors.

The citizens of the western powers living in Shanghai also manifested some anxiety at the arrival of several thousand European refugees. The newspaper of the Jewish Sephardic community, *Israel's Messenger*, mentions that, as early as the end of December 1938, the municipal council of the international concession asked the members of the diplomatic corps to intervene with their respective governments in order to limit the departure of European Jews bound for Shanghai. But this request remained without results. Nazi Germany continued to allow its Jewish citizens to leave, while the French and Italian governments likewise preferred to see the Jews leave their countries as fast as possible.[6] As a consequence, it would be the Japanese who took the first action against permitting more refugees to land in Shanghai.

These Japanese immigration regulations were quickly copied by the English, American and French authorities. From this time on, candidates for emigration had to deposit 400 American dollars as

A WARNING

To all Chinese, Japanese and Gentiles Alike

THE "CHOSEN PEOPLE"
HAVE INVADED SHANGHAI!

Be Prepared to Resist

An Economic Invasion and

Be Prepared for

An Era of Crime, Sin and Intrigue

At a time when the Sino-Japanese undeclared war is going on in China; when in Palestine the Arabs are fighting for the deliverance of their country from the Jewish yoke imposed upon them by the British Jews; when Spain is being ravaged by civil war provoked by the Jews, and a general recuiting of states is proceeding in Europe; few people seem to be interested in the so-called "refugees" and "martyrs" of Hitler.

We mean the so-called new emigrants in China, i.e., the Austrian and German Jews who are steadily arriving in Shanghai.

Shanghai, whose business life had withered owing to the Sino-Japanese hostilities; Shanghai, where thousands of unemployed foreigners are being repatriated at the expense of their Consulates; Shanghai, where millions of Chinese refugees have to be fed at the expense of the ratepayers and foreigners, i.e. at the expense of still existing foreign enterprises; Shanghai, where 24,000 Russian emigrants have more or less settled, but are in the majority living a hand to mouth existence, this Shanghai has suddenly become the "Promised Land" for those who, in Europe, i.e., in Austria, Germany and Czechoslovakia, were doing destructive work, leading the life of parasites and, generally speaking, lived at the expense of German, Austrian, Czechoslovakian and Ruthenian workers. Briefly speaking, Shanghai has become a shelter for the Austrian and German Jewish emigrants.

How? Why? Nobody knows!

While in Shanghai thousands of unemployed foreigners, many of whom are college graduates, are living at the expense of their fathers and relatives or are supported by their governments, while the Chinese, graduated from universities of America, France, Germany, Britain, etc., are forced to work for $12.00 a month, just to keep body and soul together, Shanghai, that same Shanghai, has opened wide her gates to the Jewish emigrants.

It appears that all countries are blaming Germany, reproaching the pure Germans who had kicked out the parasites. But, at the same time, neither Britain nor France, nor the USSR, for the time being, has yet given shelter to these "sufferers". There are many projects: Some are charitably

Figure 11.1

Figure 11.2 *Antisemitic cartoon from:* The Chosen People have invaded Shanghai!

'guarantee money', a sum that refugees from the Third Reich could not pay since they were allowed to take out of Germany only 10 marks, i.e. 4 dollars. A short while later, the war in Europe brought to a rapid end all immigration to China.

How did the refugees cope with the circumstances of their life in Shanghai? Clearly, for them life in the Far East was a real 'culture shock' in the broadest meaning of the term. Everything was problematic for these newcomers: the climate, housing, food, language and cultural environment. The foreign concessions in Shanghai, with their refined luxuries, coexisted with the deep misery of the Chinese quarters of the city. Most of the refugees were, of course, accustomed to certain standards of comfort in Europe, but they were now consigned, as mentioned above, to the bombed-out Chinese quarter of Hongkou without any of the customary amenities. Under these harsh conditions the weak and the elderly were the first to succumb to the tropical diseases endemic in the poor districts of Shanghai.

Under these conditions, it was, of course, impossible for the refugees to attain a meaningful degree of social and cultural integration into the fragmented and forbidding environment that Shanghai presented in those traumatic days. The only level of participation available to the newcomers was in the economic sphere. The Chinese world was still marked by colonial norms of behaviour and the western settlers tried to keep the new arrivals at a distance. As the political situation deteriorated, moreover, even the Sephardic and Russian Jewish communities came to realize that they themselves lived only as tolerated emigrants in Shanghai. But even economic integration depended on each individual's ability to overcome the difficulties inherent in founding a new existence: how, in effect, could one recycle oneself after having been a barrister or insurance broker in Vienna for twenty-five to thirty years? Many refugees simply did not have the energy to make a completely new start and spent the entire war subsisting in the special shelters sustained entirely by the relief organizations. It was for these Austrians that the living conditions were the worst: they existed in overcrowded barracks with up to 120 beds per room. The residents of these shelters belonged to the most deprived social classes and caused many problems for the aid organizations, from whom assistance was limited to material help, food and lodging. In these miserable conditions, many inhabitants sank into apathy and indifference.[7]

But there were survivors as well: among the liberal professions, physicians and dentists had the best opportunities for integrating into the economic life of Shanghai. As indicated elsewhere in this volume, in Vienna some 50 per cent of the physicians were Jewish, although Jews accounted for only some 10 per cent of the city's total population.[8] Once their academic qualifications had been recognized by the local authorities, they quickly found positions in Shanghai's hospitals and clinics, some of which had been opened for the refugees. Some also created a private practice with their own clientele; others found teaching positions in one of the city's universities – and this despite the intervention of the association of National Socialist Physicians (Nationalsozialistischer deutscher Ärztebund, NSDAeB) who feared the *Verjudung* of Chinese universities.[9] But physicians were one of the very few professional groups which could continue to practise their accustomed occupation, even though their new working conditions were sometimes difficult and their remuneration lower than in Vienna. And often they had to augment their original professional training with special studies in tropical diseases.

Most refugees worked in small shops, but a few with the requisite linguistic skills – English being the major commercial language in Shanghai – could find employment with English, American or even Chinese firms which used English. Few of the refugees were fluent in any other language than German, however. In the major refugee area of Hongkou a number of small businesses were established to serve the needs of the immigrant community. Indeed, they gave a European flavour to this part of the city, the Viennese opening pastry shops, restaurants and coffeehouses which quickly attracted an international clientele.[10] As in Vienna, the coffeehouses played a central role in social life, even if they could not equal the standards of their Viennese predecessors. People frequented them in order to conduct business, play chess or cards, or simply in order to meet fellow Viennese. Thirty-five years later, one of these Viennese refugees was asked why the Viennese met mostly other Viennese in coffeehouses and his laconic explanation was 'Kann man mit einem deutschen Juden tarockieren?', 'How could one play Tarot with a German Jew?'[11]

Refugee cultural life, too, was rapidly organized around a few professional artists who had emigrated to Shanghai. Among them was Fritz Heller, the Viennese cabaret actor, and Jenny Rausnitz, a former student in the Rheinhardt-Seminar, who together produced, along with some of their colleagues, some very popular plays in the pure Viennese tradition. The film-maker Arthur Gottlein directed a marionette theatre which was a real success with refugee and Chinese audiences alike.[12] The Viennese artists also produced new plays, mostly light comedies, but not without criticism of National Socialism, such as *Die Masken fallen* ('The Masks Fall') by the journalist Mark Siegelberg which dealt with the subject of mixed marriages. This production, however, received only one performance since the German General Consulate threatened to retaliate against relatives of those associated with the play who remained in Europe.[13]

Viennese became very active in the local press as well. The two most important refugee periodicals were edited by Viennese. Ossi Lewin was editor-in-chief of the bilingual, German-English, *Shanghai Jewish Chronicle*, in collaboration with Ladislaus Frank and Mark Siegelberg, former journalists on the *Stunde* and the *Wiener Mittagszeitung*. A.J. Storfer, a former student of Sigmund Freud, in

1939 launched the *Gelbe Post*, a cultural magazine of high intellectual standards edited in German.[14]

These cultural activities formed an important part of the process by which the emigrants managed to sustain their specifically Viennese identity. They also attended to the education of their children, creating schools and organizing leisure activities which contributed to a sense of continuity and the maintenance of a Viennese lifestyle. After several months, most refugees found living conditions if not normal, at least tolerable. They obtained employment which enabled them to provide for the basic needs of their families and, as suggested above, an intense cultural life emerged. But in December of 1941, with the Japanese attack on Pearl Harbor, the situation was radically transformed for the worse. The Japanese occupied the international concessions zone in Shanghai and numerous British and American citizens were interned in camps on the periphery of the city. Many refugees who had found employment in the administration of British and American firms lost their jobs as these were closed down. Others, who had succeeded in creating their own small factories, went out of business as they lost both their suppliers and the export markets of the United States and south-east Asia.

The situation of refugee housing likewise deteriorated rapidly as the subsidies for the joint relief organizations ceased to arrive, or arrived only irregularly, from the United States. For the first time real hunger and suffering descended on the Shanghai refugee community. In addition, with the onset of the Pacific war hope of further emigration to the United States, which several had managed to achieve up to December 1941, was now lost. As a last resort, the self-help organizations now approached the well-off Sephardic Jews and the refugees who had succeeded economically. A sponsorship scheme was developed through which one sponsor was to take responsibility for the welfare of one or several poor families. But this scheme proved inadequate for organizing the requisite support for the most deprived families.

Although life had become very difficult, the refugees were fortunate in one circumstance of their existence: they were not considered to be enemy aliens by the Japanese, but merely as 'stateless refugees' since Nazi Germany had expatriated them in 1939 through the *Ausbürgerungsgesetz* which had reduced them to the legal status of 'stateless'. But this relatively favourable attitude toward them adopted by the Japanese, now the sole masters of Shanghai, was shortlived, lasting for only a year. On 18 February

1943, the Japanese ordered all refugees who had arrived after 1937 to be domiciled in Hongkou within three months. This regulation – certainly the consequence of pressure brought to bear by the German Consulate General – did not, however, affect the Sephardic and Russian Jews who had arrived well before 1937. But soon Hongkou would be referred to as the 'Shanghai Ghetto'. Although there were no walls or barbed wire, one could only leave this district on a special passport restrictively issued by the Japanese authorities. Only those refugees whose occupations required their presence outside of the ghetto could hope to have their permits renewed monthly, and even these were not allowed to move about freely in Shanghai, but only in precisely defined parts of the city. Additionally, outside of Hongkou the refugees were obliged to wear a badge which clearly designated them as inhabitants of the ghetto. The exits were guarded by Japanese patrols and by a Jewish auxiliary police (*baojia*). The zeal with which some of the latter applied the Japanese regulations to the letter would cause them serious trouble when the war was over.

If ghettoization brought about a drastic reduction in the human situation of the refugee community it simultaneously meant an even further reduction in their economic circumstances. Once again the refugees had experienced the loss of jobs; others, who had established small shops or enterprises outside the ghetto area, went bankrupt. However, it must be realized that, while the measures taken by the Japanese authorities against the Shanghai refugees recall the ones adopted throughout Europe by Nazi Germany against the Jews, the Shanghai measures were, in fact, incomparably milder. In Shanghai the Jews were subjected to no forced labour, no deportations and no exterminations. European Jewish refugees continued to live near the Chinese, Japanese and Russians who occupied the same part of the city.

The end of the war in the Far East in 1945 meant not only the end of the Hongkou ghetto but also a rapid improvement in the economic situation as many refugees obtained well-paid jobs with the American military administration. As the material situation became progressively normal, the main preoccupation of the refugees was with the organization of their departure for either a further point of emigration, or whether to seek repatriation, one of the first steps in either case being to become enrolled as a 'departure candidate'. Nevertheless, the worldwide political situation did not yet allow them to leave China; the first group of Austrians left the country in 1946 for Australia, and only in February 1947 – eight to nine years after their arrival in the Far East – did the first Austrians return to their home country. The departures progressively accelerated, particularly as the troops of the Chinese Communist army approached the city. Those who still remained in Shanghai in 1949 were quickly repatriated to Europe by the new local authorities.

To conclude this brief account of emigration to Shanghai, one last remark must be made. Some militants who came to China in the early 1930s and were engaged in political action in Europe, had privileged relations with the Chinese Communist Party, and afterwards criticized the Jewish refugees for not taking part in local political life.[15] As to the few dozens of social democrats and communists of Jewish origin who emigrated to Shanghai, they admitted themselves that their political activities were rather limited and achieved only a little success among the refugees.[16] The reasons for not taking part in local political life were that the Austrians in Shanghai, like Central European refugees generally, had never taken much part in politics in their own countries and the political situation in Shanghai was scarcely conducive to involvement. Armed resistance to National Socialism was hardly possible in Shanghai and joining the Chinese resistance to the Japanese invasion would have entailed leaving the city altogether. Some Austrians did so, in particular doctors – mainly Jewish – who had served with the international brigades in Spain before joining the Chinese army. The only published first-hand accounts of the Austrians' experiences among the Chinese were written by those who joined the armed resistance to the occupying forces.[17] Such politically committed Austrians were among those who, on arrival in the Far East, acquired sufficient knowledge of the language to join the Chinese forces and be accepted by them. For the many others who lived for almost ten years in Shanghai, this was a period of permanent struggle for existence during which they nevertheless maintained their cherished traditions, their principles and an attitude to life which even such a harsh exile was unable to destroy. Let us conclude with a quotation from Bruno Frei that seems very appropriate to the achievement of these Austrian refugees in Shanghai:

> The fact that Austrians, persecuted for racial reasons maintained their social cohesion under the sign of Johann Strauss was in itself a blow for Austria, a blow against the Nazi invaders, a political act performed by unpolitical people – who preserved something so distant so close to their hearts.[18]

CHAPTER 12

ANTISEMITISM BEFORE AND AFTER THE HOLOCAUST: THE AUSTRIAN CASE

Bernd Marin

This chapter will argue that a new type of antisemitism has arisen after the Nazi Holocaust.[1] For reasons to be outlined, this recent syndrome can be analysed as an *'antisemitism without antisemites'*. Although the analysis focuses on Austria, its intention is more theoretical: my chief aim is to explain some of the central and general features of antisemitism after the Nazi Holocaust as a historically different prejudice from its preceding forms, using the Austrian case as a highly salient example. This requires an approach combining historical interpretation with social science data and techniques of analysis. Thus, the nature of contemporary antisemitic prejudice in Austria cannot be assessed adequately without taking into account both its history up to the Holocaust – an objective I share with the other contributors to this volume – and its historically different character after Nazism and genocide, as revealed through a close study of the available social scientific data. I believe we must aim for insights into the magnitude, spread and intensity of antisemitic prejudice; into the reasons and dimensions for its transformation and persistence in the postwar era; into the after-effects of the Nazi past and the consequences of the Middle East conflict – as well as a review of earlier manifestations and functions of antisemitism – if we are successfully to understand and combat antisemitism's qualitatively new historical manifestations and psychosocial dynamics. Such an ambitious programme can, of course, only be postulated and briefly sketched here, and the direction of its realization only suggested.

The basic starting point of the present analysis is a rejection of ahistorical-mythical interpretations of antisemitism as a timeless 'eternal' phenomenon. Research into postwar antisemitism in

Austria, however, in my view requires a more differentiated historical periodization than the traditional distinction between 'hatred towards Jews' and a more recent 'antisemitism'. In fact, today's enduring 'post-Fascist' antisemitism seems to differ as much from its predecessor as the 'modern' antisemitism that started in the 1870s differed from the ancient, religiously justified 'anti-Judaism' that dates back to before the Middle Ages.[2] I believe, therefore, that we must distinguish four qualitatively different kinds and successive stages of hatred towards Jews in European history:

1 The hostility of Christians toward the followers of their originating religion, justified mainly on religious grounds. This hostility toward the faith was not only strongly reciprocated by Jews, but the existence of an ancient *'anti-Judaism'* even before the establishment of Christianity as a state religion points to an underlying, economically-motivated antipathy of a mainly agrarian social class toward exponents of a nonagrarian economy, as was practised by the Jews as an independent 'people-class' or commercial caste.[3]

2 A *'bourgeois antisemitism'* that came into existence during the last quarter of the nineteenth century, paralleling the world economic crisis and the appearance of mass political parties. This was a mass movement of the petty bourgeoisie. As such it was an important political weapon in the social struggles among different factions of the bourgeoisie (partly in alliance with the decaying gentry), as well as later on in the struggles against a growing labour movement.[4]

3 A *'Fascist antisemitism'*, quasi-'nationalized' during National Socialism, pointedly aimed propagandistically by a totalitarian apparatus of command, which finally led to unequalled genocide. It can be seen as calculated mass irrationality by the total state.[5] Its most immediate political consequence for the survivors and expatriates was the foundation of a Jewish national state, Israel, in Palestine, which itself was to become a new target of hostility.

4 A *'post-Fascist/post-Holocaust antisemitism'* after the Second World War and the defeat of Nazism. Its main elements are indicated briefly in the next section, but some clarifying remarks should be made in advance.

The category of 'post-Fascist antisemitism' should indicate taxonomically the continuity and discontinuity of the historically changing syndrome, which did not exist as an ideology before 1870 and was not allowed to exist as a political ideology after 1945. A post-Fascist antisemitism in the true sense of the word can be found mainly in Germany and Austria, pointing to an identifiable antisemitic tradition and its organized use by the Nazi state. In a broader sense it points to the lasting impact of a historically unprecedented genocide, therefore to a qualitatively new and more universal phenomenon: to stress the unparalleled self-denying character of the now discredited prejudice, one could speak of post-Holocaust antisemitism. I shall use the terms more or less interchangeably here with regard to the Austrian case.

Post-Fascist antisemitism in Europe is distinguishable from 'anti-Zionism' in Arab countries and the 'anticolonialist' and 'anti-imperialist' ideology of young Afro-Asian nation states. 'Anti-Zionism' in European countries (such as France, both Germanies, Austria, the Soviet Union, Poland and Czechoslovakia), on the other hand, is for historical reasons rarely free from antisemitic elements,[6] which – due to the present consciousness of the Fascist past – are not admitted as such. On the contrary, they are masked or misunderstood as 'antiracist' themselves. In most eastern European countries anti-Zionism is the present expression of political antisemitism; a fact which may at least be disputed for 'Third World' countries.[7]

More than the traditional bourgeois and Fascist antisemitism, the post-Fascist variant is a particularly strange and paradoxical phenomenon. It can be characterized briefly by some of its central features. Although exemplified by the Austrian case and differently manifested in different countries, these features (except the first) seem to be symptomatic of all forms of antisemitic prejudice after the Nazi Holocaust.

Post-Fascist antisemitism in Austria is:

1 An *antisemitism without Jews* in the sense employed by Lendvai.[8] Almost all Austrian Jews were, as Gerhard Botz has analysed in chapter 10, driven out or murdered. The Jewish population sank from approximately 2.8 per cent in the year 1934 (Vienna: 10.8 per cent in 1923) to about 0.1 per cent (Vienna: 0.5 per cent) by the 1980s. Community life, cultural activities, influence in public life were to a large extent extinguished. The remaining Jews live in isolation. Moreover, a much larger number of assimilants have been 'turned into Jews' by a hostile gentile environment.[9]

It is an 'antisemitism without Jews' in two other ways as well: it was found to be significantly stronger in those regions where there were no Jews living and never were before; and significantly stronger with those persons who did not have any personal contact with Jews and never had.[10]

2   An 'antisemitism without antisemites'. This concept points to a mass prejudice which has no legitimacy, no public subject, no propagandistic base, and lacks the self-confidence and self-evidence of an ideology. This prejudice is no longer a pattern of justification to which people can refer; instead it is discredited and 'forbidden'. In addition, as a mass prejudice, it has become embedded in the 'collective unconsciousness' through a process of cultural sedimentation, and is frequently reproduced unintentionally and unconsciously in everyday language, operative 'behind the back of subjects'.

'Antisemitism without antisemites' thus means that paradoxical state of coexistence of the crystallization of prejudice and 'official' repression, where many Austrians 'must not' express any more the prejudices they want to articulate, or else 'cannot' perceive the prejudice they express despite their intentions.[11] This contradiction holds true only for antisemitism and not for prejudices against other ethnic, religious, or social minorities in Austria; historically, it appears for the first time in the Second Republic. It refers to a newly structured prejudice, even if it seizes on traditional mystifications.

Because of its massive spread, the antisemitism now submerged in the 'underground' of privacy is not simply a private phenomenon, but has eminently political potential. It is not a political weapon in Austria any more, but still has political import. There exists no political antisemitism today but there is still antisemitism in politics. This has been manifested over the postwar years not only in neo-Nazi desecrations and neo-Fascist demonstrations, but even more in those 'affairs' in public life, culminating in 'the Waldheim affair' during the presidential elections of 1986, which have periodically drawn international attention, and opprobrium, to Austria's Nazi past.[12] Antisemitic resentments became virulent again and again even in the heart of political institutions: antisemitic utterances of Österreichische Volks Partei members of the National Assembly were treated as 'slips', and not only did not lead to the immediate resignation of the incumbents, but instead to their renewed candidacy; the former SS membership of one opposition party chairman, who was no longer prosecutable under criminal law but nevertheless severely morally discrediting, not only did not lead to his immediate resignation, but to his defence by the Socialist Chancellor

Kreisky and to his growing popularity;[13] and antisemitic propaganda was used in election campaigns against the Socialists even in the official strategy of the then-ruling Conservative People's Party.[14] Other examples of similar events could be given throughout the period of the Second Republic.

The political use of and capitalization upon antisemitism have changed with the changed conditions of reproduction of prejudice in everyday life: politics becomes antisemitic today through an ingenious 'management' of massive prejudices and through socio-technological calculations that encompass avoidance of the subject, selective attention, and even the encouragement of resentments – with, at the same time, a declared rejection of the prejudice. Such a 'management of prejudice' indicates a new phase in the development of bourgeois society and corresponding techniques of the praxis of power: this is a special case of what critical social theory has analysed as 'late capitalistic crisis-, conflict-, and motivation-management'.[15]

In contrast to the 'nationalized' syndrome of prejudice during Fascism, its '(re)privatized' existence is subject to a historically changed socio-political dynamic. It is a 'dominant prejudice' not because it is a prejudice of the dominant or 'ruling' classes as during Fascism, but because any active political opposition to it or even unintentional trespass by a power representative in public, could lead to a considerable decline in the confidence and loyalty necessary for the legitimate exercise of power. Public power holders therefore believe that they 'must take this into account'. A violation of this 'avoidance imperative' of symbolic politics could give rise to legitimacy problems concerning the authority of power-holders.

Although late bourgeois antisemitism is a 'dominant prejudice', it is no longer an ideology in the Marxian sense.[16] It is not a 'necessarily false consciousness' nor an 'ideology of the ruling classes'; even advocates of existing social conditions today reject and sometimes even combat it. Its power-stabilizing functions are peripheral at most and replaceable, not necessary and central. It is only partially effective in certain classes and strata, not generally like ideologies, and only affects the sphere of reproduction but is not relevant for the legitimation of the basic economic institutions. It is no condition or prerequisite of societal organizational principles, but a phenomenon consequent upon them; it is 'backward', 'superfluous' and 'destructive' precisely in terms of 'modern' ideologies – historically quasi – 'out of date', the product of mystified ruling conditions that came into being and continue to exist unaccidentally.

That is one of the reasons why the 'ordinary' so-called '*gemütliche*', 'everyday antisemitism' of the majority of the Austrians is the typical form of postwar antisemitism, rather than the doctrinaire, fanatical and militant antisemitism of a minority of former Nazis and neo-Fascists, although there exists a mutually conditioned connection between the two in their genesis as well as in their reaction to corresponding events.

'*Post-Holocaust antisemitism*' is quite different from its predecessors as regards its mechanisms and contents. As regards the spread and intensity of antisemitic images and attitudes, all empirical findings available show uniform tendencies.[17] Its major features are:

1 An extremely large spread of general antisemitic beliefs and attitudes; approximately three-quarters of all Austrians articulate at least slightly antisemitic attitudes, approximately one-fifth to one-fourth strong, approximately 10 per cent extreme antisemitic attitudes.[18]

2 An almost unbroken persistence of the traditional stereotype of Jews, even among persons who are relatively unprejudiced and who judge similar clichés very differently from antisemites.[19]

3 A certain degree of readiness for active discrimination, or rather an indifference *vis-à-vis* possible discriminations, on the part of approximately one-fourth to one-half of the population.[20]

4 A probably considerable decrease in the readiness to act out stereotypes in activities of discrimination since the end of the war (which is explained, of course, by the absence of real objects of aggression and the fear of their return).[21]

The most unbroken 'remnant' of Nazi Fascism, then, is the traditional antisemitic reservoir of stereotypes; less persistent are the extremely negative judgments connected with these prejudicial beliefs; most changed are the discriminating actions connected with them. As already indicated, in the Second Republic too there has been an almost continuous series of 'affairs', apart from individual neo-Nazi manifestations, in which the latent 'everyday antisemitism' broke through publicly. But in contrast to antisemitism in West Germany, it has never manifested itself in attacks against individual Jewish citizens[22] – although the amount and intensity of prejudice and resentment seem to be equally strong in a very striking way.[23]

At first glance there seems to exist something like a 'typically Austrian antisemitism'. In particular, the unexpectedly weak empirical correlation between attitude scales measuring ethno-centrism and antisemitism, between a general inclination towards prejudice and specifically antisemitic prejudice in Austria[24] may indicate the fact that this prejudice cannot be interpreted as primarily determined (socio)psychologically in Austria, probably in contrast to other countries. As one study concluded:

> Those persons who by very harsh statements in the tests exposed themselves clearly as antisemites show only a slightly higher frequency of an increased inclination to (generalized) prejudice than the average. This proves that antisemitism in Austria . . . is not merely part of a generally high inclination to prejudice which is caused psychologically, but a phenomenon *sui generis*, which has little to do with the individual sources of prejudice, but is based more strongly on socially determined phenomena.
>
> Especially among the notorious antisemites in Austria one can find a relatively high number of quite normal personalities who do not deviate so much psychologically but rather are only indoctrinated and socialized antisemitically – i.e. with a special stress on antisemitism, which outstrips the other prejudices with these persons.[25]

Compared to other prejudices in Austria, antisemitism is not a 'typical' but a kind of 'exceptional' prejudice as regards its social and demographic determinants. The study just quoted shows clearly that antisemitic dispositions tend to vary independently of general prejudices in different social, political, educational, occupational, age and regional groups.[26] For instance, the universal age-effect – decreasing tolerance against outsiders with increasing age – cannot always be proven in relation to 'Jews'. There is a highly persistent latent readiness for prejudice, if not open prejudice, and antisemitic stereotyping over all time periods and generations. Moreover, the generally significant correlation between higher education and lesser tendency toward prejudice is contradicted by certain dimensions of antipathy directed specifically against 'Jews'. Again, only towards 'Jews' and only in 'displaced', indirect and cautious ways of expression, do higher-echelon employees and self-employed people show a markedly higher inclination toward prejudice than occupational groups traditionally more prejudiced, such as unskilled workers and farmers.

Although the perception of having experienced downward social mobility in Austria, surprisingly enough, does not increase the general inclination toward prejudice, antisemitism itself does increase strongly with downwardly mobiles.[27] Bitterness because of feelings of declassement is thus largely 'channelled' by antisemitic prejudice; at the same time, it is one of the most effective determinants of this prejudice.[28] In contrast to prejudices against other minorities, antisemitism is strongly politically influenced, not only in extreme groups (people without prejudice or people extremely prejudiced) but among the average respondents. Supporters of 'left' parties are markedly less, 'rightists' markedly more antisemitic. This, of course, seems to be a historic survival: as with other prejudices, the influence of political ideologies is decreasing in this respect.[29]

Empirical findings show, on the one hand, that postwar antisemitism is spread in varying degrees throughout different social classes, and on the other hand, that it means different things in various social strata – according to which measuring instrument is used.[30] Therefore, it is possible to quote as many 'proofs' for its being a 'typical' middle-class phenomenon as for its predominance among the lower classes. The partly contradictory empirical results suggest two possible explanations. Regarding the prevalent contents of stereotypes as well as the form of articulation of the prejudice, members of all social classes seem to use 'the Jews' projectively as they need them in their daily life situations. The content of prejudice, the antisemitism of the working class, which is quite similar to S.M. Lipset's classic concept of 'working-class authoritarianism',[31] is very different from the petty-bourgeois middle-class antisemitism of the social classes privileged by property and/or education, but whose perceived status can be endangered. Differently accentuated resentments crystallize around different problems of their particular working and living worlds. Antisemitism of workers crystallizes around accusations of unbridgeable cultural differences (*Andersartigkeit*), arrogance, and in particular the suspicion of parasitic aversion to work ('Jews have a dislike for hard work, therefore they always look for comfortable, profitable positions'); antisemitism in the middle classes is often characterized by diffuse racist conceptions, fixations on a supposed and threatening 'Jewish' dominance in the most important occupations, and by a defence against any assumption of guilt, responsibility, and readiness for restitution in respect to the Nazi past, sometimes taking the form of conditional justifications for Nazi measures against the Jews, and demands for the protection of Nazi war criminals.

Regarding the forms in which the prejudice is expressed, there is the already mentioned class-specific repression effect: members of the middle class seem more observant of the taboos, especially against antisemitic prejudices, to censure more or less consciously their resentments and express them only in a socially 'permitted', harmless way. This indirect expression of ambivalence or antipathy against Jews in the 'more educated' middle or upper social classes is shown empirically, for instance, in the intense rejection of guilt and shame regarding the Nazi past, a different evaluation of stereotypes, or a mechanical 'philo-Semitic' reversal of the traditional clichés. Due to a stronger affectual control in the middle and upper classes, reservations against Jews are expressed more cautiously and in greater accordance with the prevalent ideology – i.e. in postwar times they are hardly expressed publicly any more. Prejudices were preserved more covertly in the bourgeoisie; thus they are hardly recordable with the crude measuring instruments of opinion polls or nonprojective tests and were, therefore, systematically underestimated.[32]

By taking over preformulated stereotypes, members of the working class or of marginal and lower classes seem to utter resentments against minorities more naively and openly, often without really affectively feeling the uttered hostilities. They talked in linguistic stereotypes borrowed from the upper classes, connecting with them few of their own conceptions or emotions, but also without the embarrassment and cultural hypocrisy of the middle classes toward their own prejudices. All this points to a strange and increasing autonomy of antisemitic prejudice: no other prejudice in Austria shows such a discrepancy between the magnitude of the stereotype and its irrelevance for the material interests of the bearers.

Is post-Fascist antisemitism, then, merely a kind of anachronistic 'remainder' or 'historical relic' without consequences, which will inevitably dissolve with the passage of time, or has it acquired new present-day functions? How has it reproduced itself and changed? Of what sociopolitical dynamic has it become an element?

From a sociotheoretical point of view, post-Fascist antisemitism cannot, in my view, be interpreted as only a 'historical remnant with a strong tendency to persist'[33] without any functions. It must also be understood as a functional expression of a structurally determined fragmentation of consciousness and behavioural disorders in this social order. The widespread expectation of a gradual 'dying off' of the prejudice along with the most important groups of bearers is an insufficient explanation for the extent of the 'survival' so far witnessed, and the 'historical retardation' itself; but precisely this needs some explanation. Not a loss of function, but a change of function involving newer, more modern dimensions, could explain this stubborn survival.

Generally speaking, antisemitism in Austria still enables the members of the 'ruled' social classes, especially, to absorb the 'chronic surplus of disappointment' produced systematically and necessarily in a class-constituted 'society of competition and merit' as well as the partly 'free-floating' and destructive potential of anxiety and alienation, resentment and aggression. This diffuse discomfort, which is neither institutionally channelled nor individually overcome, and which continues to exist as a tendency to irrationality, represents the individualized, 'personal costs' generated by a specific mode of social organization. These costs appear as the 'refuse' of psychic stress, especially within the smallest units of social reproduction – the nuclear family and primary groups.[34]

Antisemitism fulfils this function neither exclusively nor necessarily; but it becomes less replaceable by other prejudices (for instance against migrant or 'guest workers' or 'radicals', by 'law-and-order' hysteria, and so on) the more it is connected with material interests (as in the First Republic) or the more it is culturally embedded (as in the Second Republic). The traditional antisemitic image of 'the Jew' still serves as an especially 'suitable' pattern in the minds of the majority of Austrians to express, at least in their fantasies, the tensions and aggressions they cannot live out in everyday reality and to provide a means for interpreting incomprehensible aspects of their own living conditions by reference to mythological prototypes. The classic formulations of Allport still appear to me to be highly relevant in this regard.[35] Antisemitism may be hypothesized to fulfil the following functions. First, it provides an important cultural scheme for articulating the class resentment of the lower classes against 'those above', in which the stereotype of the Jew functions as the symbolic representation of socially desirable but structurally blocked success or efficiency, as well as a convenient framework for interpreting social inequality. Second, it may serve as a preferred explanation for the disappointment of all really declassed social classes or those threatened with an incipient decline in status.

Third, it provides symbolic satisfaction of socially suppressed – prohibited and desired – needs, using the stereotype of the Jew, as a projection of the 'forbidden' and 'unattainable'. Finally, antisemitism may act as a stabilizer of informal, 'private' small groups – the family, relatives, neighbourhood, colleagues, and so on – in so far as they have to compensate for an absence of emotional relations and solidarity by aggressive out-group definitions.

In contrast to that of the interwar period, post-Fascist antisemitism as a basically 'nonpublic' opinion no longer serves to integrate political, economic, occupational, clerical, and other associations and organizations. Still persistent, although massively repressed, with the murder or expulsion of almost all Austrian Jews antisemitism lost every basis for a revival of its 'historical' function as a demagogic weapon in social struggles, be these of various fractions of capital against each other (as in liberal capitalism), class conflicts (as in the interwar years) or means of state propaganda (as during Nazi rule). After several phases of increasing 'socialization' and 'politicization' of this prejudice, it disappears as 'religious', 'economic', 'political', and 'racial' antisemitisms from the public of the media, church, parties, occupational associations, and so on. I have termed this public disappearance without abolition as '(re)privatization' of antisemitism, a decisive turn of quite ambiguous consequences.[36] This ambiguity can be seen in the after-effects of the Nazi period, as well as in the effects and repercussions of the establishment of Israel and the Middle East conflict.

Immediately after the Second World War there existed a situation in Austria in which neither a public repudiation of the existing antisemitism as a prejudice, nor its public retention as an ideology and a political weapon seemed compatible with the reconstruction and restoration of a bourgeois society. The further changes of form and function of post-Fascist antisemitism can be explained as a gradual ossification of this contradictory postwar constellation. The components of this contradiction can be encapsulated in the formulas *'split nation'*, *'tabooization'*, and *'inauthenticity'*. By 'split nation' I mean, following suggestions put forward by Pelinka,[37] discrepancies and conflicting relations between the 'elites of the leading politicians' and the 'basis of society', that is, 'the contrast between the minority who resisted (the Nazis) and the majority who stood aside more or less . . . passively'; the gap between a more objective interpretation of history and the subjective experience of it; between the 'official' account of the history (or the self-consciousness of Austrian society) on the one hand and the social consciousness of the majority of Austrians (or their everyday picture of history) on the other; between 'published' and 'nonpublic' opinions about the 'liberation' or 'defeat' of the country by the allied forces – each of these discrepancies has made for conflicts that manifested themselves in the competition of the 'elites' for the 'people' in the democratic institution of an election, and impeded 're-education'.

However, the parallel process of 'tabooization' did not and does not touch this split in society and in the collective consciousness about the importance of the Nazi past and its consequences, but instead portrays this avoidance as necessary. By 'inauthenticity'[38] I mean a consolidation of this unsolved contradiction: 'tabooization' of the state of a 'split nation' is itself made into a taboo: the denial or palliation of unresolved problems and conflicts is itself denied and palliated.

Austria is (according to the Moscow Doctrine of 1943) a country freed from Fascism, not defeated by the Allies, but one whose inhabitants, for the most part, experienced the outcome of the war as a defeat. This paradoxical state led to the grave political consequence that the political elites of the country, who for the most part were considerably influenced by the Resistance fighters, had to campaign for the votes of the Fascist-indoctrinated majority. *Thus the Fascist-tending consciousness of the majority of Austrians, suppressed and wooed by a 'ruling' anti-Fascist minority, gradually became the dominant consciousness.* Further, contradictory demands of social integration functioned as a conserving factor of fragments of Nazi ideology: in particular, the readmittance of all Austrians (including former Nazis) into the political system in 1949 led to a disproportionate upgrading of their ideological 'baggage' because of the campaigning for marginal voters. The split in social consciousness that expressed the contrast between the Fascist-indoctrinated majority and the anti-Fascist minority resulted in a split in consensus-inhibiting themes and problems ('consensus of exclusion'): 'derealization'[39] of the consequences of antisemitism in the '*Tausendjahrige Reich*' after its defeat, the defence and rejection of guilt, and the denial of shameful reservoirs of prejudice – these were among the means of achieving a conflict-free social integration that concealed unresolved divergences.

At the same time the anti-Fascism of the elites, on which the early Second Republic partly rested, was increasingly replaced by a revived anti-Communism.[40] This cold war anti-Communism, on the one hand, took over the 'safety valve' function of antisemitic prejudices, and by giving a new, total 'enemy image' it made them sociopsychologically 'unnecessary' and 'superfluous'. On the other hand, the alliance of 'all anti-Marxists' again revalued the Nazi ideology in important aspects (including antisemitic aspects) because of its continuity with it.

As a result of this development, there is a significant contrast between the intensity of antisemitism in Austria before, during, and after Nazi rule and the strong rejection of any responsibility for antisemitism's consequences. The mass murder of Jewish citizens is interpreted as an event completely beyond people's responsibility, not as the final outcome of prejudices at least tolerated by them. Empirical findings confirm a very broad agreement in the rejection of feelings of responsibility for injustices committed, of shame, of grief, of repentance, or of responsibility for restitution for the sufferings of the Jews – quite independently of the open expression of antisemitic statements. At the same time, especially in people's attitudes about the Nazi past, antisemitic prejudices appear indirectly; in fact, attitudes regarding the past became one of the decisive points of crystallization of unadmitted tendencies toward prejudice.[41]

The 'official' measures taken to 'overcome the past' consisted mainly of (a) special laws and measures against former National Socialists in the first years after the war and the prosecution of Nazi criminals, as well as legal measures – partly determined in the State Treaty – against Nazi and racist activities;[42] (b) measures to relegate concern with the Nazi period and its after-effects to administrative or professionally specialized occupations, as a quasi-institutionalized precaution and 'restitution';[43] and also (c) measures for an ideological and programmatic 'purge' by eliminating antisemitic ideas from party programmes as a visible act of 'official' annulment of the political antisemitism of the interwar period.[44] This combination of repressive measures, treatment by specialists, and programmatic 'self-purge' was not only impeded in its execution by massively repressed reservoirs of prejudice, but has counter-productively provided an 'alibi' for its continued existence.

The mass extermination of Jews by Nazi Fascism has indirectly contributed to the creation of a Jewish national state in Palestine. What role do Israel and the conflict about Palestine play in Austrian postwar antisemitism? Here is a summary of some empirical findings.[45] First, the image of 'the Israeli' is associated surprisingly strongly and readily with the traditional stereotype of 'the Jew'. It also consists of the same image-components, but its different dimensions are judged quite differently: the supposedly similar and 'German' traits in the Israelis are valued and admired (war heroism, strength, competence, diligence, and so on); the 'Jewish' characteristics are rejected. Second, the positive image of Israel does not lead to a change of opinion about 'the Jews'. The two clichés are either isolated from each other and exist side by side, or the negative stereotype of the Jew simply carries over to provide a negative image of Israel. Third, for most Austrians, 'the Israelis' seem to represent a kind of 'non-Jewish Jews', almost another category of the always tolerated 'excepted Jew' extended to a national level.[46] 'The Arabs' (the 'Palestinians'), on the other hand, are assigned various properties of the traditional antisemitic stereotype and thus become scapegoats of a kind of 'new antisemitism'.[47] So the paradoxical constellation has come about that only in so far as they represent 'non-Jewish' properties do 'Israelis' count as 'Jews' who are accepted, whereas 'the Arabs' are rejected precisely because of the attribution of supposedly 'Jewish' properties.

This view of the Arab-Israeli conflict also seems to have the particular psychological function of foisting the responsibility for restitution onto 'the Arabs'.[48] At the same time the overwhelming partisanship for Israel in the Middle East conflict is determined by Israel's political position in the world as an ally of the 'western world' and of its changing big-power interests. This partisanship, linked to foreign policy, is mainly mediated by newspaper reporting: the influence of the press is strong because of the lack of direct experience, as well as the far-reaching unanimity of judgment of the situation.[49] The reports on Israel in the Austrian daily papers evidence the dominance of calculated-interest politics over emotional, moral, or ethical considerations, even with emotionally loaded issues. The 'turning on and off' of existing emotions by the press follows clear-cut political calculations, and provides an excellent example of journalistic management of prejudice. For example, we typically find that no genuine coherent position determined by firm principles (apart from the mentioned identification with changing bloc interests) was or is taken regarding the parties to the conflict. Therefore, there is no continuous and uniform image of Israel in the Austrian newspapers; rather, it is strategically accentuated to suit present political needs. Even where reporting about Israel is explicitly referring to the Nazi past or to moral considerations, it is not affected by them in any way. Feelings for or against the Jews/Israelis are massively used by the papers, but do not influence the papers' policies at all. They only serve as changing set-scenes of reports, as they are needed politically. This led – between 1948 and 1973 – to almost grotesque comments and position changes towards the Israelis and their Arab counterparts.[50]

The Austrian population's knowledge of 'Israelis' and 'Arabs' is produced artificially to the point of including subtle nuances of associations, images, emotions, and partisanships. To this extent these clichés differ from the traditional stereotypes of Jews as they still exist today. They are no longer – in spite of their continuing social functions – the expression of current economic or political interests; they are manipulated for given effects rather than being intentionally created as means for political aims. But images of Israel are today fabricated instrumentally, rationally goal-oriented, and circulated as symbolic weapons in current international conflicts.

The dissociation of stereotypes of Jews and Israelis in the popular mind is at the same time a result and a prerequisite of the political strategy followed by the press in the Middle East conflict, in order to be able to mobilize changing moods relatively rapidly. Only if the images of 'Jews' and 'Israelis', spontaneously connected, can be kept apart and specific aspects stressed, only if 'Israelis' are not equated continuously with the negatively judged 'Jews', can Israel and its policies be presented by the press as deserving of support – even in politically right-wing, latently antisemitic publications. The strong associative connection, of course, still harbours the danger of a revival of antisemitic prejudices in an 'anti-Zionist' version.

Ironically, the existence of the Jewish national state, Israel, in Palestine as well as the presentation of its pioneers and soldiers as a 'Jewish antitype' to the traditional antisemitic stereotype both allowed larger segments of the population to admit for the first time the feeing of guilt and the need to make restitution indirectly. In connection with Israel, they could concede parts of their guilt feelings that had arisen through the complicity, always denied, in the persecution and extermination of the Jews during Nazism. The founding, existence, and safeguarding of this Jewish national state was now itself perceived as a restitution achievement. Repressed guilt could thus be projected onto the 'Arabs', 'Palestinians' who themselves suffered injury, or 'Russians' supporting them. The siding with Israel could be interpreted as support of the ('good') Jews, which enabled many Austrians to demonstrate to themselves and others sympathy, responsibility, solidarity, and the absence of prejudice.

Every threat to the state of Israel, and even more to its right to exist, is thus at the same time always a threat to the convenient assumption that political and journalistic support of Israel is the most important compensation, the real 'restitution' achievement of Austria (and also – according to the Zionist viewpoint – the 'Solution' of the so-called Jewish question) as well as proving the absence of antisemitism. Evidence for this includes the special harshness and vehemence of attacks by the Austrian newspapers on the Arab 'hard-line states'; the fact that especially 'slight antisemites' tend to have intensive prejudices and despise 'the Arabs', and the characterization of 'strong antisemites' by their opinion that 'the Jews can go to Israel any time if they do not like it here'. Traditional antisemitic prejudices and politically calculated stereotypes about Israel mutually supplement, reinforce, and limit each other.

In conclusion, it appears to me that the concept of *cultural sedimentation* seems to be the most important key to the understanding of the continuity of antisemitic prejudice in postwar times, especially in view of its increased functional irrelevance and replaceability on other levels. The massive persistence of antisemitism – without any of the economic motivations it might have had in the past, without any special psycho-pathological function (as it probably has in other countries still today), basically replaceable in its social functions, politically 'outlived' and rather a problematical consequence than an instrument of social struggle in antagonistic structures – can be explained only by an intensive cultural sedimentation of an earlier 'Austrian ideology'.[51]

Cultural sedimentation may be defined as an embodying of antisemitic concepts and forms of expression in interactions and ways of experiencing in everyday life.[52] It is seen most clearly in colloquial speech and in texts on the subject; content analyses and depth interviews[53] show a deeply rooted deformation of consciousness and a pathology of ordinary language as an expression of the now 'privatized' former ideology.[54] The mystification process is effective in manifold ways, and should be decoded on three levels.

A stereotyped image of 'the Jews' is more widespread and more consolidated than hostile prejudices. A comparative analysis of extreme groups of antisemitic Austrians and people rather free from prejudice showed an unexpectedly high degree of conformity in the concepts of 'the Jew(s)', independent of positive and negative attitudes. In view of the dominant cliché content, there seems to exist a historically crystallized, rather uniform image of Jews, which is only judged differently: but this is exactly the key problem of the 'harmless' but very persistent Austrian antisemitism. Evidence for the everyday reality of these stereotypes is provided by the frequent attribution of 'typically Jewish' properties to personalities in public life recognized as 'Jewish' as any newspaper reading quickly confirms. For instance, ex-Chancellor Bruno Kreisky was often described as the caricature of the 'clever', 'efficient', and 'shrewd' Jew; as impressively successful, but a person whose success at the same time relied on the abundance of tricks of the unserious 'conjurer' and 'juggler', who can talk people into anything and palm it off on them.

The traditional stereotype of Jews starts independently to symbolize and to become a code for certain social functions, abilities and ways of behaviour connected with them. Evidence of this includes, for instance: (a) certain persons are considered 'Jews', independent of their beliefs or origin, only because of certain social signs. This serves, for instance, again and again as a technique of verbal propaganda against high-ranking Socialist politicians in times of election campaigns; (b) certain characteristic behavioural tendencies – such as a self-reflectiveness, social criticism, liberalism, radicalism, intellectuality in general, and so on – or concrete behaviour (from commitments to social minorities, down to 'underselling' – interview statements: 'Underselling to my mind is Jewish, harmful for the trades people, no matter who does it') is labelled as 'typically Jewish' and is defamed. This 'antisemitism without Jews' signifies a step of total mystification, because 'Jews' and 'Jewish' are pure inventions for that which should be stigmatized. (An analogous American instance, which was pointed out to me in the course of writing this paper, is the phrase 'to Jew down somebody', referring to unscrupulous bargaining practices in general.)

The cultural sedimentation of antisemitism shows itself as destruction of speech on the level of vocabulary, in which the stereotypes become elements of ordinary language, less easily recognizable than in attributions by predication: they also assert themselves despite conscious intentions regarding the choice of words, categories, and so on.[55] In Austria you can still frequently hear quite innocent remarks about 'half-Jews' or 'quarter-Jews' or 'three-eighths Jews' or 'baptised Jews'; people talk about 'the Jew' or 'Jewish fortunes', 'Jewish capital', 'Jewish money', or 'the Jewish press', about things 'in Jewish hands', of a 'Jew villa' if a villa belongs to a Jew or did at some time belong to one, or – full of admiration – of 'the Jewish medicine in Vienna' – to give just a few examples.

A comparison of texts in the present-day basic lexicon and categorization processes with those of *Der Stürmer*[56] (an unquestionably antisemitic paper) has led to the following results, among others. It was found that there is a discrepancy between speech and consciousness; persistence and continuity are stronger in the latent contents and horizons of ideas, less strong in the manifest forms of speech and expression – jargon changes more than what it expresses. Moreover, the stereotypes about the Jewish minority are quite unbroken; though the vocabulary, especially the explicit statements about 'Jews', have become 'harmless', the forms of categorization have hardly changed since the Nazi era.

In so far as such residual structures of everyday language influence individuals in an unconscious way, one really has to talk about an 'antisemitism without antisemites'. This fatal cultural sedimentation of antisemitic mystifications – scars of the past far beyond the Nazi period – reinforces the central aspect of shameful self-denial, which characterizes almost all variants of this prejudice after Nazism and the Holocaust.

CHAPTER 13

LAST WALTZ IN VIENNA:
A POSTCRIPT

George Clare

We had met in the Café Landmann: Inge Lau, young Fraulein Radziner and I. Inge, whose review of my book in *Die Presse* still is – in my opinion – the most perceptive published anywhere, had become my voluntary, unpaid and highly efficient public relations manager in Vienna. Without her I would not have had one-tenth of the media exposure I enjoyed in Austria. The purpose of our meeting in the Café Landmann was further media exposure. Fraulein Radziner, then on the staff of *Die Presse*, had come to interview me.

She started with all the usual rather boring questions like: 'Why did you write *Last Waltz* . . . why did you write in English instead of German . . . why did you dedicate it to your children?' Why do they never come up with something new, I thought. And just then it came. 'So how do you feel about Vienna now? How do you see the Vienna of today?' Fraulein Radziner asked.

'Als eine unheimlich vertraute, fremde Stadt,' was my spontaneous reply. And you know because of that one word 'unheimlich' I found it difficult to translate my answer into English. I have no idea whether this was of psychological or philological significance. Anyway the man who finally gave me an almost satisfactory translation was a Hungarian, Arthur Koestler – forgive the name-dropping. He came up with the word 'uncanny'. 'An uncannily familiar foreign city,' he said. I said 'almost satisfactory' because, although any dictionary will confirm Koestler's choice of 'uncanny', I find there is a different feel about it than there is about 'unheimlich' which it seems to me has a more sinister, a more threatening meaning.

The moment I had given that reply I got a look from Inge compared to which the stare of a basilisk is nothing but friendly coquetry. From the public relations point of view it would have been better had I been less spontaneous and less honest and – naturally 'An uncannily familiar foreign city' was its headline when the interview was published. I had said it and I had meant it, but I only began to think about it afterwards. I took my sentence to pieces and looked at it word for word.

'Unheimlich.'

Well, what is so 'uncanny' about this beautiful city? Walk through its streets and squares and you won't find anything to justify the use of that word. As a matter of fact even the chance of getting mugged is less in Vienna than in most other big cities. There's nothing 'uncanny' lurking in dark street corners there by day or night, nothing – except memories. No, I'm not talking about the days of the *Anschluss*. They were terrifying but there was nothing about them that was 'unheimlich'. It was all out in the open – the frenetic hatred and the frenetic joy. Only when I visited the city of my birth for the first time after the war in July 1947 did I get the feeling that there was something 'unheimlich' about it. I was a British occupation officer in Berlin then and I had wangled being sent to Vienna by pulling a few strings. Officially I was on a fact-finding mission, unofficially I merely wanted to see how the town had fared. That was why I wore my uniform only when I had to go to the offices of the Allied Administration in Austria, otherwise I was always in civilian clothes. Hence, as there isn't much of a true blue British look about me, and as I could talk to them in their own vernacular, the many Viennese I spoke to did not hide their true feelings.

Everywhere I found that same self-pity I was so used to from Germany, but with an added dimension of lamb-like Austrian innocence. The other difference was that although most Germans trotted out all kinds of excuses for their personal involvement with the Nazi regime they did nevertheless accept a sort of generalized national responsibility for their past. Not so the Austrians. They had mislaid the Hitler years somewhere in the most distant recesses of their minds, and Austrian patriotism – so rare a commodity in March 1938 when they welcomed 'Führer' and '*Anschluss*' so jubilantly – was now much in fashion. Its visible symbols were the ubiquitous Tyrolean and Styrian peasant hats one saw everywhere in Vienna, sprouting on many a head which, not all that long ago, had been adorned either with the brown cap of the SA or the black one of the SS.

But the Viennese had not merely exchanged their headgear together with their political convictions, they had changed the very way they spoke. Instead of 'Heims ins Reich' it was now 'Weg vom Reich' and to underline that the gentle and musical Viennese idiom I know had been replaced by the broader and coarser vowels of the vulgar dialect of the less savoury suburbs in an attempt to make their German sound less like German. Abraham Lincoln stated that one can not fool all the people all the time. How true! But a hell of a lot of people can fool themselves for a hell of a long time. The Viennese certainly could and they are still at it. All that is what I experienced as 'unheimlich'.

They also wrote themselves a libretto version of their history worthy of the make-believe world of the operetta, claiming that Austria was the first country to be invaded by German troops. Mind you, they did not actually invent that one themselves. Although I'm sure they would not have needed foreign aid to arrive at the same conclusion, the facts are that it cropped up for the first time in a resolution by the British Labour party in February 1940, and exactly two years later – Winston Churchill too described the Austrian people as the first victims of Hitler's aggression. Nobody took much notice of what the Labour party had said. But when Churchill echoed it, much to the horror of a totally surprised Foreign Office and also of many Allied governments, it had considerable impact and as the Prime Minister had said it, it became official policy. Winston's impromptu performance took place on 18 February 1942 outside number 10 Downing Street. The Austrian Association in Great Britain, at least 90 per cent Jewish in its membership, had collected money to buy a mobile canteen for the British forces, and its chairman, Sir George Frankenstein, had managed things so cleverly that the Prime Minister had agreed personally to accept this donation. In happier days when Sir George was still Baron Georg von Frankenstein and the first Republic's last ambassador to the Court of St James he gave the most exquisite musical soirées at his embassy and thus made many influential friends in high places and some of those had arranged matters with the Prime Minister.

History does not record whether the timing of that little ceremony in Downing Street was merely good luck or whether it was Sir George's last diplomatic masterstroke, but the choice of the early afternoon immediately after lunch when Churchill was at his mellowest could not have been bettered. In heavy overcoat, muffler, Homburg hat and what is discreetly called a 'happy' mood, Winston Churchill stepped out into the street, accompanied only by his wife.

'It is not without deep emotion', he said after accepting the canteen, 'that I attend this simple ceremony. Here we see the heart of Austria although trampled down under the Nazi and Prussian yoke. We can never forget here in this island that Austria was the first victim of Nazi aggression. . . .'

That the Austrians eagerly seized upon these words is understandable, but what I find 'unheimlich' is that they have been perpetuated without any qualifications by people who know better and that this pap has been fed unremittingly to Austria's postwar generations. Is there a change coming now, perhaps as the one welcome by-product of the Reder-Frischenschlaeger affair? Hans Rauscher, deputy editor of the *Kurier*, said in an article published in *Profil* magazine: 'The outrageous pretence of the Austrians that they were the first victims of Hitler's policy of aggression cannot be kept up forever.' Is Rauscher merely the proverbial swallow which does not make a summer or is he the tip of an emerging iceberg of cold truth? If the latter is the case then I shall be delighted to strike the sinister word 'unheimlich' from my sentence.

'Vertraut.'

A familiar city! Oh yes, that Vienna for me most certainly is. Although it was not unexpected I was still surprised in July 1947, as I walked through streets and boulevards remembered as wide and endless, how narrow and short they had become, and how that huge St Stephen's Square had shrunk so much one could almost spit across it from where Karntnerstrasse ends to where Rothenturmstrasse begins at the far side. But I recognized every façade, knew every stone, nearly every monument had some personal meaning for me. How sharply and painfully those familiar sights brought home to me the brevity and frailty of human life when measured against the timeless endurance of stone.

I thought of my dead parents and of how often we had walked together past those buildings and how my father, who loved his Vienna and knew its history so well, had told me when they had been erected, who had lived in them, what they commemorated. There they stood as firm and solid as ever, having survived the war, but where was he? I crossed the very kerbstone over which my mother in her shortsightedness had stumbled when I was what – four or five? Seeing her suddenly sprawled on the pavement before me was so terrifying to the little boy that I had dirtied myself and we had to go back and change my clothes. Yes, that kerbstone was there, but where was she?

A familiar city indeed, but how then could it be 'foreign' at the same time?

Many great artists – Gustav Mahler is an example – never get the recognition they deserve in their lifetime. They usually have to wait about fifty years for their posthumous fame. Indeed Mahler's is a case in point. He died in 1908 but he only became truly world-famous in 1959 after the director who filmed Thomas Mann's *Death in Venice* selected a movement from Mahler's Fifth Symphony for his theme music. When did my Vienna die? Friedrich Torberg wisely said not really in 1918 but finally only in 1938. And now, almost fifty years later, what do we find if we look around? As I am writing this Claudio Abbado is conducting the first concert of a Vienna and Mahler cycle in London, Arthur Schnitzler's plays are on the British stage, and the overall theme of last year's Edinburgh Festival was 'Vienna', and here we are in Paris discussing one aspect of its history.

Vienna is in. In books, in plays, in music its fame is spreading all over the world. But what is being celebrated is not the Vienna of today, but the Vienna which died nearly fifty years ago and exists no more. We are experiencing the posthumous recognition of the Vienna that was.

The city where I was born still had more than a shimmer of the metropolitan and cosmopolitan glitter of its great past. Where, except for the famous buildings and splendid boulevards designed by generations long dead, is that now? Hitler, who hated Vienna, has had his revenge on the city which he thought had spurned him. And his Gauleiter Baldur von Schirach wrote its epitaph with his telegram 'My Führer I report to you that Vienna has been cleansed of Jews'. Not only the few Jews of genius who were driven from Vienna – Freud, Zweig, Schoenberg, Roth – were responsible for the greatness of my Vienna, it was also the many who, unless they fled for their lives lost them, those unknowns who provided its cultural infra-structure on which men and women of great gifts, whether Jewish or not, could develop their genius and find a ready response for what they created.

Not only on my first postwar visit but also on each subsequent one it became more and more obvious how provincial and, therefore, foreign Vienna now was. One little incident which sharply defined this for me occurred in the late 1950s. I went to see Karl Farkas at the 'Simpel'. I well remembered the hilarious evenings I had spent at this cabaret as a youth when Farkas and Gruenbaum had sprayed us with their bubbling wit. What I saw in the late 1950s was a pathetic, a lifeless, copy. No, not even that – a poor imitation rather. How could Farkas be so witless, how could he be so dull? Had he grown old and tired, had I become blasé? I asked around. The answers I got can be summed up in these words: 'Look at the audience he nowadays has to play down to. What response would he get if he were as sparkling as he used to be? They wouldn't know what he is talking about.'

I bought a copy of Hugo Bettauer's *Stadt ohne Juden* in Vienna and re-read it. The poor man was not much of a seer. He prophesied economic ruin without Jews. How wrong he was! The Viennese and the Austrians are more prosperous than they have ever been. Good luck to them, but there seems to me to be a connection between provinciality and prosperity, between financial security and cultural tepidity. There is nothing wrong with it. It is merely that Vienna in its present provincialism – just another well-heeled German-speaking city – is foreign to me. Not to me only. Although I have spoken of my own feelings and reactions, what I have said about myself is true of many former Viennese of my generation.

Must it remain as it is or are there, somewhere, not yet discernible, signs that Vienna may one day regain its lost intellectual horizons? I cannot give an answer but I can relate another experience I had in Vienna four or five years ago when my wife and I attended a discussion at the second – or is it the third? – stage of the Burgtheater on Schwartzenbergplatz after the performance of Peter Weiss's Auschwitz play. It did not go well, but that was not the fault of the young and highly interested audience. It was more that of their discussion partners, survivors of Auschwitz. Sadly they were not, and why should they have been, good communicators. But one sensed, except for the usual left-wing nit who could see no difference between Kreisky's Austria and Hitler's Ostmark, the eagerness of those young people for the truth which had been kept from them. They did want to know whether their parents and grandparents had really been Hitler's first victims, they did want to know what had really happened to Vienna's Jews, they were open-minded and open-hearted.

Perhaps, if the pretence Hans Rauscher referred to ceases and young Austrians could confront the historic truth instead of its fudged version, there might return some of that inner restlessness to Vienna without which there can be no creativity. If that happens then the day may come when 'Herr Karl', Qualtinger's profound characterization of that odious provincial,* can finally be laid to rest.

Friends, historians, ex-countrymen let's bury 'Karl': no good is to be said after him. If that happens Vienna would not be foreign any more.

(Presented to the Colloquium, *Les Juifs Viennois*, Institut Autrichien, Paris, 27 March 1985)

*P.S. 1987: Meanwhile they have elected him Federal President.

NOTES

CHAPTER 1

The Jews of young Hitler's Vienna: Historical and sociological aspects

1 Robert S. Wistrich, *Hitler's Apocalypse: Jews and the Nazi Legacy*, London, Weidenfeld & Nicolson, 1985, p. 14. An interesting work of 'faction' on Hitler's Vienna years is J. Sydney Jones, *Hitler in Vienna, 1907–1913*, New York, Stein & Day, 1983. But William A. Jenks in *Vienna and the Young Hitler*, New York, 1960, supplied the first extended account of this subject.

2 Ian Kershaw, *The Nazi Dictatorship: Problems and Perspectives of Interpretation*, London, Edward Arnold, 1985, p. 104 *et passim*.

3 Wistrich, op. cit., provides a particularly lucid account of the influences shaping broad parameters of Hitler's early *Weltanschauung*; see esp. pp. 12–26, 'Laboratory of World Destruction'.

4 The following historical synopsis leans most heavily on Anna Drabek, Wolfgang Häusler, Kurt Schubert, Karl Stuhlpfarrer, Nikolaus Vielmetti, *Das österreichische Judentum*, Vienna and Munich, Jugend und Volk, 1974.

5 Ilsa Barea, *Vienna: Legend and Reality*, London, Secker & Warburg, 1966, p. 39.

6 Arthur J. May, *The Hapsburg Monarchy, 1867–1914*, Harvard, 1951, p. 8.

7 According to Christine Klusacek and Kurt Stimmer, *Leopoldstadt*, Vienna, Verlag Kurt Mohl, 1978, p. 50.

8 *The Encyclopedia Judaica*, Jerusalem, 1974, vol. 9, p. 503.

9 Barea, op. cit., pp. 44–5.

10 Nikolaus Vielmetti, 'Vom Beginn der Neuzeit bis zur Toleranz', in Drabek *et al.*, *Das österreichische Judentum*, op. cit., pp. 64–5.
11 *Ibid.*, p. 68.
12 John P. Spielman, *Leopold I of Austria*, London, Thames & Hudson, 1977, pp. 75–6.
13 Robert A. Kann, *A Study in Austrian Intellectual History: From Late Baroque to Romanticism*, London, Thames & Hudson, 1960, p. 79. See also Allan Janik's remarks about this archetypal Viennese figure in chapter 4 of the present volume.
14 Vielmetti, op. cit., p. 78.
15 Loc. cit.
16 Klaus Lohrmann, 'Das österreichische Judentum zur Zeit Maria Theresias und Josephs II', *Studia Judaica Austriaca*, Bd. VII (Ausstellungskatalog), Eisenstadt, 1980, pp. 6–8.
17 Lohrmann, op. cit., p. 12.
18 Vielmetti, op. cit., pp. 80–1.
19 Wolfgang Häusler, 'Toleranz, Emanzipation und Antisemitismus. Das österreichische Judentum der bürgerlichen Zeitalters (1782–1918)', in Drabek *et al.*, op. cit., p. 88.
20 *Ibid.*, p. 84.
21 Loc. cit.
22 Robert S. Wistrich, *Socialism and the Jews: The Dilemmas of Assimilation in Germany and Austria-Hungary*, Associated University Presses, 1982, p. 180.
23 Marsha L. Rozenblit, *The Jews of Vienna 1867–1914: Assimilation and Identity*, State University of New York Press, 1983, p. 71.
24 Peter Schmidtbauer, 'Zur sozialen Situation der Wiener Juden im Jahre 1857', *Studia Judaica Austriaca*, Bd. VI, pp. 57–90.
25 Gary B. Cohen, 'Jews in German Society: Prague, 1860–1914', *Central European History*, vol. 10, March, 1977, pp. 47–9.
26 *Mein Kampf*, London, Hutchinson, 1969, pp. 48–52.
27 Loc. cit.
28 Rozenblit, op. cit., p. 129.
29 Loc. cit. A more extended report of the findings in this chapter obtained through research in Vienna and Jerusalem is provided in Ivar Oxaal and Walter R. Weitzmann, 'The Jews in Pre-1914 Vienna: An Exploration of Basic Sociological Dimensions', in *Leo Baeck Institute Year Book Vol. XXX*, 1985, pp. 395–432.
30 Peter G.J. Pulzer, *The Rise of Political Anti-Semitism in Germany and Austria*, New York, John Wiley, 1964, pp. 14–15.

31 Rozenblit, op. cit., p. 63.

32 *Ibid.*, p. 68.

33 On page 64 she appears to have thought that private business employees were lumped together in a catch-all category with 'Public Service and Free Professions', but this was true only of clerks, bookkeepers, and the like, employed in private homes. The vast majority of *Angestellte* although only identified by *religion* once, in the 1910 occupational census in the global comparison shown in Table 1, nevertheless were reported in every branch of industry.

34 Robert Wistrich has written extensively on this subject, and provides further insights in chapter 6 of the present volume. See his *Socialism and the Jews*, op. cit., and *Revolutionary Jews from Marx to Trotsky*, London, Harrap, 1976.

CHAPTER 2

Class, culture and the Jews of Vienna, 1900

1 Broch's essay is reproduced in Hermann Broch, *Schriften zur Literatur 1*, ed. P.M. Luetzeler, Frankfurt, 1975, pp. 111–284. An English translation is forthcoming from Michael Steinberg. Among the major works on the subject which have appeared since that essay are: Ilsa Barea, *Vienna*, London, 1966; Frank Field, *The Last Days of Mankind*, London, 1967; William M. Johnston, *The Austrian Mind: an Intellectual and Social History 1848–1938*, Berkeley, 1972; Allan Janik and Stephen Toulmin, *Wittgenstein's Vienna*, New York, 1973; William McGrath, *Dionysian Art and Populist Politics in Austria*, New Haven, 1974; Peter Vergo, *Art in Vienna 1898–1918*, London, 1975; Frederic Morton, *A Nervous Splendour: Vienna 1888–9*, London, 1979; Carl E. Schorske, *Fin-de-Siècle Vienna: Politics and Culture*, London, 1980 (this includes a number of Schorske's pioneering articles from the 1960s); Michael Pollak, *Vienne 1900: une identité blessée*, Paris, 1984. The latest study on the subject, not the best, is *The Viennese Enlightenment*, ed. Mark Francis, Beckenham, Kent, 1985.

2 Schorske, op. cit., p. 7.

3 *Ibid.*, pp. 8–9.

4 Professor Steiner's most recent exposition of this thesis occurred during his televised lecture on *fin-de-siècle* Vienna on the 'South Bank Show', London Weekend Television, 16 June 1985.

5 Stefan Zweig, *Die Welt von Gestern*, Frankfurt, 1982, p. 37.

6 Schorske, op. cit., pp. 148–9.

7 *Ibid.*, p. 7.

8 On Hofmannsthal, see Hermann Broch's approach, in *Hofmannsthal und seine Zeit*, published in Hermann Broch, *Schriften zur Literatur 1*, Frankfurt, 1975, esp. pp. 176–221; on Wittgenstein see Ludwig Wittgenstein, *Culture and Value*, Oxford, 1980, pp. 1–22 passim, esp. p. 18.

9 Dennis B. Klein, *The Jewish Origins of the Psychoanalytic Movement*, New York, 1981, p. vii.

10 On Wittgenstein's Jewish descent see William Bartley III, *Wittgenstein*, 2nd edn, La Salle, Illinois, pp. 198–200. On the Vienna Circle, I rely on the information of Professor Paul Neurath (Vienna and New York); Dr Eckehart Koehler (Vienna); Professor K.R. Fischer (Vienna), and Dr Renate Heuer (Frankfurt am Main).

11 See, for example, the comments of Hans Mayer, in *Aussenseiter*, Frankfurt, 1981, p. 438. See also Robert Wistrich, *Socialism and the Jews*, London, 1982, pp. 173–347, esp. p. 332.

12 According to the leading genealogist in the field, Dr Hannes Jaeger-Sunstenau, rumours about the Jewish descent of Carl Menger are false.

13 The list of members appears in Ludwig von Mises, *Erinnerungen*, Stuttgart, 1978, p. 65. Information on the Jewish origins of the members comes from Dr Renate Heuer; Dr Jaeger-Sunstenau (Vienna); Professor A. Lauterbach (Vienna); and Professor Martha Steffy Browne (New York), a member of the seminar itself.

14 The list is printed in eds Bernhard Zeller, L. Greve, W. Volke, *Jugend in Wien: Literatur um 1900: Katalog*, Stuttgart, 1974, p. 119. Information on the ethnic origins of the members comes from Dr Renate Heuer; Professor Harry Zohn (Brandeis); and the *Geburtsbücher* of the Israelitische Kultusgemeinde, Vienna.

15 Zemlinsky's origin is confirmed in the *Geburtsbücher* in Vienna, although it seems that his father was a convert *to* Judaism. Alban Berg, although often taken to be Jewish, even today, was not.

16 Information supplied by Otto Breicha (Salzburg) on Gerstl; on Strnad, see Sigmund Kaznelson, ed., *Juden im deutschen Kulturbereich: Ein Sammelwerk*, Berlin, 1962, Index.

17 James Shedel, *Art and Society*, Palo Alto, 1981, p. 61.

18 John Boyer, *Political Radicalism in Late Imperial Vienna*, Chicago, 1981.

19 This is what it was called in the leading article in the *Neue Freie Presse*, 23 August 1895, Morning Edition, p. 1.

20 For the voting of teachers and officials see the *Neue Freie Presse*,

23 September 1895, Evening Edition, p. 1; 2 March 1896, Evening Edition, p. 2; 3 March 1896, Morning Edition, p. 1. Kronawetter is quoted in *Neue Freie Presse*, 11 March 1898, Morning Edition, p. 4. See Boyer, op. cit., pp. 349–57, 396–403.

21 This point is made in William Johnston, *The Austrian Mind*, op. cit., p. 18.

22 On the antisemitic voting behaviour among the various groups, see Boyer, op. cit., pp. 401–2 (on *Hausbesitzer*); pp. 305–12 (on private and railway employees).

23 The percentage of members of *Concordia* is based on my analysis of the list of living members given in the *Festschrift* by Julius Stern, *Werden on Walten der Concordia*, Vienna, 1909, pp. 239–58. For physicians and lawyers, see Hans Tietze, *Die Juden Wiens*, Vienna, 1935, p. 232.

24 Manfred Durzak, *Hermann Broch*, Rowohlt, Reinbek bei Hamburg, 1966, p. 23. On the special position of the *Gymnasium*, see Gustav Strakosch-Grassmann, *Geschichte des Unterrichtswesens in Österreich*, Vienna, 1905, pp. 249, 276. See also the discussion by Marsha L. Rozenblit on the importance of the *Gymnasium* as an agency of Jewish assimilation into German classical culture in her study *The Jews of Vienna 1867–1914: Assimilation and Identity*, New York, 1983, pp. 99–125.

25 See the *Statistisches Jahrbuch der Stadt Wien*, 1885–1910.

26 This figure is calculated from data on the eighth class in the *Jahresberichte* of the schools. For the character of the *Theresianum*, see Eugen Guglia, *Das Theresianum in Wien*, Vienna, 1912, pp. 175–7.

27 The actual figures can be calculated from the *Statistisches Jahrbuch der Stadt Wien*, 1886–1910.

28 Corrected calculation from the eighth class figures from the *Jahresberichte* of the schools involved.

29 These facts are fairly well known, and can be confirmed by examining any of the standard biographical dictionaries such as the *Österreichische Biographische Lexikon*, or the *Neue Österreichische Biographie*.

30 I have attempted to deal with such questions in my doctoral thesis, 'Jews in Viennese Culture 1867–1938' (forthcoming as book). An intelligent discussion of the problems involved in studying the process of assimilation and intellectual innovation is included in Ivar Oxaal, *The Jews of Pre-1914 Vienna: Two Working Papers*, Hull, 1981, pp. 1–53.

31 P.G.J. Pulzer, *The Rise of Political Anti-Semitism in Germany and Austria*, New York, 1964, p. 5.

CHAPTER 3

Cultural innovation and social identity in fin-de-siècle *Vienna*

1 For these statistical tendencies, see chapters 1 and 2 of the present volume and M.L. Rozenblit, *The Jews of Vienna, 1867–1914: Assimilation and Identity*, Albany, State University of New York Press, 1983, especially pp. 47 ff.

2 G. Herlitz, B. Kirchner, eds, *Jüdisches Lexikon*, vol. 1, Berlin, Jüdischer Verlag, 1927, pp. 519–20.

3 See the studies on antisemitism in Hungary: V. Karady, 'The Hungarian Jews in the Face of the Antisemitic Laws', *Actes de la recherche en sciences sociales*, 56, 1985, pp. 3 ff.; V. Karady, I. Kemeny, 'University Antisemitism and Class Competition', *Actes de la recherche en sciences sociales*, 34, 1980, pp. 67–96.

4 Letter from Anastasius Grün to Count Leo von Thun-Hohenstein, Dornau, 6 August 1866, quoted in: Catalogue of the exhibition 'Jugend in Wien, Literatur um 1900', Marbach, Kösel, 1974, p. 17.

5 C.E. Schorske, 'Generation Conflicts and Cultural Change. Reflections on the Case of Vienna', *Actes de la recherche en sciences sociales*, 26/27, 1979.

6 See the commentaries between 7 and 9 March 1883 in the important liberal dailies, *Presse, Neue Freie Presse* and *Fremdemblatt*.

7 A. Klose, *Katholisches Soziallexikon*, Innsbruck, Tyrol, 1964, pp. 775 ff.

8 G. Wolf, 'Die Völker Österreich-Ungarns', vol. VII, *Die Juden*, Vienna, Teschen, 1883, p. 169.

9 All the disarray in the face of this situation can be seen in J.S. Broch's *Der nationale Zwist und die Juden in österreich*, Vienna, 1886.

10 See K. Paupie, *Handbuch der österreichischen Pressegeschichte*, vol. 1, Vienna, Braumuller, 1960.

11 For these conflicts see M. Rozenblit, op. cit., p. 175. See also W. Weitzmann, chapter 7 in the present volume.

12 M. Rozenblit, op. cit., p. 136; see also data in chapter 1 of the present volume.

13 M. Rozenblit, op. cit., pp. 145–6.

14 Th. Herzl, *L'Etat juif*, Paris, Stock, 1981, p. 41.

15 C.E. Schorske, *Vienne, Fin-de-Siècle*, Paris, Le Seuil, 1983, pp. 180 ff.

16 Th. Herzl, op. cit., p. 34.

17 S. Freud, 'Der Widerstande gegen die Psychoanalyse', *Imago*, 2, 1925, pp. 232 ff.

18 The effects of antisemitism on Victor Adler and the relation with his son Friedrich are studied in detail by R.G. Ardelt, 'Friedrich Adler; Probleme einer Persönlichkeitsentwicklung um die Jahrhundertwende', habilitation – thesis, Salzburg University, 1982.

19 M. Pollak, *Vienne 1900*, Paris, Gallimard, 1984.

20 H. Bahr, *Studien zur Kritik der Moderne*, Frankfurt, Rutten und Loning, 1894, p. 4.

21 H. von Hofmannsthal, L. Andrian, *Briefwechsel*, Frankfurt, Fischer, 1969, p. 105.

22 *Ibid.*, p. 176.

23 H. von Hofmannsthal, A. Schnitzler, *Briefwechsel*, Frankfurt, Fischer, 1964, p. 63.

24 H. von Hofmannsthal, R. Beer-Hofmann, *Briefwechsel*, op. cit., p. 145.

25 See C. Magris, *Il Mito absburgico nella literatura austriaca moderna*, Turin, Giulio Einaudi, 1963.

26 It was only after 1963 that opinion polls in Austria indicated a rapid identification with an 'Austrian nation' and a rapid decline in any attraction for a 'German' identification. In 1965, 22 per cent of Austrians believed in the existence of an 'Austrian nation'; in 1979, they were more than 50 per cent. 'SWS Meinungsprofile', *Journal für Sozialforschung*, 20 (3–4), 1980, p. 57. See the discussion of the ambiguities of Austrian nationality during the 1930s in chapter 9 by Richard Thieberger.

27 Herzl calls his work a work of 'combination', Th. Herzl, *Gesammelte zionistische Werke*, Tel Aviv, Hozaah Ivrith, 1934, vol. 1, p. 17; L. Flem has analysed Freud's work from the angle of the mediation between Jewish culture and Greek and European traditions. L. Flem, 'Freud between Athens, Rome and Jerusalem. The Geography of a Glance', *Revue française de Psychanalyse*, 2, 1983, pp. 591 ff. For the 'combination' of different traditions in literature, see M. Pollak, op. cit.

28 See J. Katz, *Tradition and Crisis*, London, Oxford University Press, 1961 and J. Katz, *Hors du ghetto*, Paris, Hachette, 1984, p. 24.

CHAPTER 4

Viennese culture and the Jewish self-hatred hypothesis: A critique

1 Allan Janik, 'Must Anti-Modernism Be Irrational?', *How Not to Interpret a Culture: Essays on the Problem of Method in the Geisteswissenschaften* (Filosofisk Institut Stencilserie Nr. 73; Bergen, Norway, 1986), pp. 66–84.

2 Frederick Morton, *A Nervous Splendor*, London, Weidenfeld & Nicolson, 1980.

3 Carl Schorske, *Fin-de-Siècle Vienna*, New York, Knopf, 1980. See also my 'Schorske's Vienna' in *How Not to Interpret a Culture*, op. cit., pp. 1–18.

4 Allan Janik, 'Creative Milieux: The Case of Vienna', in *How Not to Interpret a Culture*, *ibid.*, pp. 114–15. See also my 'How Not to Write Austrian Intellectual History – Again', *ibid.*, pp. 50–65. Robert Kann, in his classic *A Study in Austrian Intellectual History: From Late Baroque to Romanticism*, London, Thames & Hudson, 1960, devotes a major section of his book to Abraham a Sancta Clara, pp. 50–89.

5 I am grateful to Ivar Oxaal for information about these critiques.

6 The episode was related to me by the student's thesis adviser; but I want to make it clear that the university in question was not Professor Peter Gay's Yale University.

7 Peter Gay, *Freud, Jews and Other Germans: Masters and Victims in Modernist Culture*, London, Oxford University Press, 1978, pp. 187–230. Unfortunately, Sander Gilman's magisterial *Jewish Self-Hatred: Anti-Semitism and the Hidden Language of the Jews*, Baltimore, Johns Hopkins University Press, 1986, was published after the present critique was in press, but I hope to have occasion to comment on the many additional issues it raises in the future.

8 Gay, op. cit., p. 196.

9 Theodor Lessing, 'Otto Weininger', reprinted from *Der Jüdische Selbsthass* in Otto Weininger, *Über die letzten Dinge*, Munich, Mathes & Seitz, 1980, p. 206.

10 Alexander Centgraff, *Ein Jüde Treibt Philosophie*, Berlin, Paul Hochmuth, n.d.

11 Gay, op. cit., p. 195.

12 *Ibid.*, p. 196.

13 Kurt Lewin, *Resolving Social Conflicts: Selected Papers on Group Dynamics*, Gertrud Weiss Lewin, ed., New York, Harper, 1948, pp. 186–200.

14 *Ibid.*, p. 187.

15 Loc. cit. (italics added).

16 I have criticized various aspects of the ways in which liberal commitments (broadly construed in the American sense of the term) enter into the history of ideas in 'Must Anti-Modernism Be Irrational?', op. cit., presented at the University of Trondheim's conference on Modernity, 20 October 1983; and at the Collège Internationale de Philosophie in Paris on 15 April 1985. See also my 'Therapeutic Nihilism: How Not to Write About Otto Weininger', *Structure and Gestalt*, Barry Smith, ed., Amsterdam, Benjamins, 1981.

17 See my *Essays on Wittgenstein and Weininger*, Amsterdam, Rodophi, 1985, in which my view of Weininger is more fully developed.

18 Personal communication from Gerald Stieg. I have learned a great deal about the reception of Weininger in German letters from conversations with Dr Stieg.

19 George Klaren, *Otto Weininger*, Vienna and Leipzig, Braumüller, 1927.

20 François de Fontette, *Sociologie de l'Antisemitisme*, Paris, Presses Universitaires de France, 1984, p. 10.

21 I owe this example to Professor Jon Levinson of the Divinity School of the University of Chicago; and I have profited greatly from conversations about self-hatred with Professor Levinson.

22 This information comes from Professor Ramirez of the Department of Mathematics at the National University of Mexico. Among Professor Ramirez's qualifications as a 'native informant' is the fact that both of his parents are psychoanalysts.

23 Personal communication from Gershon Weiler, author of the book in question.

24 Lewin, op. cit., p. 187.

25 George Eaton Simpson and J. Milton Yinger, *Racial and Cultural Minorities*, New York, Harper & Row, 1953, p. 305.

26 See Stanley Cohen's *Images of Deviance*, London, Penguin, 1971; especially Jock Young's 'The Role of the Police as Amplifiers of Deviance, Negotiators of Reality and Translators of Fantasy', pp. 27–61.

27 I am grateful to Kurt H. Wolff and Ivar Oxaal for their helpful, if mainly critical, comments on this essay from a sociological point of view.

CHAPTER 5

The contexts and nuances of anti-Jewish language:
Were all the 'antisemites' antisemites?

1 'Vom Tage', *Arbeiter-Zeitung* (Vienna), 25 January 1898, pp. 1f.
(My translations are intended to facilitate the understanding of the
German text, not to render exactly the nuances of style, important as
they are for the grasping of the precise attitudes behind the quoted
passages.)

2 *Ibid.*, p. 1.

3 Cf. Robert S. Wistrich, *Socialism and the Jews: The Dilemmas of
Assimilation in Germany and Austria-Hungary*, London and
Toronto, Associated University Presses, 1982, p. 288. Cf. also Sigurd
Paul Scheichl, 'Österreichische Reaktionen auf die Dreyfus-Affäre',
Relations franco-autrichiennes 1870–1970,(Austriaca special
colloque) 1, 1986, pp. 241–59.

4 *Arbeiter-Zeitung* (as note 1), p. 2.

5 *Ibid.*

6 Cf. Wistrich, op. cit., et passim.

7 'Zum Dreyfus-Skandale', *Deutsches Volksblatt* (Vienna), 13
January 1898, evening edition, pp. 1f.

8 'Der Prozeß Esterhazy und das Judenthum', *ibid.*, 12 January
1898, evening edition, p. 1.

9 'Der Dreyfus-Rummel' (editorial), *Ostdeutsche Rundschau*
(Vienna), 26 January 1898, pp. 1f. Strangely enough, the
Ostdeutsche Rundschau also contains more balanced judgments on
the Dreyfus case; cf. Scheichl (as note 3), pp. 253ff.

10 'Capitän Dreyfus', *Reichspost* (Vienna), 10 November 1897,
p. 2.

11 *Ibid.*, 18 November 1897, p. 2. Cf. also 'Jüdische Momentbilder
aus der Gegenwart', *ibid.*, 12 January 1898, pp. 1f.

12 'Die Juden und Zola als Vertheidiger des Dreyfus', *ibid.*, 15
January 1898, pp. 1f (quotation from p. 2).

13 Wistrich, op. cit., p. 281.

14 *Ibid.*, p. 279. The article by Austerlitz had appeared in the *Neue
Zeit*, 1910–11, p. 510.

15 Wistrich, op. cit., p. 279.

16 Incidentally, my criticism of Wistrich's point of view also
concerns Leopold Spira, *Feindbild 'Jud'*, Vienna, Löcker, 1981.

17 Hendrik de Man, *Gegen den Strom*, Stuttgart, DVA, 1953.
Quoted from Karl R. Stadler, *Adolf Schärf*, Vienna, Europa, 1982,

p. 401. Wistrich mentions Schuhmeier's 'instinctive distrust of Jews' as a reminder of the 'popular prejudice'.

18 Cf. Spira, op. cit., p. 61, on the continuation of this type of Social Democratic agitation in the First Republic.

19 Wistrich, op. cit., p. 298.

20 Peter Pulzer, 'Spezifische Momente und Spielarten des österreichischen und Wiener Antisemitismus', typescript of a paper read in the symposium 'Versunkene Welt', Vienna, 1984.

21 Cf. Stadler, op. cit., pp. 246f.; Viktor Matejka, *Widerstand ist alles. Notizen eines Unorthodoxen*, Vienna, Löcker, 1986, pp. 189ff (discussing the case of Schönberg).

22 Wistrich, op. cit., p. 191.

23 *Ibid.*, p. 189.

24 *Ibid.*, p. 116. In its original context, the passage refers to Germany.

25 Cf. the quotations in Wistrich, op. cit., pp. 191, 197, 276; of course, Karl Kraus must also be mentioned as an arch-enemy of the 'Jewish press'.

26 Otto Weininger, *Geschlecht und Charakter*, Vienna, Braumüller, 1903, pp. 418f (reprint: Munich, Matthes & Seitz, 1980).

27 *Ibid.*, p. 418. Surprisingly, Le Rider in his chapter on Weininger's 'antisemitism' does not quote this important statement (Jacques Le Rider, *Der Fall Otto Weininger*, translated from the French, Vienna, Löcker, 1985, pp. 189–219).

28 Robert Hein, *Studentischer Antisemitismus in Österreich* (Beiträge zur österreichischen Studentengeschichte, 10), Vienna, Österreichischer Verein für Studentengeschichte, 1984.

29 *Ibid.*, p. 16.

30 The *Burschenschaften* were only one type of *Verbindungen*, but certainly the most radical. Other *Verbindungen* nevertheless also tended more and more towards the exclusion of Jews.

31 *Ibid.*, p. 42. The *Burschenschaft Libertas* of Vienna was the first *Verbindung*, in 1878, to stop the admission of Jewish members.

32 Hein, op. cit., pp. 21, 20.

33 Cf. *ibid.*, pp. 30 ff, on the contacts between Schönerer and the fraternities; the growth of antisemitism must apparently also have other reasons than Schönerer's influence, who may himself have been influenced by the students' positions.

34 Quoted by Peter G.J. Pulzer, *Die Entstehung des politischen Antisemitismus in Deutschland und Österreich 1867 bis 1914*, translated from the English, Gütersloh, Mohn, 1966, p. 127.

35 Hein, op. cit., p. 39.

36 *Ibid.*, p. 25.

37 *Ibid.*, p. 55.

38 *Ibid.*, p. 47.

39 *Ibid.*, p. 68.

40 Adolf Pichler – Alois Brandl, *Ausbruch aus der Provinz. Briefwechsel (1876–1900)*, edited by Johann Holzner and Gerhard Oberkofler (Innsbrucker Beiträge zur Kulturwissenschaft, Germanistische Reihe 16), Innsbruck, Institut für Germanistik, 1983. I quote in the text the number and the date of the letter; the name of the author is only mentioned when it is not obvious from the context.

41 'Jenes energische Familiengefühl, welches das jüdische Volk seit dem babylonischen Turmbau wohl zusammengenietet und begleitet hat, tritt mir bei Frankl . . . und in literarischen Kreisen oft entgegen und nötigt mir Achtung ab. Freilich das Gefühl der Humanität ist dem Hebräer fremd und bloße Phrase, die er wie Banknoten ausspielt, ohne daran zu glauben.'

42 Cf. Johann Holzner and Gerhard Oberkofler, 'Einleitung', Pichler-Brandl (as note 40), pp. 1–15, particularly p. 8.

43 We have only a first draft of Pichler's letter; so it is not impossible (though not very likely) that the final letter did not contain Pichler's defence of the pogroms.

44 Holzner/Oberkofler, op. cit.

45 This means, of course, the family of L.A. Frankl.

46 'Einiges von Rubinstein gehört. Virtuose Technik, vordringlich, alles aufgepappt, nichts von innen, echte Judenware. Wie ganz anders sprach mich am Sonntag Palestrinas Missa brevis an: alles schlicht, einfach groß, ganz der Gegenstand.'

47 'Eine beneidenswerte, höchst üppige Phantasie flackert in *unheimlicher* Pracht, . . . schlägt aber nicht mit heiliger, reiner Flamme an das Herz. Würde er sie mit *Ihrer Gesinnung* paaren, dann erst würden mir die "Tropischen Könige" . . . volle Befriedigung gewähren. . . . Aber sympathisieren kann ich nicht. . .' 'Tropische Könige' must be a mis-reading for *Tragische Könige* (1876), of which Holzner and Oberkofler are not responsible (cf. Holzner/Oberkofler, op. cit., p. 12).

48 'Was sagt man in Wien dazu, daß Rothschild mit dem Schütteln seiner Beifeles [!] den ganzen Olymp der österreichischen Staatspapiere wackeln macht? Ist das nicht großartig?'

49 *Beifeles* must be misread for *Beikeles*; cf. note 47.

50 On the *Antisemitismusstreit* cf., e.g., Pulzer, *Entstehung*, op. cit., pp. 199f.

51 'Die Juden sind wie die Krätze; es handelt sich hier nicht um einen Kampf von Religion gegen Religion, sondern von Race gegen Race, und das wußten schon die alten Heiden.'

52 'Die Humanität Frankls ist doch nicht Humanität schlankweg; denn alle Stiftungen lauten auf Juden. Sei Ihnen noch bemerkt, daß Wien oder Berlin gerade so viele Juden zählt als *ganz* Frankreich oder England, und was jüdischer Wucher bedeutet, können Sie überall erfahren.'

53 'Die Russen haben Unrecht getan, den Juden ist aber Recht geschehen. Die Reaktion gegen diese Rasse, welche kein Volk ist, sich aber überall behufs der Ausbeutung anderer zusammenschließt, wird noch viel heftiger werden. Die Deutschen können es sich auch nicht immer gefallen lassen, daß sie ihnen den Sack leeren und dafür in Herz und Hirn scheißen. Keine Nation nähme die Verjudung ihrer Literatur so gleichgültig hin wie die Deutschen, dafür sind aber eben die Deutschen keine Nation. Sehen Sie Engländer, Franzosen, Italiener, Spanier, da dürfen die Juden höchstens mitlaufen, aber nirgends die erste Violine spielen. Dabei sind sie flach und leer, nicht ausgenommen den graußen Heine, der seinen Erfolg weniger dem verdankt, was an ihm echt und schön ist, als dem platten und trivialen Spaß, nicht zum wenigsten der jüdischen Reklame, welche wieder eines Messias bedurfte. Ich kenne einzelne treffliche Juden, mag aber die Juden nicht.'

54 'Sie wissen, daß ich gegen den Juden als Menschen nichts habe, gegen *die* Juden wird man aber wohl endlich eine Wanzentinktur erfinden müssen.' Letter of Pichler to Joseph Eduard Wackernell, quoted from J.E. Wackernell, *Adolf Pichler (1819–1900). Leben und Werke*, Freiburg i.B., Herder, 1925, p. 232.

55 Eva Gabriele Reichmann, *Hostages of Civilization. The Social Sources of National Socialist Antisemitism*, London, Gollancz, 1950.

56 The poem by Bruder Norbert [Thomas Stock?], a Capuchin monk, had appeared in the *Tiroler Volksblatt* of 15 July 1899. Quoted from Johann Holzner, *Franz Kranewitter (1860–1938)*, Innsbruck, Haymon, 1985, p. 76.

57 Marie von Ebner-Eschenbach, *Aus Franzensbad*, reprint, ed. Karlheinz Rossbacher, Vienna, Österreichischer Bundesverlag, 1985.

58 *Ibid.*, pp. 97f, 114ff.

59 *Ibid.*, pp. 115f.

60 Cf. Le Rider, op. cit., pp. 189–219 (chapter 'Ein antisemitischer Jude').

61 Cf. Sigurd Paul Scheichl, 'Karl Kraus und die Politik (1892–1919)', doctoral dissertation, Innsbruck, 1971, pp. 813–1074; Harry Zohn, 'Karl Kraus: "Jüdischer Selbsthasser" oder "Erzjude"?', *Modern Austrian Literature* 8 (1975), no. 1/2, pp. 1–19; Caroline Kohn, 'Karl Kraus und das Judentum', *Im Zeichen Hiobs*, ed. Gunter E. Grimm and Hans-Peter Bayerdörfer, Königstein/Ts., Athenäum, 1985, pp. 147–60, is ridiculously erroneous.

62 Sigurd Paul Scheichl, 'Aspekte des Judentums im "Brenner" (1910–1937)', *Untersuchungen zum "Brenner". Festschrift für Ignaz Zangerle*, Salzburg, Otto Müller, 1981, pp. 70–121.

63 E.g., in the case of Kraus, by Wilma Abeles Iggers, *Karl Kraus*, Den Haag, Nijhoff, 1967, pp. 171–91.

64 Weininger, op. cit., p. 441.

65 Cf. Richard Grunberger, 'Jews in Austrian Journalism', *The Jews of Austria. Essays on Their Life, History and Destruction*, ed. Josef Fraenkel, London, Vallentine, Mitchell, 1967, pp. 83–95.

66 *Die Fackel* (Vienna), no. 381–3, 1913, p. 67.

67 *Die Fackel*, no. 418–22, 1916, p. 9.

68 E.g., *Die Fackel*, no. 386, 1913, p. 2. Cf. Scheichl, 'Karl Kraus', op. cit., pp. 927f.

69 *Die Fackel*, no. 368–9, 1913, p. 40.

70 Karl Kraus, *Die letzten Tage der Menschheit* (Kraus, *Werke*, 5), Munich, Kösel, 1957, pp. 750–4; cf. also the frontispiece of *Die Fackel*, no. 326–8, 1911.

71 Cf. Scheichl, 'Aspekte des Judentums', op. cit., pp. 110ff.

72 *Der Brenner*, vol. 14, 1933, p. 18.

73 Michael Lazarus, 'Nachwort', Karl Kraus, *Briefe an Sidonie Nádherný von Borutin 1913–1936*, Munich, dtv, 1977, vol. 1, pp. 691–5 (see p. 695).

74 Scheichl, 'Karl Kraus', op. cit., pp. 886f.

75 Cf. Georg Knepler, *Karl Kraus liest Offenbach*, Vienna, Löcker, 1984.

76 Kraus, *Briefe*, op. cit., pp. 608ff.

77 The sentence (*Die Fackel*, no. 890–905, 1934, p. 38) is so intricate that it has been completely misunderstood by Iggers, op. cit., p. 191. A translation seems impossible to me.

78 Hein, op. cit., p. 60.

79 Quoted from Spira, op. cit., pp. 50f: 'Es ist selbstverständlich,

daß es niemandem verübelt werden darf, wenn er gerade keine besonderen Sympathien für die Juden aufbringen kann: Zur Liebe wie zum Haß läßt sich nicht zwingen. Ein solcher, rein persönlicher Gefühlsantisemitismus ist Privatsache und steht jedermann frei wie die Abneigung gegen Stotternde oder Glatzköpfige. Von da bis zum politischen Antisemitismus unserer Tage ist aber ein sehr weiter Weg, und dieser kann von keinem Standpunkt aus gebilligt oder auch nur verteidigt werden.'

80 Anonymous, *Der Widerhall*, vol. 20, no. 13, 29 March 1919, pp. 3f: 'Der individuelle, gefühlsmäßige Antisemitismus ist eine Selbstverständlichkeit. Der politische ist eine Dummheit.'

81 Quoted from Bernhard Natter, 'Die "Heimat" und die "Tiefen der Seele." Volksbildungsliteratur im "Ständestaat" am Beispiel der Zeitschrift "Ruf der Heimat" (1935–8)', doctoral dissertation, Innsbruck, 1984, p. 46: '*Auch ich bin ein alter Antisemit.* Ich wünschte, daß der Kulturantisemitismus, der mich erfüllte, mehr Allgemeingut der katholischen Politiker werde. Nicht der Antisemitismus der Gewalt und der Pogrome ist es, der uns helfen kann, sondern der *Kulturantisemitismus*, der sich gegen die jüdische Kulturinflation auf allen Gebieten wendet.'

82 Cf. Robert S. Wistrich, 'Karl Lueger and the Ambiguities of Viennese Antisemitism', *Jewish Social Studies*, 44, 1983, pp. 251–62; p. 257 on 'the long-term cultural and political legitimization of antisemitism in Austrian public life', which is not only a consequence of Lueger's politics.

83 Wistrich, *ibid.*, p. 252. Wistrich asks this question about Lueger, of course.

84 *Ibid.*, pp. 252, 253.

85 *Ibid.*, p. 260f.

86 Scheichl, 'Aspekte des Judentums', op. cit., p. 72. This differentiation has been taken up by Allan Janik, 'Comment écrire sur Weininger', *Austriaca* (Rouen), no. 16, 1983, pp. 185–90 (see pp. 188f).

87 Jacques Le Rider, 'Réponses à Allan Janik', *ibid.*, pp. 190–3 (see esp. p. 192).

88 John W. Boyer, *Political Radicalism in Late Imperial Vienna. Origins of the Christian Social Movement 1848–1897*, Chicago, University of Chicago Press, 1981, p. x.

89 Spira, op. cit., p. 54, has the same argument but uses it for the opposite purpose: Pernerstorfer is not an antisemite if compared with Hitler, but he should be called one if measured by the standards of

his time. By these standards, there would have been very few non-antisemites in Austria outside of the Jewish community.

90 Wistrich, 'Lueger', op. cit., p. 261.

91 Le Rider, 'Réponses', op. cit., p. 193.

92 Colin Walker, 'Nestroy's *Judith und Holofernes* and Antisemitism in Vienna', *Oxford German Studies*, 12, 1981, pp. 85–110 (see p. 108).

93 This paper, read in Paris in German, has been entirely re-written in English. The mediocre style is not due to a translator nor to the editors (whom I thank for having corrected the worst), but to myself. I am grateful particularly to Ivar Oxaal for his editorial suggestions about how to present the nuances of the original German to a largely English-reading public.

CHAPTER 6

Social democracy, antisemitism and the Jews of Vienna

1 Joseph Roth, *Juden auf Wanderschaft*, Berlin, 1927, quoted in his *Romane-Erzählungen-Aufsätze*, Cologne, 1964, pp. 559 ff.

2 *Ibid.*

3 Robert S. Wistrich, *Socialism and the Jews: The Dilemmas of Assimilation in Germany and Austria-Hungary*, London/Toronto, 1982.

4 Paul Massing, *Rehearsal for Destruction. A Study of Political Antisemitism in Imperial Germany*, New York, 1949, p. 151; also Peter Pulzer, *The Rise of Political Antisemitism in Germany and Austria*, London, 1964, p. 259; and more recently Reinhard Rurup, 'Sozialismus und Antisemitismus in Deutschland vor 1914' in *Juden und Judische Aspekte in der Deutschen Arbeiterbewegung 1848–1918*, Tel Aviv, 1976, pp. 203–27 for examples of this viewpoint.

5 See Avram Barkai, 'The Austrian Social Democrats and the Jews' in *Wiener Library Bulletin*, 24 (1 and 2), 1970, new series, nos 18 and 19, pp. 32–40, 16–22. For a more detailed analysis, Robert S. Wistrich, 'Austrian Social Democracy and Antisemitism 1890–1914', *Jewish Social Studies*, 38 (Summer-Fall 1975), pp. 323–33.

6 See, for example, *Verhandlungen des sechsten österreichischen sozial-demokratischen Parteitages*, Vienna, 1897, pp. 91–2 and the discussion in Robert S. Wistrich, *Socialism and the Jews*, op. cit., pp. 265–8.

7 Kautsky to Engels, 23 June 1884, in *Friedrich Engels Briefwechsel*

mit Karl Kautsky, Vienna, 1955, p. 125.

8 Kautsky-Engels, 22 December 1884, in *Engels Briefwechsel, ibid.*, p. 159.

9 Wilhelm Ellenbogen, 'Der Wiener Antisemitismus', *Sozialistische Monatshefte* (September, 1899), pp. 418–25.

10 John Bunzl, ' "Arbeiterbewegung", "Judenfrage" und Antisemitismus. Am Beispiel des Wiener Bezirks Leopoldstadt', in G. Botz, H. Hautmann, H. Konrad, J. Weidenholzer, eds, *Bewegung und Klasse. Studien zur österreichischen Arbeitergeschichte*, Vienna, 1978.

11 *Arbeiter-Zeitung* (Vienna), 9 May 1890.

12 Bunzl, op. cit., p. 760.

13 Robert S. Wistrich, *Socialism and the Jews*, op. cit., pp. 250 ff.

14 For an elaboration of this point see Robert S. Wistrich, 'Victor Adler: a Viennese socialist against philosemitism', *Wiener Library Bulletin*, 27 (1974), no. 32, pp. 26–33.

15 On the occupational structure of the Jewish and gentile population in the Leopoldstadt, see Bunzl, op. cit., pp. 743 ff.

16 See Marsha L. Rozenblit, *The Jews of Vienna 1867–1914*, Albany, 1983, pp. 78–9, for a valuable statistical analysis of Jewish residential distribution in Vienna and the important article by Ivar Oxaal and Walter R. Weitzmann, 'The Jews of Pre-1914 Vienna. An Exploration of Basic Sociological Dimensions', *Leo Baeck Institute. Year Book XXX* (1985), pp. 395–432.

17 Robert S. Wistrich, 'Austrian Social Democracy and the Problem of Galician Jewry', *Leo Baeck Institute. Year Book XXVI* (1981), pp. 89–124.

18 Robert S. Wistrich, *Socialism and the Jews*, op. cit., pp. 332–4.

19 Bunzl, op. cit., pp. 746–50.

20 See Ber Borochov, *Ketavim*, Tel Aviv, 1955–66, vol. 3 (in Hebrew), pp. 496–500, 534, 536 for further details.

21 On the massive electoral swing towards the Social Democrats among Viennese Jews during the First Austrian Republic, see Walter B. Simon, 'The Jewish Vote in Austria', *Leo Baeck Yearbook*, 16 (1971), pp. 97–123.

22 John W. Boyer, *Political Radicalism in Late Imperial Vienna. Origins of the Christian Social Movement 1848–1897*, Chicago/London, 1981.

23 See John W. Boyer, 'Karl Lueger and the Viennese Jews', *Leo Baeck Institute. Year Book XXVI* (1981), pp. 139–40 and Robert S. Wistrich, 'Karl Lueger and the Ambiguities of Viennese

Antisemitism', *Jewish Social Studies* (Summer-Fall 1983), vol. XLV, nos 3–4, pp. 251–62.

24 Adolf Hitler, *Mein Kampf*, Boston, 1942, p. 61.

25 See the biographical chapters on Victor Adler and Otto Bauer in Robert S. Wistrich, *Revolutionary Jews from Marx to Trotsky*, London, 1976.

26 Otto Bauer, 'Sozialismus und Antisemitismus', *Der Kampf*, 4 (1910–11).

27 *Verhandlungen des sechsten österreichischen sozialdemokratischen Parteitages*, Vienna, 1897, op. cit., p. 87.

28 See, for example, Friedrich Austerlitz, 'Karl Lueger', *Die Neue Zeit* (1900–1), 2, pp. 36–45.

29 'Die Neue Freie Presse', *Arbeiter-Zeitung* (Vienna), 30 June 1893.

30 *Verhandlungen*, op. cit., p. 87.

31 *Ibid.*, p. 92.

32 *Ibid.*, p. 101.

33 *Ibid.*, p. 103.

34 'Christlich-sozialer Schwindel', *Volkstribune*, 21 February 1906, p. 2.

35 *Arbeiter-Zeitung* (Vienna), 6 April 1900.

CHAPTER 7

The politics of the Viennese Jewish community, 1890–1914

1 See Ivar Oxaal and Walter R. Weitzmann, 'The Jews of pre-1914 Vienna: an exploration of basic sociological dimensions', *Leo Baeck Institute Year Book*, vol. XXX, 1985, p. 398 and the literature cited in the article; Marsha L. Rozenblit, *The Jews of Vienna, 1867–1914: Assimilation and Identity*, Albany, N.Y., State University of New York Press, 1983, chapter 3.

2 Gesetz vom 21. März, 1890, no. 57, Stück XVIII. *Reichsgesetzblatt für die im Reichsrathe vertretenen Königreiche und Länder*, Wien, 1890, pp. 109–13.

3 *Bericht des Vorstandes der Israelitischen Kultusgemeinde in Wien über seine Thätigkeit in der Periode 1890–1896*, Wien, Verlag. d. isr. Kultusgemeinde, 1896, p. 14, henceforth cited as *Tätigkeitsbericht*.

4 On the legal status of the IKG see Dr Leopold Stern, *Der Haushalt der Israelitischen Kultusgemeinde nach dem geltenden österreichischen Rechte*, Wien, R. Löwith Verlag, 1914, Central Archives for the History of the Jewish People (Jerusalem), *Archiv der*

*Israelitischen Kultusgemeinde zu Wien, A W/*10, henceforth cited in
the form: CAHJP, *A W/*10. See also Sigmund Husserl, 'Die
israelitische Kultusgemeinde Wien', *Ost und West*, 1910, vol. 10
(Nr. 8/9, August-September), pp. 494–520.

5 A list of Jewish organizations can be found in *Kalendar für
Israeliten*, Wien, published annually by the
Oesterreichisch-Israelitische Union, 1892/3–1910; beginning with
1911, the lists were published as the *Jahrbuch der israelitischen
Kultusgemeinde Wien für das Jahr 1911*, CAHJP, *A W/*732,13; a very
useful compilation of the more important organizations and a
description of their purposes is in J. Kreppel, *Juden und Judentum
von Heute übersichtlich dargestellt. Ein Handbuch*, Zürich, Wien,
Leipzig, Amalthea Verlag, 1925, esp. chapter XI.

6 Husserl, op. cit., p. 497.

7 The OIU was against the plutocratic new curia. It was defended by
IKG board members with the argument that since the board was not
a political body, the number of seats given to the wealthy did not
matter. The important thing was to get their financial co-operation.
Oesterreichische Wochenschrift (henceforth cited as *OW*), vol. XVII,
16 February 1900, p. 119; *OW*, 23 February 1900, pp. 142–3.

8 *Statut der Israelitischen Kultusgemeinde in Wien*, Wien, Verlag d.
isr. Kultusgemeinde, n.d. [1913]; *Tätigkeitsbericht, 1890–1896*.

9 *Tätigkeitsbericht, 1912–1924*, Tabelle XIV.

10 A typical contemporary view is provided in the following
definition of 'modern' assimilation, by Ludwig Philippson, writing in
the *Jahrbuch für Israeliten*, in 1854: 'For the Jewish tribe to become
one with the rest of the world [das Aufgehen des jüdischen Stammes
in die übrige Welt] in all matters of intellectual, material and
social import, excepting those that make Jewry a religious and ethnic
community [mit Ausnahme der Glaubens-und
Stammesgenossenschaft]', cited by Wolfgang Häusler,
' "Orthodoxie" und "Reform" im Wiener Judentum in der Epoche
des Hochliberalismus', *Studia Judaica Austriaca*, vol. VI, 'Der Wiener
Stadttempel, 1826–1975', Eisenstadt, Edition Roetzer, 1976,
pp. 32–3.

11 Ivar Oxaal and Walter R. Weitzmann, op. cit., pp. 400–1; Hans
Tietze, *Die Juden Wiens: Geschichte-Wirtschaft-Kultur*, Leipzig,
Wien, E.P. Tal, 1933, p. 156: 'Vienna's Jews were composed of those
who were already rich or had the stuff to become so if they could
gain a foothold in the new land; nothing connected them to their
kind except a remnant of oppression and nothing connected them to

Judaism except a fading memory of their hometown ghettos, whose obscure darkness contrasted sharply with the brightness of their new milieu.' On the rapid integration of Galician Jews, see Max Grünwald, *Vienna*, Philadelphia, Jewish Publication Society, 1936, pp. 416–20.

12 On the Hungarian split, see Nathaniel Katzburg, 'The Jewish Congress of Hungary, 1868–1869', in Rudolph L. Braham, ed., *Hungarian-Jewish Studies*, New York, World Federation of Hungarian Jews, 1969, vol. II, pp. 1–34; Emil Marton, 'The family tree of Hungarian Jews', loc. cit., vol. I, pp. 54–6.

13 Jacob Allerhand, 'Die Rabbiner des Stadttempels von J.N. Mannheimer bis P.Z. Chajes', *Studia Judaica Austriaca*, vol. 6, pp. 5–28.

14 Gerson Wolf, *Vom Ersten bis zum Zweiten Tempel, Geschichte der Israelitischen Kultusgemeinde in Wien (1820–1860)*, Wien, W. Baumüller, 1861, pp. 8, 51.

15 Quoted by Wolfgang Häusler, 1976, op. cit., p. 42.

16 *Vorstandsprotokoll*, 1 November 1907, *AW/71*, 12. Even the Zionists believed that their alliance with the *minyanim* movement had 'diluted their wine'. *Jüdische Zeitung*, 27 November 1908, pp. 2–3. See also *OW*, vol. XXV, 14 February 1908, p. 130.

17 Community rabbi David produced a flurry of excitement among Galician Jews when, on the occasion of the trial of a Galician swindler named Schapira, he commented unfavourably on the behaviour of 'Ostjuden' in one of his sermons. *Vorstandsprotokoll*, 1 November 1906, *AW/71*, 12. On Ludwig Gomperz, an extreme assimilationist, see the edition of his letters and essays by Robert A. Kann, ed., *Theodor Gomperz: Ein Gelehrtenleben im Bürgertum der Franz-Josefs-Zeit*, passim. Gomperz's alienation from all things Jewish is reflected in many of his letters, indicating an almost physical repulsion for the appearance and behaviour of Ostjuden.

18 Wolfgang Häusler, 1976, op. cit., pp. 49–52.

19 *Tätigkeitsbericht, 1890–1896*, p. 14.

20 Grünwald, op. cit., p. 416.

21 On Rabbi Dr Josef Samuel Bloch, see his own reminiscences, *Erinnerungen aus meinem Leben*, Wien und Leipzig, 1922; there exists an English translation, *My Reminiscences*, Vienna and Berlin, R. Lowith, 1922; for biographical information see the short article' on Bloch in the *Encyclopedia Judaica*, s.v. 'Josef S. Bloch' and in *Neue Deutsche Bibliographie*, s.v. 'Josef S. Bloch'; the most recent discussion of his influence can be found in Jacob Toury, 'Josef

Samuel Bloch und die jüdische Identität im Österreichischen
Kaiserreich', in Walter Grab, ed., *Jüdische Identität und Integration
in Deutschland und Österreich 1848–1918*, Internationales
Symposium, April, 1983, *Jahrbuch des Instituts für Deutsche
Geschichte*, Beiheft 6, Tel-Aviv, Tel-Aviv University, 1983,
pp. 41–63; an indefatigable journalist, Bloch wrote thousands of
editorials and articles and this remarkable productivity can best be
traced in the pages of *Oesterreichische Wochenschrift* which he
founded in 1884 and published until 1922. See also the tribute paid
to him by his son-in-law, Max Grünwald, a Viennese community
rabbi, in *Vienna*, op. cit. and in Sigmund Mayer, *Ein jüdischer
Kaufmann, 1831 bis 1911, Lebenserinnerungen*, Leipzig, Duncker &
Humblot, 1911, pp. 308–9.
22 Bloch, op. cit., pp. 289–96; cf. Brian Quigley, 'Ernst Schneider,
the Vienna Guilds Assembly and the Austrian Reform Club', Verein
für Geschichte der Stadt Wien, *Jahrbuch*, vol. 34, 1978, pp. 329–41.
Quigley completely ignores Schneider's hate-filled antisemitism and
concentrates on his craft guild based anticapitalism.
23 Bloch, op. cit., pp. 163–4; *OW*, vol. XXV, 3 July 1908, p. 483;
Central Zionist Archives (Jerusalem), Schalit Papers. Typewritten
manuscript of Schalit's reminiscences, p. 629, CZA A 196/62.
Grünwald, op. cit., p. 442.
24 See Bloch's commentary throughout the debate over the
proposals in his journal. *OW*, vol. XVI, 1900. Interestingly enough,
Stern opposed the change, which he called plutocratic, as did most of
the notables in the OIU. It was widely believed that this was less a
matter of principle with Stern than pride in his own creation; he had
been the author of the original 1896 statute. When the debate over
tax and suffrage reform surfaced again in 1908, a much more
conservative Bloch argued strenuously against it, as opening the door
to the element that voted Social Democratic in the municipal
elections. *OW*, vol. XXV, 20 November 1908, p. 814.
25 For Bloch's views on the nationality questions, see his collection
of articles, *Der nationale Zwist und die Juden in Österreich*, Wien,
M. Gottlieb, 1886; the phrase, 'only the Jews are unqualifiedly
Austrian [die Juden allein [sind] Österreicher sans phrase]' can be
found on p. 40. Jacob Toury disputes the originality of his thoughts,
ascribing them to Fischhoff and Dr Bernhard Münz, an early
collaborator with Bloch in the *Oesterreichische Wochenschrift*,
Toury, 1983, op. cit., p. 55.
26 Jacob Toury, 'Herzl's newspapers: the creation of *Die Welt*',

Zionism, vol. 1, 1980, p. 159.

27 OW, vol. I, 15 October 1884, pp. 1–2.

28 OW, vol. II, 17 April 1885, pp. 1–2; 8 May 1885, p. 1.

29 Under Sigmund Mayer who discovered his own Jewishness only after the antisemites had made it impossible to ignore it, the ÖIU became more political in its activities. Sigmund Mayer's plea for greater political activity may be found in a memorandum he submitted to the Executive Board of the OIU as early as 1894, Mayer, op. cit., pp. 309–10. Sigmund Mayer was instrumental in creating and backing the ill-fated Sozialpolitische Partei, which was supposed to replace the failing Democratic Party of Vienna. For the history of this venture, see Eva Hollis, *Die Sozialpolitische Partei: Sozialpolitische Bestrebungen in Wien um 1900*, München, 1978.

30 OW, vol. XV, 11 November 1898, p. 822.

31 *Monatsschrift der OIU*, Nr. 11 (November 1908), CAHJP, *AW/ 71,3*.

32 OW, vol. XXXV, 22 November 1918, p. 725.

33 See the typewritten transcript of Stern's 1900 election speech in *AW/ 50,5*.

34 *Ibid.*

35 The deficit problem had caused a reclassification of the tax structure in 1896. See *Tätigkeitsbericht, 1890–1896*, pp. 10–11. By 1908–9, the budget was again in disarray. In May 1909, Max Frank, the chairman of the IKG Finance Commission, warned that the large deficit facing the organization was the result of the chronic problem of 'expenditures rising steadily, while income remains stable', OW, vol. XXVI, 21 May 1909, pp. 371–3.

36 The provisions of the *Heimatrecht* are described in Jiri Klabouch, *Die Gemeindeselbstverwaltung in Österreich, 1848–1918*, München, R. Oldenbourg, 1968, pp. 68–9. By the law of 1896, those who had not been born to fathers who had Viennese citizenship had to acquire it formally. It had to be granted to anyone who had resided in Vienna for ten consecutive years and during that time had not claimed public aid. *Statistisches Jahrbuch der Stadt Wien für 1910*, p. 114.

37 Whatever municipal poor relief there was is described in Hannes Stekl, 'Armenversorgung im liberalen Wien', in Herbert Knittler, ed., *Wirtschafts-und sozialhistorische Beiträge*, München, Oldenbourg, 1979, pp. 431–50; the annual report of the *Zentralstelle* is reported in OW, 26 March 1909, pp. 222–4.

38 In 1901, the last year for which detailed records exist, the

Armenstelle listed a total of 2,730 persons receiving relief payments in amounts ranging from 2–40 Kronen, the majority receiving 6–10 Kronen. An analysis of a sample of the recipients' addresses showed that 58 per cent lived, predictably, in district 2, but that only 3 per cent resided in district 20, the Jewish proletarian district. Quite clearly, the relief offered by the IKG did not reach the poorest of the Jewish community. In 1907, the IKG *Vorstand* approved regular support payments totalling 55,224 Kronen to 394 dependants of former IKG taxpayers, an average of 140 Kronen per person. CAHJP, *AW*/72,10.

39 See the report of the IKG Board meeting in O*W*, vol. XXII, 13 June 1905, pp. 22–4. Even in the OIU there were demands for limiting the welfare role of the *Kultusgemeinde*. See the report of the OIU meeting of 30 July 1900, O*W*, vol. XV, no. 31, 3 August 1900, pp. 562–4.

40 In 1904 the IKG paid out 45,100 Kronen in subsidies to district synagogues; in 1905 the amount was 50,000 Kronen, and by 1912 had reached the extraordinary amount of 183,000 Kronen, occasioned by a large construction subsidy for a new temple in the second district. *Tätigkeitsbericht, 1904–1905*; *ibid.*, 1912–24, p. 16.

41 After giving permission to build a second temple in the Leopoldstadt, the Ministry of Religion and Education in 1854 directed the IKG to sanction no more 'private prayer rooms' to prevent 'sect-mongering' and uncivil behaviour, but a decade later, there were still 30 unregulated prayer rooms in the Leopoldstadt alone, and the IKG was never able to stop the spread of *minyanim*. Wolf, op. cit., p. 6; Häusler, 1976, op. cit., p. 45. In 1907, Stern reported to his board that in the past year 69 requests for exemption from the rule had been received and 43 had been granted by the special *minyanim* committee established by the board to control their proliferation. CAHJP, *AW*/ 71,13.

42 See *Vorstandsprotokoll*, meeting of 6 October 1908, CAHJP, *AW*/ 71,13.

43 See the excellent article by Robert Wistrich, 'Karl Lueger and the ambiguities of Viennese antisemitism', *Jewish Social Studies*, vol. 45, Summer-Fall, 1983, pp. 251–62.

44 O*W*, vol. XXV, 11 November 1898, pp. 821–2.

45 Lucy Dawidowicz, *The Jewish Presence: Essays on Identity and History*, New York and London, Harcourt, Brace, Jovanovich, 1978, p. 8.

46 For the definitive monograph on the Jewish press in Austria, see Jacob Toury, *Die Jüdische Presse im österreichischen Kaiserreich: Ein Beitrag zur Problematik der Akkulturation, 1802–1918*, Tübingen, J.C.B. Mohr (Paul Siebeck), 1983, esp. Part II, chapters 13–16. On the early history of nationalist student organizations, see Harriet Pass, 'Kadimah: Jewish Nationalism in Vienna before Herzl', in *Columbia Essays in International Affairs*, vol. 5, 1970, pp. 119–38.

47 On Lueger's speech and Jewish reaction to it, see CAHJP, *AW/* 328. In the Viennese city council, Klebinder, one of the few Jewish members left, mildly admonished Lueger for his remarks, which, the speaker said, were so unlike Lueger's usual fairness; he reminded Lueger that as mayor he had no right to call for an economic war against the Jews since they were taxpayers like other citizens. Lueger dismissed the attack by saying that since his speech calling for a boycott of Jewish stores had been made at a Christian Social election rally he was accountable for his remarks only to his voters not to opposition council members. See *Amtsblatt*, Nr. 100, 15 December 1905.

48 The action of the IKG presidium to mobilize Jewish world leaders foundered on their unwillingness to join in an international action that might leave them open to the accusation of not being loyal nationals of their country. See Joel Raba, 'Reaction of the Jews of Vienna to the Russian pogrom of 1905', *Michael*, vol. II, 1973, pp. 135–44. The handwritten replies to Stern's invitation can be found in CAHJP, *AW/* 348.

49 *Vorstandsprotokoll*, 15 November 1905, *AW/* 71, 12.

50 Eduard März, *Österreichische Industrie und Bankpolitik in der Zeit Franz Josephs I*, Wien, Frankfurt, Zürich, Europa Verlag, 1968, pp. 191, 323.

51 *Vorstandsprotokoll*, 10 May 1906, *AW/* 71, 12.

52 Robert Stricker's shrewd remark that 'Herzlian Zionism, was, in the first instance, an appeal not to the Jewish world, but to the Gentiles', was not far off the mark. Josef Fraenkel, ed., *Robert Stricker*, London, Claridge, Lewis & Jordan, 1950, p. 83. Herzl was most anxious not to rouse the masses against authority but to gain the ear of those with political power. His tendency to sacrifice what some of his radical followers saw as principle to advance the cause of 'political' Zionism, i.e. the winning of a charter or land grant from Turkey, and later, Great Britain, led to early defections. Saul Raphael Landau, *Sturm und Drang im Zionismus*, Wien, Verlag Neue

National-Zeitung, n.d. [1937]; Jacques Kornberg, 'Theodore Herzl: A Reevaluation', *Journal of Modern History*, vol. 52, 1980, pp. 226–52.

53 There is a paucity of literature on the Austrian Zionist movement. An early effort by M. Landau, 'Geschichte des Zionismus in Österreich und Ungarn', diss. phil., University of Vienna, 1932, is based on some interviews and available issues of the Zionist press. But even by 1932, most of the records of the Central Zionist office including the minutes of its meetings had disappeared. What exists is scattered in various private papers in the Central Zionist Archives, collected since Landau's dissertation was written. A recent dissertation, A. Gaisbauer, *Zionismus und jüdischer Nationalismus in Zisleithanien (1882–1918)*, Vienna, 1981, was not available to me.

54 The programmatic declarations of the Austrian Zionists can be found in M. Landau, op. cit., pp. 156–67. During the debate on Austrian suffrage reform when the Zionists raised the demand for a separate Jewish curia, the OIU came out vigorously against a political *Sonderstellung*, i.e. a separate curia, for eastern Jews. *OW*, vol. XXIII, 19 January 1906, pp. 37–8.

55 The IKG Board held a protest meeting against Sombart's appearance, at which presidium and Zionist hecklers nearly came to blows, *Jüdische Zeitung*, 1 March 1912, pp. 2–3. The issue of how best to maintain and foster a separate Jewish identity appeared as early as 1898, when Oskar Marmorek came out for separate schools for Jewish children, a position that seemed to align him with the Christian Socials who, with a very different intent, had tried to introduce the 'confessional' school. See his letter to the *Oesterreichische Wochenschrift*, vol. XV, 18 November 1898, and his speech at an OIU meeting, *Die Welt*, vol. II, 21 October 1898, pp. 8–9. In the years before the war, the issue of Jewish separateness turned around the question whether the Jews constituted a 'race'. While the anthropologists Felix von Luschan and Maurice Fishberg denied that the Jews were a race, Zionists, like Ignaz Zollschan and Robert Weltsch, argued that they were. In their desire to counter the pan-German claim for Germanic racial superiority, some Zionists developed a concept of race based on history, 'genealogy' and 'will'. Ignaz Zollschan did believe that Jews were a biological race and argued that its present degenerate state could only be revitalized by the acquisition of a homeland where its potentialities could freely develop. See Zwi Bacharach, 'Ignaz Zollschans *Rassentheorie*', in

Walter Grab, ed., op. cit., pp. 183–4; Joachim Doron, 'Rassenbewusstsein und Naturwissentschaftliches Denken im deutschen Zionismus während der wilheminischen Ära', *Jahrbuch des Instituts für deutsche Geschichte*, Tel Aviv, 1980, pp. 388–427. The ambiguities of the Zionist view on race can also be followed in the discussions in *Die Welt*.

56 *OW*, vol. XXV, 20 November 1908, p. 814.

57 On the Marmorek affair, see the document entitled 'Die Affaire Marmorek' in the Central Zionist Archive (Jerusalem), Egon Zweig Papers, CZA A 41/3 and the correspondence found in CZA A 41/3.

58 Central Zionist Archives (Jerusalem), Marmorek Papers. Letter from Max Nordau to O. Marmorek, 5 August 1908, CZA A 41/3. The *Neue National-Zeitung*, vol. X, 7 June 1907, p. 10 reported the district meeting which passed the no-confidence vote against both Oskar Marmorek and Dr Jakob Kahn.

59 *Neue National-Zeitung*, vol. XIV, 8 November 1912, pp. 1–2. Böhm had also written an appreciation of Christianity for its ethical message and denigrated the value of old, i.e. biblical Judaism for the development of a Zionist morality, for which he was publicly denounced at the Zionist Congress by the representative of Misrachi, the faction of religious Jews. *Die Welt*, Congress Issue VI, 1913, p. 116.

60 *OW*, vol. XXV, 7 February 1908, p. 98; *Neue National-Zeitung*, vol. X, 7 February 1908, p. 6; 14 February, p. 5.

61 Central Zionist Archives (Jerusalem), Schalit Papers. Typewritten manuscript of Schalit's reminiscences, p. 400. CZA A 196/62.

62 'Politics in a new key: an Austrian triptych', *Journal of Modern History*, vol. 39, 1967, pp. 343–86.

63 Walter Frankl, 'Erinnerungen an Hakoah Wien 1909–1938', *LBI Bulletin*, vol. 64, 1983, p. 55; Erich Jahn, 'The sports movement in Austria', in Josef Fraenkel, ed., *The Jews of Austria*, London, Vallentine, Mitchell, 1967, pp. 161–2; from 1911 on, the IKG gave Hakoah a subsidy of 50 Kronen, and the Zionists organization, 200. *Neue National-Zeitung*, vol. XIII, Nr 26, 31 December 1911, p. 7 and *ibid.*, 14 January 1912, p. 5.

64 Although the *Jüdische Zeitung* boasted in 1907 that its early problems had been overcome, that it was no longer dependent upon and dominated by its student sector, the accounting given at district and all-Austrian congresses belie this claim. In the first decade of the twentieth century the district of Inner Austria, i.e. the territory that would become the Austrian republic, had only 30 branch

organizations. Of these, 12 were affiliated student corporations, 2 were Poale Zion branches, reflecting the socialist wing of the Zionist movement, and only 8 were membership branches in Viennese districts; the *Jüdischer Volksverein* of the second district, headed by Robert Stricker, had only 360 members. *Die Welt*, Nr 4, 31 January 1913, p. 151 and Nr 8, 24 February 1913, p. 119. In the elections to the social insurance board, the *Oesterreichische Wochenschrift* had to advise the thousands of Jewish members of the commercial employees organization to vote for the Social Democratic candidate, a Jew named Pick, as against a converted Galician Jew, Biedermann, who ran on the antisemitic Pan-German ticket. *OW*, vol. XXVII, 17 March 1911, pp. 172–3. Wilhelm Häusler, *Das galizische Judentum in der Habsburgermonarchie*, München, R. Oldenbourg, 1979, pp. 86–7, quite correctly characterizes the Austrian Zionist movement as a bourgeois organization with few roots in the Jewish working class. In 1908, the Zionists reassured their critics that the implementation of their proposal of universal suffrage would 'not bring the small number [Häuflein] of propertyless to power', for many of them were orthodox and thus no threat to social stability. *Jüdische Zeitung*, Nr 42, 15 September 1908, pp. 2–3.

65 It was not only the 'old Zionists' who fell by the wayside. I. Margulies, Isidor Schalit, Adolf Böhm resigned Viennese leadership positions to take up other Zionist work. Robert Stricker, one of its ablest leaders, resigned as vice-president of the *Aktions Komité* in 1924; Robert Stricker, *Wege der jüdischen Politik*, Wien, R. Löwith, 1929, pp. 203–9. Stricker, following the sectarian tradition of Viennese Zionism, joined the Radical Opposition within the World Zionist Organization, then the Revisionists and finally, splitting from Jabotinsky's movement, he participated in the Jewish State Party which remained without influence. See 'Robert Stricker', *Encyclopedia of Zionism and Israel*, New York, McGraw-Hill, 1971.

66 Fritz Fellner, ed., *Das politische Tagebuch Josef Redlichs*, Graz-Köln, Verlag Böhlau, 1953, vol. I, p. 90. In his bitterness, Mahler spoke to Redlich of the 'unbridgeable chasm that separates the western cultured person from those from the east', a gulf that not even a common Jewishness could overcome.

67 Richard Charmatz, *Deutsch-österreichische Politik*, Leipzig, Duncker & Humblot, 1907, pp. 97, 102.

68 *Neue National-Zeitung*, vol. XIV, 8 November 1912, pp. 1–2. As early as 1908, at the Western Austrian district conference, questions were raised against the destructive radicalism of the

leadership. One delegate from 'Kadimah' said that the district committee was completely discredited because of its policy of continually 'batting their head against a stone wall. We should meet our opponents half-way.' And Dr Hermann Kadisch, of Bohemia, spoke for the majority when he said that a new wind must blow through the organization if it was to expand; he pleaded for recruiting more diverse and less pre-committed elements and for an attitude of greater intra-Jewish harmony. *Jüdische Zeitung*, 21 February 1908, pp. 5–7. At the second Austrian Zionist Party Congress, in 1910, a new policy toward the *Kultusgemeinden* was adopted. The word 'Gewinnen', which could be interpreted more easily as 'winning over' peacefully, was substituted for the term 'Erroberung', or conquest. A detailed programme for the democratization of the *Kultusgemeinden* was accepted and the paragraph that spoke of 'open struggle' to gain 'power' was eliminated. This cleared the way for a different tactic which prevailed in the elections of 1912. *Jüdische Zeitung*, 1 April 1910, pp. 3–6.

69 As usual, Bloch reflected the attitude of the moderate reformers perfectly. Looking back on twenty years of publication, Bloch listed as one of the main accomplishments of the *Oesterreichische Wochenschrift* that 'it has always preached harmony within and undivided combat with the enemy outside. We have always held high the flag of Jewish unity.' O*W*, vol. XXI, 1 January 1904, pp. 1–2.

70 *Neue National-Zeitung*, 5 November 1913, pp. 35–6.

71 O*W*, vol. XXXIV, 8 November 1918, pp. 705–8; 15 November 1918, pp. 724–6.

72 *Tätigkeitsbericht, 1929–1932*, p. 3; *ibid.*, 1933–6, p. 9.

73 On Stricker, see Josef Fraenkel, ed., 1950, op. cit.; Robert Stricker, op. cit., *Tätigkeitsbericht, 1912–1924*; Moritz Rosenfeld, *Oberrabbiner Hirsch Perez Chajes; sein Leben und Werk*, Wien, 1933.

CHAPTER 8'

Political antisemitism in interwar Vienna

1 Among the exceptions are E. Mendelsohn, *The Jews of East Central Europe Between the World Wars*, Bloomington, Indiana University Press, 1983; C. Heller, *On the Edge of Destruction: Jews of Poland Between the Two World Wars*, New York, Schocken Books, 1980; D. Weinberg, *A Community on Trial: The Jews of Paris in the 1930s*, Chicago and London, University of Chicago

Press, 1977; and P. Hyman, *From Dreyfus to Vichy: The Remaking of French Jewry, 1906–1939*, New York, Columbia University Press, 1979.

2 See Mendelsohn, op. cit., chapters 1, 2, 5.

3 Dr E. Führer, 'Antisemitismus in neuem Österreich' in R. Körber and T. Pugel (eds), *Antisemitismus der Welt in Wort und Bild*, Dresden, M.O. Grol, 1935, p. 184.

4 M. Grunwald, *History of the Jews in Vienna*, Philadelphia, Jewish Publication Society, 1936, p. 460; J. Katz, *From Prejudice to Destruction: Anti-semitism, 1700–1933*, Cambridge, Mass., Harvard University Press, 1980, p. 176.

5 J. Ornstein, *Festschrift zur Feier des 50 jährigen Bestandes der Union österreichischer Juden*, Vienna, Union, 1937, p. 9.

6 G. Fellner, *Antisemitismus in Salzburg 1918–1938*, Vienna, Salzburg, Veröffentlichungen des Historischen Institut der Universität Salzburg, 1979, p. 84.

7 Ornstein, op. cit., p. 10.

8 J. Bunzl, *Klassenkampf in der Diasara: Zur Geschichte der jüdischen Arbeiterbewegung*, Vienna, Europa Verlag, 1975, pp. 127–8.

9 J. Moser, 'Die Katastrophe der Juden in Österreich, 1918–1945 – ihre Voraussetzung und ihre Überwindung' in vol. 5: *Der gelbe Stern in Österreich*, Eisenstadt, in Kommission bei Edition Roetzer, 1977, pp. 70–1.

10 All the above statistics are from A. Tartakower, 'Jewish Migration Movements in Austria in Recent Generations', in J. Fraenkel (ed.), *The Jews of Austria: Essays in their Life, History and Destruction*, London, Vallentine, Mitchell, 1967, pp. 286, 287, 293.

11 S. Maderegger, *Die Juden in österreichischen Ständestaat 1934–1938*, Vienna, Salzburg, Verlag Geyer, 1973, p. 1; *Bericht des Präsidiums und des Vorstandes der israelitischen Kultusgemeinde Wien über die Tätigkeit in den Jahren 1933–1936*, Vienna, Verlag der israelitischen Kultusgemeinde, 1936, p. 109.

12 K.R. Stadler, *Austria*, New York, Washington, Praeger, 1971, p. 138.

13 Maderegger, op. cit., p. 1.

14 *Die Wahrheit*, 30 January 1931, p. 3.

15 See, for example, R. Körber, *Rassensieg in Wien: Der Grenzfest des Reiches*, Vienna, Wilhelm Braunmüller, 1939, p. 217; *Deutschösterreichische Tages-Zeitung* (Dötz). *Unabhängiges Blatt für völkische Politik* (Vienna), 14 June 1932, p. 4; B. Bangha, O.

Trebitsch and P. Kris, *Klärung in der Judenfrage*, Vienna-Leipzig, Paul Kris, Reinhold Verlag, 1934, p. 138; and Allgemeines Verwaltungsarchiv (AVA) Bundeskanzleramt (BKA), Grossdeutsche Volkspartei (GVP) VI–36 (Judenausschuss), 7 May 1921.

16 Führer, op. cit., p. 203; *Der Stürmer. Unabhängiges Wochenblatt für alle Schaffenden* (Vienna), 3 March 1934, p. 7.

17 G. Glockemeier, *Zur Wiener Judenfrage*, Leipzig and Vienna, Günther, 1936, p. 115.

18 *Die Wahrheit*, 29 May 1931, p. 1; *Die Stimme, Jüdische Zeitung* (Vienna), 2 March 1934, p. 1; J. Wassermann, *My Life as a German and a Jew*, New York, Unwin, 1933, pp. 186–7.

19 Maderegger, op. cit., p. 220; H. Rosenkranz, 'The Anschluss and the Tragedy of Austrian Jewry, 1938–1945' in Fraenkel, op. cit., p. 480.

20 H. Andics, *Der ewige Jude: Ursachen und Geschichte des Antisemitismus*, Vienna, 1968, p. 292.

21 Glockemeier, op. cit., p. 109.

22 *Ibid.*, p. 66.

23 M. Grunwald, op. cit., pp. 298–9.

24 *Die Wahrheit*, 13 February 1931, p. 4; *Die Stimme*, 2 March 1934, p. 1.

25 Maderegger, op. cit., p. 156; *Die Stimme*, 2 March 1934; p. 1; W. Boerner, *Antisemitismus, Rassenfrage, Menschlichkeit*, Vienna, Flugschrift der Ethischischen Gemeinde, 1936, p. 12.

26 Sozius (pseudonym for Eli Rubin), *Die Juden in Österreich: Schädlinge oder wertvolle Staatsburger?*, Vienna, Selbstverlag, 1923, pp. 6, 9, 21.

27 Bangha, op. cit., p. 176; letter by Josef Födinger to the *Kampfruf*, 30 October 1932, Nationalsozialistische Parteistellen (NS–P), Karton (K) 8.

28 *Die Stimme*, 22 October 1931, p. 2.

29 B. Frei, *Jüdische Elend in Wien: Bilder und Daten*, Vienna, R. Löwit, 1920, p. 40.

30 Maderegger, op. cit., p. 54.

31 *Die Wahrheit*, 8 March 1935, p. 1; *Die Stimme*, 5 March 1935, p. 2.

32 Glockemeier, op. cit., p. 50.

33 J. Bunzl, 'Arbeiterbewegung und Antisemitismus in Österreich vor und nach dem Ersten Weltkrieg', *Zeitgeschichte*, vol. 4 (1976–7), p. 167.

34 *Die Wahrheit*, 29 April 1927, p. 1.

35 W. Simon, 'The Jewish Vote in Austria', *Leo Baeck Institute Yearbook*, vol. 16 (1971), pp. 103, 108.

36 R. Schwarz, 'Antisemitism and Socialism in Austria 1918–1962', in Fraenkel, op. cit., pp. 445–6; G. Zernatto, *Die Wahrheit über Österreich*, New York, Longman's Green & Co., 1939, p. 67.

37 *Die Stimme*, 21 April 1932, p. 1.

38 Bunzl, 'Arbeiterbewegung', op. cit., p. 167.

39 *Ibid.*, p. 168.

40 Fellner, op. cit., p. 124.

41 *Ibid.*, p. 121; Simon, op. cit., p. 110.

42 Bunzl, 'Arbeiterbewegung', op. cit., pp. 168–70; Katz, op. cit., p. 6; D. Niewyk, *The Jews in Weimar Germany*, Baton Rouge and London, Louisiana State University Press, 1980, p. 70.

43 A. Staudinger, *Christlichsoziale Judenpolitik in der Grundungsphase der österreichischen Republik*. Reprinted in Avshalom Hodik, Peter Malina and Gustav Spann (eds), *Juden in Österreich, 1918–1938*, Vienna, Institut für Zeitgeschichte, 1982 (typescript), p. 54; see also Katz, op. cit., p. 288.

44 Andics, op. cit., p. 387.

45 Fellner, op. cit., pp. 72–3; J. Bunzl, *Antisemitismus in Österreich: historische Studien*, Innsbruck, Inn-Verlag, 1983, p. 48.

46 Ornstein, op. cit., p. 34.

47 K. von Klemperer, *Ignaz Seipel: Christian Statesman in a Time of Crisis*, Princeton, Princeton University Press, 1972, p. 256.

48 J. Moser, 'Von der antisemitischen Bewegung zum Holocaust', in Klaus Lohrmann (ed.), *1,000 Jahre österreichisches Judentum*, Eisenstadt, Edition Roetzer, 1982, p. 257.

49 A. Pelinka, *Stand oder Klasse*. Reprinted in Hodik *et al.*, op. cit., pp. 51–3.

50 E. Weinzierl, 'Antisemitismus in Österreich', *Austriaca* (July, 1978). Reprinted in Hodik *et al.*, op. cit., p. 1.

51 H. Tietze, *Die Juden Wiens: Geschichte, Wirtschaft, Kultur*, Vienna, E.R. Tal, 1933, p. 255.

52 F. Heer, *Gottes erste Liebe: 2000 Jahre Judentum und Christentum; Genesis des österreichischen Katholiken Adolf Hitler*, Munich, Bechtle, 1967, p. 363.

53 Glockemeier, op. cit., p. 106.

54 Heer, op. cit., pp. 363–5.

55 Moser, op. cit., p. 265.

56 H. Pfarrhofer, *Friedrich Funder: Ein Mann zwischen Gestern und Morgen*, Graz, Vienna, Cologne, Verlag Styria, 1978, pp. 203, 295–301.

57 K. Stuhlpfarrer, 'Antisemitismus, Rassenpolitik in Österreich, 1918–1938.' Reprinted in Hodik *et al.*, op. cit., p. 145; P.G.J. Pulzer, 'The Development of Political Antisemitism in Austria', in Fraenkel, op. cit., p. 441.

58 For a history of the Heimwehr see C.E. Edmondson, *The Heimwehr and Austrian Politics, 1918–1936*, Athens, The University of Georgia Press, 1978. For its pan-German and racist wing see B.F. Pauley, *Hahnenschwanz und Hakenkreuz: Steirischer Heimatschutz und österreichischer Nationalsozialismus, 1918–1934*, Vienna, Munich, Zürich, Europa Verlag, 1972.

59 C.A. Macartney, 'The Armed Formations of Austria', *International Affairs*, London, vol. 7 (November, 1929), p. 630; M. Bullock, *Austria, 1918–1938: A Story of Failure*, London, Macmillan, 1939, pp. 185–6; see also *Die Wahrheit*, 4 October 1929, p. 24.

60 Excerpt from the *Arbeiter-Zeitung* (Vienna), 26 October 1930, *Tagblatt* Archive, Arbeiterkammer (Vienna), folder entitled 'Heimwehr-Antisemitismus'.

61 Quoted in F. Winkler, *Die Diktatur in Österreich*, Zürich, Orell Füsseli, 1935, p. 40.

62 *Die Stimme*, 2 March 1934, p. 1.

63 *Ibid.*, 27 March 1934, p. 2.

64 *Ibid.*, 27 February 1934, p. 2.

65 Katz, op. cit., p. 287; Sachar, op. cit., p. 238; A.G. Whiteside, *The Socialism of Fools: Georg von Schönerer and Austrian Pan-Germanism*, Berkeley, Los Angeles, London, University of California Press, 1975, p. 305.

66 Whiteside, op. cit., pp. 304–5.

67 Stuhlpfarrer, op. cit., p. 36.

68 K. Berchtold (ed.), *Österreichische Parteiprogramme 1868–1966*, Munich, 1967. Reprinted in Hodik, op. cit., pp. 70, 72.

69 R. Ardelt, *Zwischen Demokratie und Faschismus: Deutschnationales Gedankengut in Österreich, 1919–1930*, Vienna, Salzburg, Geyer, 1972, pp. 88, 98; Glockemeier, op. cit., p. 90.

70 Minutes of the Fachausschuss für die Judenfrage der GVP, 7 February 1924, p. 1 and 22 February, p. 3, AVA, GVP, VI–36.

71 Minutes of 21 April 1921, p. 6 and 7 February 1924, p. 1, *ibid*.

72 Fellner, op. cit., pp. 102, 128, 134.

73 *Ibid.*, p. 133.

74 *Ibid.*, p. 128; see also K. Peter, *Der Antisemitismus*, Vienna, Peter, 1936, 24pp.

75 · Unsigned letter from the Antisemitenbund to the security director of Lower Austria dated 27 April 1935, AVA, BKA, doc.33000 4 GD 2/1935.

76 Report dated 13 January 1937 on a meeting of the Antisemitenbund, Dokumentationsarchiv der österreichischen Widerstandes (DÖW), folder 6895.

77 Report dated 28 January 1938, *ibid.*

78 L. Jedlicka, 'Aus dem politischen Tagebuch des Unterrichtsministers a.D. Dr Emmerich Czermak, 1937 bis 1938', *Österreich in Geschichte und Literatur*, vol. 8 (1964), p. 359.

79 Draft for a poster entitled 'Ihre Existenz ist in Gefahr!', AVA, NS–P, K.14, Plakat Entwurfe; Führer, op. cit., p. 190.

80 Führer, op. cit., p. 188.

81 *Ibid.*, p. 189.

82 *Ibid.*, p. 191; *Der Stürmer*, 3 March 1934, p. 1.

83 Klemperer, op. cit., p. 257.

84 Glockemeier, op. cit., p. 121; Ornstein, op. cit., p. 29.

85 11 November 1933, p. 1.

86 Moser, op. cit., p. 257; see also E. Czermak and O. Karbach, *Ordnung in der Judenfrage: Ständigung mit dem Judentum*, Vienna, Reinhold Verlag, 1933.

87 *Die Wahrheit*, 27 October 1933, p. 1.

88 Fellner, op. cit., pp. 106–7, 136–7.

89 Minutes of the Judenausschuss, 19 May 1921, p. 2, AVA, BKA, GVP; Führer, op. cit., p. 204.

90 *Die Wahrheit*, 1 February 1923, p. 11; Marsha L. Rozenblit, *The Jews of Vienna 1867–1914: Assimilation and Identity*, State University of New York Press, 1983, p. 159.

91 *Der Stürmer*, 30 December 1933, p. 2; Peter, op. cit., p. 16; Maderegger, op. cit., p. 197; *Die Stimme*, 21 December 1933, p. 3.

92 Stuhlpfarrer, op. cit., p. 37.

93 Letter of J.H. Furth to the author, 24 June 1979, p. 5.

94 Führer, op. cit., p. 190.

95 Letter with an illegible signature from the Bundes-Polizeidirektion in Vienna to the BKA, Generaldirektion für die öffentliche Sicherheit, Staatspolizeiliches Büro in Vienna, 17 November 1935, 2pp., AVA, BKA Inneres 1933, K32, doc.219.644; *Bericht der IKG, 1933–1936*, op. cit., p. 73.

96 H. Busshoff, *Das Dollfuss-Regime in Österreich im geistesgeschichtlicher Perspektive unter besonderer Berüchtsichtigung der 'Schöneren Zukunft' und Reichspost*, Berlin, Dunckert &

Humblot, 1968, p. 280.

97 N.H. Tur-Sinai, 'Viennese Jewry', in Fraenkel, op. cit., p. 318.

98 Mendelsohn, op. cit., p. 110.

99 Ornstein, op. cit., p. 37; O. Karbach, 'Die politische Grundlagen des deutsch-österreichischen Antisemitismus', *Zeitschrift für die Geschichte der Juden*, vol. 4, Tel Aviv, 1964, p. 176.

100 Fellner, op. cit., p. 200.

101 *Der Stürmer*, 20 January 1934, p. 1 and 17 February 1934, p. 1.

102 *Die Stimme*, 21 September 1934, p. 1 and 26 October 1934, p. 1.

103 Bunzl, 'Arbeiterbewegung', op. cit., pp. 47–8; Karbach, op. cit., p. 175.

104 *The Ambassador in Germany* (Wilson) *to the Secretary of State*, 30 March 1938, United States Department of State, *Foreign Relations of the United States: Diplomatic Papers, 1938*, p. 471.

105 Maderegger, op. cit., pp. 230, 241.

106 M. Fuchs, *Showdown in Vienna*, New York, G.B. Putnam's Sons, 1939, pp. 71–2, 221.

107 At the beginning of 1938 there were nearly 40,000 Jewish-owned businesses in Nazi Germany, some of which had contracts with the government and were enjoying boom conditions. See J. Boas, 'German-Jewish Internal Politics under Hitler, 1933–1938', *Leo Baeck Institute Yearbook*, 1984, p. 4.

108 (Vienna, Bratislava), 24 May 1935, p. 1.

109 28 September 1934, p. 1.

110 21 September 1934, p. 1.

111 *Die Wahrheit*, 8 March 1935, p. 2.

112 Maderegger, op. cit., pp. 116–27.

113 Letter of Franz von Papen to the German Foreign Ministry, 5 August 1935, National Archives (Washington), microfilm T–120, reel 5415, frames K287371–72.

114 Moser, op. cit., p. 264.

115 Frei, op. cit., pp. 25, 29.

116 *Die Wahrheit*, 13 May 1932, p. 1.

117 Avshalom Hodik, 'Die israelitische Kultusgemeinde, 1918–1938', in Hodik *et al.*, op. cit., p. 31.

118 *Ibid.*, p. 30; see also, *Die Wahrheit*, 15 November 1929, p. 3.

119 *Die Wahrheit*, 18 December 1931, p. 4; Körber, *Rassensieg*, op. cit., p. 236.

120 *Die Stimme*, 20 February 1934, p. 2; *Die Neue Welt* (Vienna), 1 March 1938, p. 1.

121 *Die Wahrheit*, 2 December 1932, p. 2.
122 On the Reichsbund see U. Dunker, *Der Reichsbund jüdischer Frontsoldaten, 1919–1938*, Düsseldorf, Droste, 1977 and Boas, op. cit., pp. 10–11.
123 *Drei Jahre Bund jüdischer Frontsoldaten Österreichs*, Vienna, Selbstverlag der Bund jüdischer Frontsoldaten Österreichs, 1935, pp. 17–37; Maderegger, op. cit., p. 56.
124 Maderegger, op. cit., pp. 4–5.
125 Karbach, vol. 1, op. cit., p. 8.
126 *Die Wahrheit*, 10 February 1933, p. 1.

CHAPTER 9

Assimilated Jewish youth and Viennese cultural life around 1930

1 For a lively history of this work see Werner Wilhelm Schnabel, ' "Professor Bernhardi" und die Wiener Zensur', in *Jahrbuch der Deutschen Schiller-Gesellschaft* XXVIII, Stuttgart, 1984, pp. 349–83.
2 In his essay *Das erste Buch: Die Blendung*, Canetti speaks of the genesis of this work, in which the hero was originally named 'Brand'. This all too direct ('*Überdeutlich*') allusion to the fire at the Palace of Justice dissatisfied the author, however, and the character was finally named 'Kant'. He concluded the manuscript four years after the dramatic events in Vienna: 'In August, 1931, four years after the fifteenth of July, Kant set fire to his library and perished in the flames.' Elias Canetti, *Das Gewissen der Worte*, Munich and Vienna, Hanser, 1975.
3 The dramatic works of Hochwälder have been published in four volumes in the Styria edition, Graz. On this author see Wilhelm Bortenschlager, *Der Dramatiker Fritz Hochwälder*, Innsbruck, Universitätsverlag Wagner, 1979; also, R. Thieberger, *Gedanken über Dichter und Dichtungen. Les textes et les auteurs*, Berne, Peter Lang, 1982, pp. 267–311.
4 Csokor (1885–1969) was a non-Jew and well-known opponent of National Socialism who succeeded in leaving Austria in 1938, and returned in 1946. He was subsequently elected president of the Austrian branch of PEN. Csokor was one of the established writers who came to discuss with us in the framework of the 'Gruppe des Jungen'.
5 This occurred in February 1933.
6 Before his emigration he published under the name of Otto Brand;

much later he signed himself as Thomas O. Brand. Born in Vienna in 1906, he taught at Colorado Springs until 1965. He died in 1967 at his new post at the University of New Hampshire. See, among his publications of literary criticism, *Die Vieldeutigkeit Berthold Brechts*, Heidelberg, Lothar Stiehm, 1968. One finds there both the poet and the analyst of language.

7 Heinz Politzer, *Parable and Paradox*, Ithaca, Cornell University Press, 1962; for the German edition, *Franz Kafka, der Künstler*, Frankfurt am Main, M. Fischer, 1965.

8 For Elise Richter, see Hans Helmut Christmann, *Frau und 'Jüdin' an der Universität: Die Romanisten Elise Richter (Wien 1865 – Theresienstadt 1943)*, Mainz and Wiesbaden, Franz Steiner, 1980. I have reviewed this well-documented book in *Literatur und Kritik*, Number 157/58, Salzburg, Otto Müller, 1981, pp. 495–7.

CHAPTER 10

The Jews of Vienna from the Anschluss *to the Holocaust*

1 See for instance the otherwise comprehensive histories of Austria since the First World War: E. Weinzierl and K. Skalnik (eds), *Österreich 1918–1938: Geschichte der Ersten Republik*, Graz, Styria, 1983, 2 vols; E. Weinzierl and K. Skalnik (eds), *Österreich: Die Zweite Republik*, Graz, Styria, 1972, 2 vols; P. Dusek, A. Pelinka, E. Weinzierl, *Zeitgeschichte im Aufriß: Österreich von 1918 bis in die achtziger Jahre*, Vienna, Jugend und Volk, 1981; N. Schausberger, *Österreich: Der Weg der Republik 1918–1980*, Graz, Leykam, 1980. This is true also for scholarly researched specialized studies like H. Rosenkranz, *Verfolgung und Selbstbehauptung: Die Juden in Österreich 1938–1945*, Vienna, Herold, 1978; *Widerstand und Verfolgung in Wien 1934–1945: Eine Dokumentation*, ed., Dokumentationsarchiv des österreichischen Widerstands, Vienna, Österr. Bundesverlag, 1975, 3 vols (and the subsequent vols on Upper Austria, Burgenland and Tyrol).

2 This contribution is based mostly on my own earlier publications: G. Botz, *Wohnungspolitik und Judendeportation in Wien 1938 bis 1945: Zur Funktion des Antisemitismus als Ersatz nationalsozialistischer Sozialpolitik*, Vienna, Geyer, 1975; idem, *Wien vom 'Anschluß' zum Krieg: Nationalsozialistische Machtübernahme und politisch-soziale Umgestaltung am Beispiel der Stadt Wien 1938/39*, Vienna, Jugend und Volk, 2nd edn, 1980.

3 Cf. G. Hirschfeld and L. Kettenacker (eds), *Der 'Führerstaat':*

Mythos und Realität, Stuttgart, Klett-Cotta, 1981; I. Kershaw, *The Nazi Dictatorship: Problems and Perspectives of Interpretation*, London, Edward Arnold, 1985, pp. 82–105; K. Hildebrand, *Das Dritte Reich*, Munich, Oldenbourg, 1979, pp. 175–80; M. Broszat, ' "Holocaust" und die Geschichtswissenschaft', *Vierteljahrshefte für Zeitgeschichte*, vol. 27, no. 2 (1979), pp. 285–98; J. Hiden and J. Farquharson, *Explaining Hitler's Germany: Historians and the Third Reich*, London, Batsford, 1983, pp. 43–7.

4 G. Fleming, *Hitler und die Endlösung: 'Es ist des Führers Wunsch'*, Munich, Limes, 1982; L. Dawidowicz, *The War Against the Jews 1933–45*, Harmondsworth, Penguin, 1977; S. Gordon, *Hitler, Germans, and the 'Jewish Question'*, Princeton, Princeton University Press, 1984, pp. 128–45.

5 H. Mommsen, 'Die Realisierung des Utopischen: Die "Endlösung der Judenfrage" im Dritten Reich', *Geschichte und Gesellschaft*, vol. 9, no. 3, 1983, pp. 381–420; M. Broszat, 'Hitler und die Genesis der "Endlösung": Aus Anlaß der Thesen von David Irving', *Vierteljahrshefte für Zeitgeschichte*, vol. 25, no. 4 (1977), pp. 739–75; K.A. Schleunes, *The Twisted Road to Auschwitz: Nazi Policy Toward German Jews, 1933–1939*, Urbana, University of Illinois Press, 1970.

6 Mommsen, op. cit., pp. 394–5.

7 P.G.J. Pulzer, *The Rise of Political Antisemitism in Germany and Austria*, New York, Wiley, 1964, pp. 144–7, 279–87; idem, 'The Development of Political Antisemitism in Austria', J. Fraenkel (ed.), *The Jews of Austria: Essays on their Life, History and Destruction*, London, Vallentine Mitchell, 1967, pp. 429–43; D. von Arkel, 'Antisemitism in Austria' (unpublished) phil. Diss., University of Leiden (1966), pp. 67–185; A. Pelinka, *Stand oder Klasse? Die christliche Arbeiterbewegung österreichs 1933 bis 1938*, Vienna, Europa-Verlag, 1972, pp. 213 ff; K. Stuhlpfarrer, 'Antisemitismus, Rassenpolitik und Judenverfolgung in Österreich nach dem Ersten Weltkrieg', *Das österreichische Judentum: Voraussetzungen und Geschichte*, Vienna, Jugend und Volk, 1974, pp. 141–64; E. Weinzierl, *Zu wenig Gerechte: Österreicher und Judenverfolgung, 1938–1945*, Graz, Styria, 1969.

8 A.G. Whiteside, *The Socialism of Fools: Georg Ritter von Schönerer and Austrian Pan-Germanism*, Berkeley, University of California Press, 1975, esp. pp. 107–40.

9 J.W. Boyer, *Political Radicalism in Late Imperial Vienna: The Origins of the Christian Social Movement 1848–1897*, Chicago,

University of Chicago Press, 1981, pp. 184 ff; idem, 'Karl Lueger and the Viennese Jews', *Leo Baeck Institute Year Book*, vol. 26 (1982), pp. 125–44; K. Skalnik, *Dr Karl Lueger: Der Mann zwischen den Zeiten*, Vienna, Herold, 1954.

10 I. Oxaal and W.R. Weitzmann, 'The Jews of Pre-1914 Vienna: An Exploration of Basic Sociological Dimensions', *Leo Baeck Institute Year Book*, vol. 30 (1985), pp. 395–432; cf. also: W. von Weisl, *Die Juden in der Armee Österreich-Ungarns*, Tel Aviv, Olamenu, 1979, pp. 1–22; W. Häusler, 'Toleranz, Emanzipation und Antisemitismus: Das österreichische Judentum des bürgerlichen Zeitalters (1782–1918)', *Das österreichische Judentum*, op. cit., pp. 83–140; Leo Goldhammer, *Die Juden Wiens: Eine statistische Studie*, Vienna, 1927; G. Glockemeyer, *Zur Wiener Judenfrage*, Leipzig, 1937.

11 Botz, *Wohnungspolitik*, op. cit., pp. 117–24; idem, ' "Arisierungen" und nationalsozialistische Mittelstandspolitik in Wien (1938–1940)', *Wiener Geschichtsblätter*, vol. 29, no. 1 (1974), pp. 122–36.

12 *Völkischer Beobachter*, Vienna, 26 April 1938, pp. 2, 4.

13 H. Genschel, *Die Verdrängung der Juden aus der Wirtschaft im Dritten Reich*, Göttingen, 1966, pp. 165–6; D. Adam, *Judenpolitik im Dritten Reich*, Düsseldorf, 1972, pp. 195 ff; also K. Drobisch *et al.*, *Juden unterm Hakenkreuz*, Frankfurt/M., 1973, pp. 50 ff.

14 G.E.R. Gedye, *Die Bastionen fielen: Wie der Faschismus Wien under Prag überrannte*, Vienna, 1947, pp. 294–309; D. Wagner and G. Tomkowitz, *Ein Volk, ein Reich, ein Führer: Der Anschluß Österreichs 1938*, Munich, 1968.

15 Botz, *Wien*, op. cit., pp. 93–106.

16 J. Bunzl, 'Arbeiterbewegung, "Judenfrage" und Antisemitismus. Am Beispiel des Wiener Bezirks Leopoldstadt', G. Botz *et al.* (eds), *Bewegung und Klasse*, Vienna, Europa-Verlag, 1978, pp. 743–63; R. Beckermann, *Die Mazzesinsel*, Vienna, Löcker, 1984.

17 For literary accounts see: H. Hilsenrad, *Brown was the Danube*, New York (1966), pp. 275 ff; G. Clare, *Last Waltz in Vienna*, London, 1983.

18 Botz, *Vienna*, op. cit., pp. 98–105; Rosenkranz, *Verfolgung*, op. cit., pp. 39–41; wrong figures are still derived from Gedye, op. cit., pp. 300, 309.

19 *Neues Wiener Amtsblatt*, Vienna, 5 April 1938, p. 8.

20 MD 3872/38, Archive of the City and Land of Vienna (abbreviated: AdStuLW), letter of J. Bürckel to Göring, 19 July 1938,

R. 104/Pak/Bundesarchiv, Koblenz (abbreviated: BA).
21 *Wiener Zeitung*, Vienna, 3 March 1938, p. 4; M.D. 2802/38,
AdStuLW.
22 *Gesetzblatt für das Land Österreich*, Vienna 327/1938; E.
Mannlicher, *Wegweiser durch die Verwaltung unter besonderer
Berücksichtigung der Verwaltung im Reichsgau Wien*, Berlin, 1942,
pp. 210–11, 233.
23 *Amtsblatt der Stadt Wien*, vol. 46, no. 27, p. 2; 'Stadtchronik
1938/1940', *Handbuch Reichsgau Wien*, vol. 63/64, Vienna, 1941,
pp. 975–6.
24 M. Rieser, *Österreichs Sterbeweg*, Vienna, 1953, p. 131; R.
Luza, *Austro-German Relations in the Anschluss Era*, Princeton,
Princeton University Press, 1975, p. 217.
25 Genschel, op. cit., p. 162.
26 K. Schubert, 'Die Entjudung der ostmärkischen Wirtschaft und
die Bemessung des Kaufpreises im Entjudungsverfahren',
(unpublished) Diss., University of World Trade, Vienna, 1940, p. 10;
D. Walch, *Die jüdischen Bemühungen um die materielle
Wiedergutmachung durch die Republik Österreich*, Vienna, 1971,
p. 3; cf. A. Krüger, *Die Lösung der Judenfrage in der deutschen
Wirtschaft*, Berlin, 1940, pp. 64–5; L. Wittek-Saltzberg, 'Die
wirtschaftspolitischen Auswirkungen der Okkupation Österreichs',
(unpublished) phil. Diss., Vienna, 1970, p. 225.
27 *Der Prozeß gegen die Hauptkriegsverbrecher vor dem
Internationalen Militärgerichshof*, Nuremberg, 1947 seq. vol. 27,
p. 163 (doc. 1301–PS) (abbreviated: IMT).
28 *Ibid.*, vol. 28, p. 525 (1816–PS); R 104/Pak/,BA.; F. Romanik,
Der Leidensweg der österreichischen Wirtschaft 1933–1945, Vienna,
1957, pp. 24–8; Adam, op. cit., pp. 195 ff; Rosenkranz, Verfolgung,
op. cit., pp. 60–70.
29 IMT, vol. 28, doc. 1816–PS.
30 Letter of Eichmann to Herbert Hagen, 8 May 1938, Microfilm
T 175, R 413, 2,938.501, National Archives, Washington, D.C.; cf.
also R.M.W. Kempner, *Eichmann und Komplizen*, Zurich, 1961,
pp. 42–9; Rosenkranz, *Verfolgung*, op. cit., pp. 71–7.
31 Rosenkranz, *Verfolgung*, op. cit., pp. 105–25, 168–78. J. Moser,
Judenverfolgung in Österreich 1938–1945, Vienna, 1966, pp. 6 ff.
32 Cf. T.W. Mason, *Arbeiterklasse und Volksgemeinschaft:
Dokumente und Materialien zur deutschen Arbeiterpolitik
1936–1939*, Opladen, Westdeutscher Verlag, 1975, pp. 119–58.
33 H. Rosenkranz, *'Reichskristallnacht': 9. November 1938 in*

Österreich, Vienna, 1968; idem, *Verfolgung*, op. cit., pp. 159–67; cf.
H. Graml, *Der 9. November 1938: Reichskristallnacht*, Bonn, 1955;
L. Kochan, *Pogrom: 10. November 1938*, London, 1957.

34 Botz, *Wien*, op. cit., pp. 402 and 533.

35 Quotation see: *Widerstand und Verfolgung*, Wien, op. cit.,
vol. 3, pp. 279–80.

36 MD 3300/1938, AdStuLW.

37 F. Czeike, *Liberale, christlichsoziale und sozialdemokratische
Kommunalpolitik (1861–1934), dargestellt am Beispiel der
Gemeinde Wien*, Vienna, 1962, p. 104; cf. P. Feldbauer,
Stadtwachstum und Wohnungsnot, Vienna, Verlag für Geschichte
und Politik, 1977, pp. 209–86; cf. also A. Lichtblau, *Wiener
Wohnungspolitik 1892–1919*, Vienna, Verlag für Gesellschaftskritik,
1984, pp. 24–32.

38 See G. Botz, 'National Socialist Vienna: Anti-semitism as a
Housing Policy', *Wiener Library Bulletin*, vol. 29, no. 39/40 (1976),
pp. 47–55.

39 Memorandum E. Becker's, mat. reg., file 235 (2315/6),
Reichskommissar, Allgemeines Verwaltungsarchiv, Vienna
(abbreviated: Rk. AVA) and Letter of Bürckel to Göring, 8 July
1939, file 235 (2315/7) Rk. AVA, see: Botz, *Wohnungspolitik*,
op. cit., pp. 146–8, 172–3.

40 H. Krausnick, 'Judenverfolgung', *Anatomie des SS-Staates*, vol. 2,
Munich, 1967, p. 289.

41 File 235 (2315/7), Rk. AVA.

42 Memorandum 12 October 1939, Rk. AVA (see Botz,
Wohnungspolitik, op. cit., p. 164).

43 A. Hitler, *Mein Kampf*, New York, Reynal & Hitchcock, 1939,
pp. 73–9; see also F. Heer, *Der Glaube des Adolf Hitler*, Munich,
1968, pp. 51 ff; J.S. Jones, *Hitler in Vienna 1907–1913*, New York,
Stein & Dau, 1983, pp. 115–21; W.A. Jenks, *Vienna and the Young
Hitler*, New York, 1976; W.J. McGrath, *Dionysian Art and Populist
Politics in Austria*, New Haven and London, Yale University Press,
1974, p. 241.

44 File, mat. reg. 31 (1710), Rk. AVA. See Botz, *Wohnungspolitik*,
op. cit., pp. 85–6.

45 The non-Jewish population was involved in and profited by
Nazism's antisemitic measures in eastern central Europe to a higher
extent than usually admitted; cf. B. Vago and G.L. Mosse (eds), *Jews
and non-Jews in Eastern Europe*, New York, Wiley, 1974.

46 Moser, op. cit., pp. 17 ff.

47 Hitler, op. cit., pp. 419–25; cf. an antisemitic pamphlet from 1923, G. Botz, *Gewalt in der Politik*, 2nd edn, Munich, 1983, p. 406.

48 According to the Nuremberg Racial Laws of 15 September 1935, a Jew was a person who descended from at least three so-called racially full Jewish grandparents. Under certain circumstances (Jewish denomination, marriage to a Jew, illegitimate birth), this definition of 'Jew' applied also to 'half-castes' with only two Jewish grandparents (H. Pfeifer, *Die Ostmark: Eingliederung und Gestaltung*, Vienna, 1941, pp. 173–4). This definition of 'Jew by race' (*Rassejude*) was wider than the 'Jew of denomination' (*Glaubensjude*), which comprised only members of the Jewish religious community.

49 Rosenkranz, *Verfolgung*, op. cit., passim.

50 *Ibid.*, pp. 297–300; 'Die Juden in Wien' (1941), Botz, *Wohnungspolitik*, op. cit., pp. 605–10.

51 IMT, vol. 29, p. 176 (PS 1950).

52 R 43 II/1361a, BA.

53 For more details see: G. Botz, *Wohnungspolitik*, op. cit. and my forthcoming study *Wien im Zweiten Weltkrieg*.

54 H. Gold, *Geschichte der Juden in Wien*, Tel Aviv, Olamenu, 1966, p. 102, H.G. Adler, *Die verwaltete Mensch, Studie zur Deportation der Juden aus Deutschland*, Tübingen, S. Mohr, 1974, pp. 380 ff.

55 Rosenkranz, *Verfolgung*, op. cit., pp. 282–95.

56 Moser, op. cit., pp. 22–3; H. Rosenkranz, 'The Anschluss and the Tragedy of Austrian Jews, 1934–45', Fraenkel, op. cit., pp. 512–13.

57 Rosenkranz, *Verfolgung*, op. cit., p. 310. Jews or Jewish half-castes living in 'privileged' mixed marriages were, under certain circumstances, exempted from deportation if they had offspring with a non-Jewish spouse; exemptions were occasionally given also because of war decorations, non-Jewish appearance, etc.; *ibid.*, p. 289.

58 Moser, op. cit., pp. 47–52; Rosenkranz, *Anschluss*, op. cit., p. 526.

59 E. Weinzierl, *Zu wenig Gerechte, Österreicher und Judenverfolgung 1938–1945*, Graz, Styria, 1969, pp. 145–6.

60 Memorandum of S. Wiesenthal of 12 October 1966, sent to the Austrian Federal Chancellor Josef Klaus; copy in: Dokumentationszentrum des Bundes jüdischer Verfolgter des

Naziregimes, Vienna.
61 See also: H. Buchheim, 'Die SS – das Herrschaftsinstrument. Befehl und Gehorsam', *Anatomie des SS-Staates*, vol. 1, Munich, dtv, 1965. A similar mechanism seems to govern South Africa's Apartheid policy (cf. J. Lelyveld, *Move Your Shadow South Africa, Black and White*, New York, NY Times, 1985).

CHAPTER 11

Avenues of escape: The Far East

1 Jakob Lechner, 'Emigranten in Shanghai', *Arbeiter-Zeitung*, 18 June 1977.
2 'Arrival of Austrian Refugees', *Israel's Messenger*, 20 September 1938.
3 For the 1939 regulations see David Kranzler, *Japanese, Nazis and Jews: The Jewish Refugee Community of Shanghai (1938–1945)*, New York, Yeshiva University Press, 1976, pp. 267–76; see also 'Japanese to Restrict Jews' and 'SMC ban Jewish Refugees', *North China Herald*, 16 August 1939, and 'Shanghai Municipal Council bans Jewish Refugees arriving here after August 21st', *Israel's Messenger*, 12 September 1939.
4 *Israel's Messenger*, 5 May 1939.
5 See the numerous articles published at the beginning of 1939 in *Israel's Messenger*.
6 'Refugees continue to flock here in large numbers', *Israel's Messenger*, 17 March 1939.
7 See M. Rosenfeld's manuscript on the history of the Shanghai refugee community, Yivo, New York.
8 See also Heinz Gstrein, *Jüdisches Wien*, Vienna and Munich, Herold, 1984, p. 78.
9 Zentrales Staatsarchiv Potsdam, *Deutsche Botschaft in China*, No. 3495.
10 Gerd Kaminski, Else Unterrieder, *Von Österreichern und Chinesen*, Vienna, Europa-verlag, 1980, p. 786.
11 *Ibid.*, p. 792.
12 Testimony of Arthur Gottlein, Vienna: Dokumentationsarchiv des österreichischen Widerstandes, 11547.
13 Alfred Dreifuss, 'Shanghai – Eine Emigration am Rande', in Eike Middell, *Exil in den USA*, Leipzig, Ph. Reclam, 1979, p. 497.
14 *Ibid.*, pp. 502–3.
15 Interview with Anna Wang, December 1984.

16 A. Dreifuss, *Ensemblespiel des Lebens*, Berlin, Buchverlag der Morgen, 1985, pp. 198 and 201.

17 See the publications of: Walter Freudmann, *Tschi-lai! Erhebet Euch*, 1947; Fritz Jensen, *China siegt*, 1949; Susanne Wantoch, *Nan-Lu: Die Stadt der verschlungenen Wege*, 1948; and Klara Blum, *Der Hirte und die Weberin*, 1951.

18 'Wenn Österreicher, aus Rassengründen vertrieben, ihr geselliges Zusammensein unter die Devise von Johann Strauss stellten, so war auch das eine Demonstration für Österreich, eine Demonstration gegen die Nazi-Invasoren, ein politischer Akt, gesetzt von unpolitischen Menschen – auch sie die ferne Nähe im Herzen.' Bruno Frei, 'Exil und Widerstand', in *Österreicher im Exil, 1934 bis 1945*, Protokoll des Internationalen Symposium zur Erforschung des Österreichichen Exils von 1934 bis 1945, Vienna, Österreichischer Bundesverlag, 1977, p. XIV.

CHAPTER 12

Antisemitism before and after the Holocaust: The Austrian case

1 In different stages of preparing and revising this chapter I received critical comments, valuable suggestions, and ample opportunities for interesting discussions with many generous people, including Larry Beeferman, Peter Brod, John Bunzl, Peter J. Katzenstein, Michael Freund, Walter Grab, Jane Hilowitz, Irving Louis Horowitz, Marion Kaplan, Peter J. Katzenstein, Dalia Marin, Bruce Mazlish, Reinhard Rürup, Alphons Silbermann, Alan Silver, Walter B. Simon, Angela Yergin and Ivar Oxaal, who did an excellent job in improving the earlier version of this paper. Though most of them disagree with some aspects and generalizations developed in this essay, their disagreements stimulated some necessary clarifications. To what extent the aftermath of 'the Waldheim affair' of 1986 changes the parameters discussed here remains, of course, to be seen.

2 For a comprehensive history of antisemitism see L. Poliakov, *The History of Anti-Semitism*, 4 vols, Paris and London, 1955–64; but in regard to periodization and terminology see R. Rürup, *Emanzipation und Antisemitismus: Studien zur 'Judenfrage' der bürgerlichen Gesellschaft*, Göttingen, 1975, p. 95.

3 On this concept see A. Leon, *The Jewish Question: a Marxist Interpretation*, New York, 1970. Beyond this stage I can only partially follow the author's reasoning.

4 Compare especially P.W. Massing, *Rehearsal for Destruction: A*

Study of Political Anti-Semitism in Imperial Germany, New York, 1949; and P.G.J. Pulzer, *The Rise of Political Anti-Semitism in Germany and Austria*, New York, 1964; for an opposite conclusion calling into question the historical continuity stressed by these authors see R.S. Levy, *The Downfall of the Anti-Semitic Parties in Imperial Germany*, New Haven, 1975. On Austria see, for example, L.A. Hellwing, *Der konfessionelle Antisemitismus im 19. Jahrhundert in Österreich*, Vienna-Freiberg-Basel, 1972; S. Maderegger, *Die Juden im österreichischen Standestaat, 1934–1938*, Vienna-Salzburg, 1973; John Bunzl and Bernd Marin, *Antisemitismus in Österreich: Historische und Soziologische Studien*, Innsbruck, 1983.

5 For a counterargument see, for example, S. Friedlander, *L'Antisemitisme Nazi: Histoire d'une psychose collective*, Paris, 1971, who denies the 'functionality' of Nazi antisemitism for the Nazi rulers and stresses only its irrational and pathological character; nevertheless, he sees antisemitism as the central element in Nazi Fascism, which inevitably developed toward the 'Final Solution'. Just this idea, on the other hand, is denied by E.G. Reichmann in his *Hostages of Civilization: The Social Sources of National Socialist Anti-Semitism*, Westport, 1970. The literature on Fascist antisemitism has become immense, without having yet achieved convergent interpretations. For a penetrating theoretical analysis of antisemitism, which attempts to understand it as neither an accidental nor inevitable consequence of the decay and totalitarian self-transformation of European bourgeois society, see Max Horkheimer and Theodore W. Adorno, 'Elemente des Antisemitismus, Grenzen der Aufklarung', in their *Dialektik der Aufklarung*, Frankfurt am Main, 1969, pp. 177–217. For a reconstruction of antisemitism's historical roots in relation to the decay of nation-states see Hannah Arendt, *The Origins of Totalitarianism*, New York, 1951.

6 Examples of evidence for this can be found in the contributions of J. Amery, H. Broder, P. Lendvai and B. Lewis to J. Bunzl, E. Hacker and B. Marin (eds), *Der Nahost-Konflikt. Analysen, Perspektiven, Dokumente*, Vienna, 1980. The partially undisguised antisemitic character of 'anti-Zionism' in the Soviet communist power domain is described in H. Abosch, *Antisemitismus in Russland, Eine Analyse und Dokumentation zum sowjetischen Antisemitismus*, Darmstadt, 1972; P. Lendvai, *Antisemitismus ohne Juden*, Vienna, 1972; W. Korey, *The Soviet Cage: Anti-Semitism in Russia*, New York, 1973;

and B.A. Hazan, *Soviet Propaganda: A Case Study of the Middle East Conflict*, Jerusalem, 1976. These are only some elements of more and more consolidated evidence concerning the principally reactionary character of Soviet rule even in the post-Stalinist era.
7 This is denied, on the other hand, mainly by Israeli authors, who try to prove a special antisemitic tradition in Arab countries; see, among many examples, Y. Harkaby, *Arab Attitudes to Israel*, Jerusalem, 1972. Just as the practice of branding all (radical) critiques of Israel as antisemitic is intellectually untenable or obviously strategically motivated, the existence of an openly antisemitic anti-Zionism on the extreme right and within the Soviet power domain as well as the impossibility of genuine disinterested reflection on the Jewish state in all those countries that had or still have strong antisemitic prejudice, is equally undeniable. This historical burden rests as well on those who neither made history nor experienced it during Nazism, and this includes young people and the left.
8 Lendvai, op. cit. For a similar phenomenon in another epoch, see B. Glassman, *Anti-Semitic Stereotypes Without Jews: Images of the Jews in England, 1290–1700*, Detroit, 1975. Significantly enough, the existence or non-existence of an important Jewish minority seems to be quite irrelevant to antisemitic attitudes.
9 In the representative poll of October 1973 (IMAS, 'Die Meinung über die Juden Ergebnisse einer reprasentativen Bevolkerungsumfrage', unpublished research memorandum, Linz, 1973) 3 per cent of the people questioned still indicated that they were either 'themselves of Jewish descent' or that they 'had Jewish relatives'; this would correspond to a population of approximately 230,000 persons. Even if relations were interpreted very extensively, it becomes clear that to a minute minority of under 10,000 'Israelites' organized in the Jewish community, '*Kultusgemeinde*', would have to be added a far larger group of assimilants, who according to self-conception (identity) or to socially effect attributions (labelling, stigmatization) are considered 'Jews' by a hostile environment.
10 See IMAS, 1973, Tab 16 and pp. 32, 36.
11 The concrete manifestations of this strangely unfolding 'uneigentlich' and enduringly shameful self-denying syndrome of prejudice are described from an existentialist-phenomenological perspective in R. Misrahi, 'L'antisemitisme latent', in P. de Comarond and C. Duchet (eds), *Racisme et Société*, Paris, 1969, pp. 219–31. This inauthenticity is, along with its cultural

sedimentation, its symbolic independence, and its nation-state-global-political references, one of the central components of the historically new postwar antisemitism.

12 Three earlier such 'affairs' have been analysed extensively. For the conflicts that arose concerning an antisemitic university professor, see the documentation in H. Fischer (ed.), *Einer im Vordergrund: Taras Borodajkewycz*, Vienna, 1966; for the conflict between the head of the 'jüdisches Dokumentation-szentrum', Simon Wiesenthal, and Federal Chancellor Bruno Kreisky concerning the SS past of former FPÖ party chairman Peter, see the critical journalistic work by M. van Amerongen, *Kreisky und seine unbewaltigte Gegenwart*, Graz, 1976; for the conflict over the series of antisemitic articles in the *Kronen-Zeitung* – Austria's most widely read newspaper – about 'Die Juden in Österreich' see A. Zwergbaum, 'Information or antisemitic incitement? The Case of the Viennese Kronenzeitung', in *Forum*, Jerusalem, No. 23, 1975, pp. 112–13 and the content analysis by B. Marin, 'Die Juden in der "Kronen-Zeitung": Textanalytische Fragment zur Mythenproduktion', in J. Bunzl and B. Marin, op. cit., 1983, pp. 89–169. The controversial antisemitic nature of the series was upheld by a court decision, thus ending litigation between the author of the articles – the writer Viktor Reimann – and journalists of the Socialist *Arbeiter-Zeitung* (*AZ*). The lawyers for the *AZ*, as well as the court itself, referred extensively to this content analysis as scientific evidence, stating that the readers of the *Kronen-Zeitung* were bound to receive a generally negative image of the Jews, and therefore the series could be called an appeal to antisemitic prejudices, whether or not the author personally intended this.

13 See the report about survey results in *Journal für angewandte Sozialforschung* 62, 1976, p. 6.

14 In this way a tough Dr Klaus, at this time ruling Federal Chancellor, was presented as a 'genuine Austrian' and contrasted to the obviously not genuinely Austrian Dr Kreisky. The CSTU Academy in Munich analysed this as a prototype of antisemitic agitation: 'The tough way of presentation and the text "A genuine Austrian" evoke associations with Kreisky's Jewish background. . . . Because the attack on Kreisky is not made explicit . . . the observer does not realize that thereby possibly persistent antisemitism is being addressed' (Hans Seidel-Stiftung (ed.), *Politische Plakate der Gegenwart*, according to profile no. 23, 1977, my translation). For another example see N. Holzl, *Propaganda-schlachten. Die*

Österreichischen Wahrkampfe 1945–1971, Vienna, 1974, p. 46.
15 See in particular C. Offe, *Strukturprobleme des Kapitalistichen Staates*, Frankfurt am Main, 1972. On the concept of the 'management of prejudice' relating to antisemitic prejudices, see B. Marin, 'Nachwirkungen des Nazismus: Ein Reproduktionsmodel Kollektiver Mentalitat', in *Die Tribune* 19, 1980; relating to a 'law and order' mentality, see B. Marin 'Alltagserleben und "Sicherheitspolitik" in Krisenperioden. Zur Produktion von Angst und "innerer Sicherheit" in Österreich', in Marin (ed.), *Wachstumskrisen in Österreich*, vol. II, *Szenarios*, Vienna, 1979 and Marin, 'Zur Psychotechnik von "Angst-Management" ' and ' "Sicherheits-Agitation". Exemplarische Beobachtungen zur Formierung "innerer Sicherheit" im politischen Alltag', in *Kriminalsoziologische Bibliografie*, vol. 4, no. 14–15, 1977, pp. 38–53. Conceptualizing 'dominant prejudices' by 'avoidance imperatives' of symbolic-expressive politics modifies ideas of C. Offe in 'Politische Herrschaft und Klassenstrukturen. Zur Analyse spätkapitalistischer Herrschaftssysteme', in G. Kress and D. Senghaas (eds), *Politikwissenschaft*, 2nd edn, Frankfurt am Main, 1973, pp. 135–64.
16 Compare Karl Marx and Friedrich Engels, *Die deutsche Ideologie*, in *Marx-Engels-Werke*, vol. 3, Berlin, 1973, pp. 9 ff.
17 See in particular the Institut für empirische sozialforschung (IFES), 'Messingstrumente zur Erfassung von Out-group-Stereotypien', unpublished research report, Vienna, 1969 (1969b); IFES, 'Der Politisch Indifferente', unpublished research report, Vienna, 1969 (1969b); IFES, 'Antisemitismus und Personlichkeit', unpublished research report, Vienna, 1970; IFES, *Vorurteile in Österreich*, Vienna, 1972; IMAS, Linz, 1973, op. cit., as well as only about Vienna (Sozialwissenschaftliche studiengesellschaft), 'Vorurteile in der Wiener Bevolkerung', unpublished research paper, Vienna, 1969, and H. Weiss, 'Antisemitismus. Inhalte und Ausmass antijudischer Einstellungen in der Wiener Bevolkerung' (I)–(II), in *Journal für angewandte Sozialforschung*, vol. 17, no. 3, vol. 17, no. 4, 1977 and vol. 18, no. 1, 1978.
18 See in particular IMAS 1973, Table 6.
19 For the reservoir of stereotypes compare, e.g., the inventories of B. Marin in Bunzl and Marin, 1983, pp. 225 f; on the extent of common ideas regardless of opposite attitudes, see the comparison of extreme groups in H. Weiss, 'Die Beziehungen zwischen Juden- und

Israelstereotypen in der antisemitischen und nicht-antisemitischen Einstellung', in A. Holl and O. Saipt (eds), *Jahrbuch der Österreichischen Gesellschaft für Soziologie*, Vienna, 1974, pp. 31–43.

20 To this IFES 1969a, pp. 9 ff or, graduated according to its behavioural relevance, B. Marin in Bunzl and Marin, 1983, p. 208. Discriminatory attitudes, of course, vary strongly according to whether a more general understanding or conditional support for Nazi measures is expressed, or, on the other hand, a concrete 'Berufsverbof' or present discrimination against Jews in firms today is favoured.

21 For an estimate of attitude change towards 'the Jews' between 1946 and 1973 see B. Marin in Bunzl and Marin, 1983, p. 256. But source and quality of immediate postwar survey data are questionable and could not be checked.

22 At the Historians Meeting about 'Vorurteil ohne Ende?' of the Evangelische Akademie Loccum (18–20 November 1977), several events of this kind, especially in schools and partly in personal experience, were reported. Attacks of this kind have not become known in Austria up to the Waldheim affair.

23 See A. Silbermann and H.A. Sallen, 'Latenter Antisemitismus in der Bundesrepublik Deutschland', in *Kölner Zeitschrift für Soziologie und Sozialpsychologie*, 28, 1976, pp. 706–23. The similarity of results between the Federal Republic of Germany and Austria – e.g. FRG, Austria: Strong antisemitism 30 per cent, 24 per cent; slight antisemitism 46 per cent, 46 per cent; no antisemitism 24 per cent, 30 per cent – is even more striking given that the research in both countries was done completely independently and involved methodologically different conceptions.

24 IFES 1969a, pp. 42 ff.

25 D. Bichlbauer and E. Gehmacher, 'Vorurteile in Österreich', *Kölner Zeitschrift für Soziologie und Sozialpsychologie*, 24 (1972), p. 736.

26 For the following results see IFES 1972, Table 2 and B. Marin, 'Antisemitismus unter Arbeitern? Einige Daten und Thesen zum "Klassencharakter" des nachfaschistischen Antisemitismus in Österreich', in G. Botz *et al.* (eds), *Bewegung und Klasse, Studien zur österreichischen Arbeitergeschichte*, Vienna, 1978, pp. 765–90, esp. pp. 767–72.

27 Bruno Bettelheim and M. Janowitz in *Dynamics of Prejudice*, New York, 1950, pp. 59–150 show e.g. that in the United States,

downward social mobility in the course of the Second World War
resulted in increased prejudice against Jews and Blacks (Negroes).
28 According to the only representative and comparative study in
Austria, antisemitism is the only significant reaction of prejudice to
the experience of social declassement; beyond that, antisemitism is –
comparing the percentage differences – not determined as much by
any other factor with the exception of political preferences for right-
wing and protest parties like the FPO and DFP. These data confirm
the repeatedly corroborated empirical hypothesis that neither
objective social position nor objective change of social position
(mobility), but instead experienced downward mobility, or blocked
upward mobility in the case of strong status orientation, most likely
causes antisemitic prejudice. See W.C. Kaufman, 'Status,
Authoritarianism, and Anti-Semitism', in *American Journal of
Sociology*, vol. 62, no. 4, 1957, pp. 379–82; F.B. Silberstein and M.
Seeman, 'Social Mobility and Prejudice', in *American Journal of
Sociology*, vol. 65, no. 2, 1959, pp. 258–64; or earlier, but less
specific at this point, A.A. Campbell, 'Factors Associated with
Attitudes Towards Jews' in G. Swanson, T.M. Newcomb and E.L.
Hartley (eds), *Readings in Social Psychology*, New York, 1952,
pp. 603–12.
29 On the strength of the 'interaction effect', the mutual
reinforcement of age and political attitude, see IFES, 1972. Political
preference determines antisemitic attitudes especially in the older
generations, age especially in the national-liberal camp.
30 For the following compare B. Marin in G. Botz *et al.* (eds), 1978.
31 Seymour Martin Lipset, *Political Man*, London, 1960, pp. 97 ff.
32 This is manifested in different responses to direct, open and
indirect projective questions. For such class-specific repression
differences see B. Marin, 1978, pp. 784–5.
33 As by, e.g., D. Bichlbauer and E. Gehmacher, op. cit., p. 737,
who incidentally also wrongly speak about an 'ideological
antisemitism of the Austrians', whereas the real problem is precisely
the persistence of a 'deideologized' antisemitism.
34 Particularly interesting in this respect is O. Fenichel, 'Elements of
a Psychoanalytic Theory of Anti-Semitism', in E. Simmel (ed.), *Anti-
Semitism: A Social Disease*, New York, 1946, pp. 11–32. Other
aspects of a depth-psychological interpretation of antisemitism are
covered by B. Bettelheim, 'Dynamism of Anti-Semitism in Gentile
and Jew', in *Journal of Abnormal and Social Psychology*, vol. 42,
no. 2, 1947, pp. 153–68; N.W. Ackerman and M. Jahoda, *Anti-

Semitism and Emotional Disorder: A Psychoanalytic Interpretation, New York, 1950, as well as hypotheses in all other volumes of M. Horkheimer and S.H. Flowerman (eds), *Studies in Prejudice*, New York, 1950; or R.M. Loewenstein, *Psychoanalyse des Antisemitismus*, 3rd edn, Frankfurt am Main, 1971.

35 These and other social psychological functions are generally discussed in G.W. Allport, *The Nature of Prejudice*, New York, 1954.

36 On that see B. Marin, in *Die Tribune*, 19, 1980. 'Reprivatization' means on the level of social psychological analysis that post-Fascist antisemitism cannot be viewed any more as a mass psychosis, as was done regarding Fascist antisemitism by E. Simmel, 'Anti-Semitism and Mass Psychopathology' in idem, (ed.), 1946, pp. 33–78, but at most as a collective neurosis. Compare to this, e.g., R. Bain, 'Sociopathy of Anti-Semitism', in *Sociometry*, vol. 6, no. 4, 1943, pp. 460–4.

37 Compare the contribution to the discussion by A. Pelinka in 'Österreicher im "Tausendjahrigen Reich" ', Podiumsdiskussion an der Innsbrucker Universität am 25 Oktober 1976, hrsg. von der Österreichischen Lagergemeinschaft Auschwitz, Vienna, 1976.

38 On the concept of inauthenticity in social theory see A. Etzioni, *The Active Society*, New York, 1968, pp. 617–66; as an implicit 'Leitgedanke', but not as a concept. It was first used in analysing antisemitism by Jean-Paul Sartre in *Betrachtungen zur Judenfrage. Psychoanalyse des Antisemitismus*, Zürich, 1948.

39 This is one of the basic concepts of A.M. Mitscherlich, *Die Unfähigkeit zu trauern*, Munich, 1967.

40 On this see W. Neugebauer, 'Antifaschismus – von der Esten zur Zweiten Republik', paper presented at the Colloque deux fois l'Autriche Université de Haute Normandie. Centre d'Etudes et de Recherche Autrichienne, November 1977, published in *Austriaca, Cahiers universitaires d'information sur l'Autriche*, numero special, no. 3, Rouen, 1979.

41 For different attitudes to the Nazi past see the list in B. Marin, 1976, part III/2.

42 Here there is a precise report but with too strong a justification of the Austrian system of justice by K. Marschall, 'Volksgerichtsbarkeit und Verfolgung von nationalsozialistischen Gewaltverbrechen in Österreich 1945–1972', unpublished manuscript, Federal Ministry of Justice, Vienna, 1973. Up to the abolition of the law about Nazi war criminals in 1957, legal

proceedings were started against more than 130,000 persons; more than 23,000 ended with a verdict, more than 13,000 of those with a verdict of guilty; 30 of the 43 death sentences were executed. This was in addition to the activities of the allied military courts. But special measures against National Socialists and Nazi war criminals were gradually eliminated, especially by a number of saving clauses (for 'less incriminated persons', young people, late war returnees) and amnesties (e.g. forfeiture of property amnesty); in 1955, after the State Treaty, the popular jurisdiction was terminated, and the Nazi amnesty of 1957 changed or abolished clauses of the National Socialist Law ('Verbotsgesetz' 1947, 'Kriegsverbrechergesetz' 1945 and 1948 respectively).

43 As representative of the interests of the Resistance fighters and the victims of Fascism – after the abolition of the unified 'KZ-Verband' by the then Interior Minister Helmer – the 'Bund Sozialistischer Freiheitskampfer', the 'ÖVP-Kameradschaft der Politisch Verfolgten', as well as the communist-oriented 'KZ-Verband' were legally recognized. As a scientific institution for research into the Resistance, persecution, and the 1934–45 exile as well as Neofascism, there is the 'Dokumentationsarchiv des österreichischen Widerstandes', while more practical political activity is carried out by the 'Österreichische Widerstandsbewegung'. There are only a few independent commissioned researches by a few historians and social scientists at a few institutes within and outside the universities; laudable exceptions are the institutes for contemporary history founded in Salzburg by Professor Erika Weinzierl and in Linz by Professor Karl R. Stadler. Prof. Stadler was until recently head of the 'Ludwig Boltzmann Institut zur Geschichte der Arbeiterbewegung' which is also important in this respect.

44 On antisemitism in party programmes of the 'Christian-Conservative camp' see K. Berchtold, Österreichische Parteiprogramme 1868–1966, Munich, 1967, pp. 178, 357, 364–5, 376; on party programmes of the 'Liberal-German National camp', pp. 204, 444, 456, 478–83.

45 Compare H. Weiss, op. cit., 1975.

46 However, 'The events of recent years have proved that the "excepted Jew" is more the Jew than the exception; no Jew feels quite happy any more being assured that he is an exception' (Hannah Arendt, 'The Moral of History', excerpted from 'Privileged Jews', in Jewish Social Studies, vol. 8, no. 1, January 1946, pp. 3–7, reprinted in her The Jew as Pariah: Jewish Identity and Politics in the Modern

Age, New York, 1978, p. 107.

47 'The Arabs' are seen in hostile stereotypes as exploitative, lazy, immoral, rich and powerful, fanatical and fraudulent, plaintive, intolerant, cunning, boastful, impertinent, sensuous, cowardly, etc. Most recently, with the OPEC cartel, which particularly affected the advanced capitalist industrial societies, the media have also represented them as symbols of an overly powerful, fabulously rich, parasitic and decadent, internationally forceful and bizarre clique of capitalists. Their support of 'the Palestinians' is thought to finance a threatening and pugnacious 'gang of terrorists' or 'subversives' or at best a desperate people responsible for its own misery. The reporting even addresses stereotypes which have some structural analogies with the antisemitic myth of a 'Jewish-Bolshevik conspiracy'. These observations, while important, have not yet been empirically tested; to talk of a 'new' anti-Arab antisemitism should not be over-interpreted by reference to the somewhat similar fates of the Jewish and Palestinian peoples (a 'Palestinian Diaspora'), as is sometimes done.

48 As H. Weiss (1975, p. 38) remarks: 'In psychological associations regarding Israel there are many more guilt feelings than in the more direct context of questions relating to Jews.' Whereas shame and guilt about negligence contributing to Nazi domination, and its consequences for the Jews, is rejected by most Austrians, the 'Wiederkehr des Verdrangten' (Freud) returns through the back door in attitudes toward the Middle East conflict. For most Austrians, support for the Jewish national state in the Arab-Israeli conflict obviously means, on a social-psychological level, requesting a kind of delayed restitution by the Palestinians (who themselves, contradictorily, were also indirect victims of the Nazi terror). But the rejection of Palestinian demands against Israel is perceived by Austrians as true restitution for the Jews.

49 For these and other themes, compare E. Hindler, 'Die Entwicklung der Haltung der österreichischen Publikationen zu Israel', unpublished report as part of the study on 'Vorurteile und Gesellschaft in Österreich', Vienna, 1976.

50 E. Hindler, 1976, demonstrated, e.g., that the 'bourgeois' papers in Austria sided with the Arabs in 1948 when they refused to recognize the UN partition decisions and attacked the newly founded state of Israel. During the Yom Kippur War of 1973, which the Arabs started in order to regain the occupied territories, the press, formerly intensely pro-Israel, took Israel's position only hesitantly

and conditionally. When Israel in alliance with France and Great Britain attacked Egypt in 1956, this was interpreted as an understandable and necessary attempt to free itself from permanent threat (even if there were some critical voices of this support, such as the Socialist *Arbeiter-Zeitung*). Israel's successful preventive attack on Egypt, Syria and Jordan in 1967 – when it had become, in contrast to the political configuration during the founding years, an important ally of US interests – was justified and supported by the Austrian press enthusiastically and without reservation. Even more interesting are the arguments advanced and their modifications, and the feelings mobilized, at this change of stance. The bourgeois boulevard press in 1967, more than 20 years after the end of the war and the founding of Israel, used for the first time exactly and explicitly those pro-Israeli legitimations and emotions which the Communist press had put forward for the newly founded state earlier – and which they were now trying to forget. In most of the other Austrian papers, on the other hand, there has been a remarkable lack of sympathy for the persecuted and of understanding for their wish to have a state of their own immediately after the war, despite the exposure of the horrors committed, and the renewed threat to Jews in Palestine. In 1956 there was still almost no consideration of the tragic Jewish past, but there was a slow production of admiration for its heroic soldiers at this time – and not during the war of independence against the British colonial empire. The images of Israelis and Arabs, as fabricated by the press, are obviously extremely contradictory, and it is just these inconsistencies that make them particularly suitable for the manipulative 'management of prejudice'; they make it possible to stress or repress different dimensions, depending on the political preferences of the moment. This partisanship was determined up to now exclusively by the question of which politics best served the supposed interests of the 'Western World'.

51 Compare the quotation cited in note 25.

52 On the pointedly ideological penetration of everyday life by Nazi propaganda and 'culture', see the impressive evidence in G.L. Mosse, *Nazi Culture*, New York, 1966. For Austria see the ORF Broadcasting series (in 16 parts) by P. Dusek, 'Alltagsfaschismus in Österreich', Vienna, 1978–9.

53 On the following see B. Marin, in Bunzl and Marin, 1983, op. cit., p. 89, and H. Weiss, 1975.

54 For a conceptualization in a psychoanalytic framework, see A.

Lorenzer, *Sprachzerstörung und Rekonstruktion*, Frankfurt am Main, 1970; for a structuralist critique of ideology, compare C. Guillaumin, *Ideologie raciste, genèse et langage actuel*, Paris, 1972.
55 For this and the following findings compare my extensive analysis of the *Kronen-Zeitung* series of 1975, Part 1.
56 On this see the most interesting doctoral dissertation by N. Feldman, 'Motive des "Stürmer". Anatomie einer Zeitung', Vienna, 1966. On Nazi jargon, see also, e.g., V. Klemperer, LTI, Darmstadt, 1949; J. Wulf, *Aus dem Lexikon der Mörder, 'Sonderbehandlung' und verwandt Wörter im nationalsozialistischen Denken*, Gütrsloh, 1963; or C. Berning, *Vom 'Abstammungsnachweis' zum 'Zuchtwart' Vokabular des Nationalsozialismus*, Berlin, 1964.

INDEX